NEW ESSAYS ON PLATO

NEW ESSAYS ON PLATO

Language and Thought in Fourth-Century Greek Philosophy

Editor
Fritz-Gregor Herrmann

Contributors
Stefan Büttner, Patricia Clarke, Stephen Halliwell,
Verity Harte, Antony Hatzistavrou, Fritz-Gregor Herrmann,
Andrew S. Mason, Vasilis Politis, Richard Stalley

The Classical Press of Wales

First published in 2006 by
The Classical Press of Wales
15 Rosehill Terrace, Swansea SA1 6JN
Tel: +44 (0)1792 458397
Fax: +44 (0)1792 464067
www.classicalpressofwales.co.uk

Distributor in the United States of America:
The David Brown Book Co.
PO Box 511, Oakville, CT 06779
Tel: +1 (860) 945-9329
Fax: +1 (860) 945-9468

© 2006 The contributors

All rights reserved. No part of this publication may be reproduced, stored in a retrieval system, or transmitted, in any form or by any means, electronic, mechanical, photocopying, recording or otherwise, without the prior permission of the publisher.

ISBN 1-905125-10-0

A catalogue record for this book is available from the British Library

Typeset by Ernest Buckley, Clunton, Shropshire
Printed and bound in the UK by Gomer Press, Llandysul, Ceredigion, Wales

―――――――

The Classical Press of Wales, an independent venture, was founded in 1993, initially to support the work of classicists and ancient historians in Wales and their collaborators from further afield. More recently it has published work initiated by scholars internationally. While retaining a special loyalty to Wales and the Celtic countries, the Press welcomes scholarly contributions from all parts of the world.

The symbol of the Press is the Red Kite. This bird, once widespread in Britain, was reduced by 1905 to some five individuals confined to a small area known as 'The Desert of Wales' – the upper Tywi valley. Geneticists report that the stock was saved from terminal inbreeding by the arrival of one stray female bird from Germany. After much careful protection, the Red Kite now thrives – in Wales and beyond.

CONTENTS

	Page
Preface *Fritz-Gregor Herrmann*	vii
1. Law and justice in Plato *Richard Stalley* (University of Glasgow)	1
2. Beware of imitations: image recognition in Plato *Verity Harte* (Yale University)	21
3. ΟΥΣΙΑ in Plato's *Phaedo* *Fritz-Gregor Herrmann* (University of Wales Swansea)	43
4. The tripartition of the soul in Plato's *Republic* *Stefan Büttner* (Universität Konstanz)	75
5. Happiness and the nature of the philosopher-kings *Antony Hatzistavrou* (University of Cyprus)	95
6. Appearance and belief in *Theaetetus* 151d–187a *Patricia Clarke* (University of Aberdeen)	125
7. The argument for the reality of change and changelessness in Plato's *Sophist* (248e7–249d5) *Vasilis Politis* (Trinity College Dublin)	149
8. Plato on eternity *Andrew S. Mason* (King's College, London)	177
9. An Aristotelian perspective on Plato's dialogues *Stephen Halliwell* (University of St Andrews)	189
Index rerum	213
Index locorum	217
Index verborum	225

PREFACE

This collection of essays derives from a panel on Plato at the Second Celtic Conference in Classics, held in Glasgow from September 4–7, 2002. The panel was not 'themed', but it is worth highlighting one strand that runs through the chapters here presented, which lends a unity regardless of the academic traditions or current affiliations of their authors, and regardless of the topics addressed and the dialogues studied. Each of the contributions has at its core discussion of a word or concept – or set of words or concepts – which constitute the point of departure for a philosophical interpretation.

RICHARD STALLEY addresses the question of the relationship of νόμος, 'law', and δικαιοσύνη, 'justice', and outlines Plato's discussion of this relationship in the *Euthyphro*, the *Apology*, the *Crito* and the *Gorgias*, which marks a new stage in the Greek debate of the opposition of νόμος, 'convention', and φύσις, 'nature'. Primarily in the context of the argument at *Phaedo* 72–7 – that recollection involves being reminded of something by something else – VERITY HARTE reflects on the concept of 'likeness of something' and its role in the logic of the argument. 'οὐσία in Plato's *Phaedo*' approaches the philosophy of Plato's middle period through tracing the history and application of a key term. ANTONY HATZISTAVROU arrives at his conclusion that in Plato's *Republic* philosopher-kings *are* happy by establishing two senses in which Socrates talks of a φύσις, a 'nature' of man. Central to STEFAN BÜTTNER's discussion of the function of the tripartition of the soul in the *Republic* is the identification of 'the concept of κρίνειν as the unifying element of the recognizing soul'. An interpretation of range of meaning and application of φαίνεσθαι provides the key to an understanding of a central epistemological issue in Plato's *Theaetetus* in PATRICIA CLARKE's essay. VASILIS POLITIS demonstrates how 'the argument for the reality of change and changelessness in Plato's *Sophist*' 'depends crucially on…one phrase, τὸ παντελῶς ὄν'. ANDREW MASON's discussion of timeless eternity in Plato's *Timaeus* focuses on the conceptual difficulties involved in applying terms like αἰώνιος, ἀίδιος and ἀεὶ ὄν to the eternal in contradistinction to the everlasting, before offering a definitional solution in the context of Plato's ontology. By setting into context the expressions which Aristotle employs in his characterization of Plato's texts at *Politics* 2.6.1265a10–13, STEPHEN

Fritz-Gregor Herrmann

Halliwell arrives at a nuanced interpretation of Aristotle's response to Plato as a writer and as a philosopher, which sheds light on the complexities any reader and interpreter of Plato is faced with.

This shared aspect of these otherwise very different treatments of problems surrounding Plato's philosophy may mark a convergence of approaches, or it may be grounded in the nature of Plato's philosophy as presented in the dialogues, or it may simply be necessitated by the distance that separates the modern reader from the ancient author. At any rate, each interpretation here advanced is the result of a close reading of a passage, or set of selected passages, of Greek text. Care has been taken, though, that the volume be accessible to the reader with little or no knowledge of Ancient Greek. Words, phrases and passages of text are accompanied by English translations and precise references to the texts quoted. The only concession asked of the reader is an acquaintance with the Greek alphabet.

Anton Powell must be thanked for the conception and organization of the Celtic Conference in Classics, and for much subsequent support and encouragement. I should also like to express my gratitude to all contributors to the original panel, for their own papers as well as the friendly and stimulating discussion that ensued, and to the authors for their patience. Lastly, our thanks to Ernest Buckley, typesetter to the Press and a true man of letters, are not perfunctory.

FGH
Swansea,
September 2006

1

LAW AND JUSTICE IN PLATO

Richard Stalley

Introduction

In this chapter I shall use the noun 'justice' to stand for the Greek δικαιοσύνη and the adjectives 'just' and 'unjust' to stand for its cognates δίκαιος and ἄδικος. Although these translations are quite standard they could be misleading in some respects. As commentators on the *Republic* often point out, the Greek terms have a wider range than the English ones.[1] For example, the Greeks would have described a mugger who steals someone's purse as ἄδικος whereas we would be unlikely to describe him as 'unjust'. Aristotle explains the situation by distinguishing between a narrower conception of δικαιοσύνη which is primarily a matter of getting your fair share of goods and evils and a broader conception in which it embraces all the other virtues, at least in so far as they concern our behaviour towards others (*NE* 1129a26–1130a14). I shall be concerned with this broader conception.

There are similar problems with the term 'law'. I have in mind here the Greek word νόμος. From around the end of the sixth century the Athenians used this in place of the older word θεσμός to refer to what we would call 'statute law',[2] but it can, of course, refer to any kind of law, custom or social practice. For example, Herodotus (1.196) praises the excellent νόμος concerning marriage of a tribe who auctioned off the pretty girls to would-be husbands and then used the proceeds to provide dowries for the ugly ones. The word can even be used to refer to the way of life of animals.[3] But famously the sophists used it in contrast with φύσις to pick out what is merely conventional as opposed to what is natural.[4]

Modern philosophers and legal theorists may think that the different usages of νόμος could be a potent source of confusion. In particular they would prevent the Greeks from drawing two distinctions which have played an important part in more recent thinking about the nature of law: (1) the distinction between laws proper and other kinds of rules or customs which may have no legal force, and (2) the distinction between normative and purely descriptive principles. But whether one regards the failure to draw these distinctions as a dangerous confusion depends to some extent on one's own philosophical position. Some philosophers would argue that a legal system necessarily rests on a foundation of pre-legal rules and customs and that, in arriving at their decisions, courts cannot avoid making use of moral or quasi-moral considerations which are not themselves encapsulated in law. If these philosophers are right, it may be the English term that is potentially misleading.[5]

The problem of law and justice

In everyday life there is a natural tendency to assume that justice and obedience to law come to much the same thing. This was as true of the Greeks as it is of ourselves. There are, for example, many passages in the orators and in other writers which associate the just and the lawful.[6] On occasion philosophers, likewise, appear to identify justice and legality. For example, Xenophon makes Socrates define justice as 'the lawful', τὸ νόμιμον (*Mem.* 4.iv.12–13). Aristotle, in distinguishing the different senses of justice, also identifies justice in its general sense with obedience to law. 'Since the law-breaker is unjust while the law-abiding person is just, it is clear that what is lawful is in a sense just. For those things prescribed by the art of legislation are lawful and each of these is called just' (*NE* 1129b11–14).[7] However, the idea that the just and the lawful are the same has obvious problems. One is that there seem to have been legal or quasi-legal methods of settling disputes before there were codes of law.[8] For example, there is no reference to law in the trial depicted on the Homeric shield of Achilles (*Iliad* 18.493–508). Hesiod, too, writes as though there are methods of seeking justice which do not rely on formal codes of law.[9] The implication would seem to be that, for the Greeks at least, justice is prior to law. One might draw the same conclusion from the Athenian juror's oath which required the jurors to use only the written laws of Athens and to decide issues which were not covered by these laws as seemed just to them.[10] This may suggest that one does not always need a law to determine issues of justice and injustice. A related point is made by Aristotle who argues, following Plato's *Statesman* 295a–b, that, because laws are necessarily general, they cannot always produce the right answers in a particular case. It is here that, according to Aristotle, we have to bring in the notion of equity (ἐπιείκεια). 'The equitable is just but not legally so; rather it is a correction (ἐπανόρθωμα) of legal justice' (*NE* 1137b11–13). Problems also arise from the fact that laws are human creations which vary from place to place and from time to time. An act may be legal in one jurisdiction or at one period and illegal in another. This is acceptable in the case of matters which seem to depend purely on convention, but common sense suggests that issues of justice and injustice can transcend the rules of a particular legal system (Aristotle *NE* 1134b18–35). Incest, for example, cannot be just in one part of the world and unjust in another (Xenophon *Mem.* 4.iv.19–25). It would follow that a particular law may be unjust, and that one can appeal to considerations of justice against the requirements of positive law. This seems to be what happens in Aeschylus' *Suppliants*, where the chorus appeals to justice against the positive law of their country which Aegyptus seeks to enforce.[11]

All this might suggest that issues of law and justice ought really to be distinguished, that there are standards of justice and injustice which are prior to and independent of any system of law. In a well-ordered community the acts required by law will, in general, be the same as those required by justice, but this will not be the case in badly-governed communities and even in the best societies justice and law may sometimes diverge. However, the Greeks seem to have been reluctant to accept this.[12] There were, I suggest, good reasons for this reluctance. A community obviously can have procedures for settling disputes which do not depend on a formal code of law. It could, for example, determine them by watching for omens, or by drawing straws. It could also allow judges to decide matters in whatever way took their fancy. But if it requires judges to decide *justly* it implies that there are standards by which they can determine what is just or unjust. The parties must be able to present arguments. In doing so they must appeal to principles which the judges can be expected to accept. The judges, for their part, must either collectively or individually have reasons for their decision. This in turn implies that there should be a measure of consistency in decision-making because what is just for one individual must be just for another unless there are significant differences between the two cases. If we recognize these points, we come close to conceding that there must be a νόμος even if that νόμος is not formalized in writing.[13]

One way to make sense of these issues is by distinguishing different kinds of law. One may, for example, appeal from the laws of a particular society to laws promulgated by the gods which apply universally and whose authority may override that of human laws. This is the strategy used by Antigone as depicted by Sophocles (447 ff.). Xenophon ascribes a similar position to Socrates. There are unwritten laws made by the gods which are observed in all countries and which are enforced by divine sanctions (*Mem.* 4.iv.19–21). Aristotle (*NE* 5.7.1134b18–35) distinguishes natural from legal justice, but this does not apparently mean that natural justice is independent of law. In the *Rhetoric* (1.13.1373b1–17) Aristotle distinguishes general laws, which are in accordance with nature and hold everywhere, from the particular laws of particular human communities. Particular laws are those established by each people for themselves. General laws are in accordance with nature (κατὰ φύσιν) and express an idea of natural justice that is common to all men. In support of this distinction he quotes Sophocles' *Antigone*,[14] Empedocles[15] and Alcidamas.[16] Elsewhere in the same work Aristotle characterizes the general laws as unwritten (1.10.1368b7–10).[17] Later he points out that an orator may appeal to written laws or to general ones as suits his case (1.15.1375a26–b18). Demosthenes, when referring to the distinction between voluntary and involuntary misdeeds, speaks of them as being recognized not only in the laws [of Athens] but as having been established by nature 'in unwritten laws and in the customs of mankind' (τοῖς ἀγράφοις νομίμοις καὶ τοῖς ἀνθρωπίνοις ἤθεσιν, 18.275). Thus, although there was not a clearly developed doctrine of natural law, it seems to have been widely recognized that justice involved more than obedience to the particular laws of a human community and that this in turn implied the existence of other kinds of law which did not derive their validity from human legislation.

I now want to consider how Plato handles these issues in the *Euthyphro*, *Apology*, *Crito* and *Gorgias*. The first three are all concerned with the events surrounding Socrates' trial and execution. The *Apology* and *Crito* are generally thought to be among Plato's earliest writings. Scholars who have speculated about the chronology of the 'early' dialogues have usually put the *Euthyphro* somewhat later.[18] But its dramatic date and subject matter suggest that Plato intended it to be read before the other two. It will be convenient to consider the dialogues in the order of their dramatic dates but my arguments do not hinge on that. I will try to show that these 'trial' dialogues individually and collectively raise important problems about the relation between law and justice without presenting any very clear solution. The *Gorgias* is longer and more complex philosophically. The conversation it describes is supposed to have taken place many years before Socrates' trial and execution but it looks forward to those events. I shall argue that we can find within it some clear indications of how Plato would deal with the problems raised in the three trial dialogues.[19]

Euthyphro

The setting and context of the *Euthyphro* suggest a relevance to issues of law and justice. The dialogue is set near the office of the King Archon, with whom Socrates has evidently had some business in connection with his forthcoming trial. It begins with a discussion of the legal cases in which Socrates and Euthyphro are involved. In the first few lines our attention is drawn to a legal nicety, the distinction between the forms of procedure known as δίκη and γραφή (2b1–2).[20] Socrates is, of course, being prosecuted by Meletus on a charge of corrupting the young and introducing new gods. Euthyphro, on the other hand, is prosecuting his own father for having brought about the death of a hired worker who had killed one of his slaves (3e6–4e3). Because there is a religious dimension to both cases, the ensuing discussion focuses on the nature of τὸ ὅσιον, the holy or the pious, but, as we shall see, the issues could equally well have been expressed in terms of the just and the lawful.

Euthyphro's willingness to prosecute his own father rests on his confidence that, an expert on religion, he knows what holiness requires (4e4–5c3). But he has difficulty in understanding quite what Socrates has in mind when the latter asks him to define holiness, as opposed to merely giving examples of holy acts. Eventually he suggests that the holy is 'what is dear to the gods' (τὸ τοῖς θεοῖς προσφιλές, 6e10–7a1). Socrates offers two main arguments to show that this cannot be adequate as an account of the nature of the holy. The first argument relies on Euthyphro's acceptance of the traditional belief that the gods quarrel among themselves. If that is right, what is dear to some of the gods may be hated by others. Thus, on Euthyphro's definition, the same thing could be both holy and unholy (7e5–8b6). This is clearly unsatisfactory, but amending Euthyphro's account so that the holy is defined as 'what is dear to all the gods' does not save the day. Socrates gets Euthyphro to agree that it is not the fact that something is loved by the gods that makes it holy. Rather the gods love certain things because they are holy (9c1–11b5). Thus, even if the possibility of disagreements among the gods is ignored, Euthyphro's attempt to define the holy as 'what is dear to the gods' was misguided. It focused on something that merely 'happens to be holy' (πάθος δέ τι περὶ αὐτοῦ...ὅ τι πέπονθε τοῦτο τὸ ὅσιον) rather than on its essential nature (οὐσία) (11a6–b1). As we might say, there must be some standard of what is holy that is prior to and independent of what the gods happen to love or hate.

Even from this brief summary it should be clear that the main arguments of the *Euthyphro* would apply to justice as much as to holiness. Anyone who attempted to define justice as 'what is commanded by the gods' and who also accepted the traditional stories of quarrels among the gods would have to concede that what is commanded by one god might be forbidden by another, and that the same act might thus turn out to be both just and unjust. If someone avoided this point by defining justice as 'what is commanded by all the gods', then the question would arise whether just acts are just because they are commanded by the gods or whether the gods command them because they are just. Adopting the latter view implies that there is a standard of what is just and unjust that is prior to and independent of any divine commands. The arguments of the dialogue would be equally fatal to any suggestion that justice is determined by laws of human provenance. Since different legal systems disagree, the claim that justice is obedience to law would imply that one and the same act may be both just and unjust. Someone might try to avoid this conclusion by arguing that there are some kinds of act that are required or forbidden in all jurisdictions. But then one could argue that it is not the fact that certain acts are required by law that makes them just. Rather, it is because these acts are believed on independent grounds to be just that they are required by the laws of all human communities.

Plato was clearly aware that the arguments of the *Euthyphro* apply to justice just as much as they do to holiness. Both Socrates and Euthyphro take it for granted that the gods will love what they believe to be just. In fact Euthyphro bases his confidence that he is behaving as holiness requires on his belief that what he is doing is just. Because he accepts without question that the gods love what is just (7e6–8), he is sure that in prosecuting his father he is doing what is dear to the gods. He gets into trouble because he also accepts the traditional stories of the gods quarrelling among themselves (7b2–8a8). Since Socrates and Euthyphro agree both that the gods love what they believe to be just and that the gods love what is holy, it looks as though the just and the holy may turn out to be the same. This possibility is explored in the final section of the dialogue (11e4–15a7). Socrates there gets Euthyphro to agree that whatever is holy is just and then asks him whether whatever is just is also holy. The issue is whether the just and the holy are identical or whether the holy is merely a part of the just. Euthyphro opts for the latter alternative, claiming that holiness is the part of justice that concerns our service to the gods (12e5–8). To say that we serve someone or something normally implies that we give it some benefit. But it is absurd to say that human beings can somehow benefit the gods (14e9–15a4). If, on the other hand, serving the gods simply means doing what is pleasing to them, we are back to Euthyphro's original definition of the holy as what is dear to the gods, a definition which has already proved unsatisfactory (15b7–c2). The dialogue thus ends in confusion, but Plato's own view is clear enough. Although it does not depend on the will of the gods whether an act is or is not just, the gods, being good and wise, love justice and hate injustice. We therefore honour them by behaving justly and dishonour them when we are unjust. Justice and holiness thus coincide.[21]

From our point of view the important thing about the *Euthyphro* is its implication that justice is independent of any kind of legislation. Assuming that the gods are wise and good they will want human beings to behave justly. Thus if there are 'unwritten laws' established by the gods we may assume that those laws are just. But it is not the fact that the gods command a particular form of behaviour that makes that behaviour just. Rather the gods command that behaviour because they know it to be required by justice. The same goes for human laws. There may be laws that are common to all communities. It may be that such laws conform to the requirements of justice but there must still be some standard of justice that is independent of human legislation.

The implication of the *Euthyphro* is thus that there is no necessary relation between law and justice. Justice is prior to law and any particular law can be either just or unjust.

Apology
Issues of law and justice emerge more explicitly and with much greater urgency in the *Apology* and the *Crito*. Recent discussion of these dialogues has often been shaped by the attempt to find within them a coherent theory of civil disobedience.[22] If the dialogues contained such a theory, that would clearly be relevant to the questions we are considering, but in fact the justification of civil disobedience does not seem to have been a general issue for Plato or for his contemporaries.[23] Insofar as there is a single aim in these works, it is to honour the memory of Socrates and his commitment to philosophy while at the same time defending him against two very different kinds of accusation. The first is that he really was a trouble-maker who deserved to be executed. The second is that by accepting his fate he meekly kowtowed to public opinion and failed to live up to his own intellectual and moral standards. Since these accusations are directly opposed to one another, the task Plato sets himself in these dialogues is evidently a delicate one. Moreover, both dialogues focus on the particular case of Socrates rather than on general principles. The words Plato puts into Socrates' mouth in the *Apology* have to constitute a defence that might plausibly be offered to an Athenian court. There is little scope there for close philosophical argument. Plato presumably had a freer hand in writing the *Crito* but there he limits himself by the brevity of the dialogue, by the lack of philosophical sophistication on the part of Socrates' interlocutor and by the close focus on Socrates' own particular circumstances.

In the *Apology* Socrates' first main line of argument is that he has a divine mission to subject citizens and foreigners alike to philosophical examination. He first realized this when the Delphic oracle told his friend Chaerephon that no one was wiser than Socrates (21a4–7). This puzzled him, because he was not conscious of being wise at all. With a view to refuting the oracle he began questioning those, such as politicians and poets and craftsmen, who had a reputation for wisdom. But he discovered that none of these really understood anything about the most important matters. He then realized what the oracle really meant: that the wisest human beings are those who recognize that they have no real wisdom (23a5–b4). Since then he has spent his time questioning those who seem to be wise and showing that they are not really so. He has tried to persuade his fellow citizens that they should care for themselves rather than for their property, in other words, that they should seek to make themselves as good and wise as possible. Similarly they should care for the city rather than for its possessions (36c5–9). His task is thus to act as a 'gadfly' to Athens (30d5–31b5). In describing this mission Socrates asserts repeatedly that he is carrying out the commands of the god (21e5, 22a4, 22e1, 23b4–6, 30a5–7, 37e5–38a1). These have been expressed 'in oracles, in dreams and in every manner by which a divine power has ever instructed a man to do anything' (33c4–7). He reinforces this appeal to divine commands with the rhetoric of military discipline: 'Wherever a man stations himself deeming it best to be there, or is stationed by his superior, there he must…remain and face the danger taking no account of death nor any other thing apart from disgrace' (28d6–10). Since Socrates remained at the post assigned to him by his military commanders at Potidaea, Amphipolis and Delium it would be absurd for him now to abandon the post assigned to him by the god (28d10–29a1). If the Court decided to release him on condition that he gave up philosophizing he would have to refuse (29d3–6).

Socrates' position here may look similar to that of Antigone – that divine commands override human law – but any resemblance is in fact superficial. Socrates does not accept that he has transgressed the laws of Athens. On the contrary, if he can convince the jury that he has been following the commands of a god or gods recognized by the city, he will have an answer to the charges that have been made against him, the charges of corrupting the young and introducing new gods. So in this particular case there can be no disagreement between divine and human law.[24] Another difference between Socrates and Antigone is that he cannot appeal to any widely-recognized divine law requiring him to behave as he has. Instead he relies largely on the Delphic oracle. But the oracle certainly did not give him any explicit instruction about how he should behave. All it did was to confirm that no one was wiser than Socrates (21a6–7). It was Socrates himself who interpreted this as a command to engage in his particular kind of philosophizing. When he speaks of the commands of the gods as being expressed 'in every manner by which a divine power has ever instructed a man to do anything' (33c4–7), Socrates may be referring to his divine 'sign'. But appeals to purely private manifestations of this kind will hardly help his case. Not only are they, by their very nature, incapable of corroboration but they could also be taken as showing that Socrates did indeed introduce new gods. So the evidence on which Socrates bases his claim to have a divine mission is, to say the least, somewhat suspect. One might even suggest that the mission is not so much one that has been imposed on Socrates by the gods but rather one that he has imposed upon himself. There is a hint of this in the passage cited above where he stresses the importance of staying at one's post. Someone should stay at his post, not only when he has been placed there by his commander, but also when he has *placed himself* there 'deeming it best to be there' (28d6–10).[25]

Socrates' second main line of defence is to emphasize his own commitment to justice (28b5–9; cf. 39a8–b8). This is founded on his conviction that what really matters is not wealth, power or reputation but the welfare of our own souls (29d7–30b4) and that it can therefore never benefit us to behave unjustly. Socrates' divine 'sign' has made him keep away from public life so far as possible. This is a good thing because political activity is in practice incompatible with justice (31c4–32a3). 'No man will save his life who nobly opposes you or any other populace and prevents many unjust and illegal things (ἄδικα καὶ παράνομα) from happening in the state' (31e2–4, trans. Fowler 1914). If his accusers have him put to death unjustly they will do much more harm to themselves than they do to him (30c8–d1). Indeed no evil can come to a good man either in this life or after death (41c8–d2).

As evidence of his commitment to justice Socrates cites his behaviour after the battle of Arginusae when, as prytanist, he opposed the illegal proposal to try the generals *en masse*, and also his refusal to take part in the arrest of Leon of Salamis when he was ordered to do so by the Thirty.[26] In describing the former incident Socrates makes it totally clear that he opposed trying the generals *en masse* because that was against the law. In taking this stand he saw himself as upholding law and justice (μετὰ τοῦ νόμου καὶ τοῦ δικαίου) against the unjust (μὴ δίκαια) demands of the people (32b5–c3). He thus associates justice with upholding the law. This is puzzling because the laws of Athens are presumably measures passed by the democratic assembly at the behest of the politicians. But Socrates claims to have shown that people in general and politicians in particular have no understanding of the most important things in life. For example, they value wealth and power more than the welfare of their souls (29d7–30b4). It is difficult to see why laws passed by these people should merit Socrates' respect or what obedience to them could have to do with the welfare of our souls. This point comes close to the surface when Socrates cross-examines his accuser Meletus about the allegation that he has corrupted the young. Socrates asks who makes the young better. Meletus first replies 'the laws'. When Socrates insists on being told which are the people who, knowing the laws, improve the young, Meletus ascribes this ability to the ordinary citizens of Athens (24d2–25a11).[27] Socrates responds to this by pointing out that it takes an expert to improve horses and other animals. It would therefore be strange indeed if the ordinary man can improve human beings (25a12–c4). In this passage Meletus represents the democratic view that more or less everyone can judge matters of good and bad, right and wrong and that this communal knowledge is embodied in the laws of the city. By rejecting this view Socrates implies that human law in general and the laws of Athens in particular may not always be just.[28]

Richard Stalley

The upshot of this is that, although issues of law and justice are prominent in the *Apology,* it is very difficult to extract from the dialogue a clear view of the way in which they are related to each other. Socrates sees himself as having a divine mission which apparently overrides any requirements laid on him by human authority, yet he avoids appeals to unwritten or divine laws. In places he talks as though justice requires him to obey the laws of Athens but his scepticism about the wisdom of the masses seems to imply that the laws of a democratic state may be utterly misguided. In particular it is difficult to see how any view of justice as conformity to human law could sustain Socrates' conviction that it is always in our interests to be just.

Crito

Of all Plato's dialogues the *Crito* would appear to be the one in which Plato deals most explicitly with questions about the relation between justice and law. In that dialogue Socrates argues that he should not escape from prison because justice requires him to obey the laws of Athens, even when doing so means accepting an undeserved sentence of death. In the early pages Socrates argues that we should always do what is just. In response to Crito, who has stressed the importance of public opinion (44b5–46a8), he insists that we should not worry about the views of the many but rather about those of the one man who really knows. In matters of health, for example, we trust the view of the doctor rather than that of the ignorant masses. If we do not do this we risk destroying our bodies. Similarly in matters of right and wrong, if we follow the masses rather than the one man who really knows, we risk destroying that element within us that is ruined by injustice and benefited by justice' (ᾧ τὸ ἄδικον μὲν λωβᾶται, τὸ δὲ δίκαιον ὀνίνησιν) (47e6–7). What matters is not living but living well, and living well means living honourably and justly (καλῶς καὶ δικαίως) (48b3–9). One may not commit injustice even in response to an injustice done to oneself (49b7–e2). In making these points Socrates relies heavily on claims which Crito is supposed to have accepted in previous discussions. They have agreed, at least by implication, that justice is an objective matter in which there may be recognized experts, that public opinion is therefore no guide to the truth, and that doing injustice causes immense harm to oneself. No argument has been offered for these points and there is very little to indicate what account of justice is being presupposed. Socrates avoids using the word ψυχή, 'soul', but he makes it clear that acts of injustice create some kind of disorder of the personality that is even more harmful to us than bodily disease. It is difficult to see how he could be so sure that injustice, particularly if it is identified with a failure to obey the law, must have this effect.

In the second part of the dialogue Socrates argues that if he escaped he would indeed be committing a serious injustice. The main arguments are put into the mouth of the personified laws of Athens but Socrates prepares the ground for them at 49e5–50a2:

ΣΩ. Λέγω δὴ αὖ τὸ μετὰ τοῦτο, μᾶλλον δ' ἐρωτῶ πότερον ἃ ἄν τις ὁμολογήσῃ τῳ δίκαια ὄντα ποιητέον ἢ ἐξαπατητέον;
ΚΡ. Ποιητέον.
ΣΩ. Ἐκ τούτων δὴ ἄθρει. ἀπιόντες ἐνθένδε ἡμεῖς μὴ πείσαντες τὴν πόλιν πότερον κακῶς τινας ποιοῦμεν, καὶ ταῦτα οὓς ἥκιστα δεῖ, ἢ οὔ; καὶ ἐμμένομεν οἷς ὡμολογήσαμεν δικαίοις οὖσιν ἢ οὔ;

Socrates: Next I say, or rather ask: 'Should someone do what he has agreed to do, that being just, or should he be deceitful?'
Crito: He should do it.
Socrates: Look at the matter on this basis. If we left this place, without having persuaded the city, would we be doing harm, and that to the very ones whom we ought least to harm? And would we be abiding by what we agreed as just or not?

The main point here – that justice requires us to keep agreements – is clear enough, but there is an element of ambiguity in the phrases used at 49e6 and 50a2 to convey the idea that this only applies to just agreements. The most obvious point Socrates might have in mind here is that an agreement is binding only if it is made fairly. As the laws themselves later acknowledge, there may be no obligation to keep an agreement if it has been made in response to coercion or deceit (52d8–e5). But Socrates may also mean that an agreement is void if it requires us to do something that is unjust. For example, in the *Republic* Socrates makes it clear that someone who had agreed to return weapons to a friend would not be obliged to return them if the friend had subsequently gone mad.[29] On either view, Socrates here acknowledges that the obligation to keep agreements is not absolute but presupposes a background of conventional norms which determine what constitutes a just agreement.

It is striking that Socrates offers no justification for the principle that one should keep one's agreements or for the associated background norms. One might suppose that he is relying on popular morality but that would be inconsistent with his insistence a few pages earlier that public opinion is not to be trusted. Some of his contemporaries might have sought to ground these principles on the commands of the gods. But there is no hint of that in the *Crito* and it would in any case lead directly to the problems discussed in the *Euthyphro*. So Socrates' argument rests on a conception of justice which is not clearly articulated and for which no philosophical justification is forthcoming.

Socrates now imagines himself being addressed by the laws of Athens. These deploy two main lines of argument to demonstrate that Socrates has an obligation to obey them.[30] The first, sometimes called 'the argument from just agreement', is to the effect that Socrates has made an implicit agreement to obey the laws and must therefore abide by it. The second, sometimes called 'the argument from superior status', claims that Socrates owes obedience to the laws in much the same way that a child owes obedience to his parents or a slave to his master.

To establish that Socrates has agreed to obey them the laws point out that he has remained in Athens throughout his life even though he had ample opportunity to leave. He chose to produce children in Athens and he did not accept the opportunity to go into exile at his trial. He has thus made what we would now call an 'implicit agreement' to abide by the laws (51c8–52a3, 52a8–53a7). It is tempting to see a parallel here with the arguments of more recent philosophers who have sought to base political obligation in general on a doctrine of tacit consent.[31] But in the *Crito* the arguments of the laws are directed very much to Socrates' own particular circumstances. They appeal to specific things he has done that constitute making an agreement and do not, therefore, have any purchase on someone in different circumstances or who had behaved differently – on someone, for example, who was not a citizen or on a citizen who had tried to leave the city or who had openly criticized its institutions. If the obligation to obey the law rested entirely on the kind of implicit agreement that Socrates is supposed to have made, then many people could claim that they have no such obligation.[32]

In deploying the argument from superior status the laws argue that they made it possible for Socrates' parents to marry and thus in a sense brought him into existence. Since they required his father to have him trained in music and gymnastics, they are also responsible for his upbringing and education. He is therefore their child and slave and it would be quite improper for him to claim a position of equality with them so far as justice is concerned (50d1–52c4). Indeed the obligation he owes to the city is far stronger than that he owes to his parents. He must therefore do whatever the city commands or else show it by persuasion where justice lies. By escaping he would be destroying the laws and would thus be in the same situation as a child who killed its parent or a slave who killed his master (50a9–b5, 51a2–c3, 54c1–8).

If we take this argument at all literally it is not very impressive. In so far as it seems persuasive it relies largely on the belief, which has of course been very widely held, that children have a special obligation to obey and honour their parents and that there is, therefore, something especially terrible about killing one's father or mother. The laws can apply these ideas to Socrates because in his case it is plausible to claim that they are responsible for his birth and upbringing. They would not apply to someone who was not a citizen. But, even as applied to Socrates, the argument still looks unconvincing. It is certainly not obvious that parents should have absolute authority over adult children. Few legal systems, and certainly not the laws of Athens, give them such authority. So the claim that someone is, as it were, a child of the laws does not sustain the conclusion that he or she must obey them come what may.

The claim that Socrates has a duty to obey the laws because he is, as it were, their slave looks even more dubious. In effect it derives the obligation to obey the law from the obligation of a slave to obey his master. But the relation of master and slave can exist only within a legal context. It requires laws to determine who is a slave and who is master and to specify their respective rights and duties.[33] Even if there were natural slaves, as Aristotle thought, it would still require law to determine which slave belonged to which master. So to derive the obligation to obey the law from that of a slave to obey his master is to argue in a circle.

The laws do, of course, claim that by escaping Socrates would be destroying them, so far as he could (50a–b, 50d, 51a). To a modern reader this might suggest a general argument for obedience to law. It is in everyone's interests that there should be a legal system. Disobeying the decisions of courts tends to undermine such a system. Therefore we should obey the decisions of courts. But this is not the argument deployed by the laws in the *Crito*. They argue that if Socrates refused to accept the decision of the Athenian court he would be acting as though he was equal in status to the laws and could therefore destroy them if they tried to destroy him. But in fact he is the child or slave of the laws. If he acted in a way which tended to destroy them he would be effectively committing parricide. This argument appeals to the particular status Socrates has in relation to the laws rather than to any general obligation to uphold the law.[34]

The upshot of all this is that the *Crito* is very far from making a simple identification of justice with obedience to law. It does not even provide a general argument to show that justice requires us to obey the laws of cities such as Athens. Socrates has claimed that it is always in our interests to be just but he has not offered any account of justice which could explain why this is so. He has also claimed that justice requires him to abide by the decision of the court. But the arguments he has used appeal to his particular circumstances and do not underpin any general doctrine that we should obey the law. Moreover they depend on claims about the requirements of justice whose status is unclear and for which no justification is given. This is not to deny that there are elements in the dialogue which might be developed to provide more general accounts of the obligation to obey the law. A good deal of philosophical commentary has been devoted to pursuing such points. But, as it stands, the *Crito* certainly does not contain any systematic account of the relationship between law and justice.

Gorgias

The main elements for a solution to these problems can be found in the *Gorgias*. The first move is made when Socrates, who has been challenged by Polus to give his own definition of oratory, draws a distinction between genuine arts, τέχναι, and mere 'knacks', ἐμπειρίαι. The difference between these is that the former seek the good and use reason in doing so, whereas the latter are concerned with pleasure and the appearance of good and do not therefore require rational understanding. In the case of the body there are two genuine arts, gymnastics and medicine. Corresponding to these are the two spurious arts or 'knacks' of cosmetics and cookery. In the case of the soul there are likewise two genuine arts which seek the soul's good and make use of reason. These are law-making (νομοθετική) and justice (δικαιοσύνη). Their spurious counterparts, which seek merely pleasure and the appearance of good, are sophistry and oratory (462b8–466a8). From our point of view the key idea here is that law-making and justice are seen as crafts which make use of reason and seek the good of the soul. But it is also interesting to notice that justice is identified with the art of the judge who administers the law.

These ideas are developed in the following section where Socrates argues, first, that it is always better to suffer wrong than to do wrong and, second, that, since punishment cures injustice, it is better for us to be punished for our misdeeds than to go unpunished (474c4–479c6). He expands these points through an elaborate comparison between medicine and justice. In the same way that we take the sick man to the doctor to be cured of his bodily disorder, so we take the unjust man to the judge to be cured of the evil in his soul (477c6–479c6). On the surface, at least, these claims look absurd. In Greek cities, as in modern states, plenty of legislation was not obviously designed to improve the souls of the citizens, and their courts did not in general seek to cure criminals of their wickedness. So even if there is some sense in which law-making and justice are concerned with the good of the soul, it is difficult to see any reason for obeying the laws of existing communities.

The apparent absurdity of Socrates' claims is brought out by Callicles. He protests that Socrates has systematically confused what is the case by νόμος, which here seems to have the broad sense of 'convention', with what is the case by φύσις, 'nature'. Those who make laws (νόμοι) are, in general, the weaker people; so they lay down laws and distribute praise and blame as suits their own interests. What is naturally right is that the stronger should rule and exploit the weak for his own ends (482c4–484c3). Two distinct claims are implicit here: (a) that law is the product of human convention rather than nature, and (b) that natural right consists in the domination of the stronger. The first of these is directly relevant to the problems we have been considering. If Plato thought that law was simply the product of human convention he would have to agree with Callicles that there are no rational grounds for obeying it. He has therefore to show, against Callicles, that law is in fact founded in nature. But instead of arguing this point directly he develops his own view by making Socrates attack Callicles' conception of the strong man.

At 491d Socrates asks whether Callicles' strong man will rule over himself (i.e. exercise self-restraint). Callicles insists that the strong man will brook no restraint and will devote himself to satisfying whatever desires he happens to have. As the argument of 491d4–500a6 shows, this prevents him from offering any coherent conception of the good. The underlying message of the passage is thus that human good necessarily involves restraint in the sense that to live a good life we have to exercise control over our desires. This conception of goodness is used to underpin the positive account of law and morality which Socrates goes on to develop. He argues first that in crafts, such as painting, building and ship-making, goodness consists in regularity and order (τάξις and κόσμος). Craftsmen seek to give things a certain form by fitting their elements together to create a regular and well-ordered product. A good house, for example, is one that exhibits regularity and order while a bad one exhibits disorder. The same goes for the bodies and souls of human beings. The order of the body is called 'health' while regular and well-organized states of the soul are called 'lawful' and 'law' (νόμιμόν τε καὶ νόμος). By them people are made lawful (νόμιμοι) and orderly (κόσμιοι) (503d5–504d3). These conditions of the soul are called 'justice' and 'temperance' (δικαιοσύνη and σωφροσύνη, 504d1–3). The task of a true politician is to create these conditions in the souls of the citizens (504d5–e4). A few pages later Socrates gives this view of justice a cosmological dimension. Wise men say that heaven and earth, gods and men are held together by community (κοινωνία), friendship (φιλία), orderliness (κοσμιότης), temperance (σωφροσύνη) and justice (δικαιότης). That is why they call the universe κόσμος, 'order', rather than 'disorderly' or 'dissolute' (507e6–508a4).

In this passage Socrates, in effect, offers a new conception of law which enables him to argue both that there is an intrinsic connection between law and justice and that being just is necessarily in our own interests. A key element in this conception is the association of law with the order of the universe. In itself this was not particularly novel[35] but it enables Socrates to argue that the contrast which Callicles draws between law and nature is illusory. Genuine law is part of nature. So far as human beings are concerned, it is a fact of nature that we cannot live together unless we acknowledge the need for law and restrain our desires accordingly. A second, and apparently more original, element in Socrates' account is the insistence that the good soul exhibits order in the same kind of way as the well-made artefact. This implies that law governs, not just our external behaviour, but the internal arrangement of our souls. In particular it requires that our desires are kept under control. Although this account is not developed in any detail, it could in principle provide an answer to most of the problems with which we have been concerned. Justice is identified with a condition of order within the city and the soul. Law is what makes that order possible. There can therefore be no justice without law. Equally because goodness consists in law and order and because the just individual is one with an orderly soul it is in our interests to be just. To put the matter in another way, Socrates, without making the point explicit, accepts the idea that there is unwritten law. However, he departs from traditional views because he does not attribute this law to divine commands or to human conventions. It is binding on human communities because without it there can be no civic order, but it is also binding on individuals because it alone makes possible the orderly condition of the soul which constitutes human good. The theory thus meets the difficulties suggested by the *Euthyphro* because it implies that law and justice are prior to legislation, human or divine. It solves some of the problems posed by the *Apology* and *Crito* by showing how Socrates can be sure that it is in his interests to be just where justice is understood as requiring us to uphold the principles of order embodied in systems of law.

There is one obvious problem with this theory as it stands. Socrates has argued that the genuine legislator should seek the good of his subjects. We can now understand why this should be the case. Genuine laws will be designed to create law and order within the souls of the citizens. But Socrates goes on to argue that none of the politicians whom Callicles can name have succeeded in improving the citizens. All of them have been concerned simply to gratify the desires of the populace (515c4–517a6). Paradoxically Socrates argues that he is the only true politician (521d6–8), but he acknowledges that he will be unable to save his life if he is ever brought to trial before an Athenian court. He will then be like a doctor prosecuted by a confectioner before a jury of children (521e3–522a6). However, this does not cause him alarm because what really matters is to avoid doing injustice (522c7–e3). Only then can one face with confidence the judgement that awaits all of us after death (522e3–6).

We might infer from this that the so-called 'laws' of existing cities do not really deserve the name, because they are directed to pleasure rather than to the good of the citizens. If that is the case, one might well wonder whether these 'laws' should command any respect. In other words we might ask whether Socrates' argument provides any grounds for obedience to positive law in cities like Athens. Socrates does not address this question specifically but he does have the materials for an answer. Callicles attacks the laws and customs of existing cities and the ideas of justice and temperance embodied within them for requiring us to restrain our desires. Socrates argues, in response, that such restraint is necessary for a good life. There is an implication here that existing codes of morality have merit at least to the extent that they encourage restraint. Moreover, if Socrates is committed to the idea that goodness resides in order, he must accept that an order that is in some ways defective is preferable to a condition of disorder. So the arguments of the *Gorgias* do provide reasons for upholding existing law.

Socrates could also offer more specific reasons why a just person will in general obey the laws of the city. He argues that the just man will not be motivated by appetite or fear and that his overriding concern will simply be to avoid being unjust. He will not therefore be worried about external goods, such as wealth or reputation. So, even in a defective state, the just man would seldom have reason to disobey the law. The danger comes if he begins to participate in public affairs. To survive in public life one must assimilate oneself to the dominant element in a city, to the tyrant in a tyranny and to the masses in a democracy (510a6–e2, 512d8–513c2). The implication is that it will then be almost impossible to remain just (510e3–511a3). The main thrust of the closing pages of the *Gorgias* is thus that the wise man will withdraw from public life and devote himself to philosophy. Of course, one still cannot exclude the possibility that a tyrannical regime might command one to perform an unjust act. This is presumably what happened to Socrates when he was ordered to take part in the arrest of Leon of Salamis. The implication of the *Gorgias* is that a command of that kind has none of the characteristics of a genuine law and hence has no claim upon us.

If this is right, the *Gorgias* suggests an account of justice which gives it an essential connection with νόμος while at the same time preserving the central insight of the *Euthyphro* that justice cannot depend on the will of any legislator, human or divine. It also makes good sense of the positions Socrates adopts in the *Apology* and *Crito*. It explains why it is always in our interests to be just and provides a framework within which Socrates could justify the particular stance he takes towards the laws of Athens. Some laws embody principles that are fundamental to any legal order. These may include the principle that we should adhere to just agreements and that we should accept the decisions of properly constituted courts. Others such as the hypothetical law requiring Socrates to cease philosophizing would violate a higher order. I believe that Plato retained this theory throughout his philosophical career. It underpins the account of justice in the *Republic* and the account of law and legislation in the *Laws* and is supported by the cosmology of the *Timaeus*. It was thus immensely productive in Plato's thought. But to develop that theme would be beyond the scope of this chapter.

Notes

[1] See, for example, Cross and Woozley 1964, vi–vii. Cf. Annas 1981, 10–14. See also Dover 1974, 184–7.

[2] For a detailed investigation of the replacement of θεσμός by νόμος see Ostwald 1969.

[3] An interesting case is Hesiod, *Works and Days*, 276 ff. where the poet contrasts the νόμος of wild animals who eat each other with that of human beings to whom Zeus has given justice, δίκη.

[4] For an extended account of the different uses of νόμος see Ostwald 1969, ch. 2.

[5] For an influential discussion of these issues see Hart 1960, ch. 4.

[6] For example: Demosthenes, 18.2; 19.179; 25.17; Isocrates 3.7, 15.179.

[7] Unless otherwise indicated translations from the Greek are my own.

[8] See Gagarin 1986, ch. 2.

[9] See, e.g., *Works and Days* 213–83.

[10] Demosthenes 20.118; 39.40.

[11] Contrast 388–90 with 384, 395–6, 405–6, 437, 673.

[12] On this point see Dover 1974, 184–7, 306–9. Although it seems to have been almost impossible for an Athenian to describe a law of his own city as unjust, it was possible to criticize particular decisions of the courts or assembly. It was also possible to suggest that other communities had bad laws.

[13] Some influential modern accounts of justice also incorporate an essential reference to rules. For example, J.S. Mill defines it as 'a name for certain classes of moral rules, which concern the essentials of human well-being more nearly, and are therefore of more absolute obligation, than any other rules for the guidance of life' (*Utilitarianism* ch. 5).

[14] He cites specifically lines 456–7 where Antigone having referred to 'the unwritten and unfailing statutes of the gods' (ἄγραπτα κἀσφαλῆ θεῶν νόμιμα) which no human decrees can supersede, continues:
> For their life is not of today or yesterday, but for all time, and no man knows when they were first put forth.
> οὐ γάρ τι νῦν γε κἀχθές, ἀλλ' ἀεί ποτε
> ζῇ ταῦτα, κοὐδεὶς οἶδεν ἐξ ὅτου φάνη.

The translations in this and the next two footnotes are from Freese 1926.

[15] But a universal precept, which extends without a break throughout the wide-ruling sky and the boundless earth.
ἀλλὰ τὸ μὲν πάντων νόμιμον διάτ' εὐρυμέδοντος
αἰθέρος ἠνεκέως τέταται διά τ' ἀπλέτου αὖ γῆς.   DK 31B135

[16] The relevant passage, as supplied by the scholiast commenting on 1373b18, reads:
God has left all men free; Nature has made none a slave.
ἐλευθέρους ἀφῆκε πάντας θεός· οὐδένα δοῦλον ἡ φύσις πεποίηκεν.

[17] The apparent conflict between this passage and 1.13.1373b1–17, where it is said that particular laws may be written or unwritten, can be resolved if we recognize that Aristotle uses the term 'unwritten' to apply to two quite different kinds of law: the general laws which are common to all mankind and local customs which have the force of law in particular communities but have not been formally written down.

[18] Stylometry provides no evidence as to the order in which the dialogues discussed in this chapter were written. All attempts to provide a relative chronology for them rest on questionable assumptions about the likely development of Plato's thought. See Kahn 2002.

[19] This does not imply that the *Gorgias* must mark a later stage in Plato's thought – it might well antedate the *Euthyphro*. The fact that Plato leaves a philosophical problem unanswered in a particular dialogue does not preclude his having a pretty clear idea of how it should be solved.

[20] This distinction cannot be readily captured in English. See MacDowell 1978, 51–65.

[21] On this point see, for example, Taylor 1982.

[22] This is, for example, a main concern in Kraut 1984 and Woozley 1979. For criticism of such views see Rosen 1998.

[23] Dover (1974, 308–9) writes 'the wide range of ideals, eccentricities and obsessions which we nowadays amalgamate under the name of "conscience" did not seem to Greeks to be good reason for defying law'.

[24] Brickhouse and Smith 1989, 151.

[25] For discussion of Socrates' mission and the extent to which it was religiously motivated see Brickhouse and Smith 1989, 87–100, 105–7, Reeve 1989, 21–8, 62–73, Stokes 1997, 114–24, 142–9.

[26] Some scholars take the Leon of Salamis affair to show that Socrates was willing to disobey the law. But, even though the Thirty were originally entrusted with power by a vote of the assembly, it is unlikely that Socrates, or the majority of his contemporaries, would have seen their edicts as constituting genuine *nomos*. See Brickhouse and Smith 1989, 142.

[27] In the *Meno* 91b2–93a4, a similar view is ascribed to Meletus' co-accuser Anytus.

[28] It is a separate issue whether we should ever disobey the law. It could be that we have a duty to obey even unjust law.

[29] A third reading which might seem possible is that one should keep agreements unless doing so imposes unacceptable burdens upon oneself. But this is precluded by the general context of the *Crito* since it might suggest that those unjustly condemned to death have no obligation to accept that punishment. On the interpretation of this passage see Kraut 1984, 29–33.

[30] My understanding of these arguments owes much to Weiss 1998, 98–123 and Harte 1999.

[31] The principal source for such theories is John Locke's second *Treatise of Government*, especially chapter VII sections 119–22. For the distinction between Locke's argument and that of the *Crito* see Kraut 1984, 160–1.

[32] See Kraut 1984, ch. 5 for an extended discussion of the failure of the argument from just agreement to provide a general basis for obedience to law.

[33] This is, of course, the point made by Alcidamas in the passage cited by Aristotle *Rhetoric* (1.13.1373b18). See n. 15 above.

[34] For a detailed discussion of these issues see Kraut 1984, ch. 5, especially 142–3. Kraut finds value in Socrates' argument but demonstrates that it is not a general argument against destroying legal systems.

[35] See, e.g., Anaximander, fr. DK 12B 1; Heraclitus, frs. DK 22B 30 and 114.

Bibliography

Annas, J.
    1981   *An Introduction to Plato's* Republic, Oxford.

Annas, J. and Rowe, C.J. (eds.)
  2002 *New Perspectives on Plato, Modern and Ancient*, Cambridge, Mass., and London.
Brickhouse, T.C. and Smith, N.D.
  1989 *Socrates on Trial*, Oxford.
Cross, R.C. and Woozley, A.D.
  1964 *Plato's* Republic*: A philosophical commentary*, London.
Dover, K.J.
  1974 *Greek Popular Morality in the Time of Plato and Aristotle*, Oxford.
Fowler, H.
  1914 Plato vol. 1, Loeb edn, London and New York.
Freese, J.H.
  1926 *Aristotle:* Art of Rhetoric, Loeb edn, Cambridge, Mass.
Gagarin, M.
  1986 *Early Greek Law*, Berkeley and Los Angeles.
Hart, H.L.A.
  1960 *The Concept of Law*, Oxford.
Harte, V.
  1999 'Conflicting values in Plato's *Crito*', *Archiv für Geschichte der Philosophie* 81, 117–47.
Kahn, C.
  2002 'On Platonic chronology', in Annas and Rowe (eds.) *New Perspectives on Plato, Modern and Ancient*, 93–129.
Kraut, R.
  1984 *Socrates and the State*, Princeton.
MacDowell, D.M.
  1978 *The Law in Classical Athens,* London and Ithaca.
Ostwald, M.
  1969 *Nomos and the Rise of Athenian Democracy*, Oxford.
Reeve, C.D.C.
  1989 *Socrates in the* Apology, Indianapolis.
Rosen, F.
  1998 '"A creature of modern scholarship": disobedience and the *Crito* problem', *Polis* 15, 1–12.
Stokes, M.C.
  1997 *Plato:* Apology of Socrates, Warminster.
Taylor, C.C.W.
  1982 'The end of the *Euthyphro*', *Phronesis* 27, 109–18.
Weiss, R.
  1998 *Socrates Dissatisfied*, New York.
Woozley, A.D.
  1979 *Law and Obedience: The arguments of Plato's* Crito, London.

2

BEWARE OF IMITATIONS: IMAGE RECOGNITION IN PLATO

Verity Harte

This chapter is focused on a particular kind of mistake or illusion. The mistake is that of taking an imitation or likeness of something to be, not an imitation or likeness, but the thing itself. A person makes this mistake in attempting to walk through a cunningly painted doorway or to shake a waxwork by the hand. While no doubt uncommon, I take it to be perfectly plausible that someone might make such a mistake. (It is probably best thought of as a mistake, rather than as an illusion, since it seems corrigible in a way illusions I take it are not.)[1] As is often the case with mistakes, as interesting as what goes wrong is what the mistake tells us about what is involved in getting things right – the complexity of the recognition of a likeness of something as a *likeness* and a likeness *of that thing*.

This mistake seems to me independently interesting. But the paper arises from its interest to Plato. In a number of places, Plato contrasts the epistemic condition of one who makes this mistake with that of one who avoids it. In some key passages, he uses this contrast to illustrate the difference between one who has knowledge and one who does not. My project is, first, to work out what one should think about the epistemic condition of someone who makes the mistake. Second, to use reflection on the conditions of the mistaken person to draw both a general (if sketchy) moral about Plato's epistemology (at least in those works in which he is interested in this mistake) and some particular morals for the interpretation of one very disputed passage. In other words, I propose to take Plato at his word – that the contrast between making and avoiding the mistake tells us something about the difference, in his view, between one who has knowledge and one who does not – and then to try to work out what it tells us.

Some evidence of Plato's interest in the mistake
To say that Plato is interested in the relation between likeness and original is

not news. Discussions of this interest are, however, often focused on his use of the relation between likeness and original as an image for – or, perhaps, a literal description of – an ontological contrast, between forms and their participants. He is, I think, at least as interested in the epistemological character of these relations.

Here are three examples of Plato's interest in the mistake, where his interest is at least as much epistemological as ontological. (1) *Republic* 5, where the mistake and its avoidance are central to Socrates' first account of the difference between philosophers (who have knowledge) and a group of people identified as 'lovers of sights and sounds', whom Glaucon has confused with philosophers. (2) *Republic* 7, where the analogy of the cave depicts the majority of people as occupying an epistemic position represented by making this kind of mistake.[2] (3) More controversially, the *Phaedo*'s argument that learning is recollection of forms may be taken to place weight on avoidance of the mistake as crucial to recollection as there described.
I shall discuss only the first and third examples.

First, *Republic* 5. Of several *Republic* passages that show interest in the mistake, Book 5 is significant as the first to describe the mistake and give it importance. In doing so, it puts down a marker to which later direct and indirect allusions to the mistake may be taken to refer. Further, the mistake and its avoidance are given importance both in the content of the passage and in what we may call its 'frame'.

In *Republic* 5, Socrates produces two arguments aimed at distinguishing philosophers from lovers of sights and sounds, a group of people who are devotees of (what they take to be) the finer things in life and who are first in line for every concert or festival. The first of Socrates' arguments to distinguish these groups is explicitly directed at someone like Glaucon, who is committed to forms. He is ready to agree, for example, that beauty and ugliness are each one, but appear many 'making themselves appear all over the place through their combining with actions, bodies and each other' (476a4–7). In turn, it is the failure of the lovers of sights and sounds to distinguish forms from particulars that provides the basis for Socrates' distinction between them and philosophers. Their state – that of one who can recognize beautiful things, but, respecting beauty itself, can neither recognize it, nor follow, if someone were to lead them to knowledge of it – is described as that of one who lives in a dream as opposed to being awake (476c2–4).

The lovers of sights and sounds are described as such on the basis of what is given as the hallmark of dreaming: 'that a person, whether in sleep or awake, thinks that what is like something is not like, but is the very thing to which it is like' (476c5–7).[3] In contrast, the person who is awake is one who is 'capable of seeing both [beauty] itself and the things which have a share of it and who thinks neither that the things which have a share of it are it, nor that it is the things which have a share of it' (476d1–3). This latter may rightly be said to have knowledge, where the dreamer may not.

The mistake of the dreamer is precisely the mistake in which I am interested. The characterization of one who avoids it shows the mistake to have two sides which need to be avoided: one needs both not to take the likeness to be that of which it is a likeness and not to take that of which it is a likeness to be the likeness.[4] Of course, one who is in the grip of the mistake cannot articulate any such complexity, precisely because they do not take themself to have two items in their cognition, the likeness and that to which it is like.[5]

The fact that the dreamer's mistake and its avoidance are used to distinguish the recognitional capacities of philosophers from those of non-philosophers shows this mistake to be important to the content of the passage. The frame of the passage only underlines this, when we notice that the repetition of interest in things that are not, but are like (ὅμοιος), something recalls precisely the relation between lovers of sights and sounds and genuine philosophers from which the passage began.

At 475c6–8, Socrates had characterized the philosopher as 'one who is readily willing to taste all learning; who goes with pleasure to learn and is insatiable'. Glaucon thinks that such a description will result in the inclusion of the lovers of sights and sounds among philosophers. He asks Socrates whether we should call these people philosophers. Socrates replies that we should not, but that they are *like* philosophers (475e2).

There are two important points in Socrates' response here. First, that lovers of sights and sounds are not in fact philosophers. Hence Glaucon has made a mistake in his understanding of Socrates' characterization of philosophers. Hence too there is reason to explain the difference between them. Second, Socrates says that lovers of sights and sounds are nonetheless like philosophers.[6] Since lovers of sights and sounds are not, but are like, philosophers, Glaucon's misunderstanding of Socrates' characterization has led him to make precisely the mistake that will shortly be made characteristic of the dreaming state of the lovers of sights and sounds themselves.[7] And this way of framing the passage only reinforces the passage's interest in the mistake.

One final point about this passage. Although the passage explicitly takes the relation between what is like and that to which it is like as an analogue for the relation between participant and form (476c5–d3), the dominant use of this contrast is not ontological, but epistemological. Ontological commitments are necessary to the framework in which the dreamer's mistake is said to occur. But it is the epistemological contrast that is in focus here.

Next, then, my third example: the *Phaedo*'s discussion of recollection. Here it is more controversial to say that the passage is interested in the making or avoidance of the mistake. I shall offer reasons for thinking that it is.[8]

In *Phaedo* 72–7, Socrates sets out to establish the prenatal existence of the soul by showing that we have knowledge the possession of which must predate birth. Interpretation of the argument is highly disputed. But Socrates' strategy can, I think, be outlined in a way that is neutral, as follows. He sets out to show that there is a kind of knowledge that (at least some) people can be shown to have. This knowledge cannot itself have been derived from perception. But the recollection of it is either involved in or prompted by certain acts of perception. Because of this, he argues, this knowledge must have been possessed before we first began to perceive and so before birth.

The argument of the passage falls roughly into three parts. The first part collects some general points about recollection – or, better, being reminded of one thing by another. Here Socrates offers some general conditions on being reminded, and adds an extra condition for cases in which the thing that reminds one is like what it reminds one of. The second part of the argument is focused on the recognition of forms as distinct from their particular manifestations, the example being the recognition of the form of equality as distinct from sticks or stones which are equal, as it might be, in length or weight. Here, Socrates argues that such recognition is a case of being reminded and one which meets the additional characterization of being reminded by something like that of which it reminds one. In the third part of the argument, Socrates then argues that possession of the knowledge of which one is reminded in the case of recognition of forms must predate birth. I doubt that there is any interpretation of the argument that will get it to this conclusion, even granting the existence of forms. Nonetheless, I count it an advantage for an interpretation to do as well for the argument as it can.

I shall talk mainly about aspects of the first and second parts of the argument. In the first part, Socrates begins with some general conditions for being reminded of one thing by another. He illustrates these conditions with some ordinary examples. These examples are, nonetheless, both carefully chosen and ordered. The first examples – being reminded of a man on seeing a cloak or lyre; or of Cebes on seeing Simmias – are followed by examples that largely replicate them, but in which the reminding object is now a depiction of the object used in the first examples. Thus, one may be reminded of a man on seeing a picture of a horse or lyre; of Cebes on seeing a picture of Simmias.[9] The examples culminate in that of being reminded of Simmias himself by his own picture. Like most commentators, I take this example to be the key point of comparison, when, in the second part of the argument, Socrates turns from these ordinary examples to his principal focus: the recognition of forms as distinct from their particular manifestations.

Socrates takes his ordinary examples to show that one can be reminded of something both by a thing that is like it and by a thing that is unlike it. The example of being reminded of Simmias by his picture is the only example we are given of being reminded by something like what we are reminded of. In such a case, Socrates claims, an additional experience is necessary, namely that 'one have in mind whether or not [the reminding thing] is lacking in respect of likeness to that of which it reminds one' (74a6–7). Again like most commentators, I take this additional experience to have a parallel in Socrates' subsequent discussion of the recognition of forms, in which the form of equality serves as example. It is parallel to the experience which (at least some) people have with regard to equal sticks and stones – that they are lacking in being such as the equal itself is (74d6–7). This experience is elaborated as that of 'having in mind' that what one sees 'wants to be as some other thing', but 'falls short' and 'is incapable of being such as that is', being 'inferior' (74d9–e2). This is the experience identified as recollection of forms. Quite who has this experience with regard to perceptible manifestations of forms is one focus for the interpretative dispute surrounding this passage. For the moment, I leave all such complications aside.

It has proved difficult to understand what is meant by the additional experience taken to be required in the case of recollection from things that are like and its parallel in the case of equality. What the passage appears to suggest – and what many commentators[10] have taken to be intended – is some kind of explicit act of comparison. When being reminded of Simmias by his picture, for example, the experience envisaged is some explicit consideration of whether or not it has captured the curve of his nose, the colour of his eyes, and so on. But the problem for such an understanding – a problem acknowledged by those who support it – is that it is very hard to see why Socrates should claim – and Simmias explicitly agree – that such an act of comparison is *necessary* (74a6, a8). Possible, yes: necessary, surely not.

Faced with this difficulty, one may – and it has been suggested we should – simply downplay. It is not immediately obvious that a more cautious claim would do any damage to the subsequent argument (although I think that it would). Even so, other things being equal, we ought to prefer an interpretation that makes sense of the claim to necessity. And such an interpretation is available, along lines proposed by Gosling (1965).

Consider the example of Simmias' picture more closely. Contrast two cases: first, a person who sees what is as a matter of fact a picture of Simmias, and who, being unacquainted with Simmias, does not see it as a picture *of Simmias*, but simply as a picture of some man;[11] second, a person who does see it as a picture *of Simmias*. Only this second person could be said to be reminded of Simmias by his picture. Indeed, their recognition of the picture *as* a picture *of Simmias* may be taken to constitute their being reminded of him by his picture, providing they were not already thinking about Simmias in any case.[12] Now contrast yet a third possible case. Suppose that the picture is so incredibly lifelike that a person attempts to engage it in conversation. Here again, the situation requires prior acquaintance with Simmias – at least if they think that *Simmias* is the person with whom they are attempting to talk. But it seems wrong to say that this person is reminded of Simmias by his picture. Certainly that is not how the mistaken person would describe themselves. Rather, they have the (mistaken) impression that they are seeing Simmias himself. Nor, from the perspective of one who diagnoses the mistake, does it seem natural to speak of this person as being reminded of someone whom they cannot distinguish from his picture, nor his picture from him.[13]

My proposal, following Gosling, is that the additional experience that Socrates takes to be necessary in the case of recollection from likes is what makes the difference between the person who recognizes the picture as a picture *of Simmias*, and who does not confuse his picture with him, and the person who does so confuse them. Arguably, such an experience is indeed necessary if one is to be reminded of Simmias by his picture. The experience is undoubtedly commonplace – at least in the case of pictures – so that we rarely draw attention to it. However, in doing so, Socrates recognizes the complexity of the act of recognizing Simmias from his picture: that one must both see it as picture *of Simmias*, but also as only *a picture* of him, and not as the man himself.[14]

In support of the view that the *Phaedo*'s focus is on the status of a likeness as such – and not on how well or badly it captures its object – Gosling cites a useful parallel from the *Cratylus* (432, the two Cratyluses passage). There, Socrates draws attention to the fact that an image or likeness – an εἰκών – must fall short of the original, simply in virtue of being an image. If it did not, he suggests, it would be, not an image, but a second original. The parallel is useful, not least because it uses the same terminology as is found in the *Phaedo*'s account of the experience regarding equality, which is the counterpart to the example of Simmias' picture. Both passages use the Greek verb ἐνδέω for the 'falling short' of a likeness or image from its original. (Compare *Phaedo* 74d4–e4 and *Cratylus* 432c7–d3.) So, the proposal is that what 'falling short' is meant to capture is not the degree of resemblance between image and original, but the status of an image as such.

With this in mind, let us now turn to the experience that (at least some) people have with regard to equality; that sensible equals are experienced as somehow falling short of the equal itself. In light of the comparison with Simmias' picture, how should this counterpart experience be understood?

I propose that it be understood as follows. The person who has this experience – whoever they may be – sees perceptible equals as equal, but takes themselves to be seeing, not equality itself, but merely a likeness of equality. This person contrasts with someone who sees perceptible equals as equal, but who (mistakenly) takes themselves to be seeing equality itself. In other words, the person who has the counterpart experience with regard to equality is one who avoids the mistake that, in *Republic* 5, was made characteristic of dreaming.

I said that, other things being equal, we should prefer an interpretation of the *Phaedo* experiences that makes sense of Socrates' claim that such experiences are necessary. I shall return to the question of whether other things are equal. For now, I hope to have provided an interpretation of these experiences according to which they can claim necessity if one is to be reminded of Simmias by his picture and, for the same reason, if one is to be reminded of equality also. In the latter case, it is necessary only on the assumption that there is such a thing as equality, distinct from its perceptible manifestations. That such an assumption is necessary to the argument of the *Phaedo* is something Socrates explicitly affirms.

Since the main plank of my defence of this interpretation is its ability to make sense of the claim to necessity, it is worth considering two objections to its ability to do so. In his commentary on the *Phaedo*, Gallop questions whether it is in fact necessary that, in being reminded of someone by their picture, one consider whether it falls short of them in Gosling's sense. In being reminded of someone by a pencil sketch, he asks, must one 'attend to the fact that it is black-and-white and only a few inches long'? Surely, he says, such things are simply 'taken for granted' (Gallop 1975, 119). I agree that such things are – in general – taken for granted. But I also take that to be part of the point. Irrespective of whether or not one consciously articulates this to oneself – and I take it one normally does not – one must be aware that a likeness of something is only a likeness of something in order to count as being reminded rather than as making the mistake. What shows this is not so much what we ordinarily experience when confronted with a picture of someone as the contrast between what usually happens and the one who makes the mistake.

Gallop has a second objection also (ibid.). He notes that Socrates will claim that, whenever one judges that one thing, X, falls short of another thing, Y, one must have known Y previously (74e2–5). But Gallop denies that this is in fact necessary on the interpretation of the recognition of something as falling short that Gosling proposes. Now, I agree that on the interpretation proposed the inference to *previous* knowledge is questionable. For one might have an independent source of knowledge of the object of a picture given to one at the very moment one perceives it. Such is the case when pictures come with labels. Such a label, combined with one's general knowledge of picture conventions – and avoidance of the (generalized form of the) dreamer's mistake – would enable one to make the judgement in question. And to this extent, the interpretation will leave Socrates open to an objection that is damaging to his overall goal, the establishment of the prenatal existence of the soul. However, what does seem to me necessary – and what the use of labels for pictures itself brings out – is *some* independent source of knowledge of that to which one judges the reminding object to fall short. And for the case of being reminded of forms, it will be much less obvious what alternative, contemporaneous, independent source of knowledge might be available to one. Further, since I am not convinced that there is any interpretation of the argument available that will get Socrates to the conclusion of prenatal existence, any gap of this kind remaining on the interpretation proposed seems to me an objection to the argument itself and not to the interpretation.

Some general remarks about the mistake
Let me begin by saying something about what I take to be involved in one thing being a likeness of another in the sense in which I am using the term. I do not have a snappy definition, but the following should give some indication of what I have in mind. First, although the term 'likeness' can be used to talk of something merely like something else, I do not take it to be sufficient for one thing to be a likeness of another that the two things be alike. Second, I am uncertain as to whether it is even necessary that the two things be (in some respect) alike. A likeness would thus be something like a representation in common uses of that term. However, the Platonic examples do appear to be cases of things that are in some respect alike, and a passage of the *Parmenides* I mention shortly may suggest that Plato thinks it necessary that they be so. Third, in the *Cratylus* passage, Plato appears to take it to be a necessary condition on something's being a likeness that it not be exactly similar to that of which it is a likeness, although I am not convinced he need do so. Finally, I take it to be a necessary condition on something's being a likeness that it stand in some dependent relation to the thing of which it is a likeness. Clearly not any old dependence relation will do; a likeness must in some way represent or stand in some intentional relation to that of which it is a likeness. But such a relation need not be brought about intentionally. Artefacts such as pictures provide a ready example of likeness, but examples need not be artefacts. Reflections in water or mirrors are (neutral) Platonic examples of likenesses that are not artefacts, although, in the mirror case, they occur within one.[15]

Notice, next, that there are two related, but different versions of the mistake. Distinguish (1) the case where one thing is *like* another and someone mistakes one for the other, and (2) the case where one thing is, in the sense explained, a *likeness of* another and someone mistakes one for the other. The mistakes are similar, but not, I think, the same. The difference lies in the different relations involved. The relation of being like something is a symmetrical relation. The relation of being a likeness of something is not symmetrical. This difference carries over to the respective mistakes. In the case of two things that are alike, I could make the same mistake about either one of them. In the case of a likeness and its original, to mistake the likeness for the original is one mistake; to mistake the original for the likeness another. My focus is the likeness-original case. And I think this is Plato's principal focus too.

Against this is the fact that, in the *Republic*, Socrates talks in terms of mistaking something that is *like* for that to which it is like. However, in the *Parmenides* it is argued that, if one has a case of likeness, one can infer that one has a case of being like, although not vice versa (132d5–7).[16] Thus Socrates may simply use the wider term with the more specific application in mind. Certainly, the *Republic*'s talk of 'dreaming' – whether asleep or awake – suggests that the experiences that Socrates is using as points of reference are vivid, but non-lucid dreams and/or hallucinations. (The noun for the verb involved – ὀνειρώττειν – can refer to both dreaming and hallucination.) And, while no doubt unlike pictures in many ways, the relation between dream images and hallucinatory images and the objects about which one dreams or hallucinates has the same non-symmetrical and dependent character as that between picture and object. In the case of the *Phaedo*, the talk of pictures makes clear that we are interested in likenesses.

Next, consider another distinction. Distinguish the recognition of a likeness as a *likeness* and the recognition of a likeness of something as a likeness *of that thing*. How, in general, we recognize that a likeness is a likeness is an interesting question, but it is not my question. The mistake in which I am interested is the mistake of taking the likeness of some particular object to be, not a likeness, but that very object. The successful act that corresponds to this mistake is not the recognition of a likeness of something as a likeness, but the recognition of it as a likeness and a likeness of that very object. If a person were simply incapable of recognizing a likeness as such, then such a person would make the mistake in which I am interested every time they were confronted with a likeness of something. But it is the particular mistake they make on each occasion that I am concerned with.

For my purposes, the most important feature of the mistake is that the person who mistakes a likeness of something for the original has some cognitive access to the original. (We might be tempted to say that they have knowledge of the original, but, if we do, this will need to be a weaker sense of 'knowledge' than that which Plato reserves for the avoidance of the mistake.) That the mistaken person has some cognitive access to the original is revealed in the making of the mistake. This can be seen by reflecting once more on the picture of Simmias. The person who mistakes the picture for Simmias himself draws on some independent awareness of Simmias. That they do so can be seen by contrasting them with the person who takes the picture simply as a picture of some man.

The epistemic condition of the mistaken person is undoubtedly difficult to characterize. In particular, it looks rather different from the third and first person perspective, assuming the third person is not themself in the grip of the mistake. From the third person perspective, articulation of the epistemic condition of the mistaken person involves reference to two items – the likeness and the original. From the first person perspective of the mistaken person, no such articulation is involved. This is precisely because they are in the grip of the mistake. As far as the mistaken person is concerned there is just one item involved in their cognition – the original, which they (mistakenly) take to be present in the likeness before them. Notice, however, that even as they represent their situation to themself, it is the original that features in their cognition, albeit it is the likeness that, unbeknownst to them, gives rise to their thinking of it. This goes to show, once again, that the mistaken person has some awareness of the original in question, despite the fact that they make use of it in a peculiar way.[17]

One might object to this. Imagine a person who makes the mistake wholesale, as it were. Suppose a person is 'introduced' to Simmias only through a statue of him.[18] What I have in mind here is someone who has no preconceptions about the name 'Simmias' – that it refers to a person, and not a statue, say – who is shown a statue of Simmias and told 'This is Simmias' by someone who means thereby to introduce them to Simmias the man. But suppose the person never understands that what they are being shown is only a statue of that to which they are being introduced. Such a person, one might say, has no knowledge or awareness of Simmias himself. That seems to me right. However, just because it seems right, it seems wrong to say of this person that the word 'Simmias' in their vocabulary refers to the man himself as opposed to his statue.[19] If the word 'Simmias' in this person's vocabulary refers not to the man, but to his statue, then when they identify what is, as a matter of fact, a statue of Simmias as 'Simmias', they do not make a mistake. And it is simply a coincidence, although not accidental, that what the word 'Simmias' refers to in this person's vocabulary is as a matter of fact a statue of that to which it refers in ours.

A general moral

Recall my reason for being concerned with Plato's interest in this rather peculiar mistake. If the mistake and its avoidance are somehow central to his contrast between one who knows and one who does not, then reflection on the conditions of the mistake and its avoidance should be instructive as regards Plato's epistemology, at least in those works in which he shows interest in this mistake.

Thus, consider one general way in which Plato's (middle-period) epistemology might be, and sometimes has been, characterized. Plato, it might be said, has an entirely negative attitude to the epistemic data we receive from our senses or from judgements based upon them. In order to arrive at knowledge, we must jettison such data and engage in an entirely different kind of thinking, one independent of and unrelated to our sensory experience and judgements. This, if you like, is the epistemological end of the 'two-world' reading of Plato.

An approach to Plato's epistemology of this sort might be encouraged by one important interpretation of the recollection argument in the *Phaedo*: that espoused by Dominic Scott (1987, 1995). Scott contrasts two ways of reading the recollection passage. The first – which he calls a 'Kantian' reading – takes recollection to be involved in the business of ordinary concept-formation. Against this, Scott proposes what he calls the 'Demaratus' reading, so called because of its reference to a story in Herodotus in which one Demaratus passes a message to the Greeks inscribed in wood upon a tablet, which is concealed by being overlaid by a false message inscribed in wax. The message in the wax corresponds to the information we get from our senses. The Demaratus reading is pessimistic about the value of such information. According to this reading, the opinions derived from the senses 'are to be scraped away. We discard them, not build on them' (Scott 1995, 21).

Attention to Plato's interest in the mistake brings out an element of truth in the two-world picture. Consider the difference between the first person perspective of one in the grip of the mistake and the third person perspective of one who diagnoses it. This difference translates into a wide difference between the first person perspectives of one who makes it and of one who avoids it. There is some sense in which, cognitively speaking, one in the grip of such a mistake is in a different world from one who avoids it.

On the other hand, reflection on the fact that awareness of the original is involved even in the cognition of the mistaken person calls into question some of the pessimism as regards the opinions derived from the senses. The mistaken person needs not so much to jettison the content of their epistemic judgements about the world as to distinguish the original in the likeness. They need to recognize what they see or judge as a likeness *of the original*, but as only a *likeness*; to separate out knowledge of the original independent of its likeness.

In this, I do not mean to make Plato into an empiricist. In fact, the empiricist Plato has his home in the two-world view. (See, e.g., Scott 1995, 19 and 58.) It is just that empirically-acquired judgements are taken to have no value as a source of knowledge. Rather, I imagine the process of separating out knowledge of the original from its likeness to involve the kind of intellectual conversion of soul that the *Republic*'s education programme is designed to induce. My proposal is simply that Plato takes our sensory judgements to face two ways. They can trap us in the cognitively confused world of the mistaken person. But they can also provide the starting point for our intellectual conversion. And this proposal seems to sit well with Plato's apparent ambivalence towards the senses, on which others have commented.[20] He is wont to disparage them. But he also on occasion identifies them as an important source of stimulus for the intellectual conversion required for knowledge. (I think, in particular, of *Republic* 523 and its identification of certain sense perceptions as 'summoning' the soul to inquiry.)

A particular moral for the interpretation of *Phaedo* 72–7

In the remainder of the chapter, I want to apply the lessons learnt from Plato's interest in the mistake to the interpretation of the *Phaedo*'s discussion of recollection.

Disputes about the interpretation of the recollection argument have focused on two connected questions. First, the question of how many people are taken to have the experience of recollection described in the passage: whether everyone engages in some (more or less limited) recollection, as the Kantian reading proposes; or whether recollection is the preserve of a restricted few, as Scott rather proposes. Connected to the question of the scope of recollection is disagreement as to what constitutes recollection. On Scott's reading, the knowledge recovered in recollection is definitional knowledge of forms, the kind of knowledge likely to be articulated only by Platonist philosophers. As Scott says, it is more difficult to give a unitary characterization of the content of recollection on the alternative view. The recollected knowledge is taken to be somehow involved in ordinary concept-acquisition; sometimes with the mechanism by which we come to have a grasp of the meaning of universal terms in language.[21]

One way to focus the dispute is to ask whether or not an interpretation takes the argument of the *Phaedo* to suppose it possible to perceive, for example, two sticks as being equal in length, without already involving latent knowledge of equality. On Scott's reading it is, since judgements about perceptible equality are empirically formed entirely independently of any recollected knowledge. Recollected knowledge is displayed – by the limited few who display it – in an explicit act of comparison between what is perceived when one perceives that two sticks are equal in length and one's recollected knowledge of equality. On the opposing view it is not possible to perceive that two sticks are equal in length without already involving one's knowledge of equality.

How do these issues turn out, if the experience of recollection is understood in the way which, following Gosling, I have proposed? According to this proposal, one is reminded of the form of equal when one recognizes that perceptible equals are likenesses of equality, but that they are only likenesses of it; that is, when one avoids mistaking the likeness for the original. Such an experience seems quite clearly to be that of a restricted number of folk. It involves, first, a recognition of and commitment to the existence of forms, and sufficient understanding of the form in question to be able to recognize its likenesses as likenesses of it, but to be clear that they are distinct from it; they are only likenesses.[22]

So far, so much like Scott. We differ, however, when it comes to the appraisal of the judgements of ordinary people, those who have no such commitment to the existence of forms. Go back to the picture of Simmias and my three types of person: (1) the person who looks at the picture and sees simply a picture of some man; (2) the person who looks at the picture and sees it not as a picture of Simmias, but as Simmias himself; and (3) the person who looks at the picture and sees it as a picture of Simmias, and as only a picture. The third person provides the analogue for the person who is reminded of the form of equal by their perception of sensible equals. Which of them provides the analogue for the ordinary person's judgements about sensible equality? If Simmias plays the role of equality here, it must be the second, not the first – the person who looks at the picture and thinks it is Simmias himself, as opposed to the one who sees it as a picture of some man. Simmias plays no role whatsoever in the judgement of this latter person. Thus the ordinary person's judgements are those of the *Republic*'s dreamer, the one who makes the mistake. Recall, then, that, for this person too, awareness of the original about which they are mistaken must be involved in their judgement, albeit in a confused and muddling way.

In this way, the interpretation I have offered proposes a kind of middle ground between the two alternative readings of the *Phaedo* passage. Like Scott, it supports a restricted-scope reading of the experience of recollection. Unlike Scott, and like his opponents, it takes awareness of the form of equality to be somehow involved in ordinary perceptual judgements of equality even so.

Finally, therefore, let me return to the question of whether this interpretation of the *Phaedo*'s experience of recollection can be defended in light of the argument as a whole. First, consider an apparent difficulty (although one may note that facing apparent difficulties hardly distinguishes this interpretation from other views).

The difficulty concerns what we may call 'the recognition requirement', which Socrates imposes as a condition on being reminded quite generally. At 73c6–8, Socrates says that we may rightly describe someone as being reminded 'if, on seeing, hearing or having some other perception of one thing, he not only recognizes that thing, but also gets in mind something else, knowledge of which is not the same, but different'.[23] Here, the act of recognizing the object perceived is clearly distinguished from the act of getting in mind the object recollected, that is, from the act of recollection itself. But this has been seen as presenting a serious difficulty for those who deny that an object may be perceived as equal independently of knowledge of the form of equality. If it is impossible to perceive that two sticks are equal without already involving one's knowledge of equality, and if the recognition requirement demands that one's perception of the equality of the sticks and one's recollection of equality be distinct and independent acts, then the process of recollection could never get going. Even apart from the case of the equals, both Ackrill and Gallop have suggested that the recognition requirement is already infringed by the special case of being reminded of Simmias by his picture, since 'one cannot recognize a picture of Simmias without *eo ipso* thinking of Simmias himself' (Gallop 1975, 117–18; cf. Ackrill 1973, 185–6).

Now, I think we should already be suspicious about the fact that the recognition requirement appears to be violated by the example of Simmias' picture, not least because this seems the key example for what follows. And I think we can understand the requirement and the example in such a way that no such violation results.

First, then, let us go back to the recognition requirement itself. According to this requirement, to count as being reminded of one thing by another, one must both perceive and recognize the thing that does the reminding and get in mind *something else*, knowledge of which is *not the same, but different*. This requirement matters, I take it, insofar as it prevents one from counting as cases of being reminded, cases in which the thought of the thing one takes oneself to be reminded of is either directly given in perception or can be extrapolated from it. In cases of the latter sort, one is not so much *re-minded* as 'minded' and the inference to previous knowledge cannot be drawn.

The case of Simmias and his picture can, I think, be understood in a way that satisfies this requirement. First, it is possible to see and recognize a picture of Simmias under some description (although not under the description 'picture of Simmias') without even thinking of Simmias. (Think of the person who sees such a picture simply as a picture of some man, and who might, on seeing it again, think to themself, there's that picture of that man.) *A fortiori*, the thought of Simmias is not simply given in the perception of the picture itself.

Next, think of the person who does have a thought of Simmias – a thought that, the first point suggests, they bring to the situation themself. This thought is indeed a thought of *something else* – that is, something other than the picture – for Simmias is not identical with his picture. But is it a thought of something knowledge of which is *not the same, but different*? I think that it is. There is, of course, an overlap in content between the thought, 'picture of Simmias', and the thought, 'Simmias', but overlap is not identity. Further, the difference between the two thoughts in question is one that makes a difference relevant to considerations of being reminded. What shows this is, once again, the person who makes the dreamer's mistake. In mistaking the picture of Simmias for Simmias himself, this person precisely fails to count as being reminded of Simmias himself.

One could put the point in terms of necessary and sufficient conditions. When perceiving a likeness of X, thought of X is a necessary condition on thought of a likeness of X (as a likeness of X). But thought of X is not sufficient for thought of a likeness of X (as a likeness of X), as is shown by the possibility of the dreamer's mistake. Conversely, thought of a likeness of X (as a likeness of X) is sufficient for thought of X. But thought of a likeness of X (as a likeness of X) is not necessary for thought of X. Thought of a likeness of X is certainly not generally necessary for thought of X, nor when perceiving what is as a matter of fact a likeness of X.[24] It is not even necessary for someone to count as being reminded of X, where (at least in some sense) they are reminded *by* a picture of X. Suppose the person so reminded pays no attention to what the picture is a picture of, but simply notes that it is a picture, and is put in mind of X of whom they recall taking a picture only last week. Of course, in this scenario, we precisely do *not* have a case of someone who is reminded by something *like* what it reminds them of.[25] I shall come back to this scenario below.

The fact that thought of a likeness of X (as a likeness of X) is sufficient, although not necessary, for thought of X, may make it look as if the case of Simmias and his picture violates the recognition requirement. For this implies that thought of Simmias is given in the recognition of the picture of Simmias as a picture of him. And so it is. But it is so only, I take it, because thought of Simmias is itself necessary for the recognition of the picture as a picture *of him*. In this type of case, but this type only, recognition of the thing reminding (under the description in question) and thought of the thing it reminds one of, stand or fall together. Does the simple fact of their standing or falling together violate the recognition requirement? It does not violate the spirit of that requirement, for the person who recognizes the picture and is thereby reminded of Simmias does so through bringing their knowledge of Simmias to the scene; it is neither given in perception of the picture nor extrapolated anew from it.[26]

But does it violate its letter? I think not; not if there is a contentful difference between recognizing the picture as a picture of Simmias and thinking of Simmias, even if they co-occur. That there is a contentful difference is shown, once again, by the dreamer's mistake. The dreamer is indeed thinking of Simmias. But, just as the dreamer does not count as being reminded of Simmias, so, for the same reason, they do not count as recognizing his picture as a picture of him. This person makes a mistake about the picture of Simmias (viz. they take it to be him)[27] and hence this person does not count as recognizing the picture as a picture of him.

There are, then, two rather different ways to satisfy the recognition requirement in being reminded of Simmias by his picture and one way to fail to satisfy it. One can satisfy the requirement by seeing and recognizing the picture of Simmias under some description other than that of 'picture of Simmias' and being thereby prompted to think of him. This happens, for example, in the somewhat contrived scenario I considered above. And one can satisfy the description by seeing and recognizing the picture of Simmias as a picture of Simmias and thereby thinking of him. One fails to satisfy it if one mistakes the picture for him. For, although one gets in mind something other than the thing perceived, one does not recognize what one perceives. In this way, we begin to see once again why, in this type of case, but this type only, Socrates takes there to be an additional requirement one must satisfy in order to count as being reminded; viz. one must avoid the dreamer's mistake.

If this suffices to show that the recognition requirement is not violated by the case of being reminded of Simmias by his picture, then it suffices, *mutatis mutandis*, to show that this requirement is not violated by the case of being reminded of the equal itself by equal sticks and stones. It suffices, that is, given the prevailing assumptions about this latter case, viz. that there is a form of equality relevantly distinct from equal sticks and stones, and that the relation between equal sticks and stones and the equal itself is, for the purposes of the discussion of being reminded, relevantly similar to the relation between a picture of Simmias and Simmias himself. The first assumption is made explicit. The second is implied by the carefully established correspondence between the two cases that I take the argument to involve.[28]

Having considered an apparent objection, let me conclude with two apparent advantages of the interpretation proposed.

The first turns on the point from which I began as regards the *Phaedo* passage, the undeniable fact that Socrates takes the additional experience involved in the case of recollection from likes to be *necessary* and that Simmias explicitly agrees. The interpretation I have proposed may plausibly be claimed to be necessary, if one is to be reminded of the original by its likeness as the argument requires. The alternative – according to which some explicit act of comparison is envisaged – has no such claim to necessity, a point that its proponents have not denied.

Now it has been suggested that, although Socrates insists on the necessity of the experience, he need not have done so. All the argument requires is that some people *do* have the experience, not that they must. However, although the argument does indeed exploit an example of what some people actually do, the remainder of the argument has the best chance of working, if it is necessary for them to do precisely what they do do, if, that is, they do it at all. Charity will therefore favour an interpretation in which this is the case.

The point depends on the argument's closing stages. Socrates has argued that, given what he has said, knowledge of the form of equal must predate the first occasion of seeing perceptible equals and getting in mind their falling short of the equal itself. He next argues that knowledge of the equal must predate the first occasion of perceiving at all. And this is the crux. The argument turns on the point that there is no other possible source than perception for our getting the equal itself in mind, but that it is 'from perception' (75a10) that we have the very experience that has been agreed to presuppose our knowledge of equal. I agree, in part, with both Rowe and Scott on how this must work. I quote from Scott: 'Crucial to this argument is the assumption that the *same* perception that puts us in mind of the form would also put us in mind of the comparison' (Scott 1995, 62–3; cf. Rowe 1993, 172–3). However, as Scott acknowledges, his interpretation has not got us to this position. For Scott, the experience on which the argument turns is an explicit act of comparison between the perceived equality of some sticks and one's recollected knowledge of the form. But there is no obvious reason why one could not first be prompted to think of the form and only thereafter, on a separate occasion, engage in this comparison. On Scott's reading, this remains a fundamental weakness in Socrates' argument as a whole.

In contrast, on my reading, if one recognizes the equality of perceptible equals in the manner that my interpretation of the crucial experience requires, recognition of the form and recognition of what one perceives as merely a likeness of the form must occur in one and the same act. Otherwise, one would have fallen once again into the dreamer's mistake.[29]

The second apparent advantage also involves what might be thought a gap in the argument. Like Scott, I have proposed a restricted account of who engages in the recollection described. But the argument's intended conclusion is not restricted in scope. It aims to show that all people – not just Platonists – have prenatal knowledge of forms within their soul. Now it has been objected against a restricted scope reading that it fails to ensure the prenatal existence of any but the philosopher's soul. To this, there is a natural response – and one that Scott makes: that the argument be taken to rely on an implicit generalization from the limited sample of those who display the prenatal knowledge in question. Scott proposes that this generalization is taken to go through on the grounds that all human beings may be assumed to be of the same type (1995, 69–71). However, I think one might yet worry about this generalization at least as applied to Scott's view. On Scott's view, precisely what would appear to distinguish Platonist philosophers – if there are any – from ordinary mortals is their knowledge of forms as displayed in experiences that depend on their having such knowledge. Having such experiences and knowledge need not make them a different species, of course. But it seems perilous to have the argument rely on an implied generalization that depends on denying any special significance to the very feature of the subset from which one generalizes on which the argument has thus far turned.

On my reading, in contrast, the fact that certain of one's experiences involve prior knowledge of forms is not what makes the difference between Platonist philosophers and everyone else, and so the generalization may safely go through. The ordinary dreamers' experience involves the relevant knowledge also; they simply do not access and use it in the correct way.

Acknowledgements
The interpretation of the *Phaedo* presented here has its origins in a seminar presentation to the 'Old Chestnuts' Greek Philosophy seminar series at King's College London Philosophy Department. Versions of the present paper were read to the Second Celtic Conference in Classics (Glasgow, 2002); the Philosophy Department Staff Seminar, King's College London; a Workshop on Platonic Epistemology at Cornell University (April 2003); at Princeton University; and at Heythrop College London. I am grateful to these various audiences for questions and comments that have prompted numerous improvements. For additional comments and discussion, my particular thanks to Peter Adamson, Myles Burnyeat, Ursula Coope, Gail Fine, Fritz-Gregor Herrmann, Melissa Lane and M.M. McCabe.

Notes
[1] Paradigmatic optical illusions, at least, are incorrigible in the following sense: a straight stick in water will continue to look bent to me, even though I know it is straight. In the kind of case I am interested in, it is less clear to me that this is so. Once apprised of my mistake, a cunningly painted doorway will no longer look to me like

a (real) doorway; although, of course, it may continue to look like (a very good likeness of) a doorway. In such a case, I may wonder how I was ever taken in; in the bent stick case, there is no need to wonder, for its visual presentation remains exactly the same.

[2] Especially 515a5–c3. The prisoners' condition raises tricky issues that I will not address here. On the nature of their condition, I broadly follow Adam (1902 II, 91, 179–80) and Owen (1986, 138–47). *Ex hypothesi*, they have had no direct acquaintance with realities other than the shadows upon and echoes from the wall of the cave. But Plato does not seem to take them to have a private world of their own with private terms (correctly used) for the things within it. Rather he thinks of them as having a vocabulary for real things, misapplied to their shadows and the like. I follow Adam's text of 515b4–5: οὐ ταῦτα ἡγεῖ ἂν τὰ παρίοντα αὐτοὺς νομίζειν ὀνομάζειν, ἅπερ ὁρῶμεν… Adam translates: 'Do you not suppose that they would believe that they were naming these particular passing objects which they saw?' Cf. Grube-Reeve (1992, ad loc.): 'Don't you think they'd suppose that the names they used applied to the things they see passing before them?' The point, then, is that the expressions the prisoners use in fact refer to the objects casting the shadows, but are (mistakenly) taken to refer to the shadows. As Owen puts it, the prisoners 'are possessed of a vocabulary but [mistake] the reference of the words'. This vocabulary is (somehow) independently acquired and not derived from the shadows (Owen 1986, 144–5 with n. 20). For further discussion see now Harte, forthcoming.

[3] The reference to waking dreams (hallucinations) tends to pathologise the non-philosophers. But I do not take this to be a central feature of appeal to the mistake in general.

[4] For these two sides to identification in general and two corresponding mistakes in misidentification, compare the puzzle at *Theaetetus* 188b3–5, where one who mistakes one (*ex hypothesi*, known) thing for another (*ex hypothesi*, known) thing, 'knowing both is in turn ignorant of both'; that is, such a person makes a mistake about both the thing misidentified and the thing it is misidentified as (by taking the thing misidentified to be it).

[5] And in at least one sense of 'in their cognition', they do not in fact have two items in it.

[6] A point given some emphasis by the construction with ἀλλὰ…μέν in 475e2. On the construction, see Denniston 1966, 377–8. Denniston does not explicitly identify the construction as emphatic. But the effect of delaying the positive (μέν) clause until after that with which it is contrasted has the effect of giving it (at least equal) emphasis. Denniston's other Platonic parallels – *Theaetetus* 201b, *Sophist* 240b – provide support for this point also.

[7] This despite Glaucon's apparent sophistication. It is perhaps fitting, therefore, that he should be invited to answer on behalf of the dreamers in Socrates' second argument to distinguish them from philosophers, beginning at 476e6. (This is not to say that he is a lover of sights and sounds, since, he, unlike them, acknowledges the existence of forms over and above their perceptible manifestations. But he makes a parallel mistake regarding the identity of philosophers.)

[8] This paper went to press before the appearance of two recent treatments of this *Phaedo* argument with which it may usefully be contrasted: Franklin 2005 and Sedley 2006.

[9] Unless otherwise specified, this should be understood to refer to a depiction of

Simmias occurring within a physical object such as a painted canvas and not to any such physical object. Cf. the *Phaedo*'s talk of a 'painted Simmias' (Σιμμίαν γεγραμμένον), e.g. at 73e9.

¹⁰ So, Scott 1995, 59–61; Rowe 1993, 167; Gallop 1975, 118–19.

¹¹ Here and throughout, I have in mind someone who takes the picture as a picture of some (specific, real) man (albeit unknown to them) and not someone who takes the picture to be a man-picture, where there is no assumption that the man depicted exists or existed.

¹² There are complications here: although, arguably, all cases of recognizing a picture as a picture of Simmias will require independent knowledge of Simmias (independent of the picture, that is), it is not obvious that all will be cases of being reminded. If the picture comes with a label 'picture of Simmias' and one has knowledge of the conventions regarding pictures and labels, this will do just as well. However, while these complications will be damaging to the argument's goal of establishing *pre*natal knowledge, they do not substantially affect the points I want to make.

¹³ Recall that the *Theaetetus* supposes, at least for the purpose of setting a puzzle, that, if one misidentifies X as Y (a picture of Simmias as Simmias), one makes a mistake not only about X (the picture) but also about Y (Simmias). See n. 4 above.

¹⁴ Why, in 74a5–8, is the experience described as considering 'whether *or not*' [the reminding thing] is lacking, when, on my interpretation, it looks as if it could not fail to be lacking? I suggest that the 'not' case is not offered as a viable alternative possibility for something which does remind one, but rather as the case in which a candidate reminding object does not 'remind' one at all. If something is not lacking, according to my understanding of 'lacking', it is the original itself. In other words, in order to be reminded of Simmias by something like him, it had better be a picture of him and not the man himself.

¹⁵ At *Sophist* 266bc, reflections are in fact described as artefacts produced by god, but they are so described in a context in which everything (except humanly produced artefacts) is said to be so, including the things that cast reflections.

¹⁶ At least, this is the presumption behind Parmenides' argument in this passage, from which Socrates does not demur. Parmenides' assumption that, given Socrates' claim that participants are likenesses of forms (132d1–4), participants and forms must be like (ὅμοιος) one another, is an instance of the general inferential principle at issue. Despite the context, I see no reason why this inferential principle should not be something that Plato himself (at least sometimes) endorsed.

¹⁷ My talk of the mistaken person as having 'some cognitive access to' or 'some awareness of' the original is regrettably vague. Note that I do not assume that Plato conceives of the nature and extent of such access or awareness in a uniform way across all the passages where a mistake of this sort is in question. Further, since the mistake involves a combination of success and error as regards the original, discussions of it may choose to emphasize one more than the other for local reasons; so, for example, *Republic* 5 emphasizes error over success, while the *Phaedo* emphasizes success over error.

¹⁸ I switch to a statue here, because setting up this example is more complicated for the case of pictures, since the term 'picture' may refer to the object that is the picture (the painted canvas, for example) or to the representation within it. Cf. n. 9 above.

¹⁹ Suppose they were shown lots of rather different statues and still did not understand that, on each occasion, what they were being shown was a statue of Simmias and not

Simmias himself. One could imagine such a person, on seeing a new statue, saying 'oh look, there's another Simmias'.

[20] e.g. Gulley (1962, 26), although Gulley takes this to be an inconsistency on Plato's part between a moral condemnation of the senses and a more positive epistemological appraisal of their role. This seems to me an unsatisfactory way to resolve the apparent ambivalence.

[21] Scott 1995, 53 n. 1, who gives examples of those defending the alternative view.

[22] To defend and articulate such an experience may very well require definitional knowledge of the form.

[23] It has often been noted that meeting this description does not suffice to show that a person is being reminded of, as opposed simply to inventing the 'something else' (e.g. Bostock 1986, 63). For my purposes, this will not matter, since it is the necessity of this experience that will be at issue.

[24] Thought of X is necessary when perceiving a likeness of X as a likeness of X, but only because of the necessity of thought of X to such a perception. More on this below.

[25] For this case, I exploit the ambiguity of 'picture' remarked on above, n. 18.

[26] Ignoring, that is, complications involving pictures with labels, discussed above.

[27] Again, compare the *Theaetetus* on misidentification in general; see n. 4.

[28] One might take Socrates' claim, at 74c11–d2, that it does not matter, for the purposes of establishing that the equals case is a case of being reminded, whether equal sticks and stones are like or unlike the equal itself, to create difficulties here (through creating difficulties for the claim of correspondence between the two cases). However, first, I take the position and form of this claim to be itself part and parcel of the careful correspondence. Socrates is careful to proceed in stages exactly corresponding to those he went through before in discussing the general cases of being reminded. This identification of recollection in the equals case as indifferent to the reminding thing being like or unlike the thing of which it reminds one corresponds to his claim, at 74a2–3, that recollection can occur both from things that are like, and also from things that are unlike. Second – and to address the point of substance – if I am right that one does not satisfy the recognition requirement in the case of things that are alike, if one makes the dreamer's mistake (because one in fact fails to recognize the thing that does the reminding), and if in 74c13–d1 Socrates means to recall precisely this requirement, then, formally speaking, it will be true that, provided one meets this description one counts as being reminded, whether the things in question are like or unlike, since, in the case where they are like, failure to meet this description and failure to be reminded will coincide, because of the failure to meet the additional requirement on being reminded by things that are like.

[29] But what if one does not recognize the equality of perceptible equals *in the manner* that my interpretation of the crucial experience requires? That is, one might think that the interpretation proposed leaves a similar gap, since having the experience I propose is by no means the only thing that might happen upon perceiving equal sticks; one might make the dreamer's mistake. (Of course, in doing so, I have argued, one will also fail properly to recognize the equality of the sticks.) Leaving room for this possibility does not create the same kind of difficulty. As I have argued, this experience too presupposes knowledge of the equal, and it is no more the case of the dreamer than of the one who avoids the mistake that they first perceive and only thereafter make the mistake.

Bibliography

Ackrill, J.L.
   1973   '*Anamnesis* in the *Phaedo*: remarks on 73c–75c', in E.N. Lee, A.D.P. Mourelatos and R.M. Rorty (eds.) *Exegesis and Argument*, Phronesis Suppl. vol. I, Assen, 177–95.

Adam, J. (ed.)
   1902   *The* Republic *of Plato*, 2 vols., Cambridge.

Bostock, D.
   1986   *Plato*, Phaedo, Oxford.

Denniston, J.D.
   1966   *The Greek Particles*, 2nd edn, Oxford.

Franklin, L.
   2005   'Recollection and philosophical reflection in Plato's *Phaedo*', *Phronesis* 2.4, 289–314.

Gallop, D.
   1975   *Plato*, Phaedo, Oxford.

Gosling, J.C.B.
   1965   'Similarity in *Phaedo* 73b seq.', *Phronesis* 10, 151–61.

Grube, G.M.A. and Reeve, C.D.C.
   1992   *Plato* Republic, trans. G.M.A. Grube, rev. C.D.C. Reeve, Indianapolis.

Gulley, N.
   1962   *Plato's Theory of Knowledge*, London.

Harte, V.A.
   2007   'Language in the Cave', in D. Scott (ed.) *Marensis*, Oxford.

Owen, G.E.L.
   1986   'Plato on the Undepictable', in his *Logic, Science and Dialectic: Collected papers in Greek philosophy*, ed. Martha Nussbaum, London, 138–47.

Rowe, C.J. (ed.)
   1993   *Plato. Phaedo.* Cambridge.

Scott, D.
   1987   'Platonic anamnesis revisited', *Classical Quarterly* 37, 346–66.
   1995   *Recollection and Experience: Plato's theory of learning and its successors*, Cambridge.

Sedley, D.N.
   2006   'Form-particular resemblance in Plato's *Phaedo*', *Proceedings of the Aristotelian Society* cvi.3, 309–25.

3

ΟΥΣΙΑ IN PLATO'S *PHAEDO* – THE MEANING, USAGE AND HISTORY OF A TECHNICAL TERM

Fritz-Gregor Herrmann

I

If one had to choose one passage from Plato's middle dialogues to illustrate his ontology in that period, it would probably be *Phaedo* 95a–107b.[1] In this one passage, we find united Plato's search for αἰτία or *explanation*; the method of ὑπόθεσις or *assumption*; καλόν and ἀγαθόν, *beautiful* and *good*, as central topics of Plato's concern, singled out by the phrase αὐτὸ καθ᾿ αὐτό, *itself by itself*; in addition, the relationship which the many beautiful things have with that beautiful is referred to as μετέχειν, 'having of' or *sharing*; and the relationship 'the beautiful' has with the many is: that its παρουσία, its *presence*, or its κοινωνία, its *communion*, makes them beautiful. Through 'the beautiful', beautiful things come to be beautiful. Then, the discussion widens to include things big and small as well as mathematical numbers. At 101c2 ff., not only is the verb μετέχειν repeated, but a noun μετάσχεσις is coined to highlight this important relationship; and in addition, δυάς and μονάς, the *dyad* and the *monad*, are referred to as that in whose ἰδία οὐσία, whose *own being* or *nature*, things two or one respectively 'share'. Eventually, the terms εἶδος and ἰδέα, the two words which used to be translated as 'idea' and which are now more commonly translated as 'form', are introduced at 102b1 and 104b9 respectively; the former, εἶδος, together with the notion that 'the things coming to have a share' in any one of the εἴδη, τὰ μεταλαμβάνοντα, have their name, their *be-naming* or ἐπωνυμία from those 'forms'. μορφή occurs twice. In addition, things like μέγεθος, 'bigness', are repeatedly said 'to be in', ἐνεῖναι and εἶναι ἐν, the many things around us, or in this specific case in a person who is big. Thus we have as the vocabulary of Plato's ontology in the *Phaedo*: μετέχειν, 'having of' or 'sharing', μεταλαμβάνειν, 'coming to share', μετάσχεσις, 'a sharing (in something)'; αὐτὸ καθ᾿ αὐτό, 'itself by itself', εἶδος and ἰδέα, 'idea' or 'form', μορφή, 'shape' or 'form', οὐσία, 'being'; ἐπωνυμία, 'benaming' (or 'appellation'); παρουσία, 'presence', and κοινωνία, 'communion'; ἐνεῖναι and εἶναι ἐν, 'being in'; ὑπόθεσις, 'assumption'; and αἰτία, 'cause-and-reason'.

43

These terms are not terms of Plato's making. Many of them, indeed, had been part of the philosophical terminology of others before Plato. When Plato adopted such terms, he did so consciously, indicating to his readers both his source or sources and the way in which he wanted the terms he took over to be understood by his audience. Adoption for Plato is always adaptation, and often little more seems to be left of an older system but the word or words which Plato adopted. But this borrowing on Plato's part is never arbitrary. There are always good philosophical reasons for an active engagement with the thought of one or more of Plato's predecessors in any given dialogue.[2]

This chapter provides an outline of the usage and meaning of one of these terms in the *Phaedo* and makes a tentative suggestion concerning its possible origin. οὐσία, one of the most fertile philosophical terms in post-Platonic philosophy, was, *qua* philosophical term, Plato's creation.[3] It is of course undisputed that the word existed in Attic Greek before Plato, but only with the meaning 'property' *vel sim.*, i.e. the collective noun that denotes ἅ τινι ἔστιν, 'what is (or 'is there') to (or 'for') somebody', 'someone's property or wealth'.[4] As such, the word is frequently found in the Attic dramatists and orators of the fifth and fourth centuries BC, and in Attic inscriptions.[5] But while the history of the word is well documented, it is necessary to ask again what it signifies in Plato's dialogues before the *Republic*. Only once that is established can it be decided whether the notion expressed had been anticipated by one of Plato's predecessors.

II

When Plato for the first time introduces οὐσία with its new technical, philosophical meaning of 'being' in the *Meno* and the *Euthyphro*, he marks this new usage with definitional tags:

Σωκράτης: πολλῇ γέ τινι εὐτυχίᾳ ἔοικα κεχρῆσθαι, ὦ Μένων, εἰ μίαν ζητῶν ἀρετὴν σμῆνός τι ἀνηύρηκα ἀρετῶν παρὰ σοὶ κείμενον. ἀτάρ, ὦ Μένων, κατὰ ταύτην τὴν εἰκόνα τὴν περὶ τὰ σμήνη, εἴ μου ἐρομένου μελίττης περὶ οὐσίας ὅτι ποτ' ἐστίν, πολλὰς καὶ παντοδαπὰς ἔλεγες αὐτὰς εἶναι, τί ἂν ἀπεκρίνω μοι, εἴ σε ἠρόμην· 'ἆρα τούτῳ φῂς πολλὰς καὶ παντοδαπὰς εἶναι καὶ διαφερούσας ἀλλήλων, τῷ μελίττας εἶναι; ἢ τούτῳ μὲν οὐδὲν διαφέρουσιν, ἄλλῳ δέ τῳ, οἷον ἢ κάλλει ἢ μεγέθει ἢ ἄλλῳ τῳ τῶν τοιούτων;' εἰπέ, τί ἂν ἀπεκρίνω οὕτως ἐρωτηθείς;
Μένων: τοῦτ' ἔγωγε, ὅτι οὐδὲν διαφέρουσιν, ᾗ μέλιτται εἰσίν, ἡ ἑτέρα τῆς ἑτέρας.

Socrates: I certainly seem to have good luck, Meno, if looking for one excellence I have found a swarm of excellences lying with you. But, Meno, according to the image, the one of the swarms, if when I asked you about a bee, its being, what it is,[6] you said that they are many and varied, what would you answer me if I asked you: 'Is it that through-and-in *this* you say they are many and varied and different from each other, through being bees? Or do they differ in nothing through-and-in this, but through-and-in something else, such as through-and-in beauty or size or any other of such things?' Tell me, what would you answer thus asked? Meno: This I would answer, that, in as much as they are bees, they differ in nothing from one another. *Meno* 72a6–b9

Σωκράτης: καὶ κινδυνεύεις, ὦ Εὐθύφρων, ἐρωτώμενος τὸ ὅσιον ὅτι ποτ' ἐστίν, τὴν μὲν οὐσίαν μοι αὐτοῦ οὐ βούλεσθαι δηλῶσαι, πάθος δέ τι περὶ αὐτοῦ λέγειν, ὅτι πέπονθε τοῦτο τὸ ὅσιον, φιλεῖσθαι ὑπὸ πάντων θεῶν· ὅτι δὲ ὄν, οὔπω εἶπες. εἰ οὖν σοι φίλον, μή με ἀποκρύψῃ ἀλλὰ πάλιν εἰπὲ ἐξ ἀρχῆς τί ποτε ὂν τὸ ὅσιον εἴτε φιλεῖται ὑπὸ θεῶν εἴτε ὁτιδὴ πάσχει – οὐ γὰρ περὶ τούτου διοισόμεθα – ἀλλ' εἰπὲ προθύμως τί ἐστιν τό τε ὅσιον καὶ τὸ ἀνόσιον;

Socrates: And, Euthyphro, when asked about the pious, what it is, its being you seem not to be willing to reveal to me,[7] but just to give me 'something it suffers',[8] what this 'pious' suffers, (namely) to be loved by all the gods: but *being what* (it suffers this), you have not yet said. So if that is fine by you, do not hide it from me, but say again from the beginning: *being what* is the pious either loved by the gods or whatever else it may suffer – for we do not disagree about that – but tell me freely: *what is* the pious and the impious? *Euthyphro* 11a6–b5

In both passages, οὐσία comes to stand next to the phrase ὅτι ποτ' ἐστίν, 'what (ever) it is'. As direct questions, 'what (ever) is the pious?' and 'what (ever) is excellence?' have a form familiar from other early Platonic dialogues. The *context* in which the noun οὐσία is introduced is thus not new. By juxtaposing ὅτι ποτ' ἐστίν, as an indirect question, and οὐσία, Plato therefore defines sufficiently the sense in which he wants the noun οὐσία to be taken: οὐσία is 'what something is'. And from the *Meno* and *Euthyphro* alone one can also see that Plato's giving the meaning of 'what something is' to οὐσία is motivated partly by, or at least amounts to, an etymologizing of the noun by exploiting its similarity with the feminine singular participle οὖσα, 'being'.[9] At the same time it may be noted that, in the *Euthyphro*, οὐσία is contrasted with πάθος, just as at *Meno* 71b3–4, in the passage leading up to Socrates' introduction of the word οὐσία, 'what something is' is contrasted with 'what something is like': ὃ δὲ μὴ οἶδα τί ἐστιν, πῶς ἂν ὁποῖόν γέ τι εἰδείην; 'But concerning something of which I do not know what it is, how could I possibly know of what sort it is?'[10] It may be significant that therefore οὐσία here does not mean 'that something is'.

III

This etymological interpretation of the word οὐσία – which otherwise meant 'possession, wealth, property' – as 'being' is also found in the *Phaedo*. The first of the five passages in the dialogue in which the term occurs is 65d9–e5:

> ἤδη οὖν πώποτέ τι τῶν τοιούτων τοῖς ὀφθαλμοῖς εἶδες;
> οὐδαμῶς, ἦ δ' ὅς.
> ἀλλ' ἄλλῃ τινὶ αἰσθήσει τῶν διὰ τοῦ σώματος ἐφήψω αὐτῶν; λέγω δὲ περὶ πάντων, οἷον μεγέθους πέρι, ὑγιείας, ἰσχύος, <u>καὶ τῶν ἄλλων ἑνὶ λόγῳ ἁπάντων τῆς οὐσίας ὃ τυγχάνει ἕκαστον ὄν</u>· ἆρα διὰ τοῦ σώματος αὐτῶν τὸ ἀληθέστατον θεωρεῖται, ἢ ὧδε ἔχει· ὃς ἂν μάλιστα ἡμῶν καὶ ἀκριβέστατα παρασκευάσηται αὐτὸ ἕκαστον διανοηθῆναι περὶ οὗ σκοπεῖ, οὗτος ἂν ἐγγύτατα ἴοι τοῦ γνῶναι ἕκαστον;

So have you ever yet seen any one of the things of that sort with your eyes?
Never, said he.
But have you touched them with any other sensation of those (we get) through the body? But I am talking about everything, as for example about size, health, strength, <u>and, in a word, all other things' being</u>,[11] what each happens to be: Is it the case that what is truest of them is perceived through the body, or is it as follows: whoever of us manages to the greatest extent and most accurately to *think* through[12] each thing itself about which he speculates, this (person) may well come closest to understanding each thing?

The definitional tag 'what each happens to be' echoes the similar phrases of the *Meno* and the *Euthyphro*. What is new is the range of terms or notions or concepts with whose 'being' Socrates is concerned, as well as the epistemological considerations which accompany the introduction of the term οὐσία in the *Phaedo*. The phrase 'what each happens to be' defines the term οὐσία in the same way as in the earlier two dialogues; together with the remainder of the passage, it serves as a clear indication that οὐσία here, too, denotes 'being' in the sense of 'what something is', not in the sense of 'that something is'.

The next two occurrences of οὐσία present a slightly different case (76d7–77a5):

> ἆρ' οὖν οὕτως ἔχει, ἔφη, ἡμῖν, ὦ Σιμμία; εἰ μὲν ἔστιν ἃ θρυλοῦμεν ἀεί, καλόν τέ τι καὶ ἀγαθὸν <u>καὶ πᾶσα ἡ τοιαύτη οὐσία</u>, καὶ ἐπὶ ταύτην τὰ ἐκ τῶν αἰσθήσεων πάντα ἀναφέρομεν, ὑπάρχουσαν πρότερον ἀνευρίσκοντες ἡμετέραν οὖσαν, καὶ ταῦτα ἐκείνῃ ἀπεικάζομεν, ἀναγκαῖον, οὕτως ὥσπερ καὶ ταῦτα ἔστιν, οὕτως καὶ τὴν ἡμετέραν ψυχὴν εἶναι καὶ πρὶν γεγονέναι ἡμᾶς· εἰ δὲ μὴ ἔστι ταῦτα, ἄλλως ἂν ὁ λόγος οὗτος εἰρημένος εἴη; ἆρ' οὕτως ἔχει, καὶ ἴση ἀνάγκη ταῦτά τε εἶναι καὶ τὰς ἡμετέρας ψυχὰς πρὶν καὶ ἡμᾶς γεγονέναι, καὶ εἰ μὴ ταῦτα, οὐδὲ τάδε; ὑπερφυῶς, ὦ Σώκρατες, ἔφη ὁ Σιμμίας, δοκεῖ μοι ἡ αὐτὴ ἀνάγκη εἶναι, καὶ εἰς καλόν γε καταφεύγει ὁ λόγος εἰς τὸ ὁμοίως εἶναι τήν τε ψυχὴν ἡμῶν πρὶν γενέσθαι ἡμᾶς <u>καὶ τὴν οὐσίαν ἣν σὺ νῦν λέγεις</u>. οὐ γὰρ ἔχω ἔγωγε οὐδὲν οὕτω μοι ἐναργὲς ὂν ὡς τοῦτο, τὸ πάντα τὰ τοιαῦτ' εἶναι ὡς οἷόν τε μάλιστα, καλόν τε καὶ ἀγαθὸν καὶ τἆλλα πάντα ἃ σὺ νυνδὴ ἔλεγες· καὶ ἔμοιγε δοκεῖ ἱκανῶς ἀποδέδεικται.

So, Simmias, he said, is it not consequently like this: if what we always talk about *is*, some beautiful and good <u>and the whole being of this sort</u>, and if to this we refer everything (that we get) from our sensations, finding it again as obtaining before, being ours, and if we liken those (things which we get from our sensations) to it (the whole being of this sort), then it is necessary that such as those things (i.e. the beautiful, the good and the whole being of this sort), too, are, so also is our soul even before we were: but if those things (i.e. the beautiful, the good and the whole being of this sort) are not, this account may well have to be given in a different way? Is it like this, and there is equal necessity that those things (i.e. the beautiful, the good and the whole being of this sort) are and that our souls are, even before we were, and if not this, neither that? Exceedingly, Socrates, said Simmias, does there seem to me to be the same necessity, and the account has certainly escaped to a beautiful conclusion: that equally[13] before we have come to be *is* our soul <u>and *is* the being which you now mention</u>. For I have nothing that is so clear to me as this, that all such things *are* as much as possible, beautiful and good and all the other things which you have just mentioned: and to me it seems that it is demonstrated sufficiently.

The phrase πᾶσα ἡ τοιαύτη οὐσία must be rendered 'the whole being of this sort': οὐσία here is the collective noun[14] for τὰ ὄντα, 'things'.[15] οὐσία thus does here not refer to what a particular thing is; instead, it refers to the totality of 'such' things, i.e. the totality of the things that are, the totality of what is in the way the beautiful is and the good is; but οὐσία does not mean 'the existence' of things like the good and the beautiful. That is to say, there is a semantic extension of the noun here; as is to be expected, this extension is in line with possible application of forms of the verb εἶναι, 'to be'; but the specific extension in this case is not in the direction of a so-called 'existential' εἶναι, but rather in the direction of the meaning of the plural of the substantival neuter participle, τὰ ὄντα, which was a standard word in common Greek parlance, simply denoting 'things'.[16] This helps to establish the term οὐσία by linking it more firmly to its etymological connection with εἶναι, and it may certainly help prepare further extension in meaning based on different applications of the verb εἶναι; but this further extension itself is not implied here.

IV

The next occurrence of οὐσία, at *Phaedo* 78c6–d9, is best understood against the usage in the previous context of 76d–77a:

οὐκοῦν ἅπερ ἀεὶ κατὰ ταὐτὰ καὶ ὡσαύτως ἔχει, ταῦτα μάλιστα εἰκὸς εἶναι τὰ ἀσύνθετα, τὰ δὲ ἄλλοτ' ἄλλως καὶ μηδέποτε κατὰ ταὐτά, ταῦτα δὲ σύνθετα;
ἔμοιγε δοκεῖ οὕτως.
ἴωμεν δή, ἔφη, ἐπὶ ταὐτὰ ἐφ' ἅπερ ἐν τῷ ἔμπροσθεν λόγῳ. <u>αὐτὴ ἡ οὐσία ἧς λόγον δίδομεν τοῦ εἶναι</u> καὶ ἐρωτῶντες καὶ ἀποκρινόμενοι, πότερον ὡσαύτως ἀεὶ ἔχει κατὰ ταὐτὰ ἢ ἄλλοτ' ἄλλως; αὐτὸ τὸ ἴσον, αὐτὸ τὸ καλόν, <u>αὐτὸ ἕκαστον ὃ ἔστιν, τὸ ὄν</u>, μή ποτε μεταβολὴν καὶ ἡντινοῦν ἐνδέχεται; ἢ ἀεὶ αὐτῶν ἕκαστον

ὃ ἔστι, μονοειδὲς ὂν αὐτὸ καθ' αὑτό, ὡσαύτως κατὰ ταὐτὰ ἔχει καὶ οὐδέποτε
οὐδαμῇ οὐδαμῶς ἀλλοίωσιν οὐδεμίαν ἐνδέχεται;
ὡσαύτως, ἔφη, ἀνάγκη, ὁ Κέβης, κατὰ ταὐτὰ ἔχειν, ὦ Σώκρατες.

What is always according to the same[17] and in the same way, is not this likely to be what is incomposite; but what is at one time in one way, at another in another, and never according to the same, this in turn composite?
To me, certainly, it seems so.
Let us therefore go, said he, to the same things to which we went in the previous account. This 'being' itself[18] of which we give as an account the 'it is' when we ask and answer, is it in the same way always according to the same, or at one time in one way, at another in another? Would the equal itself, the beautiful itself, each thing-that-is itself, 'what is',[19] ever admit change, even the slightest? Or (is it rather the case that) always, of those, each thing-that-is, being uniform, itself by itself, is in the same way according to the same and never in any way anyhow admits any alteration?
In the same way, said Cebes, it must be according to the same, Socrates.

Opinions on how to construe the Greek at 78d1 differ considerably.[20] Differences, though, concern mainly the syntactical and semantic analysis of the relative clause. That οὐσία here denotes what it denoted at its last occurrence is less controversial.[21] A further complication, however, is introduced by the phrase ἕκαστον ὃ ἔστιν, here translated 'each thing-that-is'. The Greek phrase ὃ ἔστιν is ambiguous. Depending on context, ὃ can either be interpreted as a relative or as an indirect interrogative pronoun; in the former case, the phrase ὃ ἔστιν may be translated 'which is' or 'which is there', in the latter, 'what it is' or 'what is'.[22] In the *Phaedo*, the phrase first occurs at 74b2, where ὃ is the indirect interrogative pronoun:

ἦ καὶ ἐπιστάμεθα αὐτὸ ὃ ἔστιν;[23]

And certainly we also understand it, what it is?

This is followed at 74d6 by αὐτὸ τὸ ὃ ἔστιν ἴσον,[24] 'the what-is-equal itself'. The phrase ὃ ἔστιν ἴσον may be part of a sentence 'we understand *what is equal*' or of a sentence 'we understand that which is equal'; but the definite article certainly favours the former analysis.[25] That ὃ ἔστιν at 74d6 is not a gloss is supported by 75b1–2, ἐκείνου τε ὀρέγεται τοῦ ὃ ἔστιν ἴσον, 'they are striving for that thing, the what-is-equal', to which may be added 75b5–6, εἰληφότας ἐπιστήμην αὐτοῦ τοῦ ἴσου ὅτι ἔστιν, 'having got understanding of the equal itself, what it is', where the indefinite pronoun rather than the relative functions as the indirect interrogative; that section of the dialogue is crowned by the memorable conclusion concerning recollection (75c10–d4):

οὐ γὰρ περὶ τοῦ ἴσου νῦν ὁ λόγος ἡμῖν μᾶλλόν τι ἢ καὶ περὶ αὐτοῦ τοῦ καλοῦ καὶ αὐτοῦ τοῦ ἀγαθοῦ καὶ δικαίου καὶ ὁσίου καί, ὅπερ λέγω, περὶ ἁπάντων οἷς ἐπισφραγιζόμεθα τοῦτο τὸ 'ὃ ἔστι' καὶ ἐν ταῖς ἐρωτήσεσιν ἐρωτῶντες καὶ ἐν ταῖς ἀποκρίσεσιν ἀποκρινόμενοι.[26]

For, consequently, now the account is no more about the equal than also about the beautiful itself and the good itself and the just and the pious and, as I say, about all those which we mark with that seal, the 'what-it-is', both in our questions when we ask and in our answers when we answer.

In all these cases, the phrase ὃ ἔστιν is thus best taken as an indirect question, 'what(-it-)is'. This poses a question for 78d3–5: should one understand Socrates' unusual usage of ὃ ἔστιν here in line with all the previous occurrences since 74b? One should then translate (78d3–5)

αὐτὸ τὸ ἴσον, αὐτὸ τὸ καλόν, αὐτὸ ἕκαστον ὃ ἔστιν, τὸ ὄν, μή ποτε μεταβολὴν καὶ ἡντινοῦν ἐνδέχεται;

as:

Would the equal itself, the beautiful itself, each what-it-is itself, 'what is' (τὸ ὄν), ever admit change, even the slightest?[27]

If this is so, it adds a dimension to *Phaedo* 78c6–d9 as an explicit reaction to Parmenides, who is the first to use τὸ ἐόν in the singular, as synonymous with εἶναι, to denote the totality of 'being'.[28] Plato's reaction, as has often been noted, is to ascribe all the attributes of Parmenides' one 'being' severally to each of the things themselves, the equal, the beautiful, etc. At 78d, οὐσία, 'being', is the collective of these 'beings'. And it is this usage that seems to be taken up at *Phaedo* 92c8: when Simmias is asked to choose between the two views 'that the soul is an attunement' and 'that learning is recollection', he decides against the former by recalling and summarizing what has been said about recollection. In conclusion, he declares (92d8–e2):

ἐρρήθη γάρ που οὕτως ἡμῶν εἶναι ἡ ψυχὴ καὶ πρὶν εἰς σῶμα ἀφικέσθαι, <u>ὥσπερ αὐτῇ ἔστιν ἡ οὐσία ἔχουσα τὴν ἐπωνυμίαν τὴν τοῦ 'ὃ ἔστιν'</u>· ἐγὼ δὲ ταύτην, ὡς ἐμαυτὸν πείθω, ἱκανῶς τε καὶ ὀρθῶς ἀποδέδεγμαι.

For it was somehow said that in that way *is* our soul also before having arrived in the body <u>as is the 'being' (οὐσία) itself which has the benaming of 'what-it-is'</u>: but I have accepted this [οὐσία], as I persuade myself, sufficiently and correctly.

Here, it is Simmias rather than Socrates speaking. Simmias may be using ἡ οὐσία collectively, he may be using a generic singular; either way, οὐσία is defined again as 'what-it-is'. Simmias is shown to have adopted Socrates' usage, conscious that it is a neologism.

Fritz-Gregor Herrmann

V

The passage containing the last occurrence of οὐσία in the *Phaedo*, 101b10–102a2, presents difficulties of a different sort.

> τί δέ; ἑνὶ ἑνὸς προστεθέντος τὴν πρόσθεσιν αἰτίαν εἶναι τοῦ δύο γενέσθαι ἢ διασχισθέντος τὴν σχίσιν οὐκ εὐλαβοῖο ἂν λέγειν; καὶ μέγα ἂν βοῴης ὅτι οὐκ οἶσθα ἄλλως πως ἕκαστον γιγνόμενον ἢ <u>μετασχὸν τῆς ἰδίας οὐσίας ἑκάστου οὗ ἂν μετάσχῃ</u>, καὶ ἐν τούτοις οὐκ ἔχεις ἄλλην τινὰ αἰτίαν τοῦ δύο γενέσθαι ἀλλ' ἢ τὴν τῆς δυάδος μετάσχεσιν, καὶ δεῖν τούτου μετασχεῖν τὰ μέλλοντα δύο ἔσεσθαι, καὶ μονάδος ὃ ἂν μέλλῃ ἓν ἔσεσθαι, τὰς δὲ σχίσεις ταύτας καὶ προσθέσεις καὶ τὰς ἄλλας τὰς τοιαύτας κομψείας ἐῴης ἂν χαίρειν, παρεὶς ἀποκρίνασθαι τοῖς σεαυτοῦ σοφωτέροις·...

And again, wouldn't you beware of saying that when one is added to one, the addition is reason for their coming to be two, or when one is divided, that division is the reason? You'd shout loudly that you know no other way in which each thing comes to be, except <u>by participating in the particular reality of any given thing in which it does participate</u>; and in those cases you own no other reason for their coming to be two, save participation in twoness: things that are going to be two must participate in that, and whatever is going to be one must participate in oneness. You'd dismiss those divisions and additions and other such subtleties, leaving them as answers to be given by people wiser than yourself;... (tr. Gallop)[29]

Before determining the meaning of οὐσία in this passage, an apparent difficulty of syntax and semantics must be discussed. All English translations and commentaries I have consulted construe the clause ὅτι οὐκ οἶσθα ἄλλως πως ἕκαστον γιγνόμενον ἢ μετασχὸν τῆς ἰδίας οὐσίας ἑκάστου οὗ ἂν μετάσχῃ in the way Gallop does; i.e. concerning the expression οἶδα with accusative plus participle, 'I know that something does/suffers something', ἕκαστον is considered to be the accusative subject and γιγνόμενον to be the participial predicate of the accusative-plus-participle construction; the translation is thus something like 'you know that each thing comes to be'. But, arguably, the phrase οἶσθα...ἕκαστον γιγνόμενον can also be construed as follows: the accusative subject is omitted and ἕκαστον γιγνόμενον represents the predicate, with ἕκαστον functioning as complement to γιγνόμενον; in traditional terminology, ἕκαστον would be the predicate adjective or predicate noun; a translation of the clause οὐκ οἶσθα ἄλλως πως ἕκαστον γιγνόμενον ἢ μετασχὸν τῆς ἰδίας οὐσίας ἑκάστου οὗ ἂν μετάσχῃ could then run 'You do not know of any other way of coming to be each than by participating in the ἰδία οὐσία of each in which it happens to participate'. The function of ἕκαστον and ἑκάστου in this sentence would be similar to that of letters used as variables in general(izing) statements since Aristotle: 'you do not know of any other way of coming to be *x* than by participating in the ἰδία οὐσία of *x* in which it participates.' To give an example, Socrates could have said: 'you do not know of any other way of becoming *beautiful* than by participating in the ἰδία οὐσία of *beautiful*, in which it participates'. This is in line with 100c,d, viz. that if anything is beautiful, it is beautiful because it participates in the beautiful itself, and that the many beautiful things are beautiful because of the presence of that beautiful.

Additional support for this construal may derive from the context of 100e8–101c9. While from 100d6 to e6 Socrates was talking about the many *beautifuls*, the *bigs* and the *smalls*,[30] which are beautiful, big or small because they participate, respectively, in the beautiful, the big and the small itself, from 100e8 onwards he reverts to *someone*'s or *something*'s being larger or smaller or more. As he had said at 100c4–5 that if *something* else is beautiful other than the beautiful itself (εἴ τί ἐστιν ἄλλο καλὸν πλὴν αὐτὸ τὸ καλόν), it is so by participation, so at 100e8 he hypothesizes that 'if someone were to say that *some one person* is taller by a head than *some other person* (εἴ τίς τινα φαίη ἕτερον ἑτέρου τῇ κεφαλῇ μείζω εἶναι)'. Anachronistically speaking, Socrates is concerned, at least *inter alia*, with predication, with somebody's being tall, somebody's being small, something's being more, and not just with *beautifuls*' being beautiful, *bigs*' being big and *smalls*' being or becoming small.

It may be objected, though, that while all this may be so in the case of qualitative adjectives, 101b10 ff. presents a different case, as we are now dealing with numbers. The objection would be that at 101b10–11 already, ἑνὶ ἑνὸς προστεθέντος τὴν πρόσθεσιν αἰτίαν εἶναι τοῦ δύο γενέσθαι should be translated with Hackforth 1955, 135: 'when one is added to one the addition is the cause of *there* coming to be two', not with Gallop as 'when one is added to one, the addition is the reason of *their* coming to be two' – i.e., we are now dealing with 'something's coming into being', not with 'something's becoming something'.[31] This thought is continued in 101c3, where the particular case of the coming into being of two is generalized to the coming into being of anything before Socrates returns at 101c4 to the specific case of two, when he says καὶ ἐν τούτοις οὐκ ἔχεις ἄλλην τινὰ αἰτίαν τοῦ δύο γενέσθαι ἀλλ' ἢ τὴν τῆς δυάδος μετάσχεσιν, which Hackforth (1955, 135) translates: 'and that in the case just mentioned you know of no other cause of there coming to be two save coming to participate in duality'.[32]

But this is unlikely. As part of the investigation 'into the cause-and-reason of generation and destruction', περὶ γενέσεως καὶ φθορᾶς τὴν αἰτίαν (95e10), the issue of 'coming to be two' was first mentioned at 96e, which is also the place at which the other examples resumed at 100e ff. are first introduced (96e6–97b7):

πόρρω που, ἔφη, νὴ Δία ἐμὲ εἶναι τοῦ οἴεσθαι περὶ τούτων του τὴν αἰτίαν εἰδέναι, ὅς γε οὐκ ἀποδέχομαι ἐμαυτοῦ οὐδὲ ὡς ἐπειδὰν ἑνί τις προσθῇ ἕν,

ἢ τὸ ἓν ᾧ προσετέθη δύο γέγονεν, <ἢ τὸ προστεθέν>, ἢ τὸ προστεθὲν καὶ ᾧ προσετέθη διὰ τὴν πρόσθεσιν τοῦ ἑτέρου τῷ ἑτέρῳ δύο ἐγένετο· θαυμάζω γὰρ εἰ ὅτε μὲν ἑκάτερον αὐτῶν χωρὶς ἀλλήλων ἦν, ἓν ἄρα ἑκάτερον ἦν καὶ οὐκ ἤστην τότε δύο, ἐπεὶ δ' ἐπλησίασαν ἀλλήλοις, αὕτη ἄρα αἰτία αὐτοῖς ἐγένετο τοῦ δύο γενέσθαι, ἡ σύνοδος τοῦ πλησίον ἀλλήλων τεθῆναι.
οὐδέ γε ὡς ἐάν τις ἓν διασχίσῃ, δύναμαι ἔτι πείθεσθαι ὡς αὕτη αὖ αἰτία γέγονεν, ἡ σχίσις, τοῦ δύο γεγονέναι· ἐναντία γὰρ γίγνεται ἢ τότε αἰτία τοῦ δύο γίγνεσθαι. τότε μὲν γὰρ ὅτι συνήγετο πλησίον ἀλλήλων καὶ προσετίθετο ἕτερον ἑτέρῳ, νῦν δ' ὅτι ἀπάγεται καὶ χωρίζεται ἕτερον ἀφ' ἑτέρου. οὐδέ γε δι' ὅτι ἓν γίγνεται ὡς ἐπίσταμαι, ἔτι πείθω ἐμαυτόν, οὐδ' ἄλλο οὐδὲν ἑνὶ λόγῳ δι' ὅτι γίγνεται ἢ ἀπόλλυται ἢ ἔστι, κατὰ τοῦτον τὸν τρόπον τῆς μεθόδου, ἀλλά τιν' ἄλλον τρόπον αὐτὸς εἰκῇ φύρω, τοῦτον δὲ οὐδαμῇ προσίεμαι.

I can assure you that I'm far from supposing I know the reason for any of those things, when I don't even accept from myself that when you add one to one, it's either the one to which the addition is made that's come to be two, or the one that's been added and the one to which it's been added, that have come to be two, because of the addition of one to the other. Because I wonder if, when they were apart from each other, each was one and they weren't two then; whereas when they came close to each other, this then became the reason for their coming to be two – the union in which they were juxtaposed.

Nor again can I any longer be persuaded, if you divide one, that this has now become a reason for its coming to be two; then it was their being brought close to each other and added, one to the other; whereas now it's their being drawn apart, and separated each from the other. Why, I can't even persuade myself any longer that I know why it is that one comes to be; nor, in short, why anything else comes to be, or perishes, or exists, following that method of inquiry. Instead I rashly adopt a different method, a jumble of my own, and in no way incline towards the other.[33] (tr. Gallop)

In this passage, there is at least initially no ambiguity concerning the syntax of γίγνεσθαι: at 96e8–97a1, Socrates reports to have wondered if either one or other (of two that have been added to each other) has come to be two, or again if both together have come to be two. Here, 'two' is complement to 'come to be', while 'the one', 'the other', or 'both the one and the other' are subjects. In what follows (97a3), Socrates states that part of his uncertainty and puzzlement relates to the fact that each of them was one, and they were not two then, while later they came to be two (97a4–5). That this is his way of perceiving the problem is unambiguously clear from the dative αὐτοῖς at the end of 97a4. Only after that (97a5–b7) does a potential ambiguity arise. When Socrates turns from addition to division, the expression τὸ δύο γίγνεσθαι, in different tenses and cases, is employed again. The sentence context alone does not allow one to decide whether Plato conceived of it as 'the fact that something comes to be two' or 'the fact that two come to be'. It should be noted, however, that on its previous occurrence οὐσία *in Plato's* Phaedo

the phrase did denote something's coming to be two, and that Plato has good reason to postpone the mentioning of a subject at 97a7: as becomes apparent at 97b2–3, he wants to present addition and division as parallel, the former as the coming together of one of two with the other of the two, the latter as the being led apart and separated of one of two from the other of the two. In order to create this parallelism, he must talk of the one thing that is to be divided as if it already consisted of the two parts which are, at least in many cases of the division of one into two, only the result of that division: the apple, while whole, has no more two halves than it has three thirds. By avoiding the mention of a subject to δύο γίγνεσθαι from 97a7 onwards, Plato deflects from this potential awkwardness. The context of the passage, however, supports the view that there is no change of construction, and that Plato lets Socrates speak consistently of something's coming to be two. This seems to me to be so regardless of the question of whether Plato would in the first place have recognized as relevant the distinction that results from translating the Greek phrase into English in the two different ways described.

In addition, it may be noted that, at 96e8–97a1, it is the one to which has been added, or the added one, or the added one together with the one added to, which has come to be two; at 97a3, it is *something* that 'is one'; in the phrase ἓν ἄρα ἑκάτερον ἦν, ἓν is predicated of ἑκάτερον. The subject of being one and becoming two is now, at least on the surface of the linguistic expression, something other than 'the one' and 'the two' of the previous sentence: this, however, does not seem to matter at all in this context; Plato lets Socrates move from one to the other without comment, as if the two ways of expressing himself were equivalent.

In applying the various observations derived from the preceding pages to 100c9–101c9, one may conclude that it may not matter whether Socrates is speaking of 'something's coming to be beautiful' or 'the beautifuls' coming to be beautiful': 'the beautifuls' are beautiful only once they have come to be beautiful, just as the two halves of an apple are 'the one and the other' only once the apple has been cleft in twain. But just as γίγνεσθαι καλά means 'coming to be beautiful', δύο γίγνεσθαι is best understood as 'coming to be two'; and this can then be generalized to ἕκαστον γίγνεσθαι, 'coming to be *each*', 'coming to be whatever', 'coming to be x'. This ἕκαστον is the same here as ἕκαστον at 78d4 discussed above, in the phrase ἕκαστον ὃ ἔστιν, where ἕκαστον referred to each of the things which are in the same way in which the equal is and the beautiful is. To return to 101b9–101c9:

τί δέ; ἑνὶ ἑνὸς προστεθέντος τὴν πρόσθεσιν αἰτίαν εἶναι τοῦ δύο γενέσθαι ἢ διασχισθέντος τὴν σχίσιν οὐκ εὐλαβοῖο ἂν λέγειν; καὶ μέγα ἂν βοῴης ὅτι οὐκ οἶσθα ἄλλως πως <u>ἕκαστον γιγνόμενον ἢ μετασχὸν τῆς ἰδίας οὐσίας ἑκάστου οὗ ἂν μετάσχῃ</u>, καὶ ἐν τούτοις οὐκ ἔχεις ἄλλην τινὰ αἰτίαν τοῦ δύο γενέσθαι ἀλλ' ἢ

53

τὴν τῆς δυάδος μετάσχεσιν, καὶ δεῖν τούτου μετασχεῖν τὰ μέλλοντα δύο ἔσεσθαι, καὶ μονάδος ὃ ἂν μέλλῃ ἓν ἔσεσθαι, τὰς δὲ σχίσεις ταύτας καὶ προσθέσεις καὶ τὰς ἄλλας τὰς τοιαύτας κομψείας ἐῴης ἂν χαίρειν, παρεὶς ἀποκρίνασθαι τοῖς σεαυτοῦ σοφωτέροις·...

This can now be translated as:

> What about this: would you not be on your guard when it came to stating that when one is added to one, the cause-and-reason of coming to be two is addition, or in the case of division the dividing? And shout out loud that you do not know of any other way of <u>coming to be each</u> than <u>by sharing in the own proper being of each (whatever it is) in which it shares</u>;[34] and in this specific case you do not have any other cause-and-reason of having come to be two than the sharing in twoness – and that it is necessary that whatever shall be two shares in that, and in unity whatever shall be one; but those dividings and additions and other such elaborate (causes-and-reasons) you would let go, leaving (them) to those more clever than you to answer (with):...

The consequences of this for an understanding of the concept of οὐσία are at least two: οὐσία at 101c3 still means the 'being' of something in the sense of 'what something is'. But οὐσία at 101c3 is made to refer to the being of that Two in which anything and everything that is or comes to be two participates. At this point in the *Phaedo*, οὐσία refers to the 'being' of what will shortly be called a 'form' (εἶδος or ἰδέα).[35] Perhaps that is why at this point the adjective ἰδία is added to οὐσία: the 'being' of a form is in a special sense 'its own' or 'its proper being'. The οὐσία of the beautiful itself is in a special way its 'own property'.

VI

In the *Meno*, the *Euthyphro* and the *Phaedo*, οὐσία is thus in the first place 'what something is'. The noun can then also refer collectively to the totality of everything that is in the same way in which the beautiful itself is. And οὐσία can be the 'being', the 'what-it-is' of that beautiful itself. From here, there are two roads leading in different directions. One is to investigate if, and if so when, Plato took the step from the meaning 'what something is' to the meaning 'that something is': has this step been taken at, e.g., *Republic* 525 or 585, or later at *Sophist* 219, etc.? I shall not go down that road now. The other line of investigation is to ask: What prompted Plato to adopt this term οὐσία in the first place? Was it his general interest in 'being' that led him to a noun which seemed to be, and in fact was, connected with the participle of the verb 'to be'? Or was οὐσία a technical philosophical term before Plato after all? And if so, with whom? – To answer these questions, it will now be necessary to look at the few instances of οὐσία in Plato's earlier dialogues where by common consent the noun does not simply mean 'property' in the sense of '(physical) possession'.

The three instances are *Charmides* 168c, *Gorgias* 472b and *Protagoras* 349b.[36] At all three places, explanation of the use of οὐσία must, I believe, start from the common Attic meaning 'possession, property'. There is no certainty concerning the order of composition of the three dialogues. I shall begin with the *Charmides*, a dialogue in which Socrates has a conversation about σωφροσύνη with the youth Charmides and subsequently his older relative Critias. In the course of their conversation, σωφροσύνη is defined as ἐπιστήμη, 'knowledge'; but it turns out not to be knowledge of any of the things of which the other arts, crafts and sciences are knowledge; so Socrates and the others arrive at a definition of σωφροσύνη as 'the knowledge of all other knowledge and of itself'. This is scrutinized by Socrates who starts in his criticism from the directedness of knowledge and builds his proof on analogy with other things which are directed towards something. At 168c4–168d7, he draws things together:

> Οὐκοῦν καὶ εἴ τι διπλάσιόν ἐστιν τῶν τε ἄλλων διπλασίων καὶ ἑαυτοῦ, ἡμίσεος δήπου ὄντος ἑαυτοῦ τε καὶ τῶν ἄλλων διπλάσιον ἂν εἴη· οὐ γάρ ἐστίν που ἄλλου διπλάσιον ἢ ἡμίσεος.
> Ἀληθῆ.
> Πλέον δὲ αὑτοῦ ὂν οὐ καὶ ἔλαττον ἔσται, καὶ βαρύτερον ὂν κουφότερον, καὶ πρεσβύτερον ὂν νεώτερον, καὶ τἆλλα πάντα ὡσαύτως, ὅτιπερ ἂν τὴν ἑαυτοῦ δύναμιν πρὸς ἑαυτὸ ἔχῃ, οὐ καὶ ἐκείνην ἕξει τὴν οὐσίαν, πρὸς ἣν ἡ δύναμις αὐτοῦ ἦν; λέγω δὲ τὸ τοιόνδε· οἷον ἡ ἀκοή, φαμέν, οὐκ ἄλλου τινὸς ἦν ἀκοὴ ἢ φωνῆς· ἦ γάρ;
> Ναί.
> Οὐκοῦν εἴπερ αὐτὴ αὑτῆς ἀκούσεται, φωνὴν ἐχούσης ἑαυτῆς ἀκούσεται· οὐ γὰρ ἂν ἄλλως ἀκούσειεν.

And if something is the double both of the other doubles and of itself, it would itself constitute a half, as would the others, if it were double, since there is not, I'm sure, a double of anything but a half.
True.
That which is the superior of itself will be the inferior of itself too, and what is heavier, lighter, and what is older, younger, and so on. Whatever relates its own faculty to itself will also have that essential nature to which its faculty was related, won't it? I mean something like this: hearing, for example, we say is the hearing of nothing other than sound, isn't it?
Yes.
If it is to hear itself, it will hear itself as possessing a *sound*, since it couldn't hear otherwise.[37]   (tr. Watt)

Of the three passages, this is perhaps the one in which the sense of οὐσία is most difficult to explain.[38] It may be fruitful to begin by asking for the contexts and connotations of the other 'technical' term in the passage, δύναμις, which Watt translates as 'faculty'. The word occurs six times between 168b and 169a. It is introduced at 168b3 as the 'capacity', 'faculty',

55

'power' or 'capability' of something 'to be *of* something';[39] as such, it is an abstract concept, not unfamiliar in medical discussions of the faculties of the body, its organs and its senses, and of medicines; indeed, the one other context in which δύναμις occurs in the *Charmides* was Socrates' referring to the 'power' of the incantation with which he promised to cure the headache of Charmides at the beginning of their conversation (156b).

At 168d, Socrates generalizes that whatever has its power directed towards itself, must also have that οὐσία towards which the given power or faculty is directed otherwise. Hearing, in order to be capable of hearing itself, would need that possession which hearing is directed towards otherwise, namely sound. That is to say, concerning the meaning of οὐσία in this context, it would be wrong to ask: 'What is the abstract noun that captures sound, sight, etc. as that which a faculty is directed towards?' Use of οὐσία is determined by the notion of having something for oneself.[40] Of course, if the *Charmides* were written after the *Republic*, one could speculate on a semantic development of the philosophical notion of 'being' via 'nature' to 'quality, property': but it should be noted that οὐσία here is not the οὐσία of something; the noun is used in an absolute way; οὐσία here is used in its everyday Attic sense of 'property, possession', not in the sense of 'the being of something', 'what something is'.

The *Protagoras* may present a case parallel in many ways. In discussing ἀρετή, 'goodness' or 'excellence', Socrates had asked Protagoras (329c3–d1):

καὶ αὖ πολλαχοῦ ἐν τοῖς λόγοις ἐλέγετο ὑπὸ σοῦ ἡ δικαιοσύνη καὶ σωφροσύνη καὶ ὁσιότης καὶ πάντα ταῦτα ὡς ἕν τι εἴη συλλήβδην, ἀρετή· ταῦτ' οὖν αὐτὰ δίελθέ μοι ἀκριβῶς τῷ λόγῳ, πότερον ἓν μέν τί ἐστιν ἡ ἀρετή, μόρια δὲ αὐτῆς ἐστιν ἡ δικαιοσύνη καὶ σωφροσύνη καὶ ὁσιότης, ἢ ταῦτ' ἐστιν ἃ νυνδὴ ἐγὼ ἔλεγον πάντα ὀνόματα τοῦ αὐτοῦ ἑνὸς ὄντος.

And then many times in your discourse you spoke of justice and soundness of mind and holiness and all the rest as all summed up as the one thing, excellence: Will you then explain precisely whether excellence is one thing, and justice and soundness of mind and holiness parts of it, or whether all these that I've just mentioned are different names of one and the same thing?[41]   (tr. Taylor)

After an inconclusive discussion, Socrates then begins a fresh attempt at agreement with a summarizing question at 349a8–c5:

ἦν δέ, ὡς ἐγᾦμαι, τὸ ἐρώτημα τόδε· σοφία καὶ σωφροσύνη καὶ ἀνδρεία καὶ δικαιοσύνη καὶ ὁσιότης, πότερον ταῦτα, πέντε ὄντα ὀνόματα, ἐπὶ ἑνὶ πράγματί ἐστιν, ἢ ἑκάστῳ τῶν ὀνομάτων τούτων ὑπόκειταί τις ἴδιος οὐσία καὶ πρᾶγμα ἔχον ἑαυτοῦ δύναμιν ἕκαστον, οὐκ ὂν οἷον τὸ ἕτερον αὐτῶν τὸ ἕτερον; ἔφησθα οὖν σὺ οὐκ ὀνόματα ἐπὶ ἑνὶ εἶναι, ἀλλὰ ἕκαστον ἰδίῳ πράγματι τῶν ὀνομάτων τούτων ἐπικεῖσθαι, πάντα δὲ ταῦτα μόρια εἶναι ἀρετῆς, οὐχ ὡς τὰ τοῦ χρυσοῦ μόρια ὅμοιά ἐστιν ἀλλήλοις καὶ τῷ ὅλῳ οὗ μόριά ἐστιν, ἀλλ' ὡς τὰ

οὐσία *in Plato's* Phaedo

τοῦ προσώπου μόρια καὶ τῷ ὅλῳ οὗ μόριά ἐστιν καὶ ἀλλήλοις ἀνόμοια, ἰδίαν ἕκαστα δύναμιν ἔχοντα.

The question, I think, was this: are 'wisdom', 'soundness of mind', 'courage', 'justice', and 'holiness' five names for the one thing, or <u>does there correspond to each of these names some separate thing or entity with its own particular power</u>, unlike any of the others? Now you said that they are not names for the one thing, but each is the name <u>of a separate thing</u>, and all of these are parts of excellence, not as the parts of gold are like one another and the whole of which they are parts, but as the parts of the face are unlike one another and the whole of which they are parts, each having its own separate power.[42]   (tr. Taylor)

The first difference that strikes the reader of these two obviously related passages is that Socrates, in asking for the status of the virtues, managed to express himself with minimal use of additional abstract nouns in the first passage, using in addition to ὄνομα, 'name', and μόριον, 'part', only pronouns and numerals. In the second passage, by contrast, he introduces as a counterpart to ὄνομα, 'name', πρᾶγμα, 'thing', where he had previously made do with ἕν τί, 'a certain one (thing)' (where 'thing' is supplied in the English translation only), and οὐσία, and he asks if this πρᾶγμα or each of the μόρια have their own δύναμις, 'power'. The second passage is therefore at least in this sense more technical. But do these nouns contribute anything to the content of Socrates' question? And in particular, what does οὐσία mean here?

The term δύναμις, 'power', which was also encountered in the *Charmides* passage above, had first been introduced in the *Protagoras* by Protagoras himself in the 'scientific' context of the myth of Epimetheus and Prometheus, where he said that Epimetheus gave to the various animals their various 'powers' or perhaps 'abilities' (320d5, e2, 321c1). But it was then reintroduced by Socrates at 330a4, to recur five more times.[43] Socrates speaks of an ἰδία δύναμις, an 'own, proper or specific power', of each of the virtues in direct analogy to the specific 'power' of each of the parts of the face, the eyes, the ears, the nose, etc. That is to say, in the context of the bodily senses, δύναμις was an established term, as at *Charmides* 168d. Immediately after introducing δύναμις in that way, Socrates then, at 330c1, asks if δικαιοσύνη, 'justice', is a πρᾶγμα, a 'thing',[44] and he uses that concession in his refutation of Protagoras' position. While both these terms have something technical about them, they are not so specialized that they would need definition; nor do the interlocutors comment on them otherwise. In the context of 349, the thing that corresponds to the name is *one* thing; as such, the thing is specific to the name. Just as Socrates speaks of an ἰδία δύναμις at 330a4, then here at 349c5, and once again at 359a7, so here at 349c1 he speaks of an ἴδιον πρᾶγμα, 'an own, proper, specific thing'; each of these things has its own power. And in this context Socrates adds a synonym: that underlying each name, there is its own οὐσία. The term is obviously redundant. What would the original audience have understood? That for each of these names, there lies by it 'its own property, that is (epexegetic καί), a thing having its own power' etc. Not only οὐσία is used metaphorically here,[45] but also the verb ὑπόκειται. 'Land' of some kind is a particularly common subject to the verb ὑπόκειμαι.[46] The metaphor serves to indicate the close connection of name and thing, which is as close as that of the old Attic landowner and his household to his land, his property. That such property is also static and stable, an aspect often seen as lying at the root of the metaphorical extension of οὐσία from a meaning of 'property' or 'real estate' to 'real being', a being which similarly is not subject to change: all this does not seem to be emphasized in the *Protagoras* passage.[47] Of course, if the *Protagoras* were written after the *Phaedo*, more would need saying.

The *Gorgias* passage, lastly, offers a different picture. In his conversation with Polus, Socrates makes a methodological point concerning the role of mutual agreement in discussion (472b3–c2):

ἀλλ' ἐγώ σοι εἷς ὢν οὐχ ὁμολογῶ· οὐ γάρ με σὺ ἀναγκάζεις, ἀλλὰ ψευδομάρτυρας πολλοὺς κατ' ἐμοῦ παρασχόμενος ἐπιχειρεῖς ἐκβάλλειν με ἐκ τῆς οὐσίας καὶ τοῦ ἀληθοῦς. ἐγὼ δὲ ἂν μὴ σὲ αὐτὸν ἕνα ὄντα μάρτυρα παράσχωμαι ὁμολογοῦντα περὶ ὧν λέγω, οὐδὲν οἶμαι ἄξιον λόγου μοι πεπεράνθαι περὶ ὧν ἂν ἡμῖν ὁ λόγος ᾖ· οἶμαι δὲ οὐδὲ σοί, ἐὰν μὴ ἐγώ σοι μαρτυρῶ εἷς ὢν μόνος, τοὺς δ' ἄλλους πάντας τούτους χαίρειν ἐᾷς.

But I, though I am but a single individual, do not agree with you, for you produce no compelling reason why I should; instead you call numerous false witnesses against me in your attempt to evict me from my lawful property, the truth. I believe that nothing worth speaking of will have been accomplished in our discussion unless I can obtain your agreement, and yours alone, as a witness to the truth of what I say; and the same holds good for you, in my opinion; unless you can get just me, me only, on your side you can disregard what the rest of the world may say.[48]   (tr. Hamilton and Emlyn-Jones)

The nature of the legal metaphor here employed has always been recognized by translators and commentators.[49] There is a temptation, though, to see more in this expression in a dialogue in which so much of the terminology of the theory of forms is employed. Of the terms mentioned in the introduction to this chapter, the *Gorgias* provides, in philosophically significant contexts, besides οὐσία at 472b6, the following: forms of μετέχειν and μεταλαμβάνειν, 'sharing and coming to share', at 448c and 467e7 (ἃ ἐνίοτε μὲν μετέχει τοῦ ἀγαθοῦ, 'what sometimes participates in the good'); παρουσία, 'presence', thrice between 497e–498e; εἶδος, 'form', at 503e4. By themselves, each of these passages allows for interpretation without reference to the theory of forms; but the cumulative weight of the philosophical terminology presents a temptation to see the dialogue as transitional. In this mode, Classen 1959a, 158, while stopping short of positing a new meaning for the word οὐσία, speaks of Socrates' 'concern for truth and in particular this aspect of οὐσία as reality'[50] – which presupposes such a concept as 'reality' and also presupposes that 'reality' could have been part of the meaning of οὐσία in the first place; that this is so, though, has not been demonstrated.

Plato may, however, have played with his language in a different fashion. In common Attic usage, οὐσία meant 'property, possession'; but while the word was derived from the root for 'being', this was not felt, or at least it did not find expression in collocation with other forms of the same root.[51] In the *Meno*, *Euthyphro* and *Phaedo*, on the other hand, Plato made that connection by re-etymologizing the word as 'what something is'. I think it conceivable that Plato may have made the connection between οὐσία and εἶναι in the *Gorgias*, but not necessarily in the way he will exploit it in later dialogues. As we have seen,[52] both the singular τὸ ὄν and the plural τὰ ὄντα could in common parlance mean 'the truth'. Plato may have made that connection: but he certainly does not dwell on it, and the context of *Gorgias* 472 does not require, or even strongly invite, such a pun.

VII

There is thus no clear indication in the early dialogues that Plato had etymologized οὐσία in the contexts of thought about 'being', a topic which had been central to philosophy since Parmenides. Does that mean that the coinage of οὐσία as 'being', 'what something is', is an *ad hoc* creation of Plato's, reflected in the *Phaedo* and the two dialogues which also otherwise presuppose large parts of the theory presented in the *Phaedo*, to wit, the *Meno* and the *Euthyphro*?[53]

There is one pre-Platonic context that may shed light on that question. It is that part of the report by Stobaeus (1.21.7a1–8.3) usually labelled as Philolaus Fragment 6:

περὶ δὲ φύσιος καὶ ἁρμονίας ὧδε ἔχει· ἃ μὲν ἐστὼ τῶν πραγμάτων, ἀΐδιος ἔσσα καὶ αὐτὰ μὰν ἁ φύσις θείαν τε καὶ οὐκ ἀνθρωπίνην ἐνδέχεται γνῶσιν, πλάν γα ἢ ὅτι οὐχ οἷόν τ' ἦν οὐθενὶ τῶν ἐόντων καὶ γιγνωσκομένων ὑφ' ἁμῶν γεγενῆσθαι μὴ ὑπαρχούσας τᾶς ἐστοῦς τῶν πραγμάτων, ἐξ ὧν συνέστα ὁ κόσμος, καὶ τῶν περαινόντων καὶ τῶν ἀπείρων. ἐπεὶ δὲ ταὶ ἀρχαὶ ὑπᾶρχον οὐχ ὁμοῖαι οὐδ' ὁμόφυλοι ἔσσαι, ἤδη ἀδύνατον ἧς κα αὐταῖς κοσμηθῆναι, εἰ μὴ ἁρμονία ἐπεγένετο, ᾡτινιῶν ἂν τρόπῳ ἐγένετο. τὰ μὲν ὦν ὁμοῖα καὶ ὁμόφυλα ἁρμονίας οὐδὲν ἐπεδέοντο, τὰ δὲ ἀνόμοια μηδὲ ὁμόφυλα μηδὲ † ἰσοταχῆ ἀνάγκα τὰ τοιαῦτα ἁρμονίᾳ συγκεκλεῖσθαι, εἰ μέλλοντι ἐν κόσμῳ κατέχεσθαι.

Concerning nature and harmony the situation is this: the being of things, which is eternal, and nature in itself admit of divine and not human knowledge, except that it was impossible for any of the things that are and are known by us to have come to be, if <u>the being</u> of the things from which the world-order came together, both the limiting things and the unlimited things, did not preexist. But since <u>these beginnings pre-existed</u> and were neither alike or even related, it would have been impossible for them to have been ordered, if a harmony had not come upon them, in whatever way it came to be. Like things and related things did not in addition require any harmony, things that are unlike and not even related nor of [? the same speed], it is necessary that such things be bonded together by harmony, if they are going to be held in an order.[54]   (tr. Huffman)

Here, the phrases ἁ μὲν ἐστὼ τῶν πραγμάτων, which Huffman translates as 'the being of things', and μὴ ὑπαρχούσας τᾶς ἐστοῦς τῶν πραγμάτων, 'if the being of the things…did not pre-exist', contain a word ἐστὼ which, like οὐσία, is formed from the Greek verbal root meaning 'to be', only that it is not derived from the participial stem *ont- but rather from *est-, the 'stem' of the third person singular present indicative active form ἔστι.[55]

In order to establish whether one may posit a link between Plato's usage in the *Phaedo* and this text of the Presocratic Philolaus, one must take into account both an interpretation of the text of Philolaus and an interpretation of Plato's strategy in the *Phaedo*. On both counts, I must be brief.[56] To begin with the *Phaedo*, Plato uses the last day of Socrates as a setting for a discussion about the immortality of the soul of the individual. But this is only a frame which allows Plato to introduce for the first time in his writings a coherent account of his ontology. This ontology is presented against the background of earlier, Presocratic conceptions of the world. The main individuals or schools of thought with whom Plato engages are Anaxagoras and his successors, notably Diogenes of Apollonia, Democritus, and Philolaus and other Pythagoreans.[57] Plato reacts to arguments of Anaxagoras, Democritus and Philolaus in particular between *Phaedo* 95a and 107b. Part of Plato's method in dealing with his predecessors consists of identifying specific items of their philosophical terminology and letting Socrates employ those items in his own speculations and considerations, in a new context, with new connections, and as a result often possibly with new meaning, but certainly with different reference. In this way, Plato's use of μετέχειν amounts to a critique of Anaxagoras.[58] His use of αἰτία from 95e onwards and of ἰδέα from 104b onwards reflects critical reception of Democritus.[59] Huffman suggests plausibly that the specific way in which ὑπόθεσις and ἀρχή are connected in the *Phaedo* amounts to criticism of *inter alia* Philolaus Fragment 3, especially at *Phaedo* 101d1 ff.;[60] in addition, use of εἶδος, 'type', and μορφή, 'shape' or 'form' from 102b onwards may reflect knowledge of Philolaus Fragment 5.[61] In this context, it is not inherently implausible to assume reaction to Philolaus Fragment 6 at *Phaedo* 101b, c (and in related passages earlier in the dialogue), given that Philolaus was mentioned at 61d, e.

As far as Philolaus Fr. 6 is concerned, whether or not the 'context' created by Stobaeus is the original context in Philolaus' book, the content is in part epistemological: what can human beings know? But Philolaus' epistemology, like Plato's, is inseparably linked with his ontology:

> ἁ μὲν ἐστὼ τῶν πραγμάτων ἀΐδιος ἔσσα καὶ αὐτὰ μὰν ἁ φύσις θείαν τε καὶ οὐκ ἀνθρωπίνην ἐνδέχεται γνῶσιν, πλάν γα ἢ ὅτι οὐχ οἷόν τ᾽ ἦν οὐθενὶ τῶν ἐόντων καὶ γιγνωσκομένων ὑφ᾽ ἁμῶν γεγενῆσθαι μὴ ὑπαρχούσας τᾶς ἐστοῦς τῶν πραγμάτων, ἐξ ὧν συνέστα ὁ κόσμος, καὶ τῶν περαινόντων καὶ τῶν ἀπείρων.

> The being of the things (ἁ...ἐστὼ τῶν πραγμάτων), being eternal, and nature itself, at least, accept divine and not human cognition, except, that is, for the fact that it would not be possible for any of the things-that-are and the things-that-are-known-by-us to be (as things that come-to-be: γεγενῆσθαι) if there had not been there (as-a-beginning: ὑπαρχούσας) the being of things (τᾶς ἐστοῦς τῶν πραγμάτων), both the limiting and the unlimiting (things), <u>from which</u> the world-order <u>came together</u> (συνέστα).

Huffman has a long note on the lemma ἁ μὲν ἐστώ (1993, 130–2), from which I quote the beginning:

> Except for this fragment ἐστώ is only found in the later Pythagorean tradition, although it is very rare even there... This might cast doubt on the authenticity of F6 but the situation is not as simple as it appears. First, although ἐστώ itself does not occur in the fifth century, a number of compounds of ἐστώ do occur, and thus suggest that ἐστώ itself is also a possibility for the fifth century. Democritus, Philolaus' contemporary, is said to have used εὐεστώ to refer to the tranquillity of mind which he regarded as the end of all human action (D.L. 9.45–6; see also DK F2c). Aeschylus uses the same compound several times where it seems to mean something like good fortune or well-being (*A.* 647, 929; *Th.* 187). Harpocration reports that Antiphon used the compound ἀειεστώ in the sense of 'eternity' in the second book of his *Truth* (F22). Finally, Herodotus uses the compound ἀπεστώ to mean 'being away' or 'absence' (9.85).
> In light of these parallels Burkert may be right to conclude that is 'obviously an Ionic formation' (1972, 256 n. 87). As he points out, Plato's *Cratylus* (401c2–4) suggests that the Doric form for οὐσία is ὠσία or ἐσσία. ἐστώ is obviously formed from the root *εσ-(εἰμί) [sic!], and this, along with the compounds discussed above, indicates that it has the general meaning of οὐσία, 'being'. As in other uses of forms of the verb 'to be' in the Presocratics, it does not seem that it is used strictly to refer to either existence or essence, but rather represents a fused notion of existence and essence...

The fifth-century parallels of the compounds of -εστω are instructive not only with regard to the Ionic origin of the word first posited by Chantraine,[62] but because they have a parallel in the many -ουσία compounds common in Attic: συνουσία, 'a being together, a gathering', παρουσία, 'a being near, at or by; presence', ἀπουσία, 'a being away; absence', ἐξουσία, 'a being possible, possibility', etc.; the significance of these compounds in Attic is that they are all closely linked in meaning to the respective composite compound verbs; the -ουσία element in them means 'being' as a 'survival' from a time when the simplex must have had that meaning; the composita of οὐσία could therefore have served as an additional starting point for Plato's etymologizing, just as the -εστω compounds could serve as a model for the coinage of ἐστώ in the sense of 'being'.

The problem is: when Philolaus wrote, οὐσία did not mean 'being', as we have seen. Philolaus, however, is unlikely to have coined the simplex ἐστώ in the first place: because it was an Ionic word! Going by the presence of the Doric nominative singular feminine of the present active participle of the verb 'to be' in Philolaus F6, ἔσσα, Philolaus would indeed have said ἐσσία, i.e. he would have used one of the two forms suggested by Plato at *Cratylus* 401c.[63] One can thus only speculate about the real origin of ἐστώ; it may indeed have been Democritus, who after all reportedly used one of the compounds of the word. But that is to some extent a separate question. Wherever Philolaus had got the word ἐστώ from, he used it in the sense of 'being', and applied it to the being of things in a way that comes very close indeed to Plato's usage in the *Phaedo*. As it can be made plausible on independent grounds that Plato had read the book of Philolaus before writing the *Phaedo*, we may therefore conclude that in the *Phaedo* the use of οὐσία as 'what something is' is not independent of Philolaus' use of ἐστώ, and indeed, Philolaus' use seems to some extent to have been the inspiration for Plato's new, etymologizing use of οὐσία. It must be noted, though, that Philolaus himself apparently had a different etymology of ἐστώ in mind: by glossing τὰς ἐστοῦς τῶν πραγμάτων with the phrase ἐξ ὧν συνέστα ὁ κόσμος he defines, in a manner of speaking, ἐστώ as that which 'stands firm' over time and as such is part and constituent of the ever-changing composites of this world. What these firm constituents were in the ontology of Philolaus cannot be discussed here.

VIII

In conclusion, let me summarize: οὐσία as 'being' is indeed Plato's coinage in the sense that the Attic word had not meant 'being' for centuries before Plato, and in the sense that there are no other writers before Plato who would have used the term with reference to 'the being of something'. There was metaphorical usage of οὐσία to the extent that what someone's property or wealth is, in a given linguistic context, need not always be the land, the physical possession, or the sum of one's countable, touchable wealth.[64] In the *Protagoras* and *Charmides*, Plato speaks of the οὐσία not of a person, but of abstract things: this may reflect usage of the word in discussions of 'meaning' by the Sophists, but we do not have the evidence to support this claim:[65] it seems, though, as if this metaphorical usage did not go back to the etymology of the word. In the *Gorgias*, Socrates may well etymologize when he refers to the truth as his patrimony; but that is not certain. In the *Meno*, the *Euthyphro* and the *Phaedo*, the picture is different: Plato clearly defines the new application of the word as 'the being' of something in the sense of 'what something is'. This seems to have been inspired by, or at least has an uncanny parallel in, the usage of Philolaus. Plato's innovation is thus partly at the level of language; but, as with the other technical terms cited in the introduction, it lies mostly in what he applies the term to. For Plato, 'what is' is significantly different from 'what is' for Philolaus. And the central role of the 'being' of things in Plato's philosophy is a world apart from the 'being' of the Pythagorean. The discovery of the concept of the οὐσία of something as 'what something is' marks the true starting point of Plato's own explanation of the world.

Notes

[1] 'Ontology' is here used as a neutral term which is intended to denote any set of beliefs, explicit or implicit, concerning what *is* or *is there*, i.e. the term is used in a way that would, e.g., allow one to speak of the differences between the ontologies of 19th century materialists and idealists.

[2] A summary of the traditional position can be found in Kahn 1996, 332–5. For a fuller treatment of the issues involved, see Herrmann 2007; for a study of μετέχειν and related terms see Herrmann 2003; for ἰδέα see Herrmann 2005; for εἶδος see Herrmann 2006. Classen 1959a and 1959b discusses evidence of Presocratic awareness of language, and shows how the Socrates of Plato's dialogues exploits metaphorical usage for philosophical purposes as well as in ordinary conversation; see also Classen 1960. For earlier fundamental considerations on the relevance of the study of semantic development in an assessment of technical terminology, see in particular Campbell 1894; Vailati 1906; Snell 1924.

[3] Cf., e.g., Thompson 1901, 255–8, in his *Excursus* I, 'οὐσία as a philosophical term in Plato (on [*Meno*] 72b22)'; the opening paragraph of this essay reads: 'We have no certain examples of οὐσία in any sense except 'wealth', 'patrimony' in any writer before Plato. [The fragments of the Pythagorean Philolaus, in which it appears as a philosophical term in the form ἐσσία (cp. *Crat.* 401c), are almost certainly spurious. See Prof. Bywater in *JP* I pp. 21 ff.; Archer-Hind on *Phaedo* 61d. For a different view see Zeller *pre-Socr.* I 314 and note: for a summary of the controversy R&P §50 c, Ueberweg-Heinze p. 58.]'; von Fritz 1938, 53: 'An Häufigkeit des Vorkommens den Wörtern überlegen, an philosophischer Bedeutung ihnen kaum nachstehend ist das Wort οὐσία, das in seiner platonischen Verwendung ebenfalls eine Bedeutungsneuschöpfung ist. Dies Wort ist zur Zeit Platons in der attischen Sprache seit langem heimisch, aber *nur* in dieser, wie schon die Bildung zeigt: οὐσίη bei Herodot ist offensichtlich eine Teilionisierung des attischen Wortes. Das Wort kommt jedoch vor Platon nur in einer ganz speziellen Bedeutung vor: "das Vermögen", "die Habe", "der Besitz". Es ist in dieser Bedeutung abgeleitet von einem ganz speziellen Gebrauch des Verbums εἶναι, in der Konstruktion εἶναι τινί. Es

bedeutet ἅ τινι ἔστιν.' Besides Thompson and von Fritz, the best discussions of the term οὐσία and its history are Hirzel 1913 and Classen 1959a, 158–64; some useful observations in Burnet 1924, 49 f.; Bluck 1961, 221–3; Berger 1961, 1–18; Marten 1962, 7–13. Dixsaut 1991 seems to consider the meaning of the term οὐσία in the *Phaedo* as being self-evident, or at least to think that Plato indicates sufficiently by his 'definitions' what is meant by οὐσία; the great virtue of her article is the argument Dixsaut provides for the priority of οὐσία over εἶδος and ἰδέα in the *Phaedo*. Cf. also the summary of a slightly different approach to the subject in Horn and Rapp (eds.) 2002, 320–4, s.v. 'ousia'.

[4] von Fritz 1938, 53.

[5] See LSJ s.v. I. Instances of οὐσία in its common, Attic sense in Plato's early dialogues are *Crito* 44e5, 53b2, *Gorgias* 486c1.

[6] The syntax of the Greek phrase μου ἐρομένου μελίττης περὶ οὐσίας ὅτι ποτ' ἐστίν is straightforward. On a first reading, however, one may be tempted to pause after the fourth word and understand μου ἐρομένου μελίττης πέρι, with πέρι as a postposition: 'when I asked about a bee'. This type of phrasing is familiar, e.g., from *Phaedo* 65d λέγω δὲ περὶ πάντων, οἷον μεγέθους πέρι, ὑγιείας, ἰσχύος, καὶ τῶν ἄλλων ἑνὶ λόγῳ ἁπάντων τῆς οὐσίας ὃ τυγχάνει ἕκαστον ὄν, 'but I am talking about everything, as for example about size, health, strength, and, in a word, all other things' being, what each happens to be'; for a discussion of this passage see below. The phrase in the *Meno*, however, μου ἐρομένου μελίττης πέρι, could be followed immediately by the indirect question ὅτι ποτ' ἐστίν, 'what it is'; the syntax would be complete without the addition of οὐσίας. That is to say, οὐσίας could be a gloss, added with hindsight on the model of *Euthyphro* 11a and in particular of *Phaedo* 65d. The sense of the *Meno* passage would not be affected; and as a sequence of composition *Gorgias, Meno, Euthyphro, Phaedo* is plausible on independent grounds, these considerations do not make a substantial difference for the history of the semantic development of the term οὐσία either. It is important to note, though, that the very fact that the term οὐσία is strictly redundant in this context in the *Meno* facilitates its introduction with a new, technical, philosophical meaning, as this redundancy excludes any ambiguity or uncertainty concerning the sense of the passage in which the term occurs. The translation given above is meant to reflect these considerations.

[7] The Greek phrase τὸ ὅσιον ὅτι ποτ' ἐστίν, τὴν μὲν οὐσίαν suggests on a first reading that τὴν μὲν οὐσίαν, 'the/its being', is in apposition to the preceding τὸ ὅσιον ὅτι ποτ' ἐστίν, 'whatever the pious is' or 'the pious, what it is'; the continuation of the sentence reveals that τὴν μὲν οὐσίαν is in fact direct object of the infinitive at the very end of the clause. The inverted word order of the translation is meant to preserve this syntactical device.

[8] There is no literal way of translating πάθος δέ τι περὶ αὐτοῦ λέγειν; 'but to say some suffering about it' makes nonsense; 'to tell me one of its affections/properties/qualities' introduces terminology derived from later, post-Platonic, contexts which may certainly go back to distinctions made here, but ones which are at the same time based on different ontological suppositions; 'something it suffers' converts the nominal πάθος δέ τι περὶ αὐτοῦ into a verbal expression but preserves the continuity with the following ὅτι πέπονθε, 'what it suffers'; the perfect in this expression indicates that this 'affection' is a necessary aspect of 'what the pious is'; Socrates' point here is not that to say 'the pious is god-beloved' fails to answer the question 'What is the pious?' on the grounds that the pious would on occasion not actually be god-beloved; the perfect thus

indicates that the πάθος in question is, in the terminology of Aristotle's *Topics* (102a,b), ἴδιον, not συμβεβηκός, a 'property', not an 'accident': the pious is indeed always already god-beloved – but that is not sufficient for Socrates' purposes.

[9] Cf. the excellent discussion of Socrates' etymologizing in Classen 1959a, esp. 1–12, 89–98, 120–37, 151–64.

[10] On πάθος see n. 8 above; Bluck 1961, 209–14 discusses in detail the development of the contrast οὐσία – πάθος in Plato.

[11] In parallel with *Meno* 72e f. and *Euthyphro* 11a f. above, the syntax of the Greek at *Phaedo* 65d at first suggests that the genitive in καὶ τῶν ἄλλων ἑνὶ λόγῳ ἁπάντων, 'and, in a word, of all the other things', depends on the previous περί of μεγέθους πέρι, 'about size'; the listener or reader is required to adjust his construal of the syntax with the appearance of the term οὐσία. This, in itself, calls attention to that term, as in the two earlier dialogues. The translation is intended to preserve this syntactical device.

[12] To render διανοηθῆναι as 'think through' is not wholly satisfactory; it is meant to convey clearly the contrast between the act of the νοῦς or ψυχή, 'mind' or 'soul', denoted by διανοηθῆναι and the act of the body denoted by αἴσθησις, 'sensation'.

[13] The adjective ὅμοιος means 'similar', ἴσος 'equal', not restricted in its application to what is quantifiable; but the adverb ὁμοίως may be either 'similarly' or 'equally', as the adverb ἴσως means 'perhaps' and cannot normally be used to mean 'equally'.

[14] Cf. Rowe 1993, 177, ad loc.: 'πᾶσα ἡ τοιαύτη οὐσία· lit. "all being of that sort": οὐσία, a noun originally derived from the verb εἶναι, is here applied collectively to a group of things in virtue of their "being", i.e. existing (hence "existents of this sort").'

[15] In the present context, these things are the good and the beautiful, and it is of course not arbitrary that this should be so. But ὄντα can be things of any description or status, things like the good and the beautiful or, in the most general way, all the things there are, eternal and transient alike, as, e.g., at *Phaedo* 79a6. *Pace* Rowe 1993, 183, ad 78d4. See also below.

[16] e.g. Euripides, *Andromache* 1068: τὰ ὄντα referring to 'events'; Isaeus 5.9.2, 5.11.12: 'possessions'. Note, though, that in Attic the plural τὰ ὄντα, like the singular τὸ ὄν, could also be a synonym for 'the truth'; e.g. Thucydides 4.108.5, 6.60.2, 7.8.2; Andocides, *De Mysteriis* 20.6, 59.2 – but Andocides, *De Mysteriis* 138.4: 'possessions'. Cf. the ambiguous use at *Phaedo* 66a3.

[17] See Vancamp 1996 for a discussion of the origin and significance of the phrase; but cf. also the interpretation by Ebert 2004, 255 f., which strongly suggests that for Plato himself the context of this phrase was Eleatic.

[18] It may be altogether preferable to read here (and at 92d9) αὕτη ἡ οὐσία, 'this being' rather than 'the being itself', letting the demonstrative pick up the last occurrence of the word at 76d–77a.

[19] The nominalized neuter participle of the verb 'be', τὸ ἐόν, had been a standard term for 'what is' in Eleatic philosophy since Parmenides (DK 28B4.8; 8.32); in Attic, τὸ ὄν is not common, but where it occurs it denotes 'what really obtains' and is, as such, a synonym of 'the truth' (e.g. Thucydides 3.22.8; Xenophon, *Cyropaedia* 5.4.7, 6.3.7). Cf. n. 16 above. Plato, writing for an educated Athenian audience, could have had both usages in mind at *Phaedo* 66a8 and here at 78d4, the first occurrences of the term in his dialogues.

[20] Geddes 1863, 62: 'ἧς λόγον δίδομεν τοῦ εἶναι : *Of which we give this account* (or explanation) *that it absolutely* is. The double genitive depends on λόγον. In 76b, περί is

inserted after λόγον διδόναι.' As far as syntax is concerned, this is correct. Archer-Hind 1883, 90, agrees: 'ἧς λόγον δίδομεν τοῦ εἶναι "as whose principle we assign being". λόγον = its definition, notion. τοῦ εἶναι is descriptive genitive after λόγον. Madvig proposes τὸ εἶναι, which Schanz adopts: but ms. authority is entirely against him, and there is no real difficulty in the genitive.' Fearenside and Kerin 1897, 104, offer two alternatives: 'ἧς λόγον δίδομεν τοῦ εἶναι: "of the existence of which we give the proofs," or perhaps better, "the definition whereof we give as BEING." In the first case ἧς depends on εἶναι; in the second, τοῦ εἶναι is epexegetical and might just as well be the accusative, τὸ εἶναι, as Madvig reads.' The grammatical explanation of their second, apparently preferred, alternative explicates the argument of Geddes and Archer-Hind. Williamson 1904, 154, argues along the same lines: 'ἧς λόγον δίδομεν τοῦ εἶναι: this is merely another way of saying οἷς ἐπισφραγιζόμεθα τὸ ὃ ἔστι. (75d): "that essence which we define as *being*". The relation of the two genitives, ἧς and τοῦ εἶναι, to λόγον should be carefully distinguished: ἧς is an objective genitive, the thing "of which" the definition is given; τοῦ εἶναι is the "genitive of definition", describing what the λόγος consists of. Wagner gives a version which is impossible in the context – "of the existence of which we give the proofs".' All of this is correct, and it is obvious that Fearenside and Kerin provided the first of their translations, quoted from Wagner 1870, 131, only as a polite way of rejecting his suggestion.

It was probably the authority of Burnet 1911 which has led subsequent editors astray; he writes, 66: 'ἡ οὐσία ἧς λόγον δίδομεν τοῦ εἶναι, "the reality the being of which we give account of". The hyperbaton of δίδομεν has misled the commentators here. We must take λόγον τοῦ εἶναι together as equivalent to λόγον τῆς οὐσίας or "definition", and as governing the genitive ἧς. For λόγος τῆς οὐσίας cp. *Rep.* 534b3 ἦ καὶ διαλεκτικὸν καλεῖς τὸν λόγον ἑκάστου λαμβάνοντα τῆς οὐσίας; The meaning then is simply "the reality which we define".' Burnet is clearly wrong, not least because his reading presupposes that Plato mixes two idioms, the established λόγον διδόναι with his own alleged coinage λόγος τῆς οὐσίας; at any rate, equating τοῦ εἶναι with τῆς οὐσίας in the way Burnet suggests is stylistically inelegant; in addition, Burnet's literal translation, which is closer to the text, suggests that there is a being of the being or reality which Socrates has just posited; this is in danger of invoking an infinite regress. Burnet's solution, however, is adopted by Bluck 1955 and Hackforth 1955. The difference between the latter two is summarized by Gallop 1975, 138 f.:

> 78d1–5. The grammar and sense of the words translated 'the Being itself, whose being we give an account of' (d1–2) are uncertain. 'The Being itself' clearly refers to the domain of Forms... But 'giving an account' could mean either 'giving a definition' or 'giving a proof'; and the use of 'being' may be either 'incomplete' or 'complete'... 'Giving an account' of a Form's 'being' may therefore mean either 'defining its essential nature' or 'proving that it exists'. Loriaux...defends the existential interpretation... Similarly Hackforth. For the view adopted here see Bluck and Burnet. The non-existential reading has been preferred, in view of the reference to 'asking and answering questions' – cf. 75d2–3. It seems far more natural to associate this with the Socratic quest for definitions than with proofs of the Forms' existence. To 'give an account of the being of *F*' is to answer the question 'what is *F*?'. Questioning and answering of this sort are familiar in Plato's writings, and typical of dialectical inquiry (cf., e.g., *Republic*

538d6–e3), whereas questioning and answering to prove that the Forms exist can hardly be said to occur in the dialogues at all.
Grammatically, this latter view, with its permutations, may not be impossible altogether; whether or not it makes any sense is a different question. I agree with the former reading and its syntactical interpretation both because it seems to me to be the natural way to take the Greek and for the semantic reasons given in the text.

[21] Rowe 1993, 183, ad loc., while otherwise taking a different view of how to interpret this sentence, is correct in stating 'οὐσία is used as at 76d8–9'.

[22] Cf. also Gallop 1975, 230, n. 31, with references.

[23] Up to a point, accentuation is a matter of taste. I follow the OCT, but would find ὅ ἐστι equally acceptable; cf. also Burnyeat 2003, 9.

[24] On balance, this seems to be the correct text.

[25] An unambiguous example, albeit dependent on an expression of ignorance rather than knowledge, is *Meno* 80d1, καὶ νῦν περὶ ἀρετῆς ὅ ἐστιν ἐγὼ μὲν οὐκ οἶδα, 'and now, concerning excellence, what it is, I for one do not know'; it is unambiguous because of the difference in gender, regardless of how one further interprets the indirect interrogative; but for controversy even there, see Bluck 1961, 271 ad loc.

[26] I follow the new OCT with slight change in punctuation.

[27] This highlights the inadequacy of 'what is' as a translation of τὸ ὄν, the nominalized neuter participle of the verb 'be', for which the alternative rendering 'being', however, would give rise to ambiguity with οὐσία.

[28] See in particular DK 28B8, 32–8. Cf. Hackforth 1955, 81, n. 2: 'The term μονοειδές recurs at 80b in close conjunction with ἀδιάλυτον, and it is used of the Form of beauty at *Symp.* 211b. It has the same force as πᾶν ὁμοῖον which Parmenides asserts of his ἓν ὄν, viz. the denial of internal difference or distinction of unlike parts.' See in particular also Solmsen 1971, esp. 67–70. The arguments by Vancamp 1996 may thus need further revision.

[29] Gallop 1975, 53 f.; Geddes 1863, 123, translates: 'You would loudly protest that you cannot conceive each thing arising in any other way than as it partakes of the particular essence of which it is a partaker', and comments: 'τῆς ἰδίας οὐσίας = τῆς ἰδέας the universal manifesting itself in, but prior to, the particular, so that the former is an οὐσία (*Seyn*), the latter a γένεσις (*Werden*)'. Hackforth 1955, 135: 'that the only way you know of, by which anything comes to be, is by its participating in the special being in which it does participate'. Rowe 1983, 245: 'you know of no other way in which each thing comes to be except by having come to share in the appropriate essence (οὐσία) of each [thing] in which it comes to share'.

[30] The discerning reader is asked to forgive these barbarisms, which are necessary to convey the fact that the nominalized adjectives in Greek are neuter plural.

[31] Perhaps it should be stated at this point that the absence of the definite article with δύο is not decisive either way, as Plato is here using δύο as generic singular; in that, the case of 100e2–3 is different; there, it is indeed the case that the subject of γίγνεται has the definite article, the complement to the predicate does not: τῷ καλῷ τὰ καλὰ γίγνεται καλά, 'through the beautiful the beautifuls come to be beautiful' (if that is the text). – The wider question of the grammar of εἶναι and γίγνεσθαι cannot be discussed here; see Burnyeat 2003, who also lists some of the most important contributions to the debate (p. 9, n. 33). My own suspicion is that εἶναι in Greek always denotes the 'is' of 'God *is*' or the 'are' of 'the gods *are*'; what is commonly regarded as the auxiliary represents that

³² It may be noted that the continuation of that sentence at 101c5–7 is ambiguous in the same way: καὶ δεῖν τούτου μετασχεῖν τὰ μέλλοντα δύο ἔσεσθαι, καὶ μονάδος ὃ ἂν μέλλῃ ἓν ἔσεσθαι: at first one may be inclined to take the phrase τὰ μέλλοντα δύο ἔσεσθαι, 'that which is to be two', as clearly indicating that there is something which is not yet two but will be two, if everything goes according to plan; one would then translate: 'and that it is necessary that that which is to be two participate in that [the dyad just mentioned], and in the monad whatever is to be one.' But there is no such certainty concerning the prior being of something not yet two (or one, respectively) but about to be two (or one, respectively): at 95b5–6 Socrates warns Cebes of boasting: μή τις ἡμῖν βασκανία περιτρέψῃ τὸν λόγον τὸν μέλλοντα ἔσεσθαι, 'lest some jinx turn around the argument which is about to be'; regardless of whether one translates 'turn around' or 'turn upside down' or 'pervert' or 'cause…to abort', and again 'is about to be' or 'wants to be' or 'intends to be': the argument is not there yet; therefore, in the parallel construction of 101c5–7, Socrates could likewise speak of 'what is to be two' in a case where there is not anything there yet which is something else at present and which will be two in time to come.

³³ Gallop 1993, 52 f.

³⁴ The (optional) addition of 'whatever it is' is meant to reflect the generic subjunctive with ἄν.

³⁵ It should be reiterated, though, that words for 'form' have not been introduced yet, and that what Socrates and his audience are thinking of as points of reference of 'each' are the beautiful itself, the equal itself, etc. See Herrmann 2005, 2006 and 2007.

³⁶ Cf. in particular Classen 1959a, 158–160.

³⁷ Watt 1987, 198.

³⁸ Thompson 1901, 255–8, omits it altogether, whether by oversight or because he considers usage here 'literal' rather than 'metaphorical'; nor is there discussion in the seminal article by Hirzel (1913). Classen 1959a, 160, only points out that, as in the *Protagoras*, the term οὐσία occurs in the summary of a preceding argument and is followed by a number of illustrative examples. Berger 1961, 28–30, deals with the *Charmides* passage in his section on 'the philosophical being' and places it after his treatment of the *Protagoras* passage; he concludes from the syntactical and philosophical context that οὐσία is what something has as its own being (*zijn*), but he presupposes, for both dialogues, that because of the etymology of the noun any Greek would have connected οὐσία with ὄντα automatically, and that all that needs doing to understand the meaning of οὐσία is to find the requisite sense of ὄντα. This etymological awareness, though, cannot be assumed; contrariwise, the way Plato introduces οὐσία in the *Meno*, *Euthyphro* and *Phaedo* is the clearest indication that no such direct link between noun and verb was felt in everyday usage.

³⁹ This is not wholly dissimilar to *Symposium* 199c, d, where a similar explanation of directedness is given; δύναμις had been used several times with reference to the specific power of the god, and Socrates will soon use it himself when questioning Diotima (202e).

⁴⁰ Cf., e.g., Herodotus 7.28, τὴν ἐμεωυτοῦ οὐσίην, 'my possession(s)', in which passage it is then explicated what these possessions are.

[41] Taylor 1976, 21.
[42] Taylor 1976, 42.
[43] After 330a4 also 330a6, 7, b1, 331d6, 333a5.
[44] The implications of that cannot be discussed here. It may be noted, however, that when Plato alludes to this passage from the *Protagoras* by letting Socrates put a very similarly phrased question to the guest from Elea at *Sophist* 217a, he uses γένος, 'kind', in place of πρᾶγμα, 'thing'. In the *Protagoras*, the term πρᾶγμα occurs after 330c1 (twice) also 330c4, d4, d5, 331a8, 332a5, 337d4 (with slightly different reference in the mouth of Hippias); after that, with the requisite reference 349b3,4, c1, and then again 352d3 in a way that combines the specific sense of the philosophical passages with the non-committal usage of 326e8 and 327c7, from where Socrates could have picked up Protagoras' usage in the first place.
[45] For this, see Classen 1959, 158 f.
[46] See LSJ s.v.
[47] Note that this is the only place in Plato at which the noun οὐσία is connected with the verb ὑπόκειμαι. Contrast Aristotle: a TLG word search produces 43 matches with an interval of up to 6 words, of which 6 exhibit direct collocation, 3 of which in the phrase τὴν ὑποκειμένην οὐσίαν. This may just be independent of the *Protagoras* passage; even Aristotle is capable of the occasional philosophical pun.
[48] Hamilton and Emlyn-Jones 2004, 45. Cf. Waterfield 1994, 45: 'all you're doing is calling up a horde of false witnesses against me to support your attempt to dislodge me from my inheritance, the truth'.
[49] Cf., in addition to the notes to the two translations cited, e.g. Dodds 1959, 245 ad loc. and 189 ad 447a3; Classen 1959a. Thompson 1894, 156 ad loc., already rightly rejects Stallbaum's suggestion that Plato is playing with a specific philosophical meaning of οὐσία; correct also is Marten 1962, 11.
[50] Classen (1959a, 158) explains in detail how Plato constructs the law-court metaphor, but then continues: 'but the addition τοῦ ἀληθοῦς indicates that οὐσία is not equivalent to τὰ ὄντα in the sense of τὰ χρήματα or ἅ τινί ἐστιν… but is to be understood as πάντα ἃ ἔστιν, i.e. things that exist or are real [or perhaps: "or that really are"]…'
[51] *Pace* Berger, *passim*.
[52] See nn. 16 and 19.
[53] This view of the *Meno* and *Euthyphro*, which is more specific than a generally 'proleptic' reading that refers everything interesting before the *Republic* to the *Republic*, cannot be defended here.
[54] For the text, this translation and thorough discussion see Huffman 1993, 123–45. The text of Stobaeus as given by Wachsmuth 1884, 188 f. and the text of Philolaus given by Diels and Kranz 1951, 408 f., as DK 44B6, differ in significant respects.
[55] For formation of that type see Fraenkel 1925, 46 f., on -εστω in particular 47; cf. also Chantraine 1933, 116–17, on -εστω in particular 117; Schwyzer 1939, vol. I, 478; Frisk 1973, vol. I, 577 s.v.
[56] For a comprehensive interpretation of Philolaus, see Huffman 1993; for Plato's method in the *Phaedo*, cf. Herrmann 2003, 2004, 2005, 2006 and 2007.
[57] This is, of course, not an exclusive list; but some thinkers are clearly more important in an assessment of the *Phaedo* than others. For Anaxagoras see, e.g., Furley, 1987, 72; Herrmann 2003, 42–7; in this context, reference should also be made to Diogenes of Apollonia; for Democritus see Herrmann 2005; for Philolaus and other Pythagoreans

see Huffman 1993, 78–92, esp. 90–2; Ebert 1994 and 2004; Kingsley 1995, esp. 79–171; Herrmann 2004 and 2006. Parmenides is in the background; Plato engages with him in more explicit fashion in the *Symposium* and, of course, from the *Parmenides* onwards; for the *Symposium*, see, e.g., Solmsen 1971.

[58] Herrmann 2003, 42–7.
[59] Herrmann 2005, 47–55.
[60] Huffman 1993, 90–2.
[61] Herrmann 2005, 45–7. For εἶδος in particular see also Herrmann 2006.
[62] Chantraine 1933, 117, who mistakenly claims that the simplex, too, is attested for Democritus.
[63] Cf. Buck 1955, 129; *pace* Sedley 2003, 99.
[64] See Hirzel 1913 *passim* and Classen 1959a, 158–64, quoted in n. 3 above.
[65] I am grateful to Myles Burnyeat for cautioning against unwarranted claims concerning Protagoras.

Bibliography

Allen, R.E. (ed.)
   1965   *Studies in Plato's* Metaphysics, London.
Baldry, H.C.
   1937   'Plato's "technical terms"', *CQ* 31, 141–50.
Berger, H.H.
   1961   *Ousia in de dialogen van Plato. Een terminologisch onderzoek*, Leiden.
Bluck, R.S.
   1961   *Plato's* Meno, Cambridge.
Brommer, P.
   1940   ΕΙΔΟΣ *et* ΙΔΕΑ. *Étude sémantique et chronologique*, Assen.
Buck, C.D.
   1955   *The Greek Dialects*, Chicago.
Burkert, W.
   1972   *Lore and Science in Ancient Pythagoreanism*, tr. E. Minar, Cambridge, Mass. German edn 1962.
Burnet, J.
   1924   *Plato's* Euthyphro, Apology of Socrates *and* Crito, Oxford.
Burnyeat, M.F.
   2003   '*Apology* 30b 2–4: Socrates, money, and the grammar of γίγνεσθαι', *JHS* 123, 1–25.
Campbell, L.
   1867   *The* Sophist *and* Politicus *of Plato*, Oxford.
   1894   'On Plato's use of language', in Jowett and Campbell, *Plato's* Republic II, 165–340.
Chantraine, P.
   1933   *La formation des noms en grec ancien*, Paris.
Classen, C.J.
   1959a *Sprachliche Deutung als Triebkraft platonischen und sokratischen Philosophierens*, Munich.

1959b 'The study of language among Socrates' contemporaries', *Proceedings of the African Classical Associations* 2, 33–49. Repr. in C.J. Classen (ed.) *Sophistik*, Wissenschaftliche Buchgesellschaft, Darmstadt, 1976, 215–47.
1960 *Untersuchungen zu Platons Jagdbildern*, Berlin.

Diels, H. and Kranz, W.
1951–2 *Die Fragmente der Vorsokratiker*, 6. Auflage, vols. I–III, Berlin.

Diller, H.
1952 'Hippokratische Medizin und attische Philosophie', *Hermes* 80, 385–409.
1971 'Zum Gebrauch von εἶδος und ἰδέα in vorplatonischer Zeit', in H.-H. Euler et al. (eds.) *Medizingeschichte in unserer Zeit*, Stuttgart, 23–30.

Dixsaut, M.
1991 'Ousia, eidos et idea dans le Phédon', *Revue Philosophique de la France et de l'Étranger* 116.4, 479–501. Reprinted in M. Dixsaut, *Platon et la question de la pensée. Études platoniciennes*, vol. I, Paris 2000, 71–91.

Dixsaut, M. and Brancacci, A. (eds.)
2002 *Platon. Source des Présocratiques*, Paris.

Ebert, T.
1994 *Sokrates als Pythagoreer und die Anamnesis in Platons* Phaidon, Stuttgart.
2004 *Platon. Phaidon*, Göttingen.

Else, G.F.
1938 'The terminology of the ideas', *Harvard Studies in Classical Philology* 20, 17–51.

Fine, G. (ed.)
1999 *Plato*, vols. 1–2, Oxford.

Fraenkel, E.
1925 'Zur baltoslavischen Grammatik II.1', *Zeitschrift für vergleichende Sprachforschung auf dem Gebiete der indogermanischen Sprachen*, 53. Band, 1. Heft, Göttingen, 36–47.

Frank, E.
1923 *Plato und die sogenannten Pythagoreer*, Halle (Saale).

Furley, D.
1987 *The Greek Cosmologists*, vol. I, Cambridge.

Furley, D. and Allen, R.E. (eds.)
1975 *Studies in Presocratic Philosophy*, vol. II, London.

Gadamer, H.G. (ed.).
1968 *Um die Begriffswelt der Vorsokratiker*, Darmstadt.

Gallop, D.
1975 *Plato. Phaedo*, Oxford.

Gillespie, C.M.
1912 'The use of Εἶδος and Ἰδέα in Hippocrates', *CQ* 6, 179–203.

Hackforth, R.
1955 *Plato's* Phaedo, Cambridge.

Hamilton, W. and Emlyn-Jones, C.
2004 *Plato. Gorgias*, London.

Herrmann, F.G.
2003 'μετέχειν, μεταλαμβάνειν and the problem of participation in Plato's ontology', *Philosophical Inquiry* 25, 19–56.

- 2004 'Socrates' views on death', in Karasmanis (ed.) *Socrates...*, 185–99.
- 2005 'Plato's answer to Democritean determinism', in Natali and Maso (eds.) *La catena delle cause*, 37–55.
- 2006 'εἶδος– Bedeutung und Gebrauch eines Fachausdruckes in Platons Phaidon', Archiv für Begriffsgeschichte 48, 7–26.
- 2007 *Words and Ideas. The roots of Plato's philosophy*, Swansea.

Hirzel, R.
- 1913 'οὐσία', *Philologus* 72, 42–64.

Horn, C. and Rapp, C. (eds.)
- 2002 *Wörterbuch der antiken Philosophie*, Munich.

Huffman, C.
- 1993 *Philolaus of Croton. Pythagorean and Presocratic*, Cambridge.
- 2005 *Archytas of Tarentum. Pythagorean, Philosopher and Mathematician King*, Cambridge.

Jowett, B. and Campbell, L.
- 1894 *Plato's* Republic, vol. II, Oxford.

Kahn, C.H.
- 1996 *Plato and the Socratic Dialogue*, Cambridge.

Karasmanis, V. (ed.)
- 2004 *Socrates: 2400 years since his death*, Delphi and Athens.

Kingsley, P.
- 1995 *Ancient Philosophy, Mystery and Magic. Empedocles and Pythagorean tradition*, Oxford.

Kirk, G.S., Raven, J.E. and Schofield, M.
- 1982 *The Presocratic Philosophers*, 2nd edn, Cambridge.

Long, A.A. (ed.)
- 1999 *Early Greek Philosophy*, Cambridge.

Mansfeld, J.
- 1987 *Die Vorsokratiker*, Stuttgart.

Marten, R.
- 1962 *ΟΥΣΙΑ im Denken Platons*, Meisenheim am Glan.

McCabe, M.M.
- 2000 *Plato and his Predecessors*, Cambridge.

McKirahan, R.D.
- 1994 *Philosophy Before Socrates*, Indianapolis.

Motte, A., Rutten, Chr. and Somville, P.
- 2003 *Philosophie de la Forme. Eidos, idea, morphé dans la philosophie grecque des origines à Aristote*, Louvain-la-Neuve.

Natali, C. and Maso, S. (eds.)
- 2005 *La catena delle cause*, Amsterdam 2005.

Onions, C.T. et al. (eds.)
- 1973 (^{3}1944) *The Shorter Oxford English Dictionary*, reset with revised etymologies and addenda, Oxford.

Ritter, C.
- 1910 *Neue Untersuchungen über Platon*, Munich.

Rowe, C.J.
- 1993 *Plato. Phaedo*, Cambridge.

Sandoz, C.
   1972   *La notion de la forme en Grec ancien*, Fribourg.
Saunders, T.J. (ed.)
   1987   *Plato. Early Socratic Dialogues*, Harmondsworth.
Schleiermacher, F.D.E.
   1996   *Über die Philosophie Platons*, ed. M. Steiner, Hamburg.
Sedley, D.
   2003   *Plato's* Cratylus, Cambridge.
Shorey, P.
   1911   'Review of A.E. Taylor, *Varia Socratica*', *CP* VI, 361–5.
Snell, B.
   1924   *Die Ausdrücke für den Begriff des Wissens in der vorplatonischen Philosophie*, Berlin.
Solmsen, F.
   1971   'Parmenides and the description of perfect beauty in Plato's *Symposium*', *AJP* 92, 1, 62–70.
Taylor, A.E.
   1911a   *Varia Socratica. First Series*, Oxford.
   1911b   'The words εἶδος, ἰδέα in pre-Platonic literature', in Taylor 1911a, 178–267.
Taylor, C.C.W.
   1976   *Plato. Protagoras*, Oxford.
Thesleff, H.
   1982   *Studies in Platonic Chronology*, Helsinki.
Vailati, G.
   1906   'A study of Platonic terminology', *Mind* 15, 473–85.
Vancamp, B.
   1996   'κατὰ ταὐτὰ ἔχειν. Zur Herkunft einer platonischen Redewendung aus dem Bereich der Ideenlehre', *Rheinisches Museum* 139, 352–4.
von Fritz, K.
   1943   'νόος and νοεῖν in the Homeric poems', *CP* 38, 79–93.
   1945   'νόος, νοεῖν and their derivatives in pre-Socratic philosophy (excluding Anaxagoras)', *CP* 40, 223–42.
   1946   'νόος, νοεῖν and their derivatives in pre-Socratic philosophy (excluding Anaxagoras)', *CP* 41, 12–34.
(von Fritz 1943, 1945, 1946 reprinted as von Fritz 1968.)
   1962   *Philosophie und sprachlicher Ausdruck bei Demokrit, Platon und Aristoteles*, Darmstadt.
   1968   'Die Rolle des Nous', German transl. of von Fritz 1943, 1945, 1946, by P. Wilpert, in Gadamer 1968, 246–363.
Watt, D.
   1987   *Lysis. Charmides*, transl. and intro. by D. Watt, in Saunders (ed.) *Plato. Early Socratic Dialogues.*
Wilamowitz-Moellendorff, U. von
   1919   *Platon*, vols. I–II, Berlin.

4

THE TRIPARTITION OF THE SOUL IN PLATO'S *REPUBLIC*

Stefan Büttner

Even though some fifty years have passed since a well-known Platonist stated that 'the problem of the tripartite soul is amongst the thorniest of all Platonic problems',[1] little has changed regarding the truth of his statement. Concerning Plato's argument in Book 4 of the *Republic* I would like to mention just three of the points which so stubbornly persist in causing trouble.

First, if Plato says that the soul of man consists of three isolated, agent-like parts, then there is no room for the person as an entity over and above those three parts, three souls or *homunculi*. This objection is in accordance with the commonly-held view, that only the modern age has discovered the unity of the self – by means of the subject's reflection on itself – and, along with that, individuality and personality.[2]

Next, the *opinio communis* holds that for Plato the parts of the soul are distinguished primarily by what they strive to attain. Yet Plato also emphasizes the great *variety* of possible desires (*Rep.* 439a1–a8) – e.g., one can simultaneously feel the desire to drink and to eat, and one can be thirsty not for just a drink, but also for a large or a small, a warm or a cold one. However, that does not lead Plato to assume that there are any further parts of the soul desiring respectively large cold or small warm glasses of beer. How precisely does Plato arrive at his division of the soul into three, rather than five or five hundred parts?[3]

Closely connected with that latter point is the third question: what does the rather peculiar θυμοειδές (*thymoeides*) stand for? The juxtaposition of reason and emotion, which Plato points at by giving an example of a man who wishes to drink, yet simultaneously – with a view to his health or due to other, similarly reasonable considerations – not to drink (*Rep.* 439b3 ff.), we tend to find more or less acceptable; but what are we to make of the θυμοειδές, a part of our soul which supposedly is capable of feeling anger or shame, which is ambitious, envious etc.? Can a single faculty cover all those different things, and if so, does it do so on the same level with reason and emotion? For many interpreters, the description of the status of the θυμοειδές seems to be at best incoherent, more often obscure; or, indeed, the introduction of this element seems to be prompted solely by Plato's desire to complete his analogy of the soul and the state.[4]

Here, I would like to re-examine those three points, proceeding from the assumption that – as is suggested by several scholars in a number of recent publications – Plato's theory of the tripartite soul may yet possess a greater consistency than has hitherto been thought. It is predominantly the following question I would like to pursue: Does his theory have its origins merely in Plato's observational talents which induced him to classify thus certain phenomena, or can it also be justified on systematic grounds? That is to say, does it tie in with other known Platonic tenets, as for instance his theory of knowledge?

The problem of Plato's argument in *Republic* 4 seems to lie in the use of the principle of contradiction which, though serving as a useful means to distinguish between two alternatives, on its own does not suffice to explain why the soul should be composed of precisely three parts. Plato himself seems to hint at that by having Socrates refer to the incompleteness of the argument at this point of the conversation (*Rep.* 435c9–d8), which is why interpreters often feel entitled to have recourse to Books 8 and 9, in order to try to understand what Plato might be getting at here. I shall here go even further, and drag in statements from the *Theaetetus* and the *Philebus*, proceeding from the assumption that Plato's thinking remained fairly consistent throughout the time in which those writings were produced. Although not everyone would find that easy to accept, it may yet prove worthwhile to see whether anything can thus be gained for a more systematic understanding of the tripartite soul, and especially of the function of the θυμοειδές.

The first part of what follows therefore will be an examination of the unity of the soul as it becomes apparent in Book 4 of the *Republic* (1). Subsequently the *Republic* as well as the dialogues *Theaetetus* and *Philebus* will be looked at with a view to their presentation of both the different kinds of cognition (2) and of emotion (3). Within the framework thus established I shall in a final step return to the partition theory of the *Republic* (4).

1. The unity of the soul in Book 4 of the *Republic*

First of all we must consider if Plato really maintains that the soul is separated into completely isolated parts, so that in fact it would be impossible to speak of a unity of the soul according to Plato. He prepares his argumentation with the help of the principle of contradiction (*Rep.* 436b8–c1): he claims that one and the same thing (ταὐτόν) can never effect or suffer anything opposite in respect of the same (κατὰ ταὐτόν) and in relation to the same (πρὸς ταὐτόν) at the same moment (ἅμα). If during the contemplation of all those aspects (ἐν αὑτοῖς) something like that occurs nevertheless, then it becomes clear that (sc. in one of those aspects) there is no 'same' (ταὐτόν), but a 'multiple' (πλείω).

I believe that it is rather important to read the end of this sentence as I have just paraphrased it. From a purely syntactical point, the principle of contradiction can refer to all three previously mentioned ταὐτά as well as to the ἅμα (which again implies identity); that is to say, it is by no means clear from the outset that oppositions are to be resolved only by multiplying the object in question.

Socrates' examples, too, used later to illustrate the division of the soul into desire and reason, can be seen to support that interpretation. In all of them, man, spinning top, and archer, Socrates distinguishes a *prima facie* antithesis by drawing attention to how, as regards any given object (ταὐτόν) in relation to anything outside it (πρός τι), one must distinguish two aspects, the one opposed to the other, so that the 'multiple' (πλείω) must be found in the κατά τι, i.e. in respect of something belonging to or being within the object itself.

This becomes especially clear with the example of the spinning top that is at once in motion and at rest (*Rep.* 436d4–437a3). One and the same spinning top (= ταὐτόν) in relation to the same ground (= πρός τι, outside the spinning top) and at the same moment (= ἅμα) is in an opposite state, depending which aspect of it one is looking at (= πλείω by two different κατά τι of the same spinning top): Socrates explicitly states that *within* the spinning top in question (ἐν αὑτοῖς), there exist both an axis and a periphery, and that the spinning top is at rest in respect of the one (κατὰ τὸ εὐθὺ ἑστάναι, 'in respect of standing straight') and in motion in respect of the other (κατὰ τὸ περιφερές, 'according to its periphery').

The two other examples have exactly the same structure: One and the same man (= ταὐτόν) can at the same moment (= ἅμα) be moving and not moving, as in relation to the same place on the floor (= πρὸς ταὐτόν, outside the man), in respect of his legs he is at rest, while in respect of his head and arms he is in motion (= πλείω by two different κατά τι of the same man). – One and the same archer (= ταὐτόν) at the same moment (= ἅμα) and in relation to the same (normal state of the string of the) bow (= πρὸς ταὐτόν, outside the man) can be in motion moving the bow forward with the one hand and at rest by not moving it forward (or even in opposite motion by moving it backwards) with the other hand (= πλείω by two different κατά τι of the same archer).

Those comparisons have in common that the *unity* of the object in question is preserved. Just as it is unnecessary to talk about two different people simply because the legs of a man are at rest while his arms are flailing wildly. In accordance with the principle of contradiction, a distinction is drawn *within* the unity (of a given object) with regard to the respect considered at the time. All three examples form the backdrop to the division of the soul into desire and reason; all of them exhibit the same pattern; the third one, the archer, moreover, is explicitly linked to the example with the thirsty man, or, indeed, even built into it. It seems only reasonable, therefore, to assume that the division of the soul will follow the same pattern:

We start with a description of how someone desires the induction of drink into his body, yet simultaneously refrains from acting upon that desire. This ambivalence does not occur due to any two different souls in his breast, but because one and the same soul (ταὐτόν) at the same moment (ἅμα) in relation to the same drink (πρός τι = outside the soul) strives to obtain it with the part related to bodily gratification (the ἐπιθυμητικόν), and wishes to avoid it with a second part that is in charge of the well-being of the person as a whole (the λογιστικόν); thus there is a πλείω of two different κατά τι within the same soul.[5]

Those who think that Plato here divides the soul into two entirely independent parts – into two souls so to speak – will be in trouble not only on account of the three analogies framing this division. As they divide the subject of the action itself into two parts (i.e. make the ταὐτόν a πλείω), in the thirst example they are left with no equivalent for the κατά τι; that differentiation would then have been introduced in vain.[6] For, the drink must be the πρός τι of the one feeling thirsty, as Socrates explains at length.[7] The difference between those two prepositions here lies in the fact that πρός denotes a relation to something else outside the given object, while κατά refers to a single aspect within a given thing.[8]

The aim of Plato's argumentation then is by no means to destroy the unity of the soul by dividing it into two or, later on, three autonomous parts, but to differentiate first two, then three aspects, three κατά τι, within the *one* soul.

Yet even if we concede all this, we will hardly be much wiser, it seems. For what we really want to know is what this unity of the soul actually consists of and if there is a systematic reason for three, rather than four or seven, parts. To find possible answers to this question, let us embark on a little detour via Plato's theory of knowledge. There we encounter a similar problem, namely that of the different cognitive capacities in the one soul. I shall eventually endeavour to show in what way these two problems are linked.

2. The concept of κρίνειν as the unifying element of the recognizing soul (*Republic, Theaetetus, Philebus*)

In Book 7 of the *Republic* Plato divides the cognitive capacities according to their objects of cognition into two main categories: perception and thinking, αἴσθησις and νόησις. In the well-known example of the three fingers, Plato gives a hint as to what the common ground of the two faculties could possibly be (a much discussed text, of which for the present purpose I wish to consider only the following aspect).

Some objects of perception, says Socrates, do not require any additional thinking (ἐπίσκεψις) to be recognized, because they are sufficiently distinguished by perception (ἱκανῶς ὑπὸ τῆς αἰσθήσεως κρινόμενα, *Rep.* 523a10–b4). For all other objects thinking must intervene; it must, as is stated a few lines later, ἐπι-κρίνειν, which means it must distinguish in addition to perception (*Rep.* 524e4).

So the common root of perception and thinking consists, if we believe these remarks, in the active distinguishing or identification of something as something (κρίνειν τι), on different levels. As we are shown in greater detail in the *Theaetetus* and the *Philebus*, the perceptible is in the first place the specific quality of each sense organ, so the sense of sight distinguishes colours, the sense of hearing sounds, the sense of taste tastes etc. (at *Tht.* 184b8–185a3; *Phlb.* 33d2–34a6).[9]

In connection with this, Socrates emphasizes in the *Theaetetus* that, strictly speaking, we do not see and hear with our eyes and ears, but that we do this with our *one* soul by means of the sense organs (as tools) (*Tht.* 184b8–d5). As in the *Republic*, he divides the ways of cognition into two related kinds (*Tht.* 185e5–e7, he uses the term ἐπισκοπεῖν as he does in the *Republic*; this term refers to the activity of the soul which can act either bound to the body or free from it).[10]

In order better to understand the meaning of κρίνειν (or ἐπισκοπεῖν), some hermeneutic comments may be in order.[11] Cognition for Plato is an active distinguishing power independent of consciousness. The partition of the soul into a receptive and preconscious sense or emotion on the one hand and a spontaneous, conscious and unemotional thinking on the other is a peculiarity of modern theories of faculty in the seventeenth and eighteenth centuries. They have their starting point in Descartes' definition of thinking as a representing and thus reserved and cold consciousness of already 'given contents' – in the sense of Kant's 'gegebene Inhalte' – which is sometimes wrongly transferred on to Plato's division of the soul into a rational and non-rational part.[12] That is why we need not be surprised that according to Plato there is no exclusive bipartition of the soul into cold thinking and blind emotion and that thinking is an activity accompanied by very pleasant emotions.

The 'homunculus problem' is caused largely by an approach to Platonic thought based on the philosophemes of the modern age. Only when one – be it explicitly or implicitly – takes 'recognition' to mean 'consciousness', and consequently thinking, feeling, and desiring to be separate faculties, can one reach the conclusion that any part of the soul said to know and feel and desire must necessarily be seen as an independent agent. Yet speaking from everyday experience, it is not at all difficult to see how recognition in the sense of κρίνειν could imply pleasure or pain without having to resort to any further faculty. Wine may taste fruity, sweet, of cork etc. (distinction of taste) and along with that either good or bad (feeling of pleasure or pain). We observe a great injustice, feel pain and feel insulted in accordance with what it was we noticed. We understand geometrical correlations and rejoice.

A radical separation of reason and desire according to the theories of the philosophy of consciousness will leave no room for a third element in the soul. That is why all those who consider the ἐπιθυμητικόν in Book 4 of the *Republic* an urge incapable of recognition can find no place in the system to offer to the θυμοειδές.

In Plato's eyes, on the other hand, all acts of distinguishing are accompanied by pleasure and pain, and thus all cognition – and especially the unconscious, immediate act of distinguishing – is at the same time of ethical relevance. For, the education of man is all about learning and becoming used to feeling the right pleasures and pains, so that one is able to decide what would be best in any given situation.[13] In this way, when all parts of the soul are capable of (their respective kind of) cognition, the θυμοειδές, too, can easily be incorporated into it.

In order to look at that in greater detail, we shall now turn once more to the aforementioned two kinds of cognition, i.e. perception and thinking. Perception in a strict sense means, for Plato, to grasp differences like 'brown', 'hard', 'rectangular' etc. Its activity stops when the perceiver poses the question what those colours and shapes actually are (τί ποτ' ἔστι τὸ φανταζόμενον, *Phlb*. 38c12–d1, also *Tht*. 163b8–c5). In order to answer this question, the thinking mind is already required to intervene. It grasps – on the occasion of the perceptible qualities – a non-perceptible, intelligible content, one only accessible to thinking (νοητόν, ἔργον);[14] in this case for instance that the brown, hard and rectangular appearance in front of me is a door.

But this kind of intervention of thinking is not yet thinking in a strict sense and does not produce knowledge (ἐπιστήμη), because it does not consider an intelligible content for itself – for example, what the specific function of door is at all, what of triangle as such, what of number as such etc.

When I say that this 'brown' and 'rectangular' thing is a *door*, I am interpreting perceptible qualities by implicit conclusions of my mind. The mind applies a certain function or ἔργον to these qualities; this 'perception' of a concrete, single object Plato is known to call opinion (δόξα); best described by the work of the so called writer (γραμματεύς) in the soul (*Phlb.* 39a1–a7). He arrives at the formulation of the δόξα as a result of a dialogue the soul holds with itself (*Tht.* 189e4–190a5).[15]

One cannot describe the ἔργον by referring to perceptible qualities: a door may also be transparent and rounded off at the edges; or someone could take this brown and rectangular thing which I consider a door, carry it outside, plant it into the ground and sit down behind it, using it as a sun-shade. Only thinking has full access to the ἔργον.

Yet even the complexity of opinions has several levels. A more difficult job than the perception of concrete objects is the evaluation of situations. In this case, several object perceptions are grasped as *one* situation, which is evaluated as good or bad, useful or dangerous, just or unjust. *These* judgements, too, Plato calls δόξα (*Rep.* 479e1–e5) and sometimes a kind of κρίνειν (*Tht.* 170d4–e3).[16]

If, for instance, one sees a young man leading an old lady across the road, one makes a lot of single distinctions (colours, forms, sounds, which one interprets as lady, street, hand etc.), but one is also able to call this observed action as a whole good and just. In that judgement, too, a lot of premises and conclusions are implied of which I now explicate only a few.

'To be just means giving everybody what he deserves.' 'Old people deserve respect.' 'Respect can be shown by complying with a person's wishes.' 'This man complies with the wishes of the old lady.' 'So he respects her.' 'So he gives her what she deserves.' 'So his action is just.' In this situation, it is even more evident than in the case of a perception of an object that the thinking mind makes a big contribution to the conversation going on in the soul, leading to opinion.

Conclusion of section 2
According to Plato there are three main kinds of cognition which reflect the actions of one and the same soul at different levels of its function: by simply using the organs of the body to distinguish certain qualities (perception), by recognizing the intelligible ἔργον in the perceptible instance (opinion), by reflecting upon those ἔργα as such (thinking). Thinking and reflection is the least determined kind of cognition, since it requires no specific external cause, and attempts to comprehend matters in all their aspects, while opinion and perception are limited kinds of cognition.

In the *Philebus,* we see Socrates compare the powers of *imagination* with a painter (ζωγράφος), and on account of that call the imaginations εἰκόνες, pictures (*Phlb.* 39b3 ff.; Aristotle is the first to call both phenomena φαντασία). Just like thinking, imagination needs no perceptible object in order to be activated. But because of the fact that imagination distinguishes single objects or situations, too, and is in that respect completely derived from perceptions and opinions, it is not a fundamentally different kind of cognition.[17]

3. The kinds of emotion (*Republic, Philebus*)

As I mentioned before, Plato thinks that the different kinds of cognition are accompanied by specific emotions. A longer discussion of emotions, and the kinds of cognition that cause them, can be found in the *Philebus*, as well as, in a condensed way, in Book 9 of the *Republic*. Among other things, the following kinds of emotion are described:

Emotions related to the body, which are caused by αἴσθησις; for example pleasure and pain, which arise from dissolution of an orderly state or restoration of a natural, orderly corporeal state, e.g. if one is cold and then comes back into the warmth (*Phlb*. 31d4–32 b8).

Plato distinguishes these emotions, which immediately accompany cognition, from those that have the structure of desires, e.g. hunger and thirst. They are the most important examples for desires of the ἐπιθυμητικόν in the *Republic* and are analysed in the *Philebus* in a more detailed way. There Socrates supposes that appetites like hunger and thirst result from the soul supported by several different cognitive faculties.

He says (*Phlb*. 31 ff.): if one is thirsty, one must first *perceive* the lack of liquid in the body (αἴσθησις), which causes pain (immediately) and a desire for compensating this lack with something to drink. But this desire cannot arise until one *imagines* the state of being filled with liquid and through that feels a pleasure in advance (a προχαίρειν)[18] which drives one towards the realization of this imagination.

One can produce the imagination of being filled with liquid only by *memory*, which, as Socrates says (*Phlb*. 34a10–a11), requires that one has previously perceived such a pleasant state (by αἴσθησις); and, in addition to that, one must have come to the conclusion – using something similar to διάνοια – that, what was good in former times, will also be good this time. So even as simple a desire as thirst is determined in its character by a specific use of (usually unconscious) distinguishing acts – perceptions, memories, imaginations, opinions, rational conclusions etc. On projecting the pleasure once experienced into the future, the simple pleasure accompanying perception becomes a more complex emotion, a desire.

The same applies to rational thinking, too. Theoretical cognitions are accompanied by a specific pleasure (*Rep*. 583a1–a3, the pleasure of the part of the soul with which we learn is the most pleasant). This in turn causes the desire for knowledge (φιλοσοφία, but also, named more drastically, ἐπιθυμία, *Rep*. 475b8–b10; ὄρεξις, *Rep*. 485d3–d8; ἔρως, *Rep*. 490b2; ὁρμή, *Rep*. 611e1–612a3).

The *Philebus* also contains some information about a third kind of emotion or affect (*Phlb.* 47d5–48a4). It consists of a mixture of pleasure and pain, which is caused only by the soul. Paradigmatically Socrates mentions anger, fear, envy and others. Anger, as the main emotion of the θυμοειδές, is explained in more detail in the *Republic*. Anger there turns out to be the opinion that one has suffered injustice – which causes pain – linked with the expectation of being able to restore a state of justice – which produces an anticipated pleasure, which in turn causes one to act (*Rep.* 440c1–d3):

> What happens, I said, if someone holds the opinion that he is acting in the wrong way (οἴηται ἀδικεῖν)? Will not he, the more virtuous he is, be the less able to be angry (ὀργίζεσθαι), even if he suffers hunger and thirst and other things at the hands of someone, who he thinks does this justly (οἴηται δικαίως ταῦτα δρᾶν), and his θυμός will not, as I say, rebel against this?

If someone holds the opinion that he is being treated justly, he will *not* be angry, even if he is made to suffer. *Vice versa* he *will be* angry, when he believes that he is being wronged. The following lines back this up:

> What happens if someone believes that he is being wronged (ἀδικεῖσθαί τις ἡγῆται)?

Then he will be boiling with rage and stick to his way of acting, says Socrates, even if it causes pain, which means that in his desire for justice he possesses a stronger motivation to act.[19]

Summary of section 3
According to Plato the different ways of cognition are accompanied by specific emotions. There exist, however, no specific or even independent faculties for them, as they are the result of the respective cognitive actions. Plato distinguishes the immediate emotion accompanying cognitive acts and emotions which are caused by a complex interaction of distinguishing faculties such as perception, imagination, memory and reason, and which desire something.

The emotions which we have just observed – hunger, thirst, anger, thirst for knowledge – are the ones Plato uses in the *Republic* to explain the tripartition of the soul. In the following fourth section I will try to use the results of our discussion to explain the tripartition of the soul rather more precisely.

4. The application of the κρίνειν-depending model of emotions to the *Republic*

The *Republic* is concerned with the happiness of the individual and the community. If everybody does what he is capable of, he and the state will do well. The *condicio sine qua non* for that is, that the different interests in each individual soul be in a reasonable hierarchy. Plato differentiates three main interests and desires in the soul, formulated lucidly at *Rep.* 580d3–d9. Each of the three parts of the soul has specific (ἴδιαι) pleasures and desires (ἐπιθυμίαι, here used in a broader sense) and specific origins (ἀρχαί) of those emotions.

Is this division purely empirical or does it have a systematic character, too? In Book 5 of the *Republic*, before the separation of philosophers from lovers of δόξαι, Socrates states a general rule for the division of desires (*Rep.* 475a5–b10):

> – Answer yes or no: whenever we call someone 'desirous of something' (τινὸς ἐπιθυμητικόν), will we say that he desires *everything* that belongs to it (παντὸς τοῦ εἴδους), or that he desires some things and others not?
> – That he desires everything.

Then Socrates goes on to apply this general rule to the lover of wine as well as to the lover of honour and the philosopher. Let us try now to transfer this rule to the tripartition of the soul.

A. The ἐπιθυμητικόν

The ἐπιθυμητικόν is said to be of mixed shape, with hunger, thirst and sexual desire as the strongest desires (esp. *Rep.* 580d10–581a1, where the desire of the ἐπιθυμητικόν for money is explained by the fact that money would be the best means to satisfy those desires). There are, however, no separate, distinct parts of the soul for hunger and thirst respectively, nor any for warm, cold, many or few drinks – though one can feel some of these appetites at the same time – as all of these desires share *one* common characteristic, which justifies treating them as one distinct whole: all of them are desires for pleasures that relate to the body (*Rep.* 442a4–b4: the ἐπιθυμητικόν aims at αἱ περὶ τὸ σῶμα καλούμεναι ἡδοναί; see also *Tim.* 70d7–d8). Thus it strives precisely for *those* pleasures which accompany perception in the strict sense.

Depending on the particular circumstances of a given situation, the ἐπιθυμητικόν when thirsty strives for a drink, or for a warm, a cold, a large, a small drink. In the conflict with the λογιστικόν described in Book 4, the ἐπιθυμητικόν strives no less for that specific drink than the λογιστικόν wishes to avoid it. The motive for both would be satisfaction, either directly or via the avoidance of dissatisfaction, which both expect from precisely that drink. Both, that is, strive for something good, even if the good of the ἐπιθυμητικόν is rather limited (that glass of wine would taste delicious, indeed, while enjoyed, yet be by no means the best option in the long run).

For the validity of the argument in Book 4, it is not necessary to assume that the ἐπιθυμητικόν desires 'blindly'; as seen above, the root of the conflict lies in the simultaneous desire and non-desire for the same glass of wine, according to the preferences of two different aspects of the one soul. Finally, that the ἐπιθυμητικόν desires particular goods is explicitly stated in the discussion about the different ways a state can fall into decline: for the oligarch, wealth is the good which he has set his eyes upon, and which consequently determines his actions (προκείμενον ἀγαθόν, *Rep.* 555b9–b10, 562b3), while the democrat is torn between necessary and unnecessary bodily desires, and sees this freedom of choice at the lowest level as his good (ἀγαθόν, *Rep.* 562b9–b10).[20]

An argument against a blindness of the lower parts of the soul may be seen in Socrates' frequent emphasis, in the *Republic*, on the capability of those parts to form opinions and even to draw conclusions.[21] The clearest evidence of that, put forward as early as Book 4, is the definition of the moderate person (σώφρων) as the person in whose soul the lower parts live in such harmony with reason that all three are in perfect agreement regarding their opinions (ὁμοδοξῶσι, *Rep.* 442d1). If the ἐπιθυμητικόν were a blind desire, it could not be educated, but would continually have to be suppressed by force. Yet it is depicted as in principle capable of listening to arguments and thus as trainable.[22]

Despite all its potential to be trained, though, the ἐπιθυμητικόν always focuses on the perceptible aspects of things. In that way, conflicts may arise even within this part of the soul. As for instance with the oligarch, who is possessed by a series of lower desires, which however he suppresses, not because he considers it just and reasonable, but out of fear for the property he would lose if his behaviour became known (*Rep.* 554c11–e2); he is – to quote a famous phrase from the *Phaedo* – moderate out of 'unrestraint' (*Phd.* 68e3). So it is obvious that Plato is quite capable of distinguishing between the objective deed and its origin within the subject. The same action can be good or bad according to why it is done.

Even the ever-changing behaviour of the democrat (esp. *Rep.* 561c6–d7) can be explained within the framework of the desire for bodily satisfaction. He alternates between excess (in unnecessary desires) and asceticism and sports (when, for recreational purposes, he places emphasis on the necessary desires). His motivation does not go beyond bodily satisfaction.[23] Not even when he pretends to study philosophy (ὅς ἐν φιλοσοφίᾳ διατρίβων), or jumps up in the assembly in order to take part in politics, does he get inspired by the delight in knowledge or the respect others will pay him on account of his clever proposals, but solely by the idea of being seen or heard, that is to say the sensual aspect of his performance.[24] He resembles someone who wears a roll-neck sweater in order to be regarded as existentialist, or a politician who desperately comments upon everything just to appear on television.

It is my thesis that the other two parts of the soul also strive each for its own specific pleasure; each for whatever accompanies the two other kinds of cognition, as we encountered them in the *Republic*, *Theaetetus* and *Philebus*, i.e. opinion and thinking respectively. The term ἀρχαί at *Rep.* 580d8 then would denote the kind of cognition causing the respective emotions.

B. The θυμοειδές

This idea may now be examined in respect of the θυμοειδές, which also in its turn can take many forms: Plato attributes to it emotions such as anger, courage and envy as well as ambition, shame and self-disgust.

If my thesis is correct, the θυμοειδές must aim at such pleasures as are felt by grasping the ἔργον of any particular (by δόξα). As mentioned before, δόξαι exist on different levels. Somebody who constructs a machine that works well, which means that it fulfils its ἔργον, and who is pleased by that, already feels a pleasure that goes beyond the mere pleasure of perception (a mechanic of Ferrari probably will be pleased not so much by the red colour of the car as by how well the car serves its function).

Yet this functionality itself is merely a consequence of a higher functionality, namely that of the capabilities of the human soul. According to Plato the actions of humans are the most important instantiation of a common element (the soul and its justice/injustice): for it is interesting to know about tools and instruments, but much more interesting to know what good can be achieved by using them (*Rep.* 504e7–505b3).

The answer to the question, what possibilities, capabilities and interests *man as such* possesses and how in principle these interests should be optimized, is known, as Plato believes, only to the λογιστικόν (*Rep.* 441e4–e5, 442c5–c8, 586d4–e3). It alone understands when the faculties of the soul fulfil their role; it knows what state of affairs represents justice in the human soul.

The θυμοειδές has no knowledge of justice, but a δόξα that is what we called *evaluation of the situation*. So to tame any inclination to act rashly, the θυμοειδές shall follow λόγος with regard to the question what one has to fear and not to fear in order to act well (*Rep.* 442 b11–c3); just as correspondingly it is said about the guardians of the city that courage, which is their specific virtue, for them means holding on to the right opinion (ὀρθὴ δόξα) with regard to the question what must be feared and what not in order to keep the city in good order (*Rep.* 429c5–d1, 430b2–b5, 433c7–c8).

So the θυμοειδές is the faculty which concerning particular cases ensures that all the parts – of the soul as well as of the city – fulfil their respective function, that is to say it strives to keep or restore that which it considers just in any given situation. The more its δόξα observes the orders of λόγος, the better a person as a whole is able to act.

Justice then becomes the crucial point of reference to the apparently diverging emotions said to belong to the θυμοειδές. When Socrates says that by means of his θυμοειδές man strives 'wholly' for *honour* (*Rep.* 475b2), he means that man wishes to be justly judged according to his faculties and capabilities (to his ἔργον). If he is underestimated in some aspect and thus wronged, he aspires to restore the honour he deserves – for his ἔργον – and becomes *angry*.

Similarly concerning *envy*: the envied person has a material, physical or intellectual advantage, which he, from the point of view of the envious person, does not deserve. A sudden adjustment of the circumstances consequently leaves the envious person to gloat, as Socrates describes in the *Philebus* (*Phlb.* 48a8–50b6).

Shame in turn is the fear of losing one's honour (that is the respect that one deserves).[25] If shame is focused only on one's own soul, self-disgust can arise, as seen with Leontios. His θυμοειδές – which knows very well that it is improper to look at corpses for the sheer sensation of it – feels ashamed before his λόγος that it is unable to hold down the ἐπιθυμία which ought not to be allowed to take the reins.

Plato's statement that even animals and children possess a θυμοειδές fits in here, too. When a cat presents its owner with a mouse it has caught it does so both thinking that it is necessary to give something to its master (as that would be his due) and claiming acknowledgement of its ability to hunt (it wishes to prove its ἔργον).

A little boy who has been given a ball, at first will return the ball only under fierce protest – not just because the ball feels smooth or looks pretty (for the ἐπιθυμητικόν), but also – as children often state – because it is his 'own'. Animals and children have no theoretical knowledge of justice, but already apply general criteria to particular cases, which means they have an *opinion* about just and unjust and thus use their θυμοειδές.

Of course, diverging desires of the θυμοειδές can appear at the same moment and run into conflict with one another, without our therefore hurrying to propose any additional parts of the soul; for example, when someone in a restaurant is filled with indignation as he has just been served a dreadful lunch, but at the same time is too afraid to express this indignation to the waiter for fear of seeming petulant to the other guests.

Both these desires belong to the θυμοειδές as each aims to preserve justice in a particular case (a just equivalent for the money, a just estimation by one's fellow men); both are desires caused by an opinion about just and unjust, both have only a partial viewpoint. Thus, the θυμοειδές is much in need of a corrective element.

For while the θυμοειδές of the citizens after being trained accordingly acts correctly, it knows the reasons for its acting in this rather than in that way only as more or less profoundly formulated norms. The λογιστικόν on the other hand is required to account for the correctness of laws and conventions, as is stated and clearly shown in the *Laws*. Only in this way is a society, as much as an individual, enabled to survive altered conditions, and to adjust or, indeed, newly formulate their laws and convictions accordingly. To sum up, the λογιστικόν is the creative faculty of the soul, the θυμοειδές is guided by the norms set up by the λογιστικόν.[26]

C. The λογιστικόν
The λογιστικόν aims at the cognition of ἔργα as such (*Rep.* 581b5–b6, 582c8). So it can be said to act as a kind of theoretical reason. Thus the λογιστικόν also knows the soul, its capabilities, its possible desires and the correct hierarchy of goods and pleasures. It therefore has the ability – by weighing the desired goods and pleasures against each other, according to kind, intensity, duration etc. – to work out and propose a decision regarding the best way to act in respect of all parts of the soul. So here, too, Plato is allowed to name knowledge (ἐπιστήμη) as the relevant result of cognition (*Rep.* 442c5–c9).

If the λογιστικόν does not assert itself, man makes mistakes, as for example Achilles, who – angry at being dishonoured by Agamemnon – refuses to listen to the reasonable proposal of his educator Phoinix to accept the new and magnificent retribution from Agamemnon; due to this one-sided view of his θυμοειδές he eventually causes the death of his friend Patroclus.

Odysseus on the other hand, when angry at the disloyal maids and wishing to strike them dead at once, although by doing that he would reveal his identity, knows to suppress this particular desire of the θυμοειδές in favour of a complete revenge and the restoration of his house (*Rep.* 441b3–c2).

This side of the λογιστικόν one could also call 'practical reason'. It is never simply an instrument for calculation, which could be used by the different desires, but itself determines which way to go; neither is it an aloof consciousness, suited only for representation and cut off from action. In either case, acting as theoretical or practical reason, however, the λογιστικόν strives for knowledge and the pleasures entailing it.

5. Summary
Socrates calls his division of the soul in the *Republic* 'just a preliminary explanation' – a more precise one would require us to travel a much longer road. I here offer the following proposals for some first steps of this longer journey.

Plato in the *Republic* presents us with a concept of the soul, the unity of which is based on the cognitive activity of κρίνειν. κρίνειν means a distinguishing at different levels, with or without the help of the body. The main kinds of cognition are perception (that is grasping perceptible qualities), thinking (grasping the ἔργα) and opinion as a combination of both, that is grasping the ἔργον on the occasion of perceptible qualities.

In contrast with the philosophy of consciousness, the concept of the *representing consciousness* does not play a key role in Plato's thinking. Nor is *emotion* separated as a faculty of its own. Its kind and intensity depend on the acts of (mostly unconscious) cognition involved.

'Emotion', then, either refers to an immediate emotion – for example when discerning something by taste that at the same time has a good or bad taste – or an emotion resulting from an imagination of the future which leads to a certain desire, for example anger, shame or envy.

The three parts of the soul as presented in the *Republic* are main divisions of such desires. What at a first glance looks like three arbitrarily composed sets of motivations, obtains its *systematic* foundation – if there is some truth in what I have said – by the division of the three main kinds of cognition.

The ἐπιθυμητικόν strives for pleasures resulting from perception (αἴσθησις), the θυμοειδές for those resulting from the opinion (δόξα) that the ἔργον of a just state or soul is being preserved or restored. Because of this it covers a broad spectrum of human activity. The two lower parts of the soul both tend to take a rather limited perspective, so they are liable to form particular interests. By contrast, the desire of the λογιστικόν looks to those pleasures that result from knowledge of the ἔργα as such (ἐπιστήμη). It is in possession of the knowledge of what most serves each part on its own as well as all three of them as a whole, so that – presupposing a good education – it is able to act as a corrective power in the soul.

Conflicts inside the soul are possible between different desires belonging to the same part of the soul as well as between desires of different parts. So Plato formulates a concept of emotion, striving and acting, based on his theory of cognition, which to my mind at least seems an altogether feasible, systematic attempt at describing the phenomena.

Consequently, *individuality* or *personality* result, as Plato believes, from a rational forming and cultivation of the psychic faculties and capabilities. So in the similes of the soul λογιστικόν appears as 'man inside man'. For instance, in the ninth book of the *Republic*, where λογιστικόν is described as a *man*, who must tame a lion and a chimera; or in the *Phaedrus*, where the charioteer, that is again a *man*, has to control the animal urges of the soul, depicted as two horses.

The λογιστικόν is, as Socrates said, the 'inner man of man' (τοῦ ἀνθρώπου ὁ ἐντὸς ἄνθρωπος, *Rep.* 589a7–b1). So Plato separates an inner self not only from external, but also from internal influences like the desires of the ἐπιθυμητικόν and θυμοειδές, that is to say from what Kant would call the 'empirical self' ('empirisches Ich'). He formulates a kind of categorical concept of self and individuality based on the ability to be aware of and justly consider all aspects important for any given situation. So according to Plato it is not at all an easy matter to become a person with a true personality, but a task for life.

Notes

[1] Hackforth 1952, 75.

[2] Compare for instance Kersting 1999, 162; Bobonich 2001, 214.

[3] For the continuing relevance of this question see for example Görgemanns 1994, 137–8; Blößner 1997, 172–6 and 238–40 and Bobonich 2001, 211–12.

[4] See the survey at Hobbs 2000, 3–4.

[5] The crucial part of the κατά τι for the argument brought out clearly by Woods 1987, 34–5 and Siewert 2001, 333–6.

[6] Compare for instance Stalley 1975, 110–18, who – although he says that the κατά τι in the spinning top example is crucial – thinks that the thirst example has a different structure. Similarly Bobonich 2001, 205, who asserts that Plato supposes two isolated subjects of action, because 'people do opposites in respect of the same thing and in relation to the same thing at the same time'. 'In relation to the same thing' means in relation to the drink, but what should 'in respect of the same thing' then refer to (in the thirst example)?

[7] See *Rep.* 438c1–c4 (in the middle of his excursus on relations) as proof for his use of the preposition πρός for the meaning 'in relation to'.

[8] The *locus classicus* for the reconciliation of a contradiction by the πρός τι can be found at *Phd.* 102a10–d4. There Simmias seems to be taller and smaller at the same moment. This problem cannot be solved by the assumption that there are two Simmiases, but instead it is said that the same Simmias is taller in respect of his height compared to the height of Socrates (who is outside of him) and smaller in relation to Phaedo's height.

[9] In the *Republic*, apart from the specific qualities, the cognitive content 'finger', too, is called a result of perception. As shown below, in order to obtain this result it is, strictly speaking, necessary that thinking is involved, too; yet for the example in the *Republic* that does not matter. That already in the *Republic* Plato assumes that this kind of cognition is not possible without the help of thinking, is perhaps hinted at by the remark that when hearing the sentence 'This is a finger' only the 'soul of the many' (τῶν πολλῶν ἡ ψυχή) is not compelled to go on asking what 'finger' really means (*Rep.* 523d3–d5; for, one and the same thing consisting of bones and flesh is always finger and not finger. Not finger, for instance, insofar as it is 10 cm long while it is not a specific property of 'finger' to have the length of 10 cm, and there are other things, too, which are 10 cm long, like noses and ears).

[10] See also *Phd.* 65b9–b11: It is not the body which perceives, but the soul upon perceiving tries to grasp the truth *by means of* the body (ἡ ψυχή...μετὰ τοῦ σώματος ἐπιχειρῇ τι σκοπεῖν).

[11] I borrow them especially from the works of Arbogast Schmitt; compare now Schmitt 2003, with regard to tripartition esp. 283–340. For an extended reconstruction of Platonic psychology see also Büttner 2000, 18–130.

[12] Concerning the problems of the application of Cartesian or Kantian concepts to ancient thought see also Gill 2001, 1–18 (on principle) and 240–60 (about Plato's psychology). In Greek thought something similar to the Cartesian dichotomy of 'conscious' and 'unconscious' started to have an impact on the philosophical discourse more than 50 years after Plato's death. Then the Stoics postulated a world radically divided into two parts in which freedom and necessity are opponents. Freedom there is found in an act of assent (συγκατάθεσις) to already received, almost mechanically given concepts (φαντασίαι), an idea similar to that of a representing consciousness in modern thought – and at the same time a completely non-platonic one.

[13] This is the tenor of Book 9 of the *Republic*; compare also *Laws* 636d7–e3, 662b2–b4.

[14] Plato uses a number of terms to refer to 'the intelligible'; besides νοητόν and ἔργον also e.g. δύναμις, ἀρετή or εἶδος, *Grg.* 503e2 and 504d5, *Rep.* 352d8–353e6, 477c1–d6, 596b7, *Cra.* 389a6–b4. In the text, I shall use ἔργον, 'specific function', as denoting the intelligible content, even though the term ἔργον itself is not employed by Plato in this sense in the passages of the *Philebus* and the *Theaetetus* referred to above.

[15] See also *Sph.* 264a10, where δόξα is called the 'result of a conversation inside the soul' (διανοίας ἀποτελεύτησις).

[16] Compare also *Tht.* 201b5–c7, where κρίνειν refers to a propositional judgement, discernible by the metaphor of the judge.

[17] The memories used by imagination are the result of perception and thinking, compare *Tht.* 191d6, *Phlb.* 34b10–b11.

[18] προχαίρειν is an imagination as an anticipated δόξα, also called προσδοκία or ἐλπίς as δόξα μελλόντων, *Phlb.* 32b9–c1, *Laws* 644c9–c10.

[19] The expressions οἴεσθαι and ἡγεῖσθαι here are used synonymously with δοξάζειν in the sense of judging situations. For we are concerned with a particular action that is judged according to the common criterion of justice (the term δόξα for the same definition of justice is found at *Laws* 717d5–d6).

[20] Concerning this topic see recently esp. Carone 2001, 116–43, and Gardner 2002, 198–201.

[21] See the various textual references in the articles of Moline 1978 and Kahn 1987–8.

[22] The assumption that the ἐπιθυμητικόν must always be suppressed by force (for instance Kersting 1999, 163–4), is simply wrong. On the contrary, Plato's plan of education in the *Republic* envisages for all citizens, including the later philosophers, that the foundation-stone is to be laid already in their youth – by benevolent persuasion, e.g. by means of figurative, poetical language – for the growth of harmony between the bodily desires and the later – or even never – independently developed rational striving. A convincing description of this co-operation between the parts of the soul is to be found in Irwin 1995, 220–2: there the rational part is able to demonstrate to the desires how in the long run a calculation of pleasures can be of interest to them, too. Thus the ἐπιθυμητικόν can become accustomed to long-term planning, even though the λογιστικόν does not aim at optimizing bodily pleasures, but has other, higher reasons for the proposed self-control. Yet the ἐπιθυμητικόν goes along with the λογιστικόν insofar as its own nature (striving for bodily pleasure) permits.

[23] Unlike the philosopher who not only trains in order to strengthen the body, but also to effect the best conditions for intellectual activity, *Tim.* 87c1–88c6.
[24] For this explanation see in detail Cooper 1984, 10–16.
[25] Compare also *Laws* 646e10–647a2: φοβούμεθα...δόξαν, ἡγούμενοι δοξάζεσθαι κακοί.
[26] Regarding this relation see also Hobbs 2000, 56–9.

Bibliography
Blößner, N.
   1997   *Dialogform und Argument. Studien zu Platons 'Politeia'*, Stuttgart.
Bobonich, C.
   2001   '*Akrasia* and agency in Plato's *Laws* and *Republic*', in E. Wagner (ed.) *Essays on Plato's Psychology*, Lanham, 203–37.
Büttner, S.
   2000   *Die Literaturtheorie bei Platon und ihre anthropologische Begründung*, Tübingen and Basel.
Carone, G.R.
   2001   '*Akrasia* in the *Republic*: does Plato change his mind?', *Oxford Studies in Ancient Philosophy* 20, 107–48.
Cooper, J.M.
   1984   'Plato's theory of human motivation', *Philosophy Quarterly* 1, 3–21.
Gardner, T.
   2002   'Socrates and Plato on the possibility of *Akrasia*', *The Southern Journal of Philosophy* 60, 191–210.
Gill, C.
   2002   *Personality in Greek Epic, Tragedy, and Philosophy. The self in dialogue*, Oxford.
Görgemanns, H.
   1994   *Platon*, Heidelberg.
Hackforth, R.
   1952   *Plato's* Phaedrus. *Translation with introduction and commentary*, Cambridge.
Hobbs, A.
   2000   *Plato and the Hero: Courage, manliness, and the impersonal good*, Cambridge.
Irwin, T.
   1995   *Plato's Ethics*, Oxford.
Kahn, C.H.
   1987–8   'Plato's theory of desire', *Review of Metaphysics* 41, 77–103.
Kersting, W.
   1999   *Platons Staat*, Darmstadt.
Lesses, G.
   1987   'Weakness, reason and the divided soul in Plato's *Republic*', *History of Philosophy Quarterly* 4, 147–61.

Moline, J.
- 1978 'Plato on the complexity of the psyche', *Archiv für Geschichte der Philosophie* 60, 1–26.

Schmitt, A.
- 2003 *Die Moderne und Platon*, Stuttgart and Weimar.

Siewert, C.
- 2001 'Plato's division of reason and appetite', *History of Philosophy Quarterly* 18, 329–52.

Stalley, R.
- 1975 'Plato's argument for the division of the reasoning and appetitive elements in the soul', *Phronesis* 20, 110–28.

Woods, M.
- 1987 'Plato's division of the soul', *Proceedings of the British Academy* 73, 23–48.

5

HAPPINESS AND THE NATURE OF PHILOSOPHER-KINGS

Antony Hatzistavrou

My aim in this chapter is to show that the philosopher-kings in Plato's *Republic* do not sacrifice their happiness when they assume the task of ruling the perfect city. My argument is, in a nutshell, the following. According to Plato, in the perfect city one receives the type of happiness most appropriate for one's developed personality. The developed personality of the philosopher-kings is defined by two fundamental character-traits: a strong tendency towards philosophical knowledge and a stable desire to benefit the city. The mixed life of philosophy and political activity is the best life for the philosopher-kings because it satisfies both these fundamental character-traits. A purely contemplative life would have left their desire to benefit the city unfulfilled and would have reduced their happiness.

Central to my argument is the attribution to Plato of an implicit distinction between two senses of 'the nature of man' (ἡ τοῦ ἀνθρώπου φύσις, 395a4). I try to show that when Plato speaks of the φύσις of a particular individual he is referring to either of two things: (a) a cluster of a particular person's natural capacities which are to be developed by a process of education, or (b) the developed personality of a particular person, i.e. basic character-traits this person has acquired after a process of education. So, I ascribe to Plato the thesis that the mixed life of philosophy and political activity accords best to their *nature* (where 'nature' is understood in the sense of 'developed personality').

I understand the question of whether the philosopher-kings sacrifice their interest in the perfect city as equivalent to the question of whether the life of the philosopher-kings is the happiest form of life *for them*, i.e. given the sort of persons they are. This question is different from the question of whether the mixed life is the happiest possible form of human life, that is, whether there is a life which is attainable by humans and better than the life suited for the philosopher-kings. Although in this chapter I will deal primarily with the first question, I will conclude the paper with some thoughts in support of the thesis that for Plato the mixed life is the happiest possible form of life attainable by humans.

1. The implications of the possible sacrifice of the philosopher-kings' interest for Plato's defence of justice

I will begin by examining the problems which a possible sacrifice of the interests of the philosopher-kings creates for Plato's defence of justice in the *Republic*.[1] An account of some basic features of Plato's defence of justice will help us appreciate the importance of these problems. According to Plato, the philosopher-kings, after a long process of education, will reach a state of psychic harmony, which will enable them to contemplate the Forms. This state of psychic harmony is equated with justice (435a1–c2). One attains psychic harmony when each of the three parts of one's soul, the reasoning part, the spirit and the appetitive part, perform their proper natural functions. A proper natural function of the reasoning part is to rule (441e4), of the spirit to assist the reasoning part's function (441e5–6) and of the appetitive part to obey the reasoning part (442a4–b3, 441b1–5). The reasoning part does not simply have an instrumental role. It does not function like the Humean reason which chooses the best means for the ends determined by the desires. For the reasoning part to rule is for the whole soul to pursue the values of the reasoning part; this means that a proper natural function of the reasoning part is to regulate and co-ordinate the mental states of the agent (desires, beliefs, emotions) in a way which will enable the agent to attain the ends the reasoning part determines. The ends or the values of the reasoning part are cognitive achievements, i.e. the attainment of knowledge and truth. Knowledge and truth are attained when the agent gains understanding of the Forms and especially of the Form of the Good. Following Kraut, I will call this type of non-instrumental rule of reason 'normative'.[2]

To reach this normative rule of reason, it is necessary for one to have supreme intellectual and conative (i.e. non-cognitive, emotional) capacities by nature (487a2–5). In addition, one should normally go through the process of education that is available only in the perfect city Plato describes in the *Republic*. A substantial part of this education aims at the psychological assimilation to just agents and the habituation in the performance of ordinary just actions (395b8–d3). Psychological assimilation to virtuous models depicted in various forms of art (401b1–402a4)[3] and performance of ordinary just actions (443c9–444a2 and 444c10–d1) are considered by Plato to generate psychic harmony, that is, the state of the soul in which the reasoning part normatively rules.[4] The possession of psychic harmony is considered analogous to the possession of bodily health (444d8–e3).

The analogy of psychic harmony to health constitutes an initial proof that justice pays (444e7–445b7).[5] It also responds to Adeimantus' and Glaucon's challenges in Book 2 of the *Republic* that Socrates shows that justice by itself (and not only its consequences) can make one happy. It suggests that psychic harmony is a primary constituent of happiness.[6]

Plato seems also to hold that, once one has attained the normative rule of the reasoning part, one need not perform any ordinary just actions to retain the normative rule of reason in one's soul. Plato claims that contemplation of the Forms is sufficient for the preservation of the normative rule of the reasoning part. At 500b9–d2 he suggests that one tries to assimilate (μιμεῖσθαι, ἀφομοιοῦσθαι) psychologically to the character of whatever one admires. The philosopher admires the Forms and thus tries to assimilate psychologically to their inner harmony. In this way he becomes as divine and ordered (κόσμιος) as a human being can be.[7]

Before gaining an understanding of the Forms, the philosopher-kings had to perform ordinary just actions and assimilate psychologically to virtuous agents in order to achieve psychic harmony. But, once they achieve psychic harmony and are able to contemplate the Forms, they come to the possession of other means for preserving their psychic harmony. So, we may credit Plato with the following two theses:

(T1) the performance of ordinary just actions and the psychological assimilation to virtuous agents are necessary for and instrumental to one's initial attainment of psychic harmony, and

(T2) the performance of ordinary just actions and the psychological assimilation to virtuous agents are not necessary for the preservation of psychic harmony once one has reached understanding of the Forms.

However, the argument of the *Republic* has an extra twist. Plato has identified the state of psychic harmony, within which the reasoning part normatively rules, with justice *proper*. He claims that 'justice' primarily applies to the agent's inner state of psychic harmony and only derivatively to the actions which preserve or produce this inner state (i.e. ordinary just actions) (443c9–444a2). In the recent literature, justice as a state of the soul is called 'Platonic' justice, and Plato is accused of equivocating in his defence of justice in the *Republic* between Platonic and ordinary or 'vulgar' justice.[8] I will not discuss this charge of equivocation. I am only concerned here with pointing out that (T1) and (T2) are equivalent respectively to:

(T1*) the performance of ordinary just actions and the psychological assimilation to virtuous agents are necessary for and instrumental to the attainment of Platonic justice by the philosopher-kings, and

(T2*) the performance of just actions and the psychological assimilation to virtuous agents are not necessary for the preservation of Platonic justice once the philosopher-kings have reached understanding of the Forms.

A further consideration worth pondering on is that for Plato psychic harmony is not the sole constituent of happiness. Plato allows that goods other than the possession of psychic harmony contribute to the philosopher-kings' overall happiness. He claims, for example, that the philosopher-kings will live a happy life because there will be no internal strife[9] in the perfect city and they will escape all the burdens associated with rearing a family and maintaining a household (465b5–d1). As I shall argue, there is another important constituent of happiness, the satisfaction of those desires which are compatible with (though not necessary for) psychic harmony.[10]

After all, if the possession of psychic harmony were the sole constituent of happiness, the question whether the philosopher-kings sacrifice their happiness upon assuming the task of ruling would not have arisen in the first place. It is clear that the philosopher-kings retain their psychic harmony while ruling, since they are able to contemplate the Forms for most of their time (520d8–9 and 540b1). So, if their happiness were reduced by ruling, this would not be due to the fact that their psychic harmony was lost, but rather due to the loss of other constituents of happiness. It is likely, for example, that their happiness would be affected in the following way: they would experience the unpleasantness of looking back in the darkness of human affairs (516e1–517e2) and of exercising the craft of ruling (see ἐπιταλαιπωροῦντας, 540b3).[11]

Finally, Plato considers the demand that the philosopher-kings rule the city a just demand (δίκαια γὰρ δὴ δικαίοις ἐπιτάξομεν, 520a7–8). He believes that it is just for the philosopher-kings to reciprocate for the education they received from the city (520a5–c1). The demand to rule stems from the principle of reciprocity of benefits which governs the distribution of goods in the perfect city (519e3–520a4) and thus becomes a fundamental principle of ordinary justice.

So, given the importance Plato attributes to the principle of reciprocity of benefits as a principle of ordinary justice, a person who would fail to fulfil it would have been grossly ordinarily unjust. The crime of the philosopher-king who would escape the burden of ruling in particular would be quite severe in terms of ordinary justice. That person would have exploited the whole city to attain the primary constituent of his happiness, psychic harmony, neglecting his obligations to the city.

We are now in a position to assess the most important implications of the possible sacrifice of the philosopher-kings' interest for Plato's defence of justice in the *Republic*.

(1) The philosopher-king would not be as happy as he could have been. He would have been happier if he had escaped the burden of ruling. And, since the philosopher-king is the maximally just person (δικαιοτάτῳ, 545a5), for Plato, being maximally just does not entail being as happy as one can be.

(2) Since the maximally just person is identified with the philosopher-king who engages in public affairs, a maximally just person is both Platonically just and grossly ordinarily just. By contrast, the philosopher in the perfect city who escapes the burden of ruling is grossly ordinarily unjust. So, if the happiest person is a philosopher who escapes the burden of ruling, then, for Plato, being maximally happy entails being grossly ordinarily unjust. This implication would be fatal for Plato's defence of justice: Plato would have identified a type of gross ordinary injustice which actually pays. This would have been a clear failure to respond to Thrasymachus', Adeimantus' and Glaucon's challenges to show that being ordinarily just benefits the agent.[12]

(3) If the philosopher who escapes the burden of ruling were the happiest person, then he would have been Platonically just, i.e. he would have psychic harmony, since he would have been able to contemplate the Forms. But, as we have seen, he would also have been grossly ordinarily unjust. So, Plato would accept that being Platonically just is compatible with being grossly ordinarily unjust. In this case, the gap between Platonic justice and ordinary justice would have been irreconcilable and Plato could not be extricated from the objection that he commits the fallacy of equivocation.

(4) The injustice of the philosopher-king who escapes the burden of ruling could be considered a paradigmatic case of πλεονεξία. So, if the philosopher-kings who engage in public affairs sacrificed their interests, Plato would have accepted what Thrasymachus was actually arguing for and Socrates was trying to refute, namely, that πλεονεξία pays. The disagreement between Thrasymachus and Plato would be about the type of things a grossly unjust person would want to have more than is his due. Thrasymachus would claim that these would be exclusively material goods while Plato would claim that these would be primarily intellectual achievements. But they would both agree that having more than is one's due pays.

So, if the philosopher-kings sacrificed their interest when ruling, then, instead of defending ordinary justice, Plato would have produced a case in which gross ordinary injustice pays. Plato would have defended only Platonic justice and shown that it pays for one to be Platonically just. But he would also have shown that it is possible to be both Platonically just and grossly ordinarily unjust and that in some cases it pays to be so. He would have failed to establish a strong link between happiness and ordinary justice, and the gap between Platonic justice and ordinary justice would have been unbridgeable.

2. Some attempts to save the coherence of Plato's defence of justice

There have been attempts to show that the philosopher-kings do not actually sacrifice their interest when ruling. The interpretations advanced mainly deal with two issues. On the one hand, they try to explain why a life which includes some political activity is better than a life which is totally devoted to contemplation of the Forms. This is an issue about the type of life which is best for the philosopher-kings. On the other hand, they try to explain why the philosopher-kings choose a life of both contemplation and political activity over a life of uninterrupted contemplation. This is an issue about the motivation of the philosopher-kings.[13]

We may distinguish three explanations of why the mixed life of contemplation and political activity is the best life (BL) for the philosopher-kings.

(BL1) The mixed life is the best life for the philosopher-kings because only in the mixed life do the philosopher-kings avoid the suffering associated with being ruled by worse people and enjoy a life of political stability.

(BL2) The mixed life is the best life for the philosopher-kings because only in the mixed life do the philosopher-kings satisfy a strong tendency of theirs to *express*[14] the Form of the Good in social arrangements.

(BL3) The mixed life is the best life for the philosopher-kings because only in the mixed life do the philosopher-kings satisfy a strong tendency of theirs to *imitate* the rational order of the Forms in social arrangements.

We may distinguish three corresponding theses about what motivates the philosopher-kings to assume the task of ruling.

(M1) The philosopher-kings are motivated by considerations of self-interest.

(M2) The philosopher-kings are motivated by a desire to *express* the Form of the Good in social arrangements.

(M3) The philosopher-kings are motivated by a desire to *imitate* the rational order of the Forms in social arrangements.[15]

BL1 faces the following objection. Since there will be a number of philosopher-kings to rule the city, if one of them escapes the burden of ruling, the stability of the regime of the perfect city will not be threatened. The free-rider would possess the greatest happiness: he would have psychic harmony, enjoy the political stability of the perfect city and avoid the burden of ruling. M1 is equally unacceptable, since Plato claims at 520d6–e1 that the philosopher-kings will choose to rule, not out of considerations of self-interest, but because they are just (i.e. ordinarily just, as I shall argue in section 4 of this chapter).[16]

There are no grounds for crediting Plato with M2.[17] First, nowhere does Plato ascribe to the rational part of the soul a desire to *instantiate the Form of the Good*. Plato claims that every soul desires to know what the Form of the Good is (505d11–506a3) and that the philosopher-kings need to have knowledge of the Form of the Good to keep the perfect city in order (506a9–b1). But a desire to *know* the Form of the Good is different from a desire to *instantiate* it. And the fact that one needs knowledge of the Form of the Good for the successful performance of a certain task does not entail that one desires to perform this task because one desires to instantiate the Form of the Good. Secondly, if the desire to instantiate the Form of the Good in society were somehow generated by the knowledge of the Form of the Good, one would expect everyone who has grasped the Form of the Good to have the relevant desire. But it is clear that Plato allows for the possibility that some may have seen the Form of the Good but feel no desire to instantiate it in society. He thinks that these people (who obviously do not follow the training prescribed in the perfect city, 519c8–d2) are totally inappropriate for the task of ruling precisely because they *will not want* to engage in human affairs (ἑκόντες εἶναι οὐ πράξουσιν) being under the impression that they have already reached the Islands of the Blest (519c4–6).[18] Plato cannot consider their lack of the relevant desire a psychological anomaly. Since he assumes that these people have reached an understanding of the Form of the Good (519c10), he must believe that they possess psychic harmony and are able to have their desires rightly regulated. Finally, if the philosopher-kings desired to rule because they desired to instantiate the Form of the Good, they would consider ruling a commendable activity. But this is not at all how they conceive of ruling. Plato explicitly says that they do not think of it as something 'fine' (οὐχ ὡς καλόν τι, 540b4).

Ascribing M3 to Plato is equally problematic. The primary evidence for it is considered to be Plato's claim at 500b8–d3 that it is impossible for those who have reached understanding of the Forms (i.e. for any philosophers and thus for the philosopher-kings) not to imitate the rational structure of the Forms, since it is impossible for one not to imitate what one is in touch with and admires. But a careful reading of this passage reveals that Plato stops short of asserting that the philosopher desires to imitate the rational order of the Forms *in social arrangements*. Plato claims that those who admire the rational order of the Forms become *themselves* as divine (θείῳ) and orderly (κοσμίῳ) as is humanly possible (500c9–d3). And it becomes clear in the immediate sequence of the argument (500d4–9) that *mimesis* of the rational order of the Forms *does not* involve any desire on the part of the philosophers to either make their fellow-citizens as divine and orderly as possible or create just social institutions. Plato claims that, if there is a requirement for the philosopher (αὐτῷ ἀνάγκη γένηται, d4) to put the rational pattern *not only into himself* (μὴ μόνον ἑαυτὸν πλάττειν, d6), but into men's public and private life (εἰς ἀνθρώπων ἤθη καὶ ἰδίᾳ καὶ δημοσίᾳ, d5), he will be the best craftsman of temperance and of justice and of the demotic virtue (δημοτικῆς ἀρετῆς, d8) in its entirety. Here, Plato clearly refers to the philosopher-king and not to any philosopher, that is, a philosopher living in a corrupted city, since there is no requirement for the latter to engage in politics. And it is equally clear that he takes what is involved in the philosopher-king's psychological assimilation to the just order of the Forms to be exactly the same as what is involved in the *mimesis* of the rational order of the Forms by any philosopher. The expression 'not only into himself' suggests that what the previous argument at 500b7–d3 established was that the philosophers' *mimesis* of the rational order of the Forms involved putting the rational order only into themselves and not into their fellow citizens. Similarly, the contrast between ἑαυτὸν πλάττειν and εἰς ἀνθρώπων ἤθη καὶ ἰδίᾳ καὶ δημοσίᾳ suggests that what the previous argument established was that the philosophers' *mimesis* did not involve the creation of the rational order *in social arrangements*. So, what Plato seems to claim is that the contemplation of the Forms creates an impulse in all philosophers, that is both those living in corrupted cities and the philosopher-kings, to become themselves as Platonically just as is humanly possible but not a desire to advance justice in the city. Thus, the imitationist interpretation has failed to produce evidence that there exists in the philosopher-kings a desire to imitate the rational order of the Forms in society.

I do not have space here to discuss in detail Kraut's elaborate defence of what I have labelled the 'imitationist' interpretation. I will only comment on his central thesis that the Forms are somehow models of human conduct and that if one does not imitate them, one therefore rejects an essential property of them. Kraut writes: '…[Plato] also believes that if one understands what justice is but none the less violates fair requirements in human relationships, one is by that very fact *rejecting* the forms as models of human behaviour'.[19] I doubt, however, that the Forms are for Plato models of conduct, at least in a sense that supports Kraut's thesis. Plato makes clear at 443c9–444a2 that justice is primarily a property of the soul and that it applies only derivatively to actions: an action is 'just' if it preserves (σῴζῃ) and helps to complete (συναπεργάζηται) justice in the soul (443e6). The Form of justice is thus primarily instantiated in human souls and not in human actions. Whether an action X of an agent Y is just is determined by whether by doing X justice is preserved in Y's soul. Justice is preserved in Y's soul if the latter continues to instantiate the Form of justice. It is in this derivative sense that the Form of justice may be considered by Plato a standard of conduct. Now

Kraut presumably assumes that the Form of justice is not instantiated only by souls but also by other structural unities such as political communities. I do not dispute this assumption but I want to question what Kraut seems to infer from it. Kraut seems to infer that an action of a particular individual which preserves justice in a political community is *therefore* just and the agent should perform it. But the inference is not valid. Plato may accept that cities may instantiate the Form of justice and nevertheless hold that the sole criterion of whether a particular *action of an individual citizen* is just is whether it preserves justice in the soul of the agent (and *not* whether it preserves justice in the city). The preservation of justice in the city might be a criterion for the justness of *collective* actions in general or collective actions of *one class* of citizens[20] (after all Plato admits that what matters for the preservation of the city is that the guardians and not the members of the working class do their job properly, 421a2–8). So, it seems that for Plato the Form of justice can be a model for conduct in a very specific derivative sense: that a particular person's action is just because it preserves justice in the soul of that person which is an instantiation of the Form of justice. It follows from this that if one refuses to perform an action which preserves justice in the city that in itself does not entail that one is refusing to imitate the Forms. Neither is one rejecting them as a model of human conduct, since what makes them models of conduct is not the fact that they preserve justice in the city (but rather that they preserve justice in the soul).

If my argument is correct, nothing follows from the fact that a particular person's action preserves justice in the city about the justness of this action and about the reasons the agent has to do it. One could further ask whether the return to the cave satisfies the proper criterion of being a 'just' action, i.e. whether it preserves and helps to complete justice in the soul of the philosopher-kings. (If it does, then on the basis of my argument in the previous paragraph, the return to the cave could be considered an act of imitation of the Forms in the sense required by Kraut's interpretation.) I think, however, that the return to the cave does not satisfy the criterion of justness of a particular person's action described at 443c9–444a2. I think that the use of σῴζειν and συναπεργάζεσθαι at 443e6 suggests that for Plato the causal relation between a specific action and justice in the soul must be very strong: in order for the action to be 'just' its performance should be *necessary* (in the specific context) for the preservation of justice in the soul (that is, unless the action is performed the soul of the agent will lose its psychic harmony). But, as what Plato says at 500b8–d9 makes clear, the philosopher-kings have another way of preserving justice in their soul, i.e. contemplation of the Forms. So, the return to the cave is not for an individual philosopher-king a 'just' action according to the proper Platonic standards of justness for a particular person's actions. An agent who instantiates the Form of justice in his soul (a Platonically just individual) is not required to return to the cave in order to preserve justice in his soul or, as Kraut would put it, in order to avoid rejecting the Forms as a model of conduct.[21]

As my objections against ascribing to Plato either of M2 or M3 must have made clear, I do not think that for Plato any desire whose fulfilment requires political activity is generated by the knowledge of the Forms. If this is so, we have no grounds for crediting Plato with either BL2 or BL3. In the rest of the paper, I shall argue that the philosopher-kings have a desire which can only be fulfilled by their engaging in political activity and which is the result of the education they have received in the perfect city *prior* to their attaining knowledge of the Forms. This desire is developed only in those philosophers who have been trained in the perfect city and not in philosophers living in corrupted cities. It is the desire to benefit the city. This desire has become a fundamental trait of their personality through the extensive and intensive education they receive in the perfect city. Living a mixed life of both contemplation and political activity is for the philosopher-kings the greatest happiness suitable for their personality. By assuming the task of ruling, the philosopher-kings do not sacrifice their happiness but attain instead the highest degree of happiness appropriate for them. So, I will argue that for Plato:

(BL4) the mixed life is the best life for the philosopher-kings because only in the mixed life do the philosopher-kings satisfy a strong tendency of theirs to benefit the city, and

(M4) the philosopher-kings are motivated by a desire to benefit the city.

3. The basic principles of the distribution of happiness in the perfect city

At the beginning of Book 4, Adeimantus raises the objection that in the perfect city the guardians (that is both the philosopher-kings and the auxiliaries) are not very happy (419a1–3). He claims that, in contrast to rulers in other cities, the guardians do not seem to enjoy possession of pieces of land and luxurious property or other goods which are commonly associated with happiness (419a4–420a1). Socrates responds as follows. He initially claims that (a) this objection is irrelevant since his aim as a founder of a city has been to try to make the whole city most happy and not only a class in it (420b4–8). But he then argues that (b) he distributes to the philosopher-kings the kind of happiness that will not make them something other than guardians of the city (420b5–e1). And that in general (c) in the perfect city 'every class participates in happiness in the way its nature allows for' (421c4–6).[22]

Despite his initial dismissal of Adeimantus' objection as a red-herring, in the end Socrates confronts the objection. His response is that the philosopher-kings are happy in the perfect city because the members of each class get in the perfect city the type of happiness their nature is suited for (c). And he relates the 'nature' of the philosopher-kings with the cluster of personal traits which make them appropriate for the task of ruling the perfect city (b).

The implication of Adeimantus' challenge is that in the perfect city the philosopher-kings are less happy than they could have been.[23] Socrates' answer is that they are as happy as they possibly can be *qua* rulers and guardians of the city. To understand Socrates' argument, I shall analyse further the import of (b) and (c): (c) clearly describes a *principle of distribution of happiness*.

(H1) Each class receives the type of happiness its nature is suited for. Since there is substantial difference in the kind of lives each of the three classes will live in the perfect city (for example, only the members of the working class will have a family life and some property, or only the philosopher-kings will engage in contemplation of the Forms), there must be different types of happiness. So, Plato also holds a *principle of differentiation of happiness*.

(H2) Each class is naturally suited for a different type of happiness. Further, the fact that Plato relates the 'nature of a class' to a particular type of happiness as opposed to the 'nature of a particular individual' suggests that by 'nature' he means, not every natural individual peculiarity, but those personal traits on the basis of which an individual belongs to a certain class. I shall say that Plato supports a *principle of class-dependence of happiness*.

(H3) A particular person's happiness depends on those personal traits which justify that person's inclusion in a certain class of the perfect city.

Insofar as the happiness of the philosopher-kings (PKH) in the perfect city is concerned, these principles should be read as follows.

(PKH1) The philosopher-kings receive the type of happiness their nature is suited for.

(PKH2) The happiness the philosopher-kings receive is different from the happiness of the auxiliaries and the happiness of the members of the working class.

(PKH3) The happiness of a particular philosopher-king depends on those personal traits which justify his inclusion in the class of the philosopher-kings.

To appreciate the import of these principles one needs to understand what Plato takes to be the 'nature' (φύσις) of the philosopher-kings. I attempt to elucidate Plato's account of the nature of the philosopher-kings in the following section.

4. The nature (φύσις) of the philosopher-kings

The Greek term φύσις normally denotes the natural order of things (as opposed to the order of things which obtains 'artificially', say, after human intervention as in the νόμος – φύσις debate). However, in some passages of the *Republic* Plato uses the term φύσις in a more specialized sense to denote the nature of man. φύσις in this specialized sense has wide applications ranging from human nature in general to the nature of a particular person. So, for example, Plato speaks at 395b3–5 of human nature in general (ἡ τοῦ ἀνθρώπου φύσις) claiming that it should be understood to be divided into smaller modules. He also speaks of the nature of particular individuals assuming that we differ substantially in our nature (πρῶτον μὲν ἡμῶν ἕκαστος οὐ πάνυ ὅμοιος ἑκάστῳ, ἀλλὰ διαφέρων τὴν φύσιν) and that for this reason each one of us can perform different tasks (370a7–b2). It is on the basis of our natural individual differences that he commends his principle of division of labour which becomes the kernel of his account of political justice (ἕνα ἕκαστον ἓν δέοι ἐπιτηδεύειν τῶν περὶ τὴν πόλιν, εἰς ὃ αὐτοῦ ἡ φύσις ἐπιτηδειοτάτη πεφυκυῖα εἴη, 433a5–6).

In this section I shall focus on Plato's account of the nature of the philosopher-kings (where 'nature' should be understood in the specialized sense I illustrated above). I shall argue that, in addition to the distinction between φύσις as the natural order of things and φύσις as the nature of man, Plato makes a further implicit distinction between φύσις as a particular person's natural abilities and φύσις as a particular person's developed personality. I will try to show how the latter distinction helps us to construct a solution to the problem whether the philosopher-kings sacrifice their interests when they assume the task of ruling.

Plato considers the philosopher-kings' nature to be completed (τελειωθεῖσι) through education (487a2–8) and warns that, if their nature receives bad training, it will turn out to be extremely bad, while if it receives appropriate training it will flourish in virtue (491d1–492a5). 'Nature' in this sense seems to signify a cluster of natural abilities and aptitudes which require appropriate training to become stable traits of character. As I shall explain, some of these natural abilities and aptitudes in the philosopher-kings' nature are universal human faculties, like the *mimetic* faculty (μίμησις). Others are special to the philosopher-kings, like the natural ability of strong memory or the natural aptitude for truth.

Plato takes human beings to be by nature mimetic creatures, that is, capable of a spectrum of mimetic experiences ranging from mere behavioural imitation (ὅμοια ποιεῖν, 388a2) to psychological assimilation (ἀφομοιοῦν ἑαυτούς, 396a4) which is involved primarily in reciting poetry, in enacting tragic roles and also in listening to music.[24] Plato's theory of education described in Books 3 and 4 of the *Republic* is built on this mimetic dimension of human nature. Plato stipulates that the future guardians of the city, if they are to fulfil properly their role as guardians of the city, should imitate only virtuous acts and psychologically assimilate only to virtuous characters and virtuous ways of life (395b8–d1; cf. 401b1–4). On the one hand, Plato believes that the behavioural imitation of models of virtuous agents leads to the performance of virtuous acts which in turn generates psychic harmony (443c9–444a2 and 444c10–d1). What is more, it is his understanding that through a process of psychological assimilation to virtuous characters, during which the agent imaginatively experiences these people's emotions, desires and perceptions of life, his soul will be moulded so as equally to achieve inner harmony. The results of this process of psychological assimilation are best exemplified in Plato's account of the effect of music, which for him is one of the mimetic arts (398b–400e), on the soul. According to Plato, 'musical rhythm and harmony enter deep into the soul and get hold of it most powerfully and bring to it good shape' (401d6–8).[25]

There are also some natural abilities and aptitudes which are special to the philosopher-kings and differentiate their nature from the nature of the members of the other classes. In Book 6 (485b10–487a8) Plato provides an account of the basic elements of the nature of the philosopher-kings. He claims that they have abilities for quick learning and for strong memory (486c1–d3). They also share a strong desire for truth and knowledge (486c3–d5), a distaste for the pleasures of the body (486d10–e5) and a tendency to be high-minded (μεγαλοπρέπεια, 486a8), an ability to rise above the fear of death (486b1–5), a tendency to be sociable and gentle (486b6–13) and an inclination towards measure and grace (486d7–12). These natural abilities need to be developed through the appropriate education in the perfect city (487a7–8).

The abilities of quick learning and strong memory can be classified as purely cognitive or intellectual abilities. The rest of the abilities mentioned are conative or a mixture of conative and cognitive abilities. The philosopher-kings' tendency to overcome the fear of death seems to be a tendency of the spirited part of their soul and is probably the most paradigmatic of its wild tendencies (375a5–b10) which need to be softened by the appropriate application of gymnastics and music (410d6–10). The other tendencies belong to the tendencies of the philosophic part of the soul. These are characterized by gentleness (375c1–e5) and the need to be equally cultivated by the correct mixture of gymnastics and music (410e1–3).

However, Plato also uses the term 'nature' to denote not simply the philosopher-kings' natural abilities and aptitudes but basic traits of their developed personality. At 395d1–3 Socrates asks: 'Haven't you noticed that imitations (μιμήσεις), if they continue from early childhood onwards, turn into habits and nature (φύσιν) of one's bodily gestures and one's tone of voice and one's state of mind?' In this passage Plato uses 'nature' to refer not to one's natural abilities which need to be developed by appropriate education but to the *outcome* of that education. 'Nature' here denotes some fundamental personality traits a person has acquired as a result of (a broadly moral) education which involves mimetic activities as its predominant feature.

'Nature$_1$', as natural abilities and aptitudes, and 'nature$_2$', as developed personality-traits, are compatible. One is in principle able to develop personality-traits because one has a *general* natural$_1$ mimetic ability. Further, one may not develop specific personality-traits, say a strong desire for learning and knowledge, unless one has a relevant natural$_1$ aptitude, for example, a natural$_1$ desire for truth. But it is not the case that the personality-traits one has are restricted to one's developed specific natural$_1$ abilities or aptitudes. First, inappropriate training impedes the development of one's specific natural$_1$ abilities or aptitudes. For example, someone who has the natural$_1$ abilities to become a real philosopher may fail to fulfil his potential outside the perfect city. That person will have the same nature$_1$ as a philosopher-king but different nature$_2$. One major difference between his nature$_2$ and the philosopher-king's nature$_2$ will be the fact that, unlike the philosopher-king, he will lack psychic harmony. Secondly, a philosopher-king and a philosopher who has managed to attain psychic harmony outside the perfect city may have the same nature$_1$, but still differ significantly in their nature$_2$. Although they will both have attained psychic harmony and be able to contemplate the Forms, on the whole they will have significantly different personalities. The philosopher-kings receive a specific training, not only in order to attain psychic harmony, but also in order to fulfil a certain task, to rule the perfect city efficiently. To be worthy of this task they will have been trained to develop a particular desire in their souls. It is the desire to pursue what benefits the city and never to deviate from this aim (412d9–e8). According to Plato, only those who after many difficult tests have proven never to compromise their commitment to the pursuit of the city's benefit will be selected to become rulers of the city (413e6–414a2). By contrast, the philosophers living in a corrupted state will have a more self-centred attitude, and try simply to save themselves from the corruption which permeates their cities (496c5–e2). Although they might have a desire to help the city (496d4–5), in the corrupted cities this desire is suppressed rather than fostered. The point is that the philosopher-kings and the philosophers

Happiness and the nature of philosopher-kings

in the corrupted cities will not differ only in their actions. They will differ also in their personalities. Suppressed desires affect one's attitudes as do constant isolation and abstinence from public life. This is why Plato claims that in the perfect city the philosopher not only saves society but he himself further grows (αὐτός τε μᾶλλον αὐξήσεται, 497a3–5).[26] So, again, while the philosopher-kings and the philosophers living in corrupted cities share the same nature₁ and, further, while they both have psychic harmony, they differ significantly in their nature₂.

Another consideration supports this account of the difference between nature₁ and nature₂. Plato argues that the education of the intellect does not involve putting knowledge into a soul which lacks knowledge in the way that someone could put sight into blind eyes (518b7–c3). The soul never loses its capacity (δύναμιν, 518c5) for learning; the aim of the appropriate education is not to bestow on the soul the capacity of learning (as one could give the capacity of sight to the eye if one could make the eye see) but to direct the soul to the study of the right things (518c4–d8). Plato appears to consider the directing of the soul to the study of the right things an illustration of the development of the virtue of wisdom (φρονῆσαι) in the soul (518e2–519a1). This account of the virtue of wisdom is contrasted with the development of the other virtues in the soul: the latter are considered to be closer to the virtues of the body in that, while the soul does not have them in advance, they are developed through education and exercise (518d9–e2).

Given that, as we have seen, Plato recognizes the existence of certain conative abilities and aptitudes in the soul, and relates them to the spirit and the philosophical part of the soul, he cannot mean that the development of the virtues of the soul other than wisdom is not built upon certain pre-existing capacities. His point must rather be that the degree of malleability of the conative capacities of the soul is far greater than the degree of malleability of the cognitive capacities. In this sense the personality traits one will develop will be primarily the result of the education one will receive. Substantial difference in the education of the conative abilities that two agents receive results in substantial difference in the nature₂ they will develop.

I want to suggest that, when Plato postulates that in the perfect city the philosopher-kings will receive the type of happiness their nature is suited for, he refers to nature₂ and not to nature₁. I take the primary evidence for this reading of PKH1 (and consequently of H1) to be Plato's warning that, if the philosopher-kings receive any other kind of happiness, they will cease to fulfil their task, that is, to be guardians of the city (420d5–e1, 421a8–b1 and b6–c2). Thus, Plato supports a distribution of happiness to the philosopher-kings in which they get the type of happiness that allows them to best fulfil their task (421c2) as well as accords with their nature₂, i.e. their developed personality (421c5–6). As we have seen, it is not simply their nature$_1$ which makes the philosopher-kings appropriate for ruling the city, but their strong desire to promote the interest of the city. The latter is developed through training in the perfect city and belongs to their nature$_2$. So, the type of happiness they will enjoy in the perfect city is the type of happiness suitable for them *qua* guardians and thus in accordance with the traits of their developed personality.

What is the type of happiness for which the nature$_2$ of the philosopher-kings is suitable? It is reasonable to assume that the philosopher-kings' happiness will have at least the following two components. First, the philosopher-kings will have attained psychic harmony which is, as we have seen, the primary constituent of human happiness. Secondly, they will live a life in which basic traits of their personality, such as their strong desire to benefit the city, are fulfilled.[27]

Why is it conducive to the agent's happiness to fulfil basic traits of his personality which have been formed by education so as to fit his social task? The association of happiness with nature$_2$ implies that for Plato a constituent of happiness is the fulfilment of desires, tendencies or traits of the personality of the agent, provided that they are compatible with psychic harmony, that is, provided that they do not threaten the primary constituent of the happiness of the agent. The philosopher-kings by satisfying their strong desire to benefit the city (which belongs to their nature$_2$) achieve a component of happiness which is compatible with their psychic harmony. Once through education they have acquired this desire (i.e., it has become part of their nature$_2$), failure to fulfil it would reduce their happiness.

There is a further question to be asked, concerning why the philosopher-kings should develop this desire in the first place. I think that Plato relies here on pragmatic considerations. The development of this desire is instrumental to the philosopher-kings' attaining psychic harmony. It is plausible to assume, for example, that this desire motivates them to undertake, after they have received training in dialectic, several military and public duties the performance of which will be their ultimate preparation for reaching an understanding of the Form of the Good (539e2–540c2). Thus, the development of this desire is an end of the educational system of the perfect city. Subsequently, the value of the development of this desire depends on the value of the educational system of the perfect city for the attainment of the primary constituent of happiness, namely, psychic harmony. It is at this stage that pragmatic considerations come into play. On the one hand, since Plato allows that some people may become true philosophers in the corrupted cities, he acknowledges that it is not, strictly speaking, 'necessary' for those endowed with a philosophic nature$_1$ to go through the educational system of the perfect city to attain psychic harmony. But, on the other, he stresses that this is highly unlikely (a sign of divine providence, θεῶν τύχῃ),[28] and that, a philosophic nature$_1$, unless it receives proper education, will be corrupted (492a1–5). Further, there seems to be no alternative educational system which will guarantee that one's philosophic nature$_1$ is fulfilled. So, there are only two possible alternatives: a) either to leave it to luck whether one fulfils one's philosophic nature$_1$ or b) to make one follow the only training through which one can fulfil one's philosophic nature (and which requires that one develops a desire to benefit the city). Plato opts for b), since b) maximizes the probability that one's philosophic nature$_1$ could be developed.

Let me summarize my argument in this section. I argued that Plato when referring to someone's 'nature' may mean two things: either a) the cluster of abilities and aptitudes that a person has by birth (nature$_1$), or b) certain basic traits of that person's personality developed by education (nature$_2$). I tried to show that, when Plato claims that in the perfect city members of each class attain the type of happiness their nature is suited for (H1), he means nature$_2$ and not nature$_1$. Further, since members of the three classes in the perfect city will develop different personalities, there will be different types of happiness corresponding to the members of the three classes (H2). And since nature$_2$ includes those features on the basis of which people belong to different classes in the perfect city, the type of happiness one receives in the perfect city is analogous to those features on the basis of which one's inclusion in a certain class is decided (H3). The happiness of the philosopher-kings in particular must include both the attainment of psychic harmony (which is the primary constituent of happiness) and the satisfaction of desires which are compatible with their psychic harmony. One such desire is the desire always to act in such a way as to benefit the city. Unless this basic desire is satisfied, the happiness the philosopher-kings entertain in the perfect city will be reduced.

Finally, the philosopher-kings will be motivated to rule by a desire to benefit the city. Socrates also takes the desire to benefit one's subjects to be the predominant motivation of the real ruler in Book 1 of the *Republic* (342e6–11).[29] Indeed he believes that every craftsman *qua* craftsman aims not at the service of his personal interest but at the service of the interest of the subject-matter of his craft (346e3–7). And he also stresses that no one possessing species of specialized knowledge (and thus no true craftsman) would like to have more than is his due in issues relating to the exercise of his specialized knowledge (350a6–9). In this respect a knowledgeable person resembles the just person: the latter does not like to have more than any other just person. So, both the knowledgeable person and the just person reject πλεονεξία (350c1–5). But so does the philosopher-king who by assuming the task of ruling the perfect city returns the benefit he received from his fellow-citizens in his upbringing (520a9–c1). Further, the rejection of πλεονεξία is a paradigmatic case of ordinarily just attitude. So, the philosopher-kings by refusing to gain more than is their due become ordinarily just (and judging by the scale of the benefit they return to the city we may say that they become grossly ordinarily just). On the interpretation I advance what motivates their rejection of πλεονεξία is their desire to benefit the city.

It is tempting to think that what motivates the philosopher-kings to assume the task of ruling is rather their valuing of the principle of the reciprocity of benefits. After all the whole argument at 520a6–d5 aims at showing that assuming the task of ruling is required by the principle of reciprocity of benefits. And Plato seems to suggest that this argument somehow convinces the philosopher-kings to return to the cave: he says that it is impossible for the philosopher-kings not to want (οὐκ ἐθελήσουσιν) to help the city when they listen to this argument (ταῦτ' ἀκούοντες) for 'we will order just things to just people' (δίκαια γὰρ δὴ δικαίοις ἐπιτάξομεν) (520d7–e1).

But it is misleading to say that the philosopher-kings return to the cave *because* they value the principle of reciprocity of benefits if we mean by this that they value it *for its own sake*. First, the principle of reciprocity of benefits is a principle of ordinary justice. As a principle of ordinary justice it gains its value from the contribution it makes to the preservation of psychic harmony or else justice in the soul. It is reasonable to expect that the philosopher-kings (being perfectly rational and fully informed) would desire to obey a principle of ordinary justice merely as an *instrumental* good (which leads to a good in itself: the preservation of justice in their soul). But, as I have already explained in section 1 of this chapter (see especially T2*), the performance of ordinarily just actions is not necessary for the preservation of the justice in the soul of the philosopher-kings after they have reached understanding of the Forms. So, the philosopher-kings should have no reason to value the principle of reciprocity of benefits as a means to the preservation of their psychic harmony and thus no relevant motivation to observe it.

Second, it could be argued that though the philosopher-kings may not desire to observe the principle of reciprocity of benefits as a means to the preservation of their psychic order, they may still desire it as a means to fulfilling some other constituent of their happiness. This line of argument is compatible with my claim that psychic harmony is not the sole constituent of the philosopher-kings' happiness. But then the only other fundamental desire that observance of the reciprocity of benefits satisfies is the desire to benefit the city which, as I have argued, is an integral part of the developed personality of the philosopher-kings. So, the philosopher-kings might desire to observe the principle of reciprocity as a means to satisfying their more fundamental desire to benefit the city. On this reading what ultimately motivates the return to the cave is their desire to benefit the city. The desire to observe the principle of reciprocity is a derivative desire and cannot fully explain their action. We need to move to their more fundamental desire to benefit the city to understand both their reasons for assuming the task of ruling and why they desire (in a derivative way) to observe the principle of reciprocity.[30]

The upshot of the above argument seems to be the following. If we are to read the passage 520a6–e3 as describing the internal point of view of the philosopher-kings and as suggesting the presence of a desire to observe the principle of reciprocity of benefits, then this desire is not a desire to observe the principle of reciprocity for its own sake. It is best understood as a desire to observe the principle of reciprocity *for the sake of benefiting the city*. To explain fully why the philosopher-kings observe the principle of reciprocity of benefits and thus assume the task of ruling we need to mention the existence in their soul of a stable desire to benefit the city which is a fundamental trait of their developed personality. The satisfaction of this desire is not related to the preservation of their psychic harmony but enhances their happiness.

5. Objections

The interpretation I have advanced consists mainly of two theses. The first is that the mixed life of philosophy and political activity is the best life for the philosopher-kings (BL4). So, the philosopher-kings do not sacrifice their interest when they assume the task of ruling. The second is that they are motivated to rule by a desire to benefit the city (M4), a desire acquired before they gained understanding of the Forms. The second thesis entails that the philosopher-kings want to live a life in which they will devote some of their time to the regulation of the public affairs of their city; in other words, they want to live the mixed life. Plato is aware of this implication. He asserts at 520d7–e1 that it is impossible for the philosopher-kings not to want (ἐθελήσουσιν) to live the mixed life. And he makes a similar point at 592a5–9 when he claims that, in sharp contrast to the corrupted states, in the perfect city the philosophers are willing to engage in politics (τά γε πολιτικὰ ἐθελήσει πράττειν).

But the thesis that the philosopher-kings want the mixed life may be contested. Three arguments may be adduced in support of the opposite thesis. The first is that Plato repeatedly claims that the philosopher-kings will be 'compelled' to rule (ἀναγκάσαι, 519c9, ἀνάγκῃ, 519e4, προσαναγκάζοντες, 520a8; ἀναγκαστέοι 539e3; cf. 500d4) implying that they do not want to rule. The second is that Plato implies at 520d2 that the philosopher-kings are least eager (ἥκιστα πρόθυμοι) to rule. The third is that Plato presents at 540b4–5 the philosopher-kings as conceiving their engagement in public affairs not as something fine (καλόν) but as something necessary (ἀναγκαῖον).

None of these objections shows, however, that the philosopher-kings do not *want the mixed life*. The first argument misrepresents Plato's thesis. In the passages cited above Plato should not be understood as referring to the motivation of the philosopher-kings and as trying to explain their action of assuming political power from the internal point of view. Rather, 'compulsion' denotes the existence of certain laws (in the perfect city) prescribing that the philosopher-kings should engage in political activities. This is clear from the fact that some of these passages are introduced by a remark indicating that Plato is speaking from the point of view of the lawgivers (οἰκιστῶν, 519c8), not from the internal point of view of the philosopher-kings.

The other two arguments, although clearly describing the internal point of view of the philosopher-kings, show only that the philosopher-kings do not prefer, or value, ruling in its own right. Yet from this it does not follow that they do not want or value the conjunction of ruling and philosophy. For example, I might not like running on its own as a type of exercise but I might love playing football (especially a technical rather than a physical game of football). So, there is no contradiction between the fact that the philosopher-kings might not want to rule for its own sake (considering ruling not something fine but something necessary) and the fact that they want the mixed life, as Plato asserted.

Another objection which could be raised against my interpretation is that Plato does not refute the point Glaucon makes at 519d8–9 that, by assuming the task of ruling, the philosopher-kings are made to live a life worse than they could have lived. On this objection, Plato implicitly accepts that the contemplative, not the mixed, life is the best life for them. My answer to this objection is that, although Plato does not directly address Glaucon's point in the relevant passage from 519e1–521b11, he gives us sufficient information about where to look for the answer. At 519e1–520a4 he reiterates a point he made at the beginning of Book 4, namely, that the aim of the lawgiver of the perfect city is not to make one class in the city happy but the whole city happy. But, as I have already argued in section 3 of this chapter, at the beginning of Book 4 Plato also claims that in the perfect city the members of each class receive the type of happiness their nature (i.e. their developed personality) is suited for. I believe that at 519e1–520a4 Plato invites us to go back to Book 4 to look for his answer to Glaucon's point. His answer seems to be not that the philosopher-kings sacrifice their happiness but that they live a life which provides them with the happiness suitable for their personality. My interpretation explains why the mixed life is indeed the best life for people with the personality traits of the philosopher-kings.

A fifth objection which could be raised against my interpretation is that the philosopher-kings value the contemplative life more than the mixed life. And, since their preferences are informed by true knowledge, it follows that the mixed life is not the best life for them. The primary evidence for this interpretation are Plato's claims at 520e4–521a2, 521b1–2 and 521b9–10 that the philosopher-kings believe that there is a life for them better than the life of politics. Plato calls it the life of 'true philosophy' (ἀληθινῆς φιλοσοφίας, 521b2).

In order for this objection to work two conditions must be satisfied: a) the life of politics is equated with the mixed life and b) the life of true philosophy is equated with the contemplative life. I am doubtful about the validity of either a) or b). On the one hand, Plato uses three different phrases to refer to the life of politics: βίον τοῦ ἄρχειν 520e4–521a1, βίον πολιτικῶν ἀρχῶν 521b1, βίον τοῦ πολιτικοῦ 521b9–10. It is more plausible to assume that these phrases refer to a life dominated by politics than to a life which merely includes some political activity. But the mixed life is not a life dominated by politics, since most of the philosopher-kings' time will be devoted to philosophy and not to public affairs. So, the life which they find less desirable than the life of true philosophy is not the mixed life. On the other hand, there is no reason to suppose that the mixed life is not a life of true philosophy. The phrase 'true philosophy' signifies the quality of the intellectual enterprise of the philosopher-kings, that is, its affinity to the true reality of the Forms (see, 486b3, 489a5–6 and 490d6), and differentiates it from the sophistic enterprise which uses the *façade* of philosophy (495b8–496a10). In this sense the philosopher-kings live a life of true philosophy, since for most of their time they engage with the true reality of the Forms. A life of true philosophy is a component of their mixed life.

So, I take Plato to say at 520e4–521b11 that the philosopher-kings prefer a life of true philosophy to a life dominated by politics. A life dominated by politics is not the mixed life, while the life of true philosophy is a component of the mixed life. If this is right, then what Plato says at 520e4–521b11 is compatible with the philosopher-kings' wanting the mixed life. And since their preferences are informed by true knowledge, the fact that they want the mixed life is evidence that this life is good for them. My interpretation tries to explain why it is in fact the best life for them.

A final worry needs to be addressed.[31] Even a maximally charitable interpretation of the *Republic*, like the one I advance, has to admit that the way Plato presents the allocation of happiness in the perfect city gives the impression that the philosopher-kings somehow sacrifice their interest. Plato is not innocent of what in my view are misunderstandings of his position. I believe that we may identify two possible causes of these misunderstandings. The first is Plato's constant attempt to avoid the charge that he is proposing a political constitution which discriminates in favour of one class of citizens. As we have seen, Socrates stresses that he is speaking from the point of view of the lawgiver. He wants to reassure his interlocutors that he is impartial as a lawgiver and does not legislate so that the philosopher-kings exceedingly benefit from the proposed political arrangements (420b4–8 and 519e1–3). But the manner in which he presents his reassurances creates the impression that the philosopher-kings are somehow harmed by the proposed political arrangements. The second is Plato's need to differentiate his account of political art from Thrasymachus' account. In *Republic* I Socrates argued for an other-directed conception of political art according to which the real statesman acts for the sake of his subjects and not in order to serve his personal interests (345d5–e4). This conception of political art is sharply contrasted with a conception of political art as narrowly focused on serving the interest of the ruler favoured by Thrasymachus. Plato needs to make clear that he is operating within the context of an other-directed conception of political art and that the philosopher-kings *qua* rulers do not aim at serving their own interests. So, he has to stress the other-directed character of their actions as rulers and downplay their contribution to the happiness of the philosopher-kings.

6. Is the mixed life the best life human beings may attain?

Till now I have been arguing that the mixed life is the best life for the philosopher-kings. Now I should like to turn briefly to the issue of whether it is the best life human beings may attain. I cannot provide a comprehensive treatment of this issue here. I will simply explore some implications of the interpretation developed in the previous sections.

Plato clearly thinks that the mixed life of the philosopher-kings is better than the timocratic, the oligarchic, the democratic and the tyrannical lives. The philosopher-kings are happier because they have psychic harmony. But the crucial question is how the life of the philosopher-kings compares with the lives of people who possess psychic harmony and do not live the mixed life. I have in mind two possible cases. The first is that of the philosophers living in corrupted states. The second is an imaginative case, which Plato does not mention in the *Republic*. I will call it the case of the ascetic philosopher.[32]

I will start with the latter case. Suppose that the philosopher-kings in the perfect city decide to make an experiment and create through appropriate education a philosopher who will not have substantial other-directed desires, such as a desire to benefit the city. His existence will not be a threat to the regime since the philosopher-kings will continue producing philosophers like themselves who want to administer public issues. The question is whether this philosopher would be happier than the philosopher-kings.

To answer the question we need to understand the respects in which the happiness of the philosopher-kings and of the ascetic philosopher differ. On the interpretation I previously advanced there was an implicit distinction between two classes of desires.

Type (a) desires: satisfaction of these desires is necessary for the preservation of one's psychic harmony (e.g. the desire for knowledge and truth).

Type (b) desires: satisfaction of these desires is compatible with, but not necessary for, the preservation of one's psychic harmony (e.g. the desire to benefit the city).

On the face of this distinction, we may say that both the philosopher-kings and the ascetic philosopher satisfy the first class of desires. Nonetheless, they differ in that the ascetic philosopher tries to minimize desires of the second type while the philosopher-king has a substantial number of these desires and tries to maximize their satisfaction. The philosopher-king's general desire to benefit the city generates a whole cluster of more specific desires (for example, to create good laws, to regulate marriages). His happiness increases as these desires are satisfied. This is an increase in happiness on top of the core constituent of happiness which is psychic harmony (that is, satisfaction of desires of the first type). So, there is a sense in which the philosopher-kings are happier than the ascetic philosopher. The latter receives only the happiness associated with his having psychic harmony while the former have added to that happiness the type of happiness associated with the satisfaction of their other-directed desires, provided that satisfying these desires does not entail losing their psychic harmony.

Is there any evidence that Plato considers satisfaction of the second type of desires as increasing the happiness of one who already possesses psychic harmony? To answer this we may turn to the case of those philosophers living in corrupted cities. Plato must think that they have understanding of the Forms and thus have achieved psychic harmony, since he is willing to entrust to them the education of the first inhabitants of the perfect city (540d1–541b5). But he also describes their lives in the corrupted cities in a way which clearly suggests that he finds it in certain respects less happy than the life of the philosopher-kings (496a11–497a5). He thinks that they live a life of seclusion from society (as if they were surrounded by wild animals, 496d3) minding exclusively their own affairs (497d6) and not achieving the type of personal development (αὐξήσεται, 497a4) they would have achieved in the perfect city. In what sense have they not achieved a full development and in what respects is their life miserable? Given that they have achieved psychic harmony, their difference in happiness from the philosopher-kings must result from the fact that they do not satisfy constituents of happiness other than psychic harmony. I believe that Plato here has in mind satisfaction of other-directed desires which are compatible with psychic harmony. This is suggested by the fact that the notion of personal development is associated with the idea of the philosophers' saving the city (497a5; cf. 496c7–d5). As we have seen, this desire has been suppressed in the corrupted cities, and the philosophers there have adopted a more self-centred attitude. Only in the perfect city can the true philosophers increase their happiness by developing and then satisfying their other-directed desires.

If my arguments are correct, then Plato could argue that the life of the philosopher-kings is the best possible life for human beings. It combines the attainment of psychic harmony with the satisfaction of (other-directed) desires compatible with psychic harmony. The philosophers in the corrupted cities and the imaginative ascetic philosopher satisfy the first and primary constituent of happiness but not the second. The timocrat, the oligarch, the democrat and the tyrant fail to satisfy even the first constituent of happiness.

7. Conclusion

In conclusion I should like to sketch some of the implications of my interpretation.

First, Plato's defence of justice avoids the four problems I described at the end of the first section of my paper. The maximally just person, that is, the philosopher-king, will be as happy as he can possibly be. The happiest person will be grossly ordinarily just; Plato's defence cannot be immediately dismissed on the grounds that it fails to answer Thrasymachus', Adeimantus' and Glaucon's challenges. The philosopher-kings are both Platonically just and grossly ordinarily just; so, there is in principle no irreconcilable gap between Platonic and ordinary justice, although further arguments are needed to show how the gap might be closed. Since the philosopher-kings are better off returning the benefit they received from the city, Plato has not produced a case in which πλεονεξία pays.

Secondly, happiness for Plato is associated with the satisfaction of fundamental desires of one's personality. The satisfaction of some of these desires is necessary for the attainment of psychic harmony, which is the core constituent of happiness. The satisfaction of some other desires compatible with psychic harmony but not necessary for the attainment of psychic harmony is a secondary constituent of happiness. The philosopher-kings by living the mixed life attain both constituents of happiness and are as happy as they can possibly be.

Finally, on the interpretation I advanced, what motivates the philosopher-kings to engage in the other-directed activity of ruling and to be ordinarily just is a desire to benefit the city, a desire developed through education in the perfect city. This desire is developed prior to the philosopher-kings' reaching an understanding of the Forms. My interpretation differs, thus, from interpretations which assume a) that the philosopher-kings are motivated by a general desire to produce goodness or justice in the world, and b) that this desire is generated somehow by their knowledge of the Forms. These interpretations take Plato to be an 'internalist' about moral motivation: knowledge of the Forms essentially motivates the philosopher-kings to engage in other-directed activity; it is impossible for anyone to know the Forms and not form the intention to engage in other-directed activities.[33] On the interpretation I advance Plato is rather an 'externalist' about moral motivation: knowledge of the Forms does not suffice to motivate the philosopher-kings to engage in other-directed activities; a further desire to benefit the city is required, and this may not be found in people who have knowledge of the Forms, like the philosophers in the corrupted cities. I reserve a fuller treatment of this issue for another paper.

Acknowledgements

I have benefited from comments on earlier drafts of this paper by Mehmet Erginel, Hallvard Fossheim, Fritz-Gregor Herrmann, David Robinson, Theodore Scaltsas and Malcolm Schofield.

Notes

[1] For the view that the philosopher-kings sacrifice their happiness, see Cooper 1977 and White 1986.

[2] Kraut 1973, 210–13.

[3] The process of psychological assimilation to various virtuous models is best depicted in Plato's account of the influence of music on the soul (401d5–402a4). In this passage it is made clear that psychological assimilation to virtuous models need not involve a cognitive component. Music is able to affect the character of one's soul before one reaches 'understanding' (λόγον) of the object of *mimesis*. In fact it appears to enable the process of understanding. The agent seems to be able to gain understanding of the object of *mimesis* because his soul has become similar to the object of *mimesis*. Psychological assimilation to virtuous models should be understood as a kind of harmonious agreement (see especially ὁμολογοῦντα and συμφωνοῦντα, 402d2–3) between conditions (ἤθη, 402d2) of the soul and virtuous models (402b9–d5; cf. 500b8–d3).

[4] *Contra* Bosanquet (1895, 167–8), I think that Plato takes justice in the soul to be an inner state of the agent which is produced by repeated action at 443c9–444e3. I consider as evidence for the causal power of actions the use of σῴζῃ and συνεργάζηται at 443e6, of λύῃ at 444a1 and of ἐμποιεῖ at 444c10. I see nothing ironic in the suggestion that one's actions are causally responsible for one's inner state of psychic harmony. I believe that here Plato intends to advance a serious philosophical point supported by an argument

from analogy. As one's actions (say, one's daily exercise) affect one's state of health so one's actions can affect one's state of the soul. (Thanks to Fritz-Gregor Herrmann for bringing to my attention Bosanquet's interpretation and suggesting the possibility that Plato is making an ironic point here.)

[5] Here I follow White 1984, 34–41 who claims that Plato's argument that justice is preferable to injustice is not completed at the end of Book 4 but continues in Book 9. I do not enter here into the debate on whether the three arguments that the just life is the most pleasant life in Book 9 are actually parts of the defence of justice. For opposing views see Gosling and Taylor 1982, 98–103 and Kraut 1993.

[6] For the implications of Glaucon's and Adeimantus' demand that justice by itself makes the just person happier than the unjust person see Irwin 1995, 192–3. For psychic harmony's being dominant in happiness, see also Irwin 1995, 254–6.

[7] I defend this interpretation of 500b9–d2 in section 2. For an intriguing analysis of Plato's account of *mimesis*, see Halliwell 2001, 72–85 and 98–117.

[8] The seminal paper is by Sachs 1971. For responses to Sachs, see, among others, Demos 1971, Vlastos 1971, Kraut 1973, Dahl 1999 and Penner 2005.

[9] Internal peace will be the result of the absence of φθόνος in the perfect city. See Herrmann 2003.

[10] See section 4, n. 27 and the distinction between two types of desires in section 6.

[11] Another possibility is that their happiness would be reduced because they would spend less time contemplating the Forms. This again does not entail loss in psychic harmony. One should distinguish the pleasure *per se* of contemplating the Forms from the state of psychic harmony. When the philosopher-kings return to the cave, they may be considered to receive a lesser amount of the true pleasure of contemplation of the Forms but their inner state of psychic harmony is not affected.

[12] See Sachs 1971, 45–51.

[13] A proper answer to the question what motivates the philosopher-kings in assuming the task of ruling should identify a motive which properly *explains* rather than simply re-describing their action while adding nothing to the explanation of the action other than that it was *intentional* (see Davidson 1980, 4–6). For example, to say that Tony Blair had a desire to put the issue of the financial debt of African countries on the agenda of the G8 meeting has no real explanatory power, if it is meant as an explanation of his action of putting the issue on the agenda. This piece of information does not enlighten us at all about the real motives (considerations, plans, desires) of Tony Blair; it only clarifies that the issue was not 'accidentally' put on the agenda. We want to know what is behind Blair's desire that the issue be discussed during the G8 summit. It is a motive with a similar explanatory power we are after when we are considering the question what motivates the philosopher-kings to assume the task of ruling. See also section 4; cf. n. 30.

[14] 'Expressing' the Form of the Good may include but is not restricted to 'imitation' of the Form of the Good. It should be understood more loosely as 'being inspired by' the Form of the Good.

[15] Supporters of BL1 and M1 include Cross and Woozley 1964, 101 and Reeve 1988, 202–3. The conjunction of BL2 and M2 is supported by Dahl 1999 and Mahoney 1992. Scholars who think that the philosopher-kings sacrifice their interest when ruling may support M2 (but not BL2): see Cooper 1977, Annas 1980, 266–8 and White 1986. BL3 and M3 are supported by Demos 1971 and more comprehensively by Kraut 1999.

[16] For an analysis of these objections, see Kraut 1999, 241–2. For my interpretation

of 520d7–e1 see section 4.

[17] It has to be noted that supporters of M2 are not clear about the origin of the desire to express the Form of the Good in social arrangements and its relation to the knowledge of the Form of the Good. A cluster of questions are pertinent and have direct bearing on the issue of whether Plato is an externalist or internalist about moral motivation. For example, is there an independent desire to instantiate what one admires of which the desire to instantiate the Form of the Good is a specification? Or is it the case that the knowledge of the Form of the Good is intrinsically connected with a desire to instantiate it to the extent that it is impossible for one who knows the Form of the Good not to desire to instantiate it?

[18] The attitude of the philosophers outside the perfect city is to be contrasted with the attitude of the philosopher-kings. Plato thinks that it is impossible for the latter not to *want* (ἐθελήσουσιν 519d7) to undertake the task of ruling (527d7–e1). So, the philosophers outside the perfect city will lack, while the philosopher-kings will possess, a *desire* to engage in human affairs. And since both the philosophers outside the perfect city and the philosopher-kings have an understanding of the Form of the Good, it cannot be the case that this other-directed desire is generated by knowledge of the Form of the Good.

[19] Kraut 1999, 729 (Kraut's italics).

[20] An example of collective action might be the co-ordination of the philosopher-kings in supervising the educational process in the perfect city.

[21] Let me make two comments to avoid possible misunderstanding of my interpretation. First, when I say that undertaking the task of ruling the perfect city is not a 'just' action according to the proper Platonic standards of justice I do not imply that it is Platonically unjust. For an action to be Platonically unjust, it must destroy justice in the soul (444a1). But, as I have already explained in section 1 of this chapter, the philosopher-kings' engagement with the political affairs of the perfect city does not threaten their psychic harmony. So, their undertaking the task of ruling the perfect city is neutral in respect of Platonic justice. Second, it is true that Plato argues that the return to the cave is a just action on the basis that it fulfils the principle of reciprocity of benefits (520a6–e3). But we should note that at 520a6–e3 there is no reference to Platonic justice and no attempt to show a link between the return to the cave and the preservation of justice in the soul of the philosopher-kings. I believe that the reciprocity of benefits is best understood to be a principle of 'ordinary' justice and that the conclusion of Plato's argument is that the philosopher-kings are ordinarily just. But the passage at 520a6–e3 is not at all informative about whether there is a necessary relation between the principle of reciprocity and justice in the soul, or whether the philosopher-kings regard the principle of reciprocity as a universal principle of conduct. The most this passage shows is that from the point of view of ordinary justice the law requiring the rulers to return to the cave is just and so is their conformity with the principle of reciprocity. For more see section 4.

[22] As I explain at the beginning of section 4, in the *Republic* Plato uses the term 'nature' (φύσις) to denote not only the natural order of the external world but also human nature in general and the 'nature' of a particular person. For example, he speaks of human nature (ἡ τοῦ ἀνθρώπου φύσις) at 395b4, and of 'natural' individual differences at 369a8–b1 (πρῶτον μὲν ἡμῶν φύεται ἕκαστος οὐ πάνυ ὅμοιος ἑκάστῳ, ἀλλὰ διαφέρων τὴν φύσιν) and at 433a5–6 (ἕνα ἕκαστον ἓν δέοι ἐπιτηδεύειν τῶν περὶ τὴν πόλιν, εἰς ὃ αὐτοῦ ἡ φύσις ἐπιτηδειοτάτη πεφυκυῖα εἴη). I take it that he similarly speaks of the nature of the members of each class and not of nature in general at 421c4–6. The

primary evidence for this reading of φύσις at 421c4–6 is the correspondence between the division of labour and the distribution of happiness which is at the kernel of the statue analogy from 420b3–421c6. The point seems to be the following: as concerns about the nature of a person govern the division of labour in the perfect city (see, for example, 369a8–b1 and 433a5–6) so concerns about the nature of the members of each class should determine the distribution of happiness. For more on Plato's reference to nature of a particular person see section 4. I am grateful to Fritz-Gregor Herrmann for pressing me to clarify the distinction between φύσις as the general natural order of things and φύσις as the nature of man.

[23] In this respect Adeimantus' challenge is similar to the challenge Glaucon puts forward at 519d8–9, namely, that the philosopher-kings are made to live worse than they could when they assume the task of ruling. But it should be noted that Adeimantus and Glaucon employ different conceptions of happiness in their challenges. Adeimantus operates with an ordinary conception of happiness; he thinks that the philosopher-kings are worse off because they do not have property, family, etc. On the contrary, for Glaucon happiness involves primarily intellectual activities, like the contemplation of the Forms.

[24] See Halliwell 2001, 72–85 and 98–117.

[25] See n. 3.

[26] To understand better Plato's point we might compare the personalities of a scientist living in a totalitarian regime and of a scientist living in a liberal society. While both may be equally devoted to their science and gain the same amount of joy out of properly exercising it, their overall mentalities may be different. The scientist living in a totalitarian regime may isolate himself from the rest of the academic community (who may follow blindly the official scientific line prescribed by the ruling party) and from political life in general. In contrast, the scientist in the liberal environment may actively engage with the rest of the academic community and feel free to take a stance on public issues. The first scientist will be closed to himself and have an introvert mentality. The second will be more open and have a stronger sense of overall self-fulfillment.

[27] One could possibly take some external goods like the absence of internal strife in a city and the escape of certain burdens such as having to raise a family and maintain a household (465b5–d1) as components of happiness. But their value is probably instrumental. They contribute to the development of the appropriate conditions in which one can attain psychic harmony and satisfy one's other desires compatible with psychic harmony.

[28] Socrates may be considered an example of a philosopher aided by divine providence. I explain the role of divine intervention in the preservation of Socrates' virtue in Hatzistavrou 2005, 108–10.

[29] For Socrates' account of justice in Book 1 of the *Republic*, see Scaltsas 1993 and Hatzistavrou 1998.

[30] To avoid possible misunderstandings: my point in this paragraph is different from the claim in n. 13 that we should look for motives with explanatory power. The desire to observe the principle of reciprocity explains in the required sense the action of assuming the task of ruling and does not simply show that the latter is an intentional action. My point is rather that the explanation provided is not complete precisely because the desire to observe the principle of reciprocity is 'derivative'. The complete explanation of the action requires the identification of the relevant more fundamental desire. This is the desire to benefit the city.

[31] I have benefited from discussions with Malcolm Schofield on this issue.
[32] I am indebted to Dory Scaltsas for discussions on the case of the ascetic philosopher.
[33] See Dahl 1999, 208–9; for the internalism/externalism debate see Smith 1994, ch. 3.

Bibliography

Annas, J.
   1980   *An Introduction to Plato's* Republic, Oxford.
Bosanquet, B.
   1895   *A Companion to Plato's* Republic. London.
Cooper, J.
   1977   'The psychology of justice', *American Philosophical Quarterly* 14, 151–7.
Cross, R.C. and Woozley, A.D.
   1964   *Plato's* Republic: *A philosophical commentary*, London.
Dahl, N.
   1999   'Plato's defence of justice', in G. Fine (ed.) *Plato*, vol. 2, Oxford, 207–34.
Davidson, D.
   1980   'Actions, reasons and causes', in D. Davidson, *Essays on Actions and Events*, Oxford.
Demos, R.
   1971   'A fallacy in Plato's *Republic*?', in G. Vlastos (ed.) *Plato*, vol. 2, New York, 52–6.
Gosling, J.B. and Taylor, C.C.W.
   1984   *The Greeks on Pleasure*, Oxford.
Halliwell, S.
   2002   *The Aesthetics of Mimesis*, Princeton.
Hatzistavrou, A.
   1998   'Thrasymachus' definition of justice', *Philosophical Inquiry* 18, 62–82.
   2005   'Socrates' deliberative authoritarianism', *Oxford Studies in Ancient Philosophy* 19, 75–113.
Herrmann, F.G.
   2003   'φθόνος in the world of Plato's *Timaeus*', in D. Konstan and K. Rutter (eds.) *Envy, Spite and Jealousy*, Edinburgh, 53–84.
Irwin, T.
   1995   *Plato's Ethics*, Oxford.
Kraut, R.
   1973   'Reason and justice in Plato's *Republic*', in E.N. Lee, A.P.D. Mourelatos, R.M. Rorty (eds.) *Exegesis and Argument*, New York, 207–24.
   1993   'The defence of justice in Plato's *Republic*', in R. Kraut (ed.) *The Cambridge Companion to Plato*, Cambridge, 311–17.
   1999   'Return to the cave: *Republic* 519–521', in G. Fine (ed.) *Plato*, vol. 2, Oxford, 235–54.
Mahoney, T.
   1992   'Do Plato's philosopher-rulers sacrifice self-interest to justice?', *Phronesis* 37, 265–82.

Penner, T.
   2005   'Platonic justice and what we mean by "justice"', *Journal of the International Plato Society* [online]. Available at: http://www.nd.edu/~plato/plato5issue/Penner.pdf.

Reeve, C.D.C.
   1988   *Philosopher-Kings: The argument of Plato's* Republic, Princeton.

Sachs, D.
   1971   'A fallacy in Plato's *Republic*', in G. Vlastos (ed.) *Plato*, vol. 2, New York, 141–58.

Scaltsas, T.
   1992   'Fairness in Socratic justice: *Republic* I', *Proceedings of the Aristotelian Society*, 247–62.

Smith, M.
   1994   *The Moral Problem*, Oxford.

Vlastos, G.
   1971   'Justice and happiness in the *Republic*', in G. Vlastos (ed.) *Plato*, vol. 2, New York, 111–39.

White, N.
   1986   'The ruler's choice', *Archiv für Geschichte der Philosophie* 68, 22–46.

6

APPEARANCE AND BELIEF IN *THEAETETUS* 151D–187A

Patricia Clarke

I want to raise some questions relating to the gloss of Protagoras' measure doctrine which is offered at *Theaetetus* 152a6–8. My discussion will also have some bearing on *Theaetetus* 184–7, where, on the face of it, in arguing that perception cannot be knowledge, Socrates draws a sharp distinction between perception on the one hand and thought, judgement, and belief on the other, and appears to allow that infants and animals can perceive, but not think, judge, and believe. However, I shall not address the argument of 184–7 directly.[1]

I

When Theaetetus suggests, at 151e1–3, that one who knows something perceives that which he knows, and that knowledge is nothing other than perception, Socrates – though perhaps with some qualification[2] – says that this is equivalent to Protagoras' measure doctrine, that is, to the view that a human being is a measure of all things, of the things that are that they are, and of the things that are not that they are not. The measure doctrine is then glossed as follows: individual things are for me such as they appear (φαίνεται) to me, and for you such as they appear to you; and you and I are human beings. The gloss is then illustrated with the example of the wind:

> SOC. Is it not the case that sometimes, when one and the same wind is blowing, one of us feels cold, the other doesn't, and one of us feels a bit cold, the other very cold?
> THEAT. Yes, indeed.
> SOC. Shall we say of such occasions that the wind by itself is cold or not cold? Or shall we be persuaded by Protagoras and say that the wind is cold for the one who feels cold, and not for the one who does not?
> THEAE. That seems right.[3]

The main question I want to raise is whether the gloss at 152a6–8 should be interpreted in terms of belief, that is, as saying that individual things are for me such as I believe them to be, for you such as you believe them to be, and both you and I are human beings. I shall argue that it should not be interpreted simply and straightforwardly in terms of judgement or belief, and also that no completely univocal interpretation can be given.[4]

Gail Fine is among those who interpret the gloss at 152a6–8 in terms of belief – given at least what we find towards the beginning of Fine 1996a, where she says, in section II, referring to the gloss: 'In the context of the measure doctrine, to say how things *appear* to me is to say how I *believe* things are' (212–13; her italics). She bases her claim in part on linguistic grounds. She says (footnote 6, and using '(P)' to refer to Protagoras' measure doctrine):

> 'Appears' (φαίνεσθαι) can be veridical or nonveridical: I can say 'It is apparent that the wind is cold', where this means that it obviously, evidently is cold; but I can also say 'The wind appears to be cold', where this means that I believe that it is cold. In Greek, the first use is indicated by an accusative plus participle, the second by an accusative plus infinitive. But sometimes, as in (P), the second verb is omitted and so one has to decide from the context which construction is intended. I take it that (P) involves the second use.

Now clearly *something* has gone wrong here, for the two references to the accusative case are out of place. If one ignores that, Fine is in effect claiming that the construction with φαίνεται in 152a6–8 is incomplete as it stands, and that either the nominative plural participle ὄντα ('being') or the infinitive εἶναι ('to be') must be understood. Understanding ὄντα would give 'things are for me such as they manifestly are for me…', understanding εἶναι 'things are for me such as they appear to me to be…'. Fine suggests that εἶναι be understood, and that the gloss should then be interpreted in terms of belief.

Understanding the gloss to be completed with εἶναι would bring it into line with the version at *Cratylus* 386a1–3, at least as it appears in the new edition of the Oxford text,[5] in which εἶναι has been released from square brackets; and I would agree with Fine that, if the choice at 152a6–8 is as she presents it, one should opt for supplying εἶναι. If one then interprets in terms of belief, however, one consequence would seem to be that the gloss cannot include things' being for someone as they look, taste, sound, and so on, to him or her, i.e., that οἷα μὲν ἕκαστα ἐμοὶ φαίνεται ('such as individual things appear to me') in 152a6–7 cannot cover things' simply looking white, tasting sweet, sounding harmonious, etc. to me, given that how something looks, sounds, tastes, etc. to a person is not necessarily how he or she believes it to be. It makes perfect sense, for example, to say 'It looks brown to me in this light, but I think it's really red'. On Fine's account, therefore, it seems that 152a6–8 would not cover things' being for someone such as they look, taste, sound, and so on to that person, or would do so only if that is how he or she believes them to be.

What Fine says about φαίνεσθαι in the passage quoted constitutes a useful peg on which to hang part of my discussion. However, since Fine elsewhere qualifies what she says there,[6] I shall call the view she expresses about φαίνεσθαι in the passage quoted 'the simple view'. It would, if correct, apply, not only to 152a6–8, but also to the repetitions of the gloss, with φαίνεσθαι used again, at 158a (first with one dative, then in effect with two), and to innumerable other passages, both in the *Theaetetus* and elsewhere. I mention just two from the *Theaetetus*: (i) 154a3–9 where Socrates asks: 'Or would you insist that each colour appears to a dog and to any animal as it appears to you?', and goes on, after Theaetetus' denial, 'Does anything appear similar to you and to another human being?', and suggests that the case is rather that nothing ever appears the same (sc. more than once) to Theaetetus owing to his never being in the same condition (more than once). This passage is obviously especially significant for 184–7, because of the apparent implication that things can appear to animals; though, since the claim being made at 154a3–5 is negative, there is no strict entailment that they can. (ii) 159c11–12, where Socrates says: 'When I drink wine when I am well, it appears pleasant and sweet to me.' Immediately after, in 159d, the wine is said both to be and to appear sweet to the healthy tongue, which might seem to pose a problem if appearing sweet is to be interpreted in terms of belief; but perhaps, where the tongue stands in for its sapient owner, it can judge as well as taste.

Accepting that in general φαίνεσθαι with a participle means 'to be manifestly being/doing such-and-such', φαίνεσθαι with an infinitive 'to appear to…', I want to ask: Can expressions in Greek in which, with use of φαίνεσθαι, something is said to appear such-and-such – e.g., expressions such as γλυκύς μοι φαίνεται ὁ οἶνος ('the wine appears sweet to me') – ever be regarded as yielding complete constructions as they stand? If they can be so regarded, how should they be interpreted? Also, when φαίνεσθαι occurs with the infinitive construction, must one in all cases interpret, simply and straightforwardly, in terms of belief? Does it make any difference whether a dative is supplied with φαίνεσθαι: for example, does τοῦτό μοι φαίνεται λευκὸν (εἶναι) ('this appears white to me/this appears to me to be white') speak of belief more than the more general τοῦτο φαίνεται λευκὸν (εἶναι) ('this appears [to be] white')?[7]

The simple view receives considerable support from Liddell and Scott, and from Liddell, Scott, and Jones. Both LS and LSJ cite the use of φαίνεσθαι with a participle and its use with an infinitive. They render the former in terms of 'being manifest' or 'manifestly being', and so on, but the latter in terms of 'appearing to...', rather than in terms of belief (though LS say at one point that φαίνεσθαι with an infinitive 'expresses an opinion *that a thing appears to be* so and so', but with a participle states a fact). Both say that both participle and infinitive can be omitted – indeed that the infinitive is often omitted. They both give other constructions for φαίνεσθαι, of course, citing, for example, the opening of the *Protagoras* (309a1): Πόθεν <ὦ Σώκρατες> φαίνῃ; ('Where did you just spring from?'); the use by philosophical writers of τὰ φαινόμενα ('the things that appear') both for things which appear to the senses, and for things which appear to the mind (and LSJ render τὸ φαινόμενον εἰπεῖν at Plutarch, *Moralia*, II.158c as 'to express one's opinion'); the Homeric 'the rosy-fingered dawn appeared', where ῥοδοδάκτυλος is in apposition to the subject, though doubtless the dawn's rosy-fingeredness was supposed to show in her appearance. They cite no passage quite like, say, 159c11–12 where the wine appears sweet to Socrates; but they do allow that where φαίνεσθαι means 'to come into being' or 'to become', it can take a complement, i.e., it can occur as a copula.

Grammar books vary in what they say; but, in general, unlike LS and LSJ, they allow that expressions of the form '*x* φαίνεται such-and-such' and equivalents can constitute syntactically complete expressions, even when φαίνεται means 'appears'. Smyth mentions and distinguishes the use of φαίνεσθαι with a participle and its use with an infinitive. He renders the former in terms of 'being plainly'; and for φαίνομαι with an infinitive he gives '*I seem* or *it appears* (but may not be true) *that I*'. He gives the examples φαίνεται τἀληθῆ λέγων, which he translates '*he is evidently speaking the truth*', and φαίνεται τἀληθῆ λέγειν, which he renders '*he appears to be speaking the truth* (but he may be lying)'. Smyth says that the distinction is not always maintained. He mentions the possible omission of the participle ὤν, but is silent on the possible omission of εἶναι.[8] Goodwin presents the distinction between the use of φαίνεσθαι with a participle and its use with an infinitive in terms of 'being manifestly...' and 'seeming to be...', but says that 'in some cases the two constructions cannot be distinguished in sense' and gives examples. He does not mention the possibility that either participle or infinitive might be omitted in appropriate cases. He counts φαίνεσθαι, in the meaning 'to appear', as a verb which, like εἶναι, can be used as a copula, but gives no example.[9] Kühner-Gerth mention and illustrate the use of φαίνεσθαι with both participle and infinitive. Like Goodwin, KG count φαίνεσθαι as a verb which can occur as copula, and cite the example: ὅστις σοι ἀδικώτατος φαίνεται ἄνθρωπος ('whoever appears to you <the> most wicked human being') from *Protagoras* 327c5 (with which one might compare ὅς τις φαίνηται ἄριστος ('whoever should appear best') from *Odyssey* 14, 106, cited by LS and LSJ as an example with infinitive omitted).[10] Translators of and commentators upon Greek texts do not always follow the line set down in the simple view.[11]

II

So the authorities are apparently not of one view on the question whether expressions of the form '*x* φαίνεται such-and-such', with φαίνεται meaning 'appears', can be syntactically complete as they stand. In addition, our survey has not thrown much light on whether such a sentence should be interpreted in terms of belief, nor on whether φαίνεσθαι with an infinitive should be so interpreted. The difference, or apparent difference, of view between LS and LSJ on the one hand and the grammar books on the other has no clear upshot for our purposes, for two reasons. (1) There need be no substantial difference of view between those who regard an expression as syntactically complete and those who do not; for example, someone who holds that γλυκύς μοι φαίνεται ὁ οἶνος ('the wine appears sweet to me') is syntactically complete may nevertheless regard it as having the same force as ὁ οἶνός μοι φαίνεται γλυκὺς εἶναι ('the wine appears to me to be sweet'), with the latter expression spelling out the meaning more fully, in which case his or her view would not differ substantially from the view that the shorter expression is incomplete, with εἶναι ('to be') needing to be understood. (2) None of the authorities consulted cites examples in which something is said φαίνεσθαι white, or sweet, and so on for other secondary qualities; i.e., none of them cites examples of a kind with which we are centrally concerned. In this situation how might one proceed? I suggest we look at five passages, one in the *Timaeus*, two in Aristotle's *De Anima*, one in the *Sophist*, and one in the *Republic*. They suggest at least that φαίνεσθαι can be used to record how things appear with the focus very heavily on the way things look, taste, sound, and so on, but perfectly compatibly with its being generally assumed that, all things being equal – which might or might not include the perceiver's not being an animal or a human infant – appearance will be accompanied by or involve a belief, or at least a tendency to believe, that things are as they appear. However, a belief which accompanies or is involved in an appearing, can, it seems, even while the appearance continues, be counteracted or overridden by beliefs based on other considerations.

The passage from the *Timaeus* is at 65d3–4, in a discussion of χυμοί (flavours, tastes). We read: τραχύτερα μὲν ὄντα στρυφνά, ἧττον δὲ τραχύνοντα αὐστηρὰ φαίνεται. D. Zeyl translates: 'When they tend to be rather rough we taste them as *sour*, when less rough as *tangy*'.[12] Galen reads λέγεται for φαίνεται, but φαίνεται is better attested. What is being described here is clearly how things taste – how different tastes are brought about.

Nevertheless, the notion of judgement is at the very least hovering in the wings; for claims about how things taste and how various flavours are secured have to be based on the verdicts of tasters. But to interpret simply in terms of belief and have the passage say: 'the rougher ones are believed to be sour, the less rough tangy' would surely be wrong; and even to have it say: 'the rougher ones appear to be sour, the less rough tangy' seems somewhat wide of the mark – and not, I think, because we should assume that the participle ὄντα is to be understood, and that the translation should be, say: 'the rougher ones are manifestly sour, the less rough tangy'.

The first passage from the *De Anima* is in 2.10.4, at 422b8–10 (in Hicks' edition). Aristotle says: καὶ οἷον τοῖς κάμνουσι πικρὰ πάντα φαίνεται διὰ τὸ τῇ γλώττῃ πλήρει τοιαύτης ὑγρότητος αἰσθάνεσθαι ('and as everything appears bitter to those who are ill because they perceive them with the tongue [when it is] full of bitter moisture'). This is a tricky passage; for, although we seem to be concerned with how things taste, it appears from the context that, according to Aristotle, those who are ill do not actually perceive by taste the things they eat and drink; rather they perceive the bitter moisture in their tongues. It is not clear, therefore, whether one can say that it is claimed here that everything *tastes* bitter to those who are ill.[13] However, if one interprets the passage as saying that everything *appears* to those who are ill *to be* bitter, it is nevertheless clear that, unless appearance and reality are assumed to coincide, any instinctive belief on the part of an invalid that what he or she is eating or drinking *is* bitter could be overridden by his or her knowledge or belief that he or she is ill and that everything, even honey-cake, appears bitter to those who are ill. Therefore, to interpret the passage straightforwardly in terms of belief would surely be wrong.

The second example from the *De Anima* is 428b2 ff. in 3.3.10. Aristotle writes: φαίνεται δὲ καὶ ψευδῆ, περὶ ὧν ἅμα ὑπόληψιν ἀληθῆ ἔχει, οἷον φαίνεται μὲν ὁ ἥλιος ποδιαῖος, πεπίστευται δ' εἶναι μείζων τῆς οἰκουμένης ('False things also appear, concerning things about which one has at the same time a true conception/supposition, as, e.g., the sun appears a foot across, but is firmly believed to be larger than the inhabited world'). The statement here that the sun appears a foot across (φαίνεται...ὁ ἥλιος ποδιαῖος) is a rather different case again. Ἡ ποδιαιότης is not a secondary quality nor an Aristotelian proper sensible, and judgement is clearly built into φαίνεται here, in the sense that if the sun appears a foot across that is because it looks as though it were a foot across, i.e., you would say, just from looking at it, and taking nothing else into account, that it was a foot or so across. To understand an εἶναι with φαίνεται ποδιαῖος here would seem completely appropriate, and to find one printed also appropriate – except that that would give repetition of εἶναι and might interfere with the emphasis which the εἶναι following πεπίστευται clearly has.

Appearance and belief in Theaetetus *151d–187a*

I think that this passage makes clear that the connection between φαίνεσθαι, including φαίνεσθαι plus infinitive, and belief is complex. It suggests, at least so far as appearance via the senses is concerned, that, all things being equal, one believes or is disposed to believe that things are as they appear (to be); but that things are not always equal, and one may know or believe that things are not as they appear (to be). Given what is said here, it would be appropriate for someone to say: 'If you didn't know any better, you would think, just from looking at it, that the sun was a foot across.' Would it make a difference if there were a dative with φαίνεται? A dative, such as 'to one', is presumably understood; and in the example from *De Anima* 2.10 we had the dative τοῖς κάμνουσι, but nevertheless any belief going with the bitter appearance seemed to be one which could be overridden. I think, however, that in some cases a dative could make a difference: compare 'It appears to be a foot across, but I don't believe it really is' with 'It appears to me to be a foot across, but I don't believe it really is', which is at least a bit odd, even if one puts a heavy emphasis on 'appears'. (However, 'It appears to me to be a foot across, but I am not sure that it is' sounds perfectly all right.)[14]

In *Sophist* 235e5–236a3 we are concerned again with misleading appearances. The Eleatic Stranger and Theaetetus agree that, if those who fashion colossal statues or produce colossal drawings fashioned or drew to scale, the upper parts would appear (φαίνοιτ' ἄν) too small, the lower too big, because of the different distances from which they are seen by us. They do not explicitly agree that the statues and drawings would appear wrong even to those in the know; but I assume that Plato thought that that was so, and that he thought that any instinctive belief going with the appearance could be counteracted by the knowledge that the statues and drawings were, in the case imagined, actually to scale.

Finally I turn to *Republic* 602c7–603a8,[15] where we find the examples of things which appear larger from closer to than from further away, and of sticks which appear straight when out of water but bent when (partly) submerged, and so on, with φαίνεσθαι used for 'appear' (602c8, d8, e5). Socrates argues that the reasoning part of the soul forms its judgements in such cases in accordance with measurement and the like, whereas another but inferior part of the soul forms its judgements contrary to measurement (and, by implication, in accordance with appearances), judging, for example, that the sticks change shape when they are (partly) immersed in water. On the view argued in this passage, a person (or at any rate a person who has carried out measurements) often holds two conflicting opinions in cases of the kind considered (see also 603c11–d2), but no one part of his or her soul does so. Moreover, the reasoning part of the soul holds sway (ἄρχειν, 602d7) – that is to say in effect, I assume, that its judgement is dominant;

the judgement in accordance with appearances remains, it appears, at least if the appearances remain, but is overridden. This passage, unlike those cited from the *De Anima* and the *Sophist*, implies that, when someone receives appearances via the senses, part of the soul forms a judgement in accordance with those appearances, and that this judgement can remain, even if it is overridden. Nevertheless, because this passage, like the others, allows that a judgement in accordance with appearances can be overridden, it too supports the view that if *x* appears/φαίνεται *F* to a person *y* it does not without qualification follow that *y* judges or believes that *x* is *F*, for *y*'s dominant belief may be that *x* is not *F* – and perhaps *y* may simply have no firm belief as to whether *x* is *F*. On the question whether a judgement in accordance with appearances is to be identified with the appearing, the passage is, in my view, at least neutral. It *may* be being assumed that the judging contrary to measurement at 603a1 has already been mentioned in the talk of things' appearing bent and straight, and so on. On the other hand, it *may* be implied at 602e4–6 that when the reasoning part of the soul has judged, for example, that a stick which appears bent is actually straight, the stick often still appears bent *to that part of the soul*, which would imply that something can appear bent to a subject without that subject's judging it to be bent. However, the lines are construed differently by different commentators and translators, the differences turning in part on whether φαίνεται implies judgement, and I do not wish to put weight on them.[16] The claim that in *Republic* 602c7–603a8 a judgement in accordance with appearances can be overridden while the appearances remain does not require the support of a particular construal of 602e4–6.[17]

Two things seem to emerge from these five passages: (a) that φαίνεσθαι can be used where the focus is on how things look, taste, sound, and so on; (b) that, at least in the case of appearance via the senses, the connection between φαίνεσθαι, even φαίνεσθαι plus infinitive, and belief is fairly complex, and more complex than is allowed for by the view that, say, τοῦτο φαίνεταί μοι λευκὸν (εἶναι) should be interpreted as saying 'I believe that this is white.' Given that the gloss at 152a6–8 is clearly intended to cover cases of appearance via the senses, it follows that the language in which it is expressed is not a ground for interpreting it simply and straightforwardly in terms of belief.

However, the gloss is clearly intended also to cover cases of metaphorical appearing, e.g., its appearing, in Theaetetus' judgement, at least for the time being, that knowledge is nothing other than perception (151e1–3), or a course of action's appearing just to someone, and so on. Consider the following four forms of declaration:

(1) This appears just.
(2) This appears to be just.

(3) This appears just to me.
(4) This appears to me to be just.

It seems to me that whereas to add to (3) or (4) 'but I don't believe it really is' or 'but it isn't really' would sound self-defeating, such additions are possible with the more open (1) and (2), particularly if 'appears' is emphasized. However that may be, at least this is surely clear, that all four forms of declaration are compatible with less than confident belief on the part of the speaker.[18] Theaetetus has no confident belief as to how knowledge should be defined when he makes his suggestion at 151e (see 148b6–8, d4–e6). Similarly, when Socrates presents 'the things which appear to him' at *Republic* 517b–c (τὰ δ' οὖν ἐμοὶ φαινόμενα οὕτω φαίνεται, b7–8), what immediately precedes b7–8 suggests less than confident belief. And interlocutors in Platonic dialogues often respond with φαίνεται; it does not always express firm agreement. However, statements that one *thinks* or *believes* that such-and-such is so need not express confident belief either, so that to interpret the gloss in application to such cases as that of its appearing to someone that knowledge is perception in terms of belief or at least an inclination to believe need not be unreasonable.[19]

III

Against the background of this brief consideration of the use of φαίνεσθαι and of 'to appear',[20] I return more fully to the *Theaetetus*. In the τόκος, or 'delivery', section of Part 1 (151d–160e), in which, at least ostensibly, a theory of perception[21] is developed as a framework in which both the measure doctrine and Theaetetus' suggestion that knowledge is perception would be true, there is almost no explicit mention of judgement or belief.[22] There is none in the initial statement of the wind example, i.e., in 152b2–9 (quoted above, p. 125). In what follows on the wind example down to 152c7, there would seem to be implicit reference to belief in the ἀψευδές ('free from falsehood', McDowell) of c5 (though the use of ἀληθής and ψευδής, 'true' and 'false', in the *Theaetetus* is something which itself requires careful examination);[23] and some might insist that the occurrence of φαντασία ('appearance'/'appearing') and φαίνεται in b10–c1 imports belief.

In the passages which develop the theory of perception, and in that, at 182a–b, in which there is reference back to it, the focus is on how the colours and so on with which we are presented in perception come about. In the delineation of the theory of perception there is no explicit mention of belief. The main passage in the τόκος section in which thought, judgement, and belief are explicitly mentioned is that dealing with the potential objection to the measure doctrine and to Theaetetus' suggestion that knowledge is perception, from what happens in illness, including madness, and in dreams

(157e1 ff.). Socrates says, using παρακούειν, παρορᾶν, and παραισθάνεσθαι, that those who are ill, and especially those who are mad, are said to mishear, to mis-see, and generally to misperceive, and he speaks of 'false perceptions' (ψευδεῖς αἰσθήσεις); and Theaetetus says that he cannot deny that those who are mad or dreaming make false judgements (or 'hold false beliefs', ψευδῆ δοξάζουσι), whenever some think (οἴωνται) that they are gods, and others think (διανοῶνται) in their sleep that they have wings and are flying about.[24] Here we most certainly have reference to thought, judgement, and belief in Theaetetus' elaboration of what is involved in the 'misperceiving' mentioned by Socrates, and it occurs in close association with the repetitions of the gloss in 158a. Equally, however, we are here presented with cases far more complex than those the theory of perception is built around, in which sticks and stones 'are filled with whiteness' (156e), and so on. One should not overlook, however, the terms in which the measure doctrine is glossed at 158e5–6, where we have: τὰ ἀεὶ δοκοῦντα...τῷ δοκοῦντι εἶναι ἀληθῆ. This is not decisive: although a natural translation would be 'that the things which on each occasion seem are true for him who so thinks', one wonders whether τῷ δοκοῦντι is intended here (and at 162d1) simply to identify the one to whom things seem, rather than the one who so thinks; in addition, I have already alluded (p. 133) to the slippery use of 'true' and 'false' in the *Theaetetus*. Less ambivalent is 160c7–d4, at the very end of the τόκος, where Socrates' declaration that his perception is true is followed by the claim that he is a Protagorean judge (κριτής) of the things that are for him that they are, and of the things that are not that they are not. Nevertheless, it seems to me noteworthy that in the actual delineation of the theory of perception in which Socrates purports to develop the suggestion that knowledge is perception and the measure doctrine, at least as it applies to cases of perception, explicit references to thought, judgement, and belief on the part of perceivers are singularly absent. No such references are apparently thought necessary in order to illustrate how things might be for each person such as they appear to him or her in perception.

Things are different when we move into the ἀμφιδρόμια (160e7 ff.), in which Theaetetus' suggestion and the measure doctrine are examined (and the measure doctrine also further developed, in Socrates' 'defence' of it, 165e8–168c5). For one thing, in the ἀμφιδρόμια Socrates is concerned much of the time with cases in which the 'appearances' or 'seemings' do not occur via perception, but in which, for example, such-and-such a course of action seems just to a city;[25] and indeed from 158e δοκεῖν, which I translate 'to seem', is frequently used in place of φαίνεσθαι, which I translate 'to appear', in references to the measure doctrine.[26] But in addition to that, it seems from passages in the ἀμφιδρόμια that it is assumed that belief accompanies, or is even part of, perception, and that it has been assumed to be involved in the cases of perception which figure in the τόκος. For instance, in 166e–167a, in Socrates' defence of Protagoras, there is reference back to the example of Socrates ill and Socrates well, with φαίνεσθαι used and then δοξάζειν: it is said that one should not 'accuse the sick man of being ignorant because he makes the sort of judgements he does, and call the healthy one wise because he makes judgements of a different sort' (translation after McDowell). The example has developed since 159: it is now concerned with eating rather than drinking (166e3–4); but we have an explicit reference back to 159, nevertheless: 'remember, for example, what was said earlier on' (166e2). More striking are remarks made in 161d2–162a3, the second part of the 'pig and baboon' speech with which Socrates opens the ἀμφιδρόμια. See, for example, 161d5–7, where Socrates says that it has often been said, presumably in the τόκος, where colours and so on are described as occurring to perceivers privately, that each alone will judge (δοξάσει) the things which are his, and they are all correct and true; to which one might respond that this was not said, explicitly, even once in the τόκος – unless, of course, one takes it to have been said in 152, by the very introduction of the Protagorean view; rather, it seems, it is being assumed that judgement accompanies, or is part and parcel of, perception.

Two passages may suggest that the connection between perception and δόξα (normally translated 'judgement' or 'belief') is taken to be so close that some element of δόξα is actually part and parcel of perception. At 161d2–3, the second part of the pig and baboon speech begins as follows: 'for, if what each judges δι' αἰσθήσεως is to be true for him…', i.e., 'if what each judges through/by means of/on the basis of/in the course of, perception is to be true for him…'. The different possible translations of δι' αἰσθήσεως express different degrees of connection; but it seems to me that the expression could, though it need not, express a very close connection. The passage reminds one of *Sophist* 264a–b, where φαντασία is said to occur when δόξα arises δι' αἰσθήσεως, and φαίνεται to denote a mixing together of αἴσθησις and δόξα.

The second passage is 158d2–4, where Socrates says that both in dreams and in waking experience διαμάχεται ἡμῶν ἡ ψυχὴ τὰ ἀεὶ παρόντα δόγματα παντὸς μᾶλλον εἶναι ἀληθῆ ('at any one time our soul insists that whatever δόγματα are then present are true'). The παρόντα δόγματα referred to here are surely whatever the individual is presented with at any one time, whether in a dream or in waking experience; it is at the time so convincing – that is the thought, surely; and it fits experiences rather than beliefs. So, I think, Waterfield, who speaks of 'impressions'; and perhaps also McDowell, who has 'what seems to be the case at the moment'.[27] If δόγματα, a word certainly redolent of judgement and belief, is used here, in a context in which belief has indeed been spoken of in connection with madness and dreams, for what one is presented with in dreams and in waking experience, it suggests a tight knitting together of what one is presented with on the one hand and judgement or belief on the other. One wonders whether δόξα can also be so used (and notes that the δόγματα of 158d4 are referred back to as δοξάσματα at 158e3).

However, none of the passages considered seems to me to show conclusively that it is being assumed in the *Theaetetus* that in cases of appearance via the senses, or of appearances in dreams and the like, a belief in accordance with the appearances does not simply accompany the appearing but is rather part and parcel of it.[28] *Sophist* 264a–b is sometimes taken to show that in the *Theaetetus* also appearance via the senses includes belief – sc. a belief in accordance with the appearances.[29] However, our earlier consideration of five passages, including one from the *Sophist*, shows that this view of what φαντασία and φαίνεσθαι imply when used in connection with perception is at the very least a simplification, and that, even if a perceiver necessarily holds a belief in accordance with the appearances while those appearances last, it was clear to Plato that it need not be his or her dominant belief. One cannot therefore simply import into the *Theaetetus* without argument (and without some comment on 152b12, where appearance is equated with perception) the account of φαντασία and of φαίνεσθαι presented in *Sophist* 264. However, it is certainly true that in the *Theaetetus* the possibility that a subject's dominant belief may not be in accordance with appearances he or she is receiving is apparently ignored, either for the sake of simplicity, or because it was ignored in the measure doctrine, or for both these reasons. Its being ignored in the measure doctrine is connected with that doctrine's leaving little room, if any, for the critical examination of one's own and other people's φαντασίαι τε καὶ δόξαι (161e8).[30] It would be a pity to make this less apparent by interpreting the gloss at 152a6–8 simply and straightforwardly in terms of belief.

If the gloss at 152a6–8 is interpreted simply and straightforwardly in terms of belief, it would seem to follow that it should make no difference to its import if one replaced the way it is expressed at 152a6–8 with one using οἴεσθαι or ἡγεῖσθαι or νομίζειν or some other Greek verb for believing which lacks φαίνεσθαι's ties to light, sight, and literal appearing. I doubt, however, whether anyone wants to suggest that it is an accident, or incidental, that φαίνεσθαι is used. If, say, οἴεσθαι were used instead, Socrates' associating Theaetetus' suggestion that knowledge is perception with the measure doctrine would have far less surface plausibility; and neither illustrating the measure doctrine with the example of the wind, nor proceeding to develop the theory of perception, would seem at all natural. However, we have seen that, although there is almost no explicit mention of judgement or belief in the τόκος section, it nevertheless seems to be assumed that a judgement or belief in accordance with the appearances will at least accompany all cases of appearing via the senses or in dreams and the like. In addition, the measure doctrine is certainly taken in the *Theaetetus* to claim that every judgement or belief is true (for those who hold it for as long as they do so).[31] I therefore do not wish to suggest that the gloss should not be interpreted in terms of belief at all, but that it should not be taken simply to be equivalent to 'individual things are for me such as I believe them to be...' One needs to tell a more complicated story than that.

IV

In section III of Fine 1996a the author lays down as one criterion among others to be satisfied, if Plato's dialectical strategy in the first part of the *Theaetetus* is to succeed, a univocity criterion, viz. that each of the three theses introduced there – that knowledge is perception, the measure doctrine, and the Heraclitean theory – 'must be interpreted in a univocal way both when it is connected to the other two, and when it is refuted' (216); and, as I understand it, in her view, the measure doctrine is to be interpreted in exactly the same way both when it is applied to cases involving perception and in other cases. However, when one says, e.g., 'The course of action you suggest appears to me unjust', or its Greek equivalent expressed with φαίνεσθαι, 'appears' and φαίνεται would be being used metaphorically. On the other hand, in τοῦτό μοι φαίνεται λευκὸν (εἶναι) and 'this appears white to me/this appears to me to be white', φαίνεται and 'appears' are being used literally, at least in so far as literal appearance is referred to, even if judgement or belief are also referred to or implied; perhaps in at least some such cases they are used both literally and metaphorically, but certainly not just metaphorically.[32] I do not see how one can give a completely univocal interpretation of the gloss at 152a6–8 which does justice both to the force of φαίνεται and to the range of application which the measure doctrine is treated as having. A completely univocal interpretation would seem to require either that φαίνεται be used always literally only, or that it be used always metaphorically only, or that it be used always in both ways and with the same weighting of literal and metaphorical.

Someone might suggest that φαίνεται is used metaphorically in all cases to which the measure doctrine applies, with a natural allusion to literal appearing, arising from the origin of the metaphor. This is not convincing, however, for such a connection with literal appearing would be too weak to make Socrates' associating Theaetetus' suggestion that knowledge is perception with the measure doctrine at all plausible, and so on. (And one would want to know whether the measure doctrine so interpreted could apply at all to infants, and,

Patricia Clarke

if suitably re-expressed, to animals – i.e., one would want to know whether the allusion to perception was sufficiently strong to allow this.)

V

The whole pig and baboon speech merits examination, not least because of its references to animals. In the speech Socrates declares himself surprised that Protagoras did not make a pig or a baboon or some yet stranger creature which has perception a measure of all things. On Protagoras' own account, he says, he (Protagoras) is no better in point of wisdom than a tadpole, let alone another human being. What should he say instead, he asks. For if every δόξα is true (for its holder), how can one make sense of anyone's, even Protagoras', being a teacher, and how can one make sense of the whole business of philosophical discussion and the critical examination of one another's φαντασίαι τε καὶ δόξαι?

That Plato is in one way wholly serious in this speech, even in its possibly hyperbolical first part, is, I think, beyond doubt. He is arguing that, on the measure doctrine, our critical powers are not allowed their proper role; and, if he cared about anything, he cared about that, especially in connection with, say, questions about the nature of justice, and about how what is just and unjust should be determined – and one thinks in this connection of the content of the main digression (172d–177b/c).[33] However, he could (a) make this serious point by suggesting that Protagoras' account of how judgements can properly be arrived at is so inadequate that he might as well have made a pig, baboon, or tadpole a measure of all things, without (b) meaning seriously to imply that, if the measure doctrine applies at all, it could apply just as well to pigs, baboons, and tadpoles, as to human beings, over the same range of cases. Certainly, if the second part of the speech is supposed simply to repeat the point made in the first, it is difficult to avoid the conclusion that the first part makes its point hyperbolically, since to take it otherwise then implies that pigs, baboons, and tadpoles have 'appearings' on the topics covered by Protagoras in his teaching and by Socrates and his associates in their discussions. It might seem in addition that those who take the first part of the speech at face value, if they also interpret the measure doctrine simply and straightforwardly in terms of belief, would be committed to the view that Socrates here attributes belief even to tadpoles. However, one needs to be careful here: for since Socrates is surely suggesting in the speech that the measure doctrine is mistaken, the most one could take him to be suggesting about pigs, baboons, and tadpoles is that, *if* the measure doctrine were correct, it should apply to them as well. But perhaps to suggest even that is to suggest things can be said to 'appear' to animals, with whatever connotations of belief that is supposed to carry. (Perhaps some δόξαι, or kinds of δόξαι, arising δι' αἰσθήσεως [161d3] might be attributed to animals.) Protagoras is allowed to address himself to the pig and baboon part of the speech. He does so, in the person of Socrates, of course, at 162e and 166c7–9 ff. He argues that he can accommodate wisdom (or 'expertise', σοφία) on his account, by allowing that some δόξαι are better than others, and adds plants to the list of things which have perceptions.[34]

I have been concerned, not with how the gloss at 152a6–8 should be translated, on which I think there would be wide agreement that one should translate in terms of appearance and stay as close as possible to the Greek; I have been concerned rather with how it should be interpreted. I do not wish to suggest that it should not be interpreted in terms of judgement and belief at all, but rather that it cannot plausibly be interpreted as saying simply that things are for each person as he or she believes them to be, and that no completely univocal interpretation is possible.

Acknowledgements

I am indebted to a number of colleagues for their questions, comments, and suggestions. I would mention in particular G.P. Edwards, F.-G. Herrmann, and R. Kamtekar.

Notes

[1] A number of scholars have turned their attention to the argument in 184–7. For example, Cooper (1970), and, with fewer reservations, Modrak, have suggested that the labelling of the colours, sounds, etc. presented in sensation with their names might, consistently with 184–7, be counted as part of perception (at least in the case of adult humans; Cooper assumes that Plato 'does not imagine that beasts and day-old babies are capable of using concepts' 362). Frede, on the other hand, claims that in *Theaet.* 184–7 perception is presented as 'a purely passive affection of the mind' (379), and suggests that 'Plato's point in introducing this very narrow notion of perception is to untangle the conflation of perception, appearance, belief, and knowledge with which the main discussion of the dialogue begins in 151d ff.'. According to Frede, on the narrow notion of perception which he claims is introduced in 184–7, we perceive colours, sounds, etc., but not that something is red. See also, e.g., McDowell 118 (n. 2 on 151d–e) and 185 ff; Burnyeat 1976a; Burnyeat 1990, 12, 42 ff., and 52–65; Kanayama; Bostock 110 ff.; Sedley 106–7 n. 29, and 158 ff.

[2] Although at 152a1–2 Socrates says '[Protagoras] says the same things but in a different way', he first says (151e8–152a1) that Theaetetus 'runs the risk' (κινδυνεύεις) of having said the same as Protagoras, which could mean that he chances to have said the same as P., or merely that perhaps he has said the same as P. Only context can pin down the force of κινδυνεύειν. If anything pins down its force here, it is what *follows* it, so that *when it actually occurs* no restriction on its meaning to 'you chance to...' has yet been given. Perhaps that suggests that Plato did not want it read here only in that sense.

[3] Here 'feels cold' translates ῥιγῷ. The root meaning of ῥιγόω seems to be 'I shudder'

or 'shake', but it and/or ῥιγέω seem standardly to be used for feeling cold, e.g. at *Rep.* 440c2 and *Phileb.* 46c7; and the agreement in 152b10–11 that 'it appears so to each of us' suggests that both Socrates and Theaetetus are supposed to be conscious.

The Greek text, from 151e8 to 152b9 in the lineation of Duke et al., reads as follows:

ΣΩ. Κινδυνεύεις μέντοι λόγον οὐ φαῦλον εἰρηκέναι περὶ ἐπιστήμης, ἀλλ᾽ ὃν ἔλεγε καὶ Πρωταγόρας. τρόπον δέ τινα ἄλλον εἴρηκε τὰ αὐτὰ ταῦτα. φησὶ γάρ που 'πάντων χρημάτων μέτρον' ἄνθρωπον εἶναι, 'τῶν μὲν ὄντων ὡς ἔστι, τῶν δὲ μὴ ὄντων ὡς οὐκ ἔστιν.' ἀνέγνωκας γάρ που;
ΘΕΑΙ. Ἀνέγνωκα καὶ πολλάκις.
ΣΩ. Οὐκοῦν οὕτω πως λέγει, ὡς οἷα μὲν ἕκαστα ἐμοὶ φαίνεται τοιαῦτα μὲν ἔστιν ἐμοί, οἷα δὲ σοί, τοιαῦτα δὲ αὖ σοί· ἄνθρωπος δὲ σύ τε κἀγώ;
ΘΕΑΙ. Λέγει γὰρ οὖν οὕτω.
ΣΩ. Ἐικὸς μέντοι σοφὸν ἄνδρα μὴ ληρεῖν· ἐπακολουθήσωμεν οὖν αὐτῷ. ἆρ᾽ οὐκ ἐνίοτε πνέοντος ἀνέμου τοῦ αὐτοῦ ὁ μὲν ἡμῶν ῥιγῷ, ὁ δ᾽ οὔ; καὶ ὁ μὲν ἠρέμα, ὁ δὲ σφόδρα;
ΘΕΑΙ. Καὶ μάλα.
ΣΩ. Πότερον οὖν τότε αὐτὸ ἐφ᾽ ἑαυτοῦ τὸ πνεῦμα ψυχρὸν ἢ οὐ ψυχρὸν φήσομεν; ἢ πεισόμεθα τῷ Πρωταγόρᾳ ὅτι τῷ μὲν ῥιγῶντι ψυχρόν, τῷ δὲ μὴ οὔ;
ΘΕΑΙ. Ἔοικεν.

[4] (i) In what follows I speak sometimes of 'judgement' sometimes of 'belief', not regarding the difference in meaning as important for my discussion. (ii) I am not directly concerned with the views of the historical Protagoras, but with how the gloss at 152a6–8 should be interpreted in the context of the *Theaet.* (iii) Few commentators address directly the question how 152a6–8 should be interpreted, and even fewer consider what interpretation would follow from the language alone. McDowell (119–20) distinguishes two possible interpretations of the gloss: (a) each thing is, for any person, the way he perceives it as being; (b) each thing is, for any person, the way he is inclined to think it is. He goes on to say that, if there were no non-perceptual predicates, it would be impossible to distinguish (b) from (a); and this may imply that he construes (a) as well as (b) in terms of inclination to believe. In discussing 152a6–8, Barnes (1979, 239–42; rev. edn, 541–4) distinguishes a 'phenomenological' and a 'judgemental' sense of φαίνεσθαι, but without clear or explicit reference to syntax. In his view, the measure doctrine is interpreted phenomenologically at 152, but is not always so interpreted later, where it is often taken judgementally. I take him to allow that the language of 152a6–8, and that of *Crat.* 386a1–3, can support either interpretation (he does not discuss whether εἶναι should be read in the *Crat.* passage). He takes 'phenomenological seeming' and 'judgemental seeming' to 'differ not in range but in kind'. What some others write implies, sometimes more sometimes less directly, that they would interpret the gloss in such a way as always to involve judgement or belief. For example: Frede takes appearance to be 'treated as if it were the same as belief' at 158a, and elsewhere from 152b12 (to, I think, 184), and I think also at 152a6–8 (379). Dancy takes belief to be involved in the wind example which illustrates the gloss. See, for example, his final paragraph on p. 66, and his claim that 'the argument [for the Protagorean position] works by suppressing the possibility that the one to whom the wind seems cold might be wrong' (67). Kanayama (53) suggests that φαντασία ('appearance'/'appearing') is understood in the *Theaet.* in the same way as at *Soph.* 263e–264b, as a mixture of perception and judgement, with the

judgement being explicit judgement in the *Theaet*. no less than in the *Soph*. Burnyeat also takes the *Soph*. account of appearing as a mixture of perception and judgement to be assumed in the *Theaet*. so far as appearances via perception are concerned (1976a, 35; 1979, 100; 1990, 43); and other remarks he makes suggest that he assumes that 152a6–8 can be interpreted in part in terms of judgement or belief – see esp. 1976b, 177–8; 1990, 49–50 (and for further reference to *Soph*. 264a–b see below, pp. 135–6). Lee may have 152a6–8 as much in mind as any later passages in the remark: 'Protagoras' claim seems to be a doctrine of relativism, according to which something is the case for one if and only if it appears so to one' (48); cf. 50. See also Notomi 263–4. Sedley is somewhat elusive, but I think he takes judgement in accordance with the appearances to be involved in appearance to the senses. For example, he distinguishes 'appearing perceptually' from 'appearing' in a broader sense 'spanning all judgement and not just narrowly perceptual "appearance"', and apparently endorses Fine's distinction between Broad and Narrow Protagoreanism, both of which Fine characterizes in terms of belief, or an inclination to believe (49–50; and see Fine 1996a; 1996b, 107). To turn for contrast to older commentators: according to Cornford, 'Protagoras' word "appears" was not confined to what appears *real* to me in sense-perception; it included...what appears true to me, what I think or judge to be true'(32–3; see also 59, 71, 76, 100). Campbell, in his running précis, glosses the gloss as follows: 'What appears to me is real to me' (36). Most commentators seem to assume that a single univocal interpretation of the gloss can be given. I think this is true even of McDowell, in so far as he seems to offer alternative single interpretations, the choice between them to rest on the range of predicates to which the thesis being glossed is intended to apply; and Fine's Narrow Protagoreanism is supposed to be included in her Broad Protagoreanism. Barnes presumably holds that the gloss is not interpreted univocally.

[5] Duke et al., where *Crat*. 385e4–386a4 reads as follows:

ΣΩ. Φέρε δὴ ἴδωμεν, ὦ Ἑρμόγενες, πότερον καὶ τὰ ὄντα οὕτως ἔχειν σοι φαίνεται, ἰδίᾳ αὐτῶν ἡ οὐσία εἶναι ἑκάστῳ, ὥσπερ Πρωταγόρας ἔλεγεν λέγων 'πάντων χρημάτων μέτρον' εἶναι ἄνθρωπον, ὡς ἄρα οἷα μὲν ἂν ἐμοὶ φαίνηται τὰ πράγματα εἶναι, τοιαῦτα μὲν ἔστιν ἐμοί, οἷα δ' ἂν σοί, τοιαῦτα δὲ σοί· ἢ ἔχειν δοκεῖ σοι αὐτὰ αὑτῶν τινα βεβαιότητα τῆς οὐσίας;

[6] Later in the article, at 233, Fine refers back to what she said at 212–13 but in more equivocal terms: 'as we have seen (in sect. 2), as appearance is understood here it includes (or is a kind of) belief'; (by 'here' she means in claims that, say, such-and-such an object appears red to such-and-such a perceiver). The view of 212–13 she expresses also at 1996b, 106, where, however, she adds (n. 4): '"Appears" can also be used both epistemically and non-epistemically: I can say that the oar appears (looks) bent in water, where I do not mean to commit myself to the belief that it is bent in water; or I can say that the wind appears cold, where I do mean to express my belief about how it is. If, as I have suggested, (P) uses "appears" to express beliefs, then it uses "appears" epistemically.' It is not clear from this whether in Fine's view 'non-epistemic' occurrences of φαίνεσθαι take infinitives expressed or understood, nor whether, in her view, 'epistemic' and 'non-epistemic' occurrences are to be identified by context, and, if so, in quite what way or ways. She refers (107, n. 6) to Barnes' distinction between 'phenomenological' and 'judgemental' seeming (see n. 4, above). She counts Barnes' phenomenological seemings' as 'non-epistemic appearances in the perceptual realm'. In fact Barnes later

takes phenomenological appearing expressible with φαίνεσθαι to include non-perceptual cases, illustrating with, e.g., 'That argument *looks* sound – but don't be taken in by it', 'Incest strikes me as wrong in Alexandria' (1982, 63–4; cf. 1980, 491, n. 1, and Annas and Barnes, 22–4). Barnes distinguishes 'non-veridical' from 'veridical' senses of φαίνεσθαι, saying that the distinction 'coincides by and large with the syntactical distinction between φαίνεσθαι + infinitive and φαίνεσθαι + participle' (1980, 491, n. 1).

[7] I ignore occurrences of φαίνεσθαι with the epexegetic infinitive, such as we find, e.g., at *Phaedo* 84c3, where ὡς ἰδεῖν ἐφαίνετο means, literally, 'as he appeared, to look at'. Notomi discusses the grammar of φαίνεσθαι (91–4), but without special reference to appearing white, or sweet, or the like.

[8] See esp. sections 2143 (p. 476), and 2119 (p. 473).

[9] For Goodwin on the use of φαίνεσθαι with a participle and its use with an infinitive see 1899, sect. 914, pp. 362–3. (On its use with a participle see also 1894, sect. 1588 (pp. 341–2), taken together with the entry for φαίνω in the Greek Index.) For Goodwin's counting φαίνεσθαι as a copulative verb see 1894, sects 907–8 (p. 199), again together with the entry for φαίνω in the Greek Index. At sect. 907 the closest example Goodwin offers to one with φαίνεσθαι is νομίζεται σοφός, which he translates 'he is thought wise'.

[10] See Kühner (ed. Gerth) vol. II, pt I, sect. 353, 3 (pp. 37–8), and sect. 355 (pp. 42–4); vol. II, pt II, sect. 473, 1 (p. 5), sect. 482, 2 (pp. 52–3), and sect. 484, 13 (p. 71).

[11] To take just two examples: (i) At *Theaet.* 174d1, in the main digression, it is said of the philosopher: ἀπορῶν οὖν γελοῖος φαίνεται ('so, being at a loss, he appears ridiculous'). Cornford, Levett-Burnyeat, McDowell, and Waterfield all translate in terms of the philosopher's looking ridiculous (or 'very comic', or 'foolish', or 'a fool'), none in terms of his appearing to be ridiculous, and none in terms of belief. This is the more striking, given that at c6 it has been said that the philosopher's awkwardness is prodigious, providing a δόξα of stupidity (ἡ ἀσχημοσύνη δεινή, δόξαν ἀβελτερίας παρεχομένη). Campbell and Cornford here render δόξα (normally translated 'judgement' or 'belief', but connected with δοκεῖν, 'to seem' or 'to believe') in terms of 'seeming', but Levett-Burnyeat, McDowell, and Waterfield, very naturally, render in terms of 'reputation'. If any had felt it natural to render φαίνεται at d1 in terms of 'belief', δόξα at c6 would have provided a strong invitation to do so, but it was not accepted. (ii) At 1070–1 in Euripides' *Hippolytus*, Hippolytus says to Theseus: αἰαῖ, πρὸς ἧπαρ, δακρύων ἐγγὺς τόδε, | εἰ δὴ κακός γε φαίνομαι δοκῶ τε σοί (Barrett's accentuation). LS and LSJ cite 1071 as an example in which φαίνομαι is joined with δοκέω. Barrett translates: 'Ah, that wounds me deep: this is near to tears, if I seem base and you think me so.' He takes φαίνομαι 'of the appearance generally', δοκῶ σοί of Theseus' own opinion.

[12] In Cooper 1997, at 1267. A more literal translation would be: 'Those which are rougher appear sour, the less rough tangy.'

[13] That is to say, it is not claimed here *by Aristotle* that everything *tastes* bitter to those who are ill, rather than that everything *appears* to them *to be* bitter. However, it seems pretty clear that we are here presented with a common opinion, which appears also at *Theaet.* 159b–e, and 166e3–4; and it seems reasonable to say that when it expresses a common opinion τοῖς κάμνουσι πικρὰ πάντα φαίνεται claims that everything tastes bitter to those who are ill.

[14] In *De Anima* 3.3 Aristotle makes various claims both about φαντασία, sometimes using φαίνεσθαι, and about ὑπόληψις ('conception'/'understanding'), and the lines

cited here occur in the course of his discussion. One might therefore wonder whether his use of φαίνεται in this context is representative of Greek usage in general. However, the view presented here that the sun appears a foot across seems to be a common view, expressed in an ordinary way. That the sun was nevertheless not a foot across seems also to have been a widespread opinion. Cf. Aristotle, *Meteorologica* 1.345b1–3; *De Insomniis* 1.458b28–29, 2.460b18–20. Cf. also *Epinomis* 983a, and see Barnes 1989. I translate πεπίστευται at *De An.* 428b4 as 'is firmly believed', which is in line with Hicks' own translation, and that of J.A. Smith in Barnes 1984. Hamlyn has more simply 'we believe'. See further n. 19 (and e.g. *Theaet.* 144e3, 170c9; *Rep.* 603a4, b10).

[15] Line references are to the new Oxford text (Slings).

[16] The lines read: τούτῳ δὲ πολλάκις μετρήσαντι καὶ σημαίνοντι μείζω ἄττα εἶναι ἢ ἐλάττω ἕτερα ἑτέρων ἢ ἴσα τἀναντία φαίνεται ἅμα περὶ ταὐτά. Grube translates: 'But when this part has measured and has indicated that some things are larger or smaller or the same size as others, the opposite appears to it at the same time.' Annas (338) also seems to allow that things appear to the reasoning part of the soul contrary to its calculations. Jowett and Campbell (1894) do not, nor does Adam. According to Jowett and Campbell, 'the dative is in a loose construction with the whole sentence, like a genitive absolute, and is not to be taken with φαίνεται' (vol. III, 452). Adam takes τἀναντία to refer to 'the contrary (in any given instance) of the impression formed without the aid of measurement' (vol. II, 407–8; see also 466–7). Others, including recently Sedley (113–14, n. 40), and, according to Sedley, now also Burnyeat (in Burnyeat 1999, at 233, n. 12), take conflicting opinions to be attributed in *Rep.* 10 to different parts of the rational part of the soul. Halliwell rejects this view; commenting on 602e4–6, he writes (134): 'in strict grammar, the rational element is the indirect object of *phainetai*; but as the sequel shows, this should not mean that the reason itself succumbs to erroneous sense impressions, only that the soul as a whole does so'. Barney suggests the datives be taken with τἀναντία, rather than with φαίνεται (287, in n. 5). For my purposes in this paper, it does not matter precisely which parts or sub-parts of the soul are being supposed to hold conflicting opinions, and on this point I have simply followed what seems the most natural reading of 602c7–603a8 (and I have taken πολλάκις, 'often', at 602e4, which Grube seems to ignore, with 'appears' and not, as some do, with 'has measured').

[17] With this passage from the *Republic* one might compare in particular *Protag.* 356c4–357a5.

[18] Compare the remarks made, p. 131, on similar forms of statement in connection with cases involving perception.

[19] At *De An.* 3.3.428a20–2 Aristotle says that being persuaded (τὸ πεπεῖσθαι) follows πίστις (*pistis*, which Hicks translates 'conviction') and πίστις follows δόξα – οὐκ ἐνδέχεται γὰρ δοξάζοντα οἷς δοκεῖ μὴ πιστεύειν ('for it is not possible for one judging not to believe firmly in the things which seem to him'). Hamlyn suggests that Aristotle may mean something less strong than conviction by πίστις, e.g. 'acceptance' (132, note on 428a16). The word suggests 'trusting belief', and one remembers its use at *Rep.* 511e1 and 534a1 in connection with the Line. (Aristotle also says here that animals lack πίστις, but that not all lack φαντασία.) See also n. 14.

[20] Not all types of appearing have been considered – not appearances in dreams and hallucinations, for example. I think, however, that the consideration has been sufficient for our purposes.

[21] I speak here of a single theory for the sake of simplicity, and do not mean to take

issue with those, like Day, who argue that no single coherent theory emerges from the relevant passages of the *Theaet.*

[22] I think I have read this observation somewhere in the literature, but cannot trace the reference. My apologies to anyone to whom acknowledgement is due here. (Since writing this I note that Chappell says of ψευδῆ δοξάσουσι at 158b2 that 'this is the first time Plato in the *Theaetetus* speaks of *beliefs* rather than *perceptions*' (80, n. 60), and (91) that in 151–60 Plato's main concern is 'perception, not *judgements about* perception', and he makes other similar remarks.)

[23] I have in mind such passages as 161d6–7, 167a7–8, 171a6–9, all of which occur in presentations of Protagoras' thought. It may be that in all of them the claim that all judgements and beliefs are true is supposed to be supported simply by a framework for which the theory of perception provides a model. Cf. 178b3–7. However, it is difficult not to see in all these passages hints both (i) of a failure to distinguish between an experience or belief-content's being ἀληθές ('true') in the sense of being genuine and its being so in the sense of being veridical, and (ii) of the paradox according to which there can be no such thing as false judgement or belief, given that to judge or believe falsely is to judge or believe something which is not. The paradox is spelled out at 188d3–189b6, as a problem requiring solution, and Plato returns to it in the *Sophist*. We meet it also at *Rep.* 478b5–c2; applied to false speaking at *Crat.* 429c7–d6; and applied first to speaking and then also to judging or believing at *Euthyd.* 283e7 ff., where at 286b8 ff. it is associated with οἱ ἀμφὶ Πρωταγόραν (c2; 'the followers of Protagoras'). The senses of ἀληθής mentioned above are to some extent distinguished at *Phileb.* 37, which might lead one to expect that, in writing the *Theaet.*, Plato might have been aware of the dangers of passing from one to the other. However, one finds slippery use of 'true' and 'false' in passages in which Protagoras' thought is not being presented. I have in mind the references, in connection with the midwifery motif, to the possibility that one of Socrates' associates might give birth to an εἴδωλον ('image') or to something ἀνεμιαῖον ('windy', 'full of wind', and so, presumably, empty). In the main midwifery section (149a1–151d3) the relevant passages are: 150a8–b4, b9–c3, e6–7, and 151c2–d3; then: 151e5–6, 157c7–d3, 160e7–161a4, and 210b4 ff. In addition, 160e2–3, 161e4 ff., and 184a9–b1 also pick up the midwifery motif, but without special reference to the possibility of εἴδωλα. In part, as the terms εἴδωλα and ἀνεμιαῖα would imply, the εἴδωλα seem to be productions which are not genuine views, in part to be genuine views which are false, as the treatment of Theaetetus' suggested definitions of knowledge would imply; and the initial claim at 150a8 ff. that there are no parallels to these εἴδωλα for the ordinary midwife is not reflected in the later passages.

[24] Or 'and others think that they are flying about in their sleep'.

[25] See, for example, 167c4–6; cf. 172a1–4.

[26] Other expressions are used as well, either in statements of the doctrine or in expressing particular applications of it: e.g., δοξάζειν (161d3), νομίζειν (167c6), οἰηθεῖσα θέσθαι (172a3 [cf. b1–2], 177d4), οἴεσθαι (178b–c), all of which connote judgement or belief.

[27] Contrast Barnes 1982, 68–9, incl. n. 40.

[28] Some might have expected reference here also to 167a6–b4, where δοξάζειν ('to judge') and φαντάσματα ('appearances'/'impressions') are certainly very closely associated. However, the φαντάσματα of b2–3 are 'the things one experiences' (ἃ ἂν πάσχῃ, a8), and are presented as the objects of judgements, i.e., as their contents or what they

are about. There is no clear identification in this passage of having something appear to one and judging. More problematic might be the implication in 151d–187a that the theory of perception can be applied to, e.g., largeness (see, for example, 154b1–6), which is not a purely phenomenal property. However, even if this implies that an element of judgement is built into something's looking big to someone, and so on for other cases, it is noteworthy that the theory of perception is *illustrated* only for whiteness, sweetness, bitterness, and, to some extent, warmth (156d–e, 159c–e, 182a–b).

It is never made explicit in the *Theaet.* precisely what the content of a belief in accordance with appearances received via the senses would be. Perhaps the δόξαι κατὰ τὰς αἰσθήσεις ('δόξαι in accordance with the perceptions') referred to at 179c3–4 would simply record the colours, tastes, sounds, and so on presented in the relevant perceptions, as might be suggested by passages on the theory of perception, and by 182d1–7. It is obviously more plausible to claim that to have something appear white, or sweet, and so on to one involves a judgement of this simple kind than to claim that, say, having a stone appear white to one involves one's identifying what appears white to one as a stone and judging that it is white.

[29] See n. 4.

[30] The 'appearings and δόξαι' referred to at 161e8 are of a kind to be examined in philosophical discussion, rather than appearances via the senses and beliefs in accordance with those appearances (see below, p. 138). It seems appropriate nevertheless to borrow the *phrase* here.

[31] This is implied in the pig and baboon speech; see also, e.g., 167d2–3 towards the end of Socrates' 'defence' of Protagoras, 170c2–4 ff. in the context of 169e8–170a5 ff., and 179c1–2. Exactly what view or views are attributed to Protagoras in the *Theaet.* is of course disputed. Here I wish only to acknowledge that, although in the τόκος a sense in which things are for one such as they appear to one is ostensibly made out, with no explicit reference to belief, in the ἀμφιδρόμια the measure doctrine is taken to imply that every judgement or belief is true for those who hold it – or perhaps to imply that every judgement or belief is true.

[32] Perhaps any extension beyond appearance to sight is to an extent metaphorical. If so, 'appears' in 'x appears cold' and 'x appears sweet' is already metaphorical – though not in the same way as in 'x appears just'. However, the main point is that φαίνεται at 152a7 must cover *both* appearing to be the case, whatever the subject-matter, *and* looking, feeling, tasting, and the like.

[33] Both here and in n. 11, I refer to 172d–177b/c as the 'main digression'. Jowett (1953, vol. III, 196) counted the midwifery passage as another. Quite apart from that, much of the meat of the *Theaet.* discussion comes in passages which, formally speaking, can be seen as digressions, e.g. 151e4–c. 184a9; 187c7–200d4; 201d4–206c2. The 'main digression' is like a chorus, as may have been Plato's own view; see esp. 173b–c.

[34] McDowell (158–9) and Campbell (76–7) appear to take the pig and baboon part of the speech at face value; so also, by implication, Burnyeat (1976b, 188, n. 18), and I think Waterfield (163–4) does too. I take Cornford (62, 70, 72) to have regarded it as valid against the measure doctrine in application to perception, not in application to judgement. To see humour in the passage, as does, e.g., Chappell (88), is not necessarily to see it as making its point hyperbolically.

Bibliography

Adam, J. (ed.)
- 1963   *The* Republic *of Plato*, 2nd edn, with critical notes, commentary and appendices, introduction by D.A. Rees, Cambridge.

Annas, J.
- 1981   *An Introduction to Plato's* Republic, Oxford.

Annas, J. and Barnes, J.
- 1985   *The Modes of Scepticism*, Cambridge.

Aristotle   *De Anima*, see Hicks.

Barnes, J.
- 1979   *The Presocratic Philosophers*, 2 vols., London. Revd edn, 1 vol., 1982, London.
- 1980   'Aristotle and the methods of ethics', *Revue Internationale de Philosophie* 133-4, 490–511.
- 1982   'The beliefs of a Pyrrhonist', *Proceedings of the Cambridge Philological Society* NS 28, 1–29. Repr. in *Elenchos* 4 (1983), 5–43, and in Burnyeat and Frede (eds.) *The Original Sceptics*, 58–91. Incorporated into J. Barnes, 'Pyrrhonism, belief and causation: observations on the Scepticism of Sextus Empiricus', *Aufstieg und Niedergang der Römischen Welt* 36.4 (1990), 2608–95. My references are to Burnyeat and Frede.
- 1989   'The size of the sun in antiquity', *Acta Classica Universitatis Scientiarum Debrecenensis* 25, 29–41.

Barnes, J. (ed.)
- 1984   *The Complete Works of Aristotle: The revised Oxford translation*, 2 vols., Princeton.

Barney, R.
- 1992   'Appearances and impressions', *Phronesis* 37, 283–313.

Barratt, W.S.
- 1964   *Euripides:* Hippolytos, edited with introduction and commentary, Oxford.

Bostock, D.
- 1988   *Plato's* Theaetetus, Oxford.

Burnyeat, M.
- 1976a   'Plato on the grammar of perceiving', *Classical Quarterly* NS 26, 29–51.
- 1976b   'Protagoras and self-refutation in Plato's *Theaetetus*', *Philosophical Review* 85, 172–95. Repr. in S. Everson (ed.) *Companions to Ancient Thought 1: Epistemology*, Cambridge, 39–59. My references are to the original.
- 1979   'Conflicting appearances', *Proceedings of the British Academy* 65, 69–111.
- 1990   *The* Theaetetus *of Plato*, introductory essay, with a translation of the *Theaetetus* by M.J. Levett, rev. Burnyeat, Indianapolis. Pp. 7–31, 39–52 of the essay are included in Fine 1999, 320–54; my references are all to the original.
- 1999   'Culture and society in Plato's *Republic*', *The Tanner Lectures on Human Values* 20, 215–324.

Burnyeat, M. and Frede, M. (eds.)
- 1997   *The Original Sceptics: A controversy*, Indianapolis.

Campbell, L.
- 1883   *The* Theaetetus *of Plato*, with a revised text and English notes, 2nd edn, Oxford. See also Jowett and Campbell.

Chappell, T.
  2004   *Reading Plato's* Theaetetus, Sankt Augustin. Also published 2005, Indianapolis.
Cooper, J.M.
  1970   'Plato on sense perception and knowledge: *Theaetetus* 184–6', *Phronesis* 15, 123–46. Reprinted in Fine 1999, 355–67. My references are to Fine.
Cooper, J.M. (ed.)
  1997   *The Complete Works of Plato*, Indianapolis. In translation, various translators, edited with introduction and notes.
Cornford, F.M.
  1935   *Plato's Theory of Knowledge*, London. The *Theaetetus* and the *Sophist* of Plato translated with a running commentary.
Dancy, R.M.
  1987   'Theaetetus' first baby: *Theaetetus* 151e–160e', *Philosophical Topics* XV, 61–102.
Day, J.M.
  1997   'The theory of perception in Plato's *Theaetetus* 152–183', *Oxford Studies in Ancient Philosophy* XV, 51–80.
Duke, E.A., Hicken, W.F., Nicoll, W.S.M., Robinson, D.B. and Strachan, J.C.G.
  1995   *Platonis Opera*, Tomus I, Oxford. Critical edn, Oxford Classical Texts.
Fine, G.
  1996a   'Protagorean relativisms', *Proceedings of the Boston Area Colloquium in Ancient Philosophy* X, Lanham Md. The colloquium was held in 1994.
  1996b   'Conflicting appearances: *Theaetetus* 153d–154b', in C. Gill and M.M. McCabe (eds.) *Form and Argument in Late Plato*, Oxford, 105–33.
Fine, G. (ed.)
  1999   *Plato*, vol. I, *Metaphysics and Epistemology*, Oxford Readings in Philosophy, Oxford. Vol. I was also published in one volume with vol. II, *Ethics, Politics, Religion and the Soul*, 2000, Oxford.
Frede, M.
  1987   'Observations on perception in Plato's later dialogues', in M. Frede *Essays on Ancient Philosophy*, Oxford. Reprinted in Fine 1999, 377–83; my references are to Fine.
Goodwin, W.W.
  1889   *Syntax of the Moods and Tenses of the Greek Verb*, 3rd edn, London.
  1894   *A Greek Grammar*, 2nd edn, Basingstoke.
Grube, G.M.A.
  1992   *Plato:* Republic (translation), 2nd edn, rev. C.D.C. Reeve, Indianapolis. Included in Cooper 1997.
Halliwell, S.
  1988 and 1993   *Plato:* Republic *10*, with translation and commentary, Warminster.
Hamlyn, D.W.
  1993   *Aristotle:* De Anima *Books II and III (with passages from Book I)*, translated with introduction and notes, Clarendon Aristotle Series, 2nd edn, with a report on recent work and a revised bibliography by C. Shields, Oxford.
Hicks, R.D.
  1907   *Aristotle:* De Anima, with translation, introduction and notes, Cambridge.

Jowett, B.
- 1953 *The Dialogues of Plato*, translated into English with analyses and introductions, 4 vols., 4th edn, Oxford.

Jowett, B. and Campbell, L.
- 1894 *Plato's* Republic, Greek text, edited, with notes and essays, 3 vols., Oxford.

Kanayama, Y.
- 1987 'Perceiving, considering, and attaining being: *Theaetetus* 184–6', *Oxford Studies in Ancient Philosophy* V, 29–81.

Kühner, R.
- 1898 *Ausführliche Grammatik der Griechischen Sprache*, vol. II, Pt I, 3rd edn, ed. B. Gerth, Hanover and Leipzig.
- 1904 *Ausfürhliche Grammatik der Griechischen Sprache*, vol. II, Pt II, 3rd edn, ed. B. Gerth, Hanover and Leipzig.

Lee, M.-K.
- 2000 'The secret doctrine: Plato's defence of Protagoras in the *Theaetetus*', *Oxford Studies in Ancient Philosophy* XIX, 47–86.

Levett, M.J.
- 1992 *Plato:* Theaetetus, Indianapolis. Translation, ed., with introduction, by B. Williams; rev. M. Burnyeat. The translation is included in Burnyeat 1990, and in Cooper 1997.

Liddell, H.G. and Scott, R.
- 1882 *A Greek-English Lexicon*, 7th edn, Oxford.
- 1968 *A Greek-English Lexicon*, 9th edn (of 1940, rev. H.S. Jones), with Supplement, Oxford.

McDowell, J.M.
- 1973 *Plato:* Theaetetus, translated with notes, Clarendon Plato Series, Oxford.

Modrak, D.M.
- 1981 'Perception and judgment in the *Theaetetus*', *Phronesis* 26, 35–54.

Notomi, N.
- 1999 *The Unity of Plato's* Sophist, Cambridge.

Sedley, D.
- 2004 *The Midwife of Platonism*, Oxford.

Slings, S.R.
- 2003 *Platonis* Respublica, critical edn, Oxford Classical Texts, Oxford.

Smyth, H.W.
- 1956 *Greek Grammar*, rev. G.M. Messing, Cambridge, Mass.

Waterfield, R.
- 1987 *Plato:* Theaetetus, translation and essay, Penguin Classics, Harmondsworth.

7

THE ARGUMENT FOR THE REALITY OF CHANGE AND CHANGELESSNESS IN PLATO'S *SOPHIST* (248e7–249d5)

Vasilis Politis

1. Introduction

Plato's metaphysics, from beginning to end, is tiered rather than tier-less.[1] This is because Plato's general account of reality is characterized by a fundamental distinction between certain things, especially the changeless forms, which he argues are perfect beings,[2] and certain other things, the changing objects of sense-perception, which he argues are something, as opposed to being nothing at all, only by virtue of being appropriately related to and dependent on those perfect beings.[3] However, in a dialogue addressed to the very question, 'What is there?' – and to the related question, 'What is being?' – he defends an answer which, so it appears, makes no reference to two tiers of reality and indicates rather a tier-insensitive ontology. This is the argument in the *Sophist* (248e7–249d5) which, together with the arguments that precede it in the dialogue, is summed up in the conclusion that any changing thing (κινούμενον), and likewise any changeless thing (ἀκίνητον, στάσιμον), is something that is.[4] There can be no doubt that this conclusion is about *any* changing thing and *any* changeless thing, and there is no suggestion, moreover, that the things referred to must occupy one or the other of two tiers of reality.

Following Julius Moravcsik and Gwil Owen, Lesley Brown has recently defended a tier-insensitive interpretation of this argument, such that the 'upshot is an all-inclusive ontology'.[5] On the other hand, a number of critics, including David Ross, Harold Cherniss, and Michael Frede, have defended a tiered interpretation.[6] It seems to me, however, that the choice between these two interpretations – which evidently is of central importance for the understanding of Plato – has not been properly characterized, much less settled. My aim in this chapter is to show, first, that the choice between these two fundamentally different and opposed interpretations of this argument, the tier-insensitive and the tiered interpretation, depends on how we read the single phrase, τὸ παντελῶς ὄν, at 248e8–249a1; and second, that the correct reading of this phrase commits us to a tiered interpretation beyond reasonable doubt, and that Plato's formulation of the conclusion (249c10–d4), which sums up both this and the previous arguments in the dialogue, does not state a commitment to a tier-insensitive ontology.

By way of clarification, I shall mean by 'a tiered ontology' the view that any answer to the question 'What is there?' requires thinking that there are tiers of reality; by 'a tier-less ontology', the view that any answer to this question requires thinking that there are no tiers of reality; and by 'a tier-insensitive ontology', the view that this question can be answered without either thinking that there are or thinking that there are not tiers of reality – it can be answered while remaining neutral on the question of whether there are tiers of reality. We shall see that the friends of the forms, to whom this argument is addressed, are committed to a tiered ontology, whereas the materialists, to whom the previous argument is addressed (246e5–247c8), are committed to a tier-less ontology. The question is whether the argument with the friends of the forms is aimed at a genuine reconciliation between them and the materialists and, therefore, aimed at a tier-insensitive ontology (the tier-insensitive interpretation) or, on the contrary, it accepts the commitment of the friends of the forms to a tiered ontology (the tiered interpretation, which I shall defend).

The argument is introduced by the question, what things should we include in 'complete being'? (τὸ παντελῶς ὄν, 248e7–249a2), and we shall see that its interpretation depends on how we read this single phrase, τὸ παντελῶς ὄν.[7] On one reading, it means 'complete being' in the sense of 'all-inclusive being', and we may refer to this as the 'unrestricted' reading. Read in this way, we shall see that the phrase requires a tier-insensitive interpretation of the argument. But while this reading may not be impossible, a restricted reading is far more plausible, such that the phrase means 'complete being' in the sense of 'perfect being'.[8] That this is a virtually unmistakable reference to the upper tier, the tier of things that are perfectly real, can be seen from what is the only other occurrence of this phrase in Plato, *Republic* 5.477a3–4, where he says: 'what is completely (τὸ παντελῶς ὄν) is completely knowable and what is in no way (μὴ ὄν μηδαμῇ) is in every way unknowable'.[9] Here the phrase τὸ παντελῶς ὄν is evidently used in a restricted sense, for it is contrasted, first, with that which 'is in no way', i.e. is nothing at all; and then with that which is so constituted as 'both to be and not to be' (εἶναί τε καὶ μὴ εἶναι, 477a6), which, it emerges, is a reference to the changing objects of sense-perception that make up the lower tier of reality. We shall see that the restricted reading of τὸ παντελῶς ὄν requires a tiered interpretation of the argument.

The conclusion of Plato's argument, on any interpretation, is that changing things, and not just the changeless forms, belong to complete being (τὸ παντελῶς ὄν). But while, on the tier-insensitive interpretation, this amounts to the relatively unexciting claim that changing things are indeed something as opposed to nothing at all,[10] on the tiered interpretation Plato is defending the altogether striking claim that changing things, or rather *some* changing things, just as much as the changeless forms, are perfect beings and belong to the upper tier. (This, we shall see, only appears to conflict with the statement of the conclusion at 249c10–d4, which is indeed about *any* changing and changeless things.) On both interpretations, changelessness (στάσις) refers to the changelessness peculiar to the forms. We shall see that both interpretations may also agree that change (κίνησις) refers, in the first instance at least, to the change peculiar to the rational soul which has the capacity to know the forms. This rationally cognizing soul is, in the first instance, our human, rationally cognizing soul. It is essentially a changing thing because both the activity of searching for knowledge is a kind of change (since it is an activity) and the process of acquiring knowledge is a kind of change (since it is a process). However, the two interpretations are divided about nothing less than what is at issue in the argument. Is the issue whether the changing soul and its change should be included simply in being and the totality of things (cf. τὸ ὄν τε καὶ τὸ πᾶν, 249d4), irrespective of whether this is an admission into a tiered or a tier-less ontology (the tier-insensitive interpretation)? Or is the issue whether the changing soul and its change should be included in perfect being and the upper tier (cf. τὸ παντελῶς ὄν), and only as a consequence should it be included in being and the totality of things (the tiered interpretation)?

One important consequence of this issue is that, on the tier-insensitive interpretation, Plato may justifiably move from 'being includes *some* changing things (namely, souls)' to 'being includes *any* changing things (that is, bodies too)' – indeed the conclusion (249c10–d4) appears to imply that he makes this move. On the tiered interpretation, on the other hand, Plato does not, and cannot justifiably, make such a move, and when he argues that τὸ παντελῶς ὄν includes, in addition to the changeless forms, changing things and change, what this means is that perfect being and the upper tier includes also changing souls and the change peculiar to them. It is true that the conclusion (249c10–d4) is about *any* kind of changing and changeless things (cf. ὅσα ἀκίνητα καὶ κεκινημένα, '*as many things as* are changeless and [*as many things as*] are changing', 249d3–4), but we shall see that this is because it is the conclusion not only of the present argument against the friends of the forms, who are committed to a tiered ontology, but also of the previous argument against the materialists, who are committed to a tier-less ontology.

The choice between the tiered and the tier-insensitive interpretation of this argument is of central importance for understanding Plato. Plato defends a tiered ontology in dialogues written, even on a most conservative estimate, both before and after the *Sophist*. How can this be reconciled with a tier-insensitive interpretation of this dialogue's defence of these two greatest kinds (μέγιστα γένη), change and changelessness? It follows from the tier-insensitive interpretation that either Plato came to reject the idea of tiers of reality and came to think that answering the question, 'What is there?', requires thinking that there are no tiers of reality – which is not at all a credible interpretation – or he came to think that the distinction between tiers of reality, though it may be required for other reasons, is not required to answer the question, 'What is there?'[11] But I wonder whether even this latter interpretation is at all plausible. We may suppose rather that Plato thought the distinction between two tiers of reality is fundamental to metaphysics and required to answer the question, 'What is there?'

2. Text, translation, basic structure

[1] 248e7–249b7

> ELEATIC STRANGER. In Heaven's name! Are we really to be so easily persuaded that change, life, soul and intelligence are not present in complete being, and that this is neither alive nor intelligent but rather, august and holy, is without reason and changeless?
> THEAETETUS. That would certainly be a terrible statement to admit.
> ES. But are we to say that although it has reason, it does not have life?
> THT. Of course not.
> ES. But if we say that both these things are present in it, must we not say that it has them in a soul?
> THT. How else would it have them?
> ES. But if we say that it has reason, life, and soul, can we still say that, though it is ensouled, it is utterly changeless?
> THT. That seems entirely unreasonable to me.
> ES. But then we must acknowledge as beings that which changes and likewise change.
> THT. Certainly.
> ES. So it turns out, Theaetetus, that if all things are changeless, there is no such thing as reason anywhere about anything.[12]
> THT. Exactly.

[2] 249b8–c9

> ES. But if, on the other hand, we admit that all things are moving and changing, then, according to this claim, too, we shall be excluding the very same thing from the things that are.
> THT. How so?
> ES. Do you think that without changelessness there could ever be such a thing as staying the same in the same condition and in the same respects?

THT. Not at all.
Es. But without this, can you make out that there is such a thing as reason anywhere, or could ever be?
THT. Not in the least.
Es. And we need to oppose with all the force of reasoning the person who in any way maintains anything about anything while doing away with knowledge, intelligence and reason.
THT. Most definitely.

[3] 249c10–d5

Es. From all this it follows, as it appears, that the philosopher, that is, he who supremely values all these things, must refuse to accept, from the defenders of either the One or the many forms, that the totality of things is changeless, and likewise he must turn a deaf ear to those who make being change throughout, rather, like a child begging for both, he must declare that being and the totality of things is as many things as are changeless and as many things as are changing, both together.
THT. Perfectly true.

The basic structure of the argument is clear enough. First ([1] 248e7–249b7) it is argued that changing things (τὸ κινούμενον) and change (κίνησις) are real (setting aside for the moment the crucial qualification, παντελῶς). The argument is that reason (νοῦς, also φρόνησις, 'intelligence') is real; and that if reason is real, then life (ζωή) is real; and that if reason and life are real, then soul (ψυχή) and something ensouled (ἔμψυχον) are real; and, finally, that if all these things are real, then change and changing things are real.

Then ([2] 249b8–c9) it is argued that changeless things (τὸ ἀκίνητον, τὸ στάσιμον) and changelessness (στάσις) are likewise real. The argument is that there is such a thing as knowledge, intelligence and reason (ἐπιστήμη, φρόνησις, νοῦς) – or at least we must maintain that there is if we are to be capable of maintaining anything at all; but there cannot be such a thing as knowledge, intelligence and reason unless there are changeless things and the changelessness peculiar to them.

Finally ([3] 249c10–d5), there is the conclusion, which says that being and the totality of things (τὸ ὄν τε καὶ τὸ πᾶν) comprises, precisely, as many things as are changeless and as many things as are changing (ὅσα ἀκίνητα καὶ κεκινημένα), both together (συναμφότερα). In particular because of the ὅσα ('as many things as'), there can be no doubt that this conclusion is about *any* changeless and changing things.[13] However, it is, as we shall see, particularly important to observe that these lines (249c10–d4) are the conclusion not only of the argument against the friends of the forms (248e7–249d5), but also of the earlier argument against the materialists (246e5–247c8). Indeed the conclusion mentions not only the friends of the forms, but also

3. The background (245e6–248e6)

The argument for the reality of change and changelessness (248e7–249d5) concludes an extended two-pronged strategy directed against two radically opposed positions about what there is (245e6–249d5). On the one hand, there is the position of the materialists, which asserts that all and only material things are real (246a8–b3). This, it is assumed, implies that only changing things are real, for it is assumed throughout that if something is a material thing, it is a changing thing. (But not the converse. For it will emerge that souls are changing things, but, at least on the view of the stranger and of the reformed materialists, they are not material.) On the other hand, there are those who believe that all and only changeless things are real (246b6–c4). This group, the immaterialists, includes, first and foremost, the so-called friends of the forms (οἱ τῶν εἰδῶν φίλοι, 248a4–5), who claim that all and only the plurality of immaterial forms are true or real beings. Indeed it appears that just these immaterialists are referred to at this point (246b6–c4). However, it emerges at the end of the argument (249c11–d1) that Plato wants to include under the immaterialists not only the friends of the forms, who are evidently pluralist immaterialists, but also monist immaterialists, such as Parmenides.[14] There is an important difference between these two groups of immaterialists, for while, presumably, Parmenides and his followers think that there are no changing things at all, what the friends of the forms assert is rather that such things are not true or real beings (cf. ἀληθινὴ οὐσία, 246b8, ὄντως οὐσία, 248a11) but only some sort of processes of becoming (cf. γένεσις φερομένη τινά, 246c1–2). For they emphatically refuse to apply the term 'true being' (ἀληθινὴ οὐσία) and the term οὐσία itself (246c2; see also 248d2 and e2) to changing, material things; rather they refer to such things generically as 'becoming' (γένεσις, 246c1, 248a7, 10, 12, b7). This shows that the friends of the forms straightaway defend a sharp distinction between two tiers of reality (see esp. 248a7–8), i.e. two tiers of what is something as opposed to being nothing at all – those above and those below. Indeed the metaphor of things above and things below is employed here in characterizing their position (see 246b7, cf. 246a8). It remains to be seen, however, just how they do want to characterize the distinction between being and becoming, for we shall see that this is not the distinction between being and not-being, but, rather, the distinction between being without qualification – true, real, and perfect being – and qualified being. In a playful allusion to the mythical battle between giants and gods (the γιγαντομαχία, 246a4), the materialists are cast in the role of giants and the immaterialists in that of the gods. But the aim is to put an end to this ceaseless and bloody battle by arguing first, against the materialists, that changeless things are real also, and then, against the friends of the forms, that changing things are real also.[15]

The argument for the reality of change and changelessness (248e7–249d5) concludes this project. We shall see that while its conclusion (249c10–d5) is addressed to all the parties, i.e. the materialists and both groups of immaterialists, the argument itself is addressed to just the one group of immaterialists, the friends of the forms. It is also notable that all parties are addressed in their absence and by drawing on second-hand reports of their views (see Brown 1998). The arguments are conducted by the Eleatic Stranger, with some help from Theaetetus especially in reporting those views. But it is hard not to be inclined to suppose that Plato is closely associated with the so-called friends of the forms. For we shall see that the position of the friends of the forms is characterized in terms that closely resemble the characterization of the theory of forms in the (so-called) middle dialogues – and, of course, Plato never ceased loving the forms. So when the Stranger sets out to persuade the friends of the forms to abandon their extreme view that only the changeless forms are real and to acknowledge that at least some changing things are real too, it seems safe to suppose that the position of these reformed friends of the forms represents Plato's own latest position. Whether in the (so-called) middle dialogues he had held the extreme or the more moderate position is a further question.

We should note that the argument for change and changelessness (248e7–249d5) is accepted as successful and as having successfully established the reality of these kinds. For the two kinds, change and changelessness, are taken up in what follows and they play a central role in the remaining part of an inquiry whose aim is to solve certain fundamental *aporiai* about being and not-being (up to 264). Indeed they are honoured with the title, 'greatest kinds' (μέγιστα γένη), a title that is otherwise conferred, first and foremost, on being itself (τὸ ὄν), and, second, on the kinds, identity (τὸ ταὐτόν) and difference (τὸ ἕτερον / θάτερον). These latter two kinds, identity and difference, are introduced because it is argued that each of the three kinds, being, change, and changelessness, is identical with itself and different from the others. Indeed, this last kind, difference, emerges as decisive for solving the *aporia* about not-being. It is, therefore, not an exaggeration if we say that the argument for change and changelessness plays a pivotal role in the whole inquiry into being and not-being in the *Sophist* (236–64).

There is a striking symmetry about the overall strategy: in the battle between giants and gods each party excludes from being what the other party includes, and the aim is to persuade each party to include what the other party includes. However, we must ask whether this symmetry is supposed to be perfect. If it is supposed to be perfect, the materialists must be persuaded to include in being precisely those changeless things that the friends of the forms include, that is, the forms along with the changelessness peculiar to them, and the friends of the forms must be persuaded to include in being precisely those changing things that the materialists include, that is, material things along with the change peculiar to them. Evidently, if it is Plato's aim that materialists and immaterialists should be reconciled and united, he must intend perfect symmetry. It is, however, far from clear whether this is his aim. The symmetry he intends may rather be of a weaker, imperfect kind, such that the immaterialists are persuaded to include *some* kind of changeless things, along with the changelessness peculiar to *them*, and the friends of the forms are persuaded to include *some* changing things, along with the change peculiar to *them*, but without each party being persuaded to include precisely the changeless things and the kind of changelessness, or the changing things and the kind of change, that the other party includes. There will still be a general symmetry about the overall strategy, for it will still be true that, on a generic level, each party is persuaded to include what the other party includes: changeless things and changelessness in the case of the materialists (i.e. *some* changeless things and *some* kind of changelessness), and changing things and change in the case of the friends of the forms (i.e. *some* changing things and *some* kind of change).

The issue of whether Plato intends perfect symmetry is of particular importance for understanding the argument for change and changelessness (248e7–249d5a). Brown (1998, 202–3), in particular, appeals to perfect symmetry to support a tier-insensitive interpretation of this argument. For it is easy to see that perfect symmetry requires a tier-insensitive interpretation, such that the argument defends a tier-insensitive ontology, whereas a tiered interpretation, such that the argument defends a tiered ontology, implies that the symmetry is less than perfect and obtains only on a generic level. To see this, we need only observe that the friends of the forms could never be persuaded to include material things and the change peculiar to them in *complete* being (τὸ παντελῶς ὄν), if this means *perfect* being and the upper tier. For material things and the change peculiar to them is just what they think makes up the lower tier. A tiered interpretation, therefore, implies lack of perfect symmetry, while perfect symmetry implies a tier-insensitive interpretation such that, in particular, the friends of the forms are persuaded to include material things and the change peculiar to them in *complete* being in the sense, rather, of *all-inclusive* being.

But there is in any case a basic problem for supposing perfect symmetry. The materialists deny that there are any changeless things, and the one group of immaterialists, Parmenides and his followers, deny that there are any changing things. Since it is argued that both are wrong and that both kinds of things are real, we may naturally form the impression that perfect symmetry is Plato's aim. So far, there would be no problem in supposing perfect symmetry. The problem, however, is that the friends of the forms, to whom the argument is primarily addressed, assert not that there are no changing things, but rather that such things are not true or real beings but only some sort of processes of becoming. This means that the very condition for perfect symmetry being Plato's aim is not satisfied: that the one party should exclude from being precisely what the other party includes. This also suggests that there is a basic problem for supposing that Plato's aim is to establish something right in both materialism and the immaterialism of the friends of the forms, and to put these two things together into a single, coherent ontology. The problem is that this would involve adding together elements in a tier-less ontology with elements in a tiered ontology, and it is not at all clear how doing this can result in a coherent position. But this problem is avoided if we suppose that perfect symmetry is not Plato's aim and that the symmetry he sets out is rather imperfect and supposed to obtain only on a generic level.

It may be thought that the argument against the materialists (246e5–247c8) supports perfect symmetry, which in turn requires a tier-insensitive interpretation of the argument against the friends of the forms. For it may be thought that what the materialists are persuaded to include in being is precisely what the friends of the forms include, that is, changeless forms. But this interpretation is unconvincing. What the materialists are persuaded to include are things such as justice and injustice and intelligence and its contrary; and they are invited to concede that these things are not visible or tangible and, therefore, not material. So they are persuaded to include some non-material qualities in being. But it is far from clear whether what they are persuaded to include are forms. After all, forms are not so much qualities as the essence of qualities, and forms are supposed to be perfect whereas sense-perceptible things and their qualities are supposed somehow to be imperfect and to depend on them. This is the theory of forms with which we are familiar from dialogues such as the *Phaedo* and the *Republic*, and the position of the friends of the forms appears to be modelled on it. But although some effort is made to persuade the materialists to include in being qualities that are not sense-perceptible and, therefore, not material, no particular effort is made to persuade them to include forms. However, even if the materialists are indeed persuaded to include changeless forms in being, we must add that if they properly realize what this admission involves, they will now commit themselves to two tiers of reality and to the view that changeless forms belong in the upper tier whereas changing, material things belong in the lower tier.

Their position will in effect have become virtually indistinguishable from that of the friends of the forms, except for the fact that, unlike them, they want to apply the term 'being' (οὐσία, see 246b1) to changing, material things also. But even on this interpretation of the reformed materialists, it is still an open question whether, when the friends of the forms are persuaded to include change in *complete* being (τὸ παντελῶς ὄν), they are persuaded to include material change in *all-inclusive* being, which supports the tier-insensitive interpretation and perfect symmetry, or they are persuaded to include non-material change in *perfect* being, which supports the tiered interpretation and lack of perfect symmetry.

There is a further important step in the dialogue (247c9–248e6), before we arrive at the argument for change and changelessness. This is the *dunamis* proposal, which says that something is real if, and only if, it has the power (δύναμις) either to act on something else or to be acted on by something else. This proposal is introduced as soon as the materialists have been persuaded to include in being, in addition to changing things, changeless ones, and it is an attempt to determine something that changing and changeless things have in common (cf. συμφυὲς γεγονός, 247d3) and which marks them out as both being real.[16] The suggestion is that both the changing and the changeless things espoused by the reformed materialists fit this proposal in some way, i.e. each of them either has the power to act on, or the power to be acted on, or both. The materialists readily accept the proposal, but the friends of the forms, to whom it is offered next, reject it for very particular reasons.

The position of the friends of the forms is characterized as involving, first, the view that there is a sharp distinction between being, and in particular true and real being, which is changeless, and becoming, which is changing (248a7–8 and 12–13); and, second, the view that we commune with, i.e. apprehend, the latter through the body and the senses whereas we commune with, i.e. apprehend, the former through the soul and reasoning (248a10–11). The *dunamis* proposal is offered to the friends of the forms in order to determine something that these two kinds of communion, and their respective objects, have in common and which marks them out as both being real. The suggestion is that both kinds of communion, and their respective objects, fit this proposal in some way, i.e. by having either the power to act on, or the power to be acted on, or both. But the friends of the forms reject the proposal and conclude that while it holds good of becoming, it does not hold good of being (248c7–9). For, they argue, if it did hold good of being, it would follow, absurdly, that being, which is changeless, is changed in so far as we, or our rational souls, commune with it and know it (248d10–e5).[17]

How does the *dunamis* proposal, and the friends of the forms' response to it, bear on the interpretation of the final argument for change and changelessness (248e7–249d5)? First of all, it shows that the argument for change and changelessness is addressed primarily to the friends of the forms and that it is supposed to persuade them on their terms. For it is because they, on their terms, reject the *dunamis* proposal that Plato sets it aside and moves on to the argument for change and changelessness. This supports a tiered interpretation of the argument. For the friends of the forms are characterized as drawing a sharp distinction between true or real being and becoming, which looks just like the two tiers of reality distinguished in dialogues such as the *Phaedo* and the *Republic*; and it appears that it is because of this sharp distinction that they reject the *dunamis* proposal.

Second, it can be argued that the *dunamis* proposal is incompatible with a tiered ontology. This is because the *dunamis* proposal is based on the view that all things without distinction have something in common which marks them out as beings, whereas it can be argued that a tiered ontology like Plato's precisely denies this. What a tiered ontology like Plato's asserts instead is that, while there is something that marks out the things in the upper tier as perfect beings (in particular, their being either changeless and rationally knowable forms or changing rational souls that can know the forms), what marks out the things in the lower tier as beings is nothing but their relation to the things in the upper tier.[18] It would be a large task to defend this interpretation of Plato's ontology, but if it is correct, it implies a tiered interpretation of the argument for change and changelessness. For it means that the underlying reason why the friends of the forms reject the *dunamis* proposal is that they reject the view that all things without distinction have something in common which marks them out as beings, and they reject this view because of their fundamental commitment to a tiered ontology. The attempt to persuade the friends of the forms on their own terms must, therefore, be conducted by relying on their fundamental commitment to two tiers of reality. Let us simply observe that there is some notable textual support for this interpretation. The Stranger offers the *dunamis* proposal to the friends of the forms precisely in order to determine something that the two kinds of communion with things – sense-perception and reason, along with their respective objects, changing and changeless objects – have in common and which marks them out as both being real (248b2–6). But it is at just this point that the friends of the forms refuse to accept the offer (248c1 f.). We may also note that this interpretation explains why the materialists accept, while the friends of the forms reject, the *dunamis* proposal: because the proposal is incompatible with a tiered ontology, which the friends of the forms accept, and naturally associated with a tier-less ontology, which the materialists accept.

Third, critics have observed that when the friends of the forms reject the *dunamis* proposal by arguing that it has the absurd consequence that being, which is changeless, is changed in so far as it is known, they appear to overlook the possibility that it is rather the cognizing soul that is changed in so far as it cognizes being. I want to emphasize that on the particular tiered interpretation of the argument for change and changelessness that we shall go on to defend, just this possibility is the one that Plato will in the end adopt. For Plato will argue that *complete* being (τὸ παντελῶς ὄν), in the sense of *perfect* being and the upper tier, includes change because the soul that cognizes perfect beings must itself be a perfect being and this soul changes in so far as it cognizes those beings.

Should we, therefore, conclude, as some of the same critics have also suggested, that the friends of the forms may after all accept the *dunamis* proposal, once they recognize what they previously overlooked?[19] Not at all. For although the friends of the forms may be happy to admit that the change peculiar to the soul in so far as it cognizes perfect being is itself perfectly real and belongs to the upper tier, they may still object to an account, such as the *dunamis* proposal, which implies that this kind of change has something in common with the change peculiar to the things in the lower tier, i.e. the change peculiar to sense-perception and its objects, which marks them out as both being real.[20]

4. 'Complete being' – τὸ παντελῶς ὄν

The argument for the reality of change and changelessness is introduced by the question, what things should we include in 'complete being' (τὸ παντελῶς ὄν, 248e7–249a1)? But this phrase, τὸ παντελῶς ὄν, is ambiguous, and we shall see that the interpretation of the entire argument depends crucially on this ambiguity. τὸ παντελῶς ὄν may mean 'all-inclusive being' or it may mean 'perfect being'.[21] On the former, unrestricted reading it denotes all beings without distinction – the totality of beings and the whole of being – whereas on the latter, restricted reading it denotes one class (or kind, or type) of beings as opposed to another, that is, perfect as opposed to imperfect beings. On the unrestricted reading of this phrase, the argument defends a tier-insensitive ontology whereas on the restricted reading it defends a tiered ontology.

One might suggest that the two meanings of τὸ παντελῶς ὄν may be associated with different aspects of the argument and that, therefore, both meanings may be in play. On the one hand, the restricted meaning is associated with the fact that the friends of the forms adopt a tiered ontology and that the argument is conducted by appealing to items which they acknowledge in their ontology. On the other hand, the unrestricted meaning is associated with the fact that the conclusion of the argument is addressed not only to the friends of the forms, but also to the materialists and the monistic immaterialists such as Parmenides, and these parties are committed to a tier-less ontology. But this suggestion is not convincing. The important issue is whether Plato thinks that engaging with the friends of the forms' commitment to a tiered ontology can establish items in a tier-insensitive ontology. If we think the phrase τὸ παντελῶς ὄν means 'all-inclusive being' and is associated with a tier-insensitive ontology, we must answer this question in the affirmative. For then the argument against the friends of the forms will evidently contain a move from a commitment to items (such as the changeless forms and the changelessness peculiar to them) that must be situated within a tiered ontology, to a commitment to items (such as changing, material things and the change peculiar to them) that need not be situated within a tiered ontology and belong simply to being and the totality of things. If, on the other hand, the phrase τὸ παντελῶς ὄν means 'perfect being', the argument against the friends of the forms will not contain any such move and will remain entirely within the ambit of a tiered ontology. (Or at least it will do so for as long as we disregard the conclusion at 249c10–d4. We shall return to this issue later.)

Both readings of this critical phrase, τὸ παντελῶς ὄν, can cite textual support. In favour of the unrestricted reading and the meaning 'all-inclusive being', one may point out that the conclusion (249c10–d4) evidently employs the unrestricted concept of being, for it is expressly about 'being and the totality of things' (τὸ ὄν τε καὶ τὸ πᾶν, 249d4). Indeed the conclusion is expressly about *any* changeless and changing things (cf. ὅσα ἀκίνητα καὶ κεκινημένα, 'as many things as are changeless and [as many things as] are changing', 249d3–4), whereas the restricted reading of τὸ παντελῶς ὄν seems to imply that it should be about only one kind of changeless and changing things. One may add that the unrestricted reading is required by the dialectic between the three parties mentioned in the conclusion, i.e. the materialists and the two kinds of immaterialists. For while the restricted reading of τὸ παντελῶς ὄν is associated with a tiered ontology, the conclusion is addressed not only to the friends of the forms, who espouse such an ontology, but also to the materialists and the monistic immaterialists such as Parmenides, who espouse a tier-less ontology. One may add further that although the argument is introduced by asking what we should include in τὸ παντελῶς ὄν, and although the phrase τὸ παντελῶς ὄν remains the grammatical subject for half a dozen lines (up to 249a10), the first conclusion reached in the argument is that we must acknowledge changing things and change as beings (ὄντα, 249b2–3). Here the qualification παντελῶς is omitted, and it continues to be absent in the remainder of the argument. One may urge that this move from τὸ παντελῶς ὄν to simply ὄν is readily intelligible if τὸ παντελῶς ὄν means 'all-inclusive being', but problematical if it means 'perfect being'. Finally, one may draw attention to the fact that there is one other occurrence of the phrase 'τὸ παντελ- X' in Plato in which it may appear to mean 'the all-inclusive X'. This is the phrase τὸ παντελὲς ζῷον in the later dialogue, *Timaeus* (31b1; see also 39e1), which, on this reading, means 'the all-inclusive living being'.

However, in favour of the restricted reading of the phrase τὸ παντελῶς ὄν and the meaning 'perfect being', we may simply point out that there is just one other occurrence of this phrase in Plato, and there it is evidently used in a restricted sense to denote perfect being and the upper tier. This is *Republic* 5.477a3–4, where he says: 'what is completely (τὸ παντελῶς ὄν) is completely knowable and what is in no way (μὴ ὂν μηδαμῇ) is in every way unknowable'.[22] Here the phrase τὸ παντελῶς ὄν is evidently used in a restricted sense, for it is contrasted, first, with something which 'is in no way', i.e. is nothing at all, and then with something which is so constituted as 'both to be and not to be' (εἶναί τε καὶ μὴ εἶναι, 477a6) – and this latter, it emerges, is a reference to the changing objects of sense-perception that make up the lower tier of reality. This occurrence of the phrase τὸ παντελῶς ὄν is of paramount importance, for it occurs in a context in which Plato makes a central attempt to characterize precisely the distinction between changeless forms, along with the way in which we grasp them, and changing things, along with the way in which we grasp them. But the characterization of the position of the friends of the forms in the immediate background to our argument in the *Sophist* is strikingly similar to the characterization of the theory of forms from this passage in the *Republic*. We may also note that, as already characterized in the *Sophist*, the friends of the forms have used a number of phrases to refer to the upper tier of things, which they identify as the realm of the forms: οὐσία ('being'), ἀληθινὴ οὐσία ('true being'), and ὄντως οὐσία ('real being'). But it is natural to suppose that when the phrase τὸ παντελῶς ὄν is introduced, it is introduced simply as a variation on ἀληθινὴ οὐσία and ὄντως οὐσία. We may note, finally, that in the *Republic* passage and the (so-called) middle dialogues generally, Plato uses all these expressions, as well as τὸ εἰλικρινῶς ὄν ('pure being'), interchangeably for the upper tier of reality.

On purely textual grounds, it seems to me the phrase τὸ παντελῶς ὄν ought to mean 'perfect being', not 'all-inclusive being'. The evidence that can be cited for the latter, unrestricted reading is entirely indirect, to the effect that this reading is required by what Plato says elsewhere and especially in the conclusion. But we shall see that the unrestricted reading is not required by what Plato says in the conclusion. With regard to the move from τὸ παντελῶς ὄν (at 248e8–249a10) to simply ὄντα (at 249b2–3), this is not really a problem for the restricted reading; for if something is a perfect being and belongs to the upper tier, then evidently it is a being. There is no direct evidence for the unrestricted reading, for nowhere does Plato use this phrase to mean 'all-inclusive being'. When he uses the phrase τὸ παντελὲς ζῷον in the *Timaeus* (31b1), what he is referring to is the model (παράδειγμα, 31a4) of the totality of living beings and the cosmos, and it is this model that is labelled παντελές. He is, therefore, referring to something in the realm of perfect being and the upper tier, and the correct translation of the phrase in the *Timaeus* is not 'the all-inclusive living being', but 'the perfect living being'. On the other hand, there is direct evidence for the restricted reading, for Plato does elsewhere, and indeed in a passage that is directly relevant for understanding the present characterization of the friends of the forms (*Republic* 5.477a3–4), use the phrase τὸ παντελῶς ὄν to mean 'perfect being', and the supposition that this is how he is using it here fits perfectly with the characterization of the friends of the forms with which we are presented in the immediate context.

5. Change – κίνησις

The aim of the argument is to persuade the friends of the forms to abandon their extreme view, which says that only changeless forms and the changelessness peculiar to them are real, and to admit that changing things and change are real too. On any reading, the changeless things and the changelessness acknowledged by the friends of the forms are the changeless forms and the changelessness peculiar to them. It is also agreed on any reading that the aim of the second part of the argument ([2] 249b8–c9) is to show why that part of the friends of the forms' view is correct which says that changeless things and changelessness are real: because without changeless things and changelessness there could be no such thing as knowledge, intelligence and reason. The underlying idea here, we may naturally suppose, is that an object of rational knowledge, i.e. something that can be known by reason, must be changeless, or at least it must be changeless in so far as it is rationally knowable. So far, the interpretation of Plato's argument is on the whole straightforward and relies by and large on ideas with which we are familiar from the *Phaedo* and *Republic* and the (so-called) middle dialogues generally.

The first part of the argument ([1] 248e7–249b7), however, which sets out to persuade the friends of the forms that changing things and change are real also, can be understood in two very different ways, depending on whether we think τὸ παντελῶς ὄν means 'all-inclusive being' or 'perfect being'. On the latter, restricted reading of this critical phrase, the conclusion is that we must include certain changing things, along with the change peculiar to them, in perfect being and the upper tier. No inference is made about what may be included in a tier-insensitive ontology. So the friends of the forms are persuaded to abandon a view which says that only changeless things, along with the changelessness peculiar to them, are perfect beings and belong to the upper tier, and that all changing things belong to the lower tier – the tier which they characterize as becoming (γένεσις). Instead, they are persuaded to accept a view which says that both changeless things, along with the changelessness peculiar to them, and some changing things, along with the change peculiar to them, are perfect beings and belong to the upper tier, and that the lower tier – which they may still characterize as becoming (γένεσις) – is made up of changing things that are distinguished by a fundamentally different kind of change.

On the unrestricted reading of τὸ παντελῶς ὄν, on the other hand, the conclusion of the argument is altogether different, for it says that changing things – *any* changing things – just as much as changeless things, must be included in the totality of beings and the whole of being. Brown (1998, 204) defends this reading as follows: 'And once they [the friends of the forms] see reason to include *some* things subject to change as *onta*, they are left with no grounds for excluding any *kinoumena*. This upshot is an all-inclusive ontology.' So the friends of the forms are persuaded to abandon a view which says that only changeless things and changelessness are beings and that changing things are merely some sort of processes of becoming (γένεσις). What they are persuaded to admit instead is that *any* changing things and *any* kind of change, just as much as changeless things and changelessness, are beings.

But we should note that on the unrestricted reading of τὸ παντελῶς ὄν, one may still think that the conclusion which says that *any* changing things are real is reached via a prior conclusion that at least *some* changing things are real.[23] The two readings, therefore, can agree that the argument for the reality of change involves the claim that *some* changing things are real. What separates them is whether just this is Plato's conclusion or there is a further step, that is, to the conclusion that *any* changing things are real. If τὸ παντελῶς ὄν means 'all-inclusive being', he is taking this further step; if it means 'perfect being', he is not. It is important to recognize why such a step is licensed on the former, unrestricted reading, but illicit on the latter, restricted reading of τὸ παντελῶς ὄν. On the unrestricted reading, and in general on a tier-insensitive ontology, one may argue as follows: the soul (which may be immaterial) is a changing thing and it is a being; any two things that are F (e.g. changing), if they are both beings, are neither more nor less beings than the other; therefore, any changing thing (including changing, material things) is a being. But such an argument is, precisely, not available on the restricted reading, since on this reading, and in general on a tiered ontology, we cannot suppose that any two things that are F (e.g. changing), if they are both beings, are neither more nor less beings than the other. For it may be that the one thing is a being without qualification – a true, real, and perfect being – whereas the other is only a qualified being, and that the former is characterized by the kind of F-ness peculiar to beings without qualification (e.g. immaterial change) whereas the latter is characterized by the kind of F-ness peculiar to qualified beings (e.g. material change).

The dialectic between the friends of the forms and the materialists also turns out very different depending on which reading we adopt. On the unrestricted reading of τὸ παντελῶς ὄν, what the friends of the forms are persuaded to include in being is, or certainly includes, precisely what the materialists include, that is, changing, material things and the change peculiar to them. Thus the dialectic is perfectly symmetrical – the one party is persuaded to include precisely what the other party includes – and perfect peace and harmony is achieved between the two parties.[24] On the restricted reading of τὸ παντελῶς ὄν, it is true that a sort of peace or at least a cease-fire is achieved, since both parties in the end sign up to the formula that being includes both changing and changeless things, but this diplomatic formula conceals fundamental underlying disagreements and indeed a lack of proper fit between their views. For while the materialists, as befits their tier-less ontology, end up thinking simply that changeless things and changing things are alike beings, the friends of the forms end up thinking that changeless things and a peculiar kind of changing immaterial things are alike perfect beings and belong to the upper tier, but that changing, material things are only some sort of processes of becoming (γένεσις).

The argument, no less than the conclusion, depends crucially on which reading of τὸ παντελῶς ὄν we adopt. On the restricted reading of this phrase, the argument will be, first, that since our soul (ψυχή), in so far as it possesses reason (νοῦς), can know things that are perfect beings and belong to the upper tier, namely the changeless forms, it must itself be a perfect being and belong to the upper tier; second, the soul, in so far as it has the capacity to know something, is essentially a changing thing. The first step would require further defence, which Plato does not offer here, but even as it stands it has considerable force. After all, if the soul can know something, it must itself be real, and on the tiered ontology of the friends of the forms, there are two and just two types of things, perfect beings and changing things. If the soul is an imperfect being and belongs to the tier of changing, material things, it will in effect be like the capacity for sense-perception. But the friends of the forms have previously argued that the forms cannot be known by anything like sense perception – again this is a view with which we are familiar from dialogues such as the *Phaedo* and *Republic*. The soul, therefore, if it is to be capable of knowing the forms, which are perfect beings and belong to the upper tier, must itself be a perfect being and belong to the upper tier.[25] The second step is also forceful, since both the activity of searching for knowledge is a kind of change (since it is an activity) and the process of acquiring knowledge is a kind of change (since it is a process). Plato may, therefore, conclude with considerable force that perfect being and the upper tier includes not only the changeless forms and the changelessness peculiar to them, but also the changing rationally cognitive soul and the change peculiar to it.

On the unrestricted reading of τὸ παντελῶς ὄν, on the other hand, the argument is, first, that since the soul can know the forms, which are evidently beings, it must itself be a being; second, the soul, in so far as it has the capacity to know something, is a changing thing (the same as on the previous interpretation); third, once the friends of the forms grant that *some* changing things are beings, they have no grounds for denying that *any* changing things, including changing, material things, are beings. Brown defends this interpretation as follows:

> On any account of this section, the Stranger's aim is to force the Friends of the Forms to accept into their ontology not just Forms…but (some or all) changing things as well. He does this by showing them that they are committed to according the title 'being' to at least some changing items: namely, souls and what is ensouled (i.e. living bodies, presumably). Since the Friends of the Forms insist that their Forms can be known, they must also acknowledge the being of that which has intelligence and knows the Forms.[26]

This tier-insensitive interpretation may cite as textual support that not only the soul (ψυχή), but also something ensouled (ἔμψυχον, 249a10) is admitted as real, and this, as Brown says, may be a reference to ensouled bodies, which obviously are material things.

There is, however, a deeper problem with the tier-insensitive interpretation, because it fails to indicate into which tier of being the changing soul is admitted when it is acknowledged as real. The friends of the forms, on any reading, distinguish sharply between two tiers of reality, so we should expect that they will be satisfied to admit the reality of the changing soul only if it is at the same time established to which tier it belongs. Evidently they cannot suppose that the changing soul, which can know the forms, belongs to the lower tier and to becoming (γένεσις). But if they suppose rather that the soul belongs to the upper tier and to true and real being (ἀληθινὴ οὐσία, ὄντως οὐσία), they cannot infer from this that *any* changing things and *any* kind of change, including material things and the change peculiar to them, are, just as much as the forms, beings – which, on the tier-insensitive interpretation, is the conclusion Plato argues for here. They may, therefore, still think that while the changing soul and the change peculiar to it belong to true, real and perfect being and the upper tier, changing, material things and the change peculiar to them are only some sort of processes of becoming (γένεσις).

As far as I can see, the only way to avoid this problem is to argue, as Brown does,[27] that the previously considered *dunamis* proposal (which says that something is real if, and only if, either it has the power to act on other things or it has the power to be acted upon by other things) has superseded the tiered ontology of the friends of the forms and replaced it by a tier-insensitive ontology; for the *dunamis* proposal was an attempt to establish a criterion of being that is neutral between a tiered and a tier-less ontology. That is to say, because of the *dunamis* proposal, the friends of the forms no longer hold the view that something can be acknowledged as real only if it is at the same time established to which tier it belongs, and they now rather believe that something can be established as real in a neutral way such that it is a further question to which tier it belongs or indeed whether it belongs to a tiered or a tier-less ontology.

This way of avoiding the problem is, however, untenable, since the friends of the forms have rejected the *dunamis* proposal. Furthermore, it would be wrong to suppose that though they have in fact rejected it, they can in principle accept it. For the question just is whether the friends of the forms can in principle accept a neutral criterion of being, such as the *dunamis* proposal, which says that whether something is real can be established independently of establishing to which tier it belongs or indeed whether it belongs to a tiered or a tier-less ontology. The conclusion that the friends of the forms end up accepting, namely that the soul is a being which changes when it knows the forms, may appear to be in conformity with the *dunamis* proposal, since that proposal makes room for the possibility that something is changed when it cognizes something. But it does not follow that the friends of the forms may after all accept the *dunamis* proposal. For if the friends of the forms include the changing soul in perfect being and the upper tier, they may still object to an account, such as the *dunamis* proposal, which implies that this kind of change has something in common with the change peculiar to the things in the lower tier that marks them out as both being real. In general, they may still object to an account, such as the *dunamis* proposal, which is neutral between a tiered and a tier-less ontology.

With regard to the point about the argument's admitting not only the soul, but also something ensouled (ἔμψυχον, 249a10) as real, this is at best inconclusive. If ἔμψυχον here means ἔμψυχον σῶμα ('ensouled body'), then evidently the friends of the forms are admitting also changing, material things into complete being, and this requires the tier-insensitive interpretation. But certainly ἔμψυχον does not by itself mean ἔμψυχον σῶμα, and when Plato uses this term here and says that τὸ παντελῶς ὄν is something ἔμψυχον, he appears to mean no more than that τὸ παντελῶς ὄν has or includes soul. But if τὸ παντελῶς ὄν means 'perfect being', as it does on the restricted reading and the tiered interpretation, it will be perfect being and the upper tier that has or includes soul, hence the use of the term ἔμψυχον will not be a reference to ensouled bodies at all.

I conclude that when Plato argues for the inclusion of changing things in being, it is the inclusion of changing things in perfect being and the upper tier that he intends, and in particular the changing, rationally cognizing soul along with the change peculiar to it.

So far, we have been supposing that it is, in the first instance at least, the ontological status of the individual human soul that is in question, and it is worth pointing out that there is good reason for this supposition. First, the argument for changelessness, which relies on the claim that knowledge is possible only if there are changeless forms, is evidently in the first instance about the knowledge sought after by the individual human soul – indeed, as the conclusion indicates, sought after by the philosopher (cf. 240c10). Second, the argument for the reality of the changing soul must be seen against the background of the friends of the forms' claim that true and real being (ἀληθινὴ / ὄντως οὐσία) is known by the soul through reasoning whereas becoming (γένεσις) is known by the body through sense-perception. But evidently this is a reference to the individual human soul and sense-perception. At the same time, however, there may be no reason to deny that Plato may, in addition, have something like a universal soul in mind – which would point towards the view of the *Timaeus*.[28] But we should note that, in our *Sophist* passage, the function of this universal soul would in the first instance be cognitive, with the forms, and indeed the forms of the physical universe as a whole, as the object of its knowledge. It would be a further question how this universal soul is related to the physical universe and in particular whether this relation is one of generation and production.

As a final point, we ought to point out that our interpretation is set against not only the tier-insensitive interpretation, but also an alternative tiered interpretation which says that it is the forms themselves that are supposed to be involved in change.[29] The main objection to this interpretation is that the friends of the forms have, immediately before the present argument, emphatically denied that the forms can be involved in change, and the present argument is addressed to them and supposed to persuade them on their own terms. Furthermore, when change is defended as real, it is, we have seen, the change of the rational soul that is so defended. But while it is entirely natural to think that this is a reference to the soul that has the power to know the forms, there is nothing to suggest that it is the forms themselves that are supposed to have a changing, rational soul.[30] This alternative tiered interpretation is largely the result of thinking that if perfect being and the upper tier are supposed to contain change, then it must be the forms that are supposed to contain change. But this is to miss the very point of the argument, which is that while certain extreme friends of the forms equate perfect being and the upper tier with the realm of the changeless forms, the truth is rather that perfect being and the upper tier includes also the changing rational soul which can know the forms.

6. Reading Plato's conclusion at 249c10–d4

We have seen that when the friends of the forms are persuaded to include, in addition to the changeless forms, changing things in τὸ παντελῶς ὄν, they are persuaded to include these things in perfect being and the upper tier. They are, of course, also persuaded to include them in being quite generally and the totality of things, but only because, evidently, if something is a perfect being and belongs to the upper tier, then it is indeed a being and belongs to the totality of things. Furthermore, what is included in perfect being is not *any* kind of changeless and changing things, but only *some* particular kinds. However, this upshot appears to be directly at odds with Plato's conclusion (249c10–d4), which says that we – and in particular the philosopher, that is, he who supremely values knowledge, intelligence and reason – must include *any* changeless and changing things (cf. ὅσα ἀκίνητα καὶ κεκινημένα, '*as many things as* are changeless and [*as many things as*] are changing') in being and the totality of things (τὸ ὄν τε καὶ τὸ πᾶν). Clearly this statement is not attached to a tiered ontology; on the contrary, it is simply about the totality of things, whether or not these belong to a tiered ontology. Moreover, it says that being and the totality of things contains *any* changeless and changing things.

There is, however, a way of overcoming this apparent tension, and this is to observe that these lines (249c10–d4) are the conclusion not only of the argument against the friends of the forms (248e7–249d5), but also of the earlier argument against the materialists (246e5–247c8). Indeed the conclusion mentions not only the friends of the forms, but also the materialists (as well as immaterialist monists such as Parmenides). We should also note that the conclusion sets out what 'the philosopher', that is, he who supremely values knowledge, intelligence and reason, ought to believe and what he ought not to believe. But it would not be generous for Plato to suggest that only friends of the forms, that is, Platonists of one variety or another, are philosophers in this sense, and it is only appropriate for him to think that materialists too, or certainly the reformed ones, deserve this title. After all, the materialists were persuaded to acknowledge the reality of changeless things partly by being invited to acknowledge the reality of intelligence (φρόνησις).

This allows us to overcome the apparent tension. Since the conclusion is addressed just as much to the materialists as to the friends of the forms, it is only appropriate that it should be formulated in such a way as to leave open whether the issue was what should be included simply in being and the totality of things (which is how the materialists conceive of the issue) or it was what should be included in perfect being and the upper tier and only as a consequence in being and the totality of things (which is how the friends of the forms conceive of the issue). It is also appropriate that the conclusion should mention not some particular kinds of changing and changeless things, but any changing and changeless things. For although the friends of the forms distinguish sharply in particular between different kinds of changing things, i.e. those in the upper and those in the lower tier, the materialists, as befits their tier-less ontology, are entirely insensitive to such distinctions (the same may be true of the immaterialist monists such as Parmenides).

It follows that Plato is not defending a tier-insensitive ontology in this conclusion (249c10–d4), that is, an ontology that is neutral between the tier-less one of the materialists and the tiered one of the friends of the forms. For the conclusion does not introduce a standpoint that is neutral between the two ontologies. What it does rather is formulate a statement with which both materialists and friends of the forms can agree, but only because it means different things to each of them. Of course, if this is how we read the conclusion, it is only a diplomatic statement of concord which conceals fundamental underlying disagreements and indeed a lack of proper fit between their views. This upshot does, naturally, mean that Plato does not at all intend that the dialectic between the materialists and the friends of the forms should exhibit perfect symmetry, i.e. that each party should be persuaded to accept as real precisely that which the other party initially accepts as real. But perfect symmetry between the materialists and the friends of the forms is in any case unlikely, since there cannot be a proper fit between a tiered ontology, such as that of the friends of the forms, and a tier-less ontology, such as that of the materialists.

But surely, one may object, Plato has taken pains to formulate the conclusion in a tier-insensitive way. After all, it is supposed to appeal equally to the materialists, who defend a tier-less ontology, and to the friends of the forms, who defend a tiered ontology. But this objection misses the point, which is that no single position is expressed through the formulation of the conclusion; rather, two very different positions are allowed for, depending on whether it is read from the standpoint of the materialists or from that of the friends of the forms. If this paper has been on the right lines, no neutral standpoint between these two positions has been argued for by Plato.

Summarily, the conclusion means the following to each of the two parties. To the materialists, it means simply that changing, material things and changeless, immaterial things together make up all the changing and changeless things there are, and together they make up being and the totality of things, as opposed to what is nothing at all. To the friends of the forms, on the other hand, the conclusion means that true, real, perfect being and the upper tier includes some kind of changing and changeless things; becoming and the lower tier includes a fundamentally different kind of changing things; together all these kinds of changing and changeless things make up all the changing and changeless things there are; and together these two tiers make up being and the totality of things, as opposed to what is nothing at all.

One may naturally object to this reading of the conclusion that it does not account for how the friends of the forms can admit that changing, material things, which, on this reading, they still conceive as belonging to becoming and the lower tier, are at the same time ὄντα – as the conclusion, on any reading, says they are. Indeed, did not the friends of the forms initially deny them the status of ὄντα? But, on the present reading, nothing has been done to persuade them otherwise. My response is that the friends of the forms assume from the start (246b6–c4) that changing, material things are ὄντα of a sort, that is, ὄντα as opposed to nothing at all. What they deny, both at the start and at the end, is that they are ὄντα without qualification – true, real, perfect beings. When they initially claim that changing, material things belong not to ἀληθινὴ οὐσία but only to γένεσις (246b6–c2), they make this claim not because they deny, or overlook, that these things are ὄντα as opposed to nothing at all, but rather because they want to emphasize that they are not ὄντα without qualification – true, real, perfect beings. It seems to me that this reading of the initial opposition between the materialists and the friends of the forms (246a8–c4) is supported by the fact that what the materialists are said to mark out as identical with body is, precisely, οὐσία (ταὐτὸν σῶμα καὶ οὐσίαν ὁριζόμενοι, 246b1). For this suggests that, certainly as they are understood by the friends of the forms, they mark out true and real being as identical with body (we recall that the friends of the forms use the term οὐσία interchangeably with ἀληθινὴ οὐσία and ὄντως οὐσία). From the start, then, it is the claim that changing, material things are οὐσίαι, in the sense of true, real, and perfect beings, that the friends of the forms oppose, rather than the claim that changing, material things are ὄντα, in the sense of not nothing at all.

7. Conclusion

We have seen that the interpretation of Plato's argument for the reality of change and changelessness, the argument against the friends of the forms, depends crucially on that one phrase, τὸ παντελῶς ὄν. But I trust it has emerged that the issue of how we read this critical phrase – whether in an unrestricted sense and as meaning 'all-inclusive being' or in a restricted sense and as meaning 'perfect being' – is of more than local textual significance. Certainly it is of deeper significance if we are entitled to suppose that Plato sees himself as a friend of the forms – after all, when did he ever cease loving the forms? – and that, although he takes issue with those extreme friends of the forms that include only the changeless forms in τὸ παντελῶς ὄν, he sees himself as belonging to a reformed party of friends of the forms which wants to include at least some changing things in τὸ παντελῶς ὄν. The philosophical upshot will be altogether different, indeed opposite, depending on which reading of τὸ παντελῶς ὄν we adopt. On the unrestricted reading of this phrase, on which it means 'all-inclusive being', the upshot is that either Plato came to reject the idea of tiers of reality and came to think that answering the question, 'What is there?', requires thinking that there are no tiers of reality, or he came to think that the distinction between tiers of reality, though it may be required for other reasons, is not required to answer the question, 'What is there?' But this, we have argued, is not the upshot at all. Rather, the upshot is the opposite, namely, that Plato thinks the distinction between two tiers of reality is fundamental to metaphysics and required to answer the question, 'What is there?' This upshot emerges if, as we must, we read τὸ παντελῶς ὄν in the restricted sense as meaning 'perfect being' and referring to the upper tier. Whether the upshot of Plato's argument, thus understood, is a genuine insight is a large and difficult question. It is the question whether we can answer the question, 'What is there?', without drawing a fundamental distinction between ontologically independent things ('perfect' beings, or what Aristotle will call 'primary' beings) and ontologically dependent ones (imperfect beings in this sense).

Acknowledgements
I am grateful to John Cleary, John Dillon, Verity Harte, Fritz-Gregor Herrmann, Kevin Mulligan, Brendan O'Byrne, Scott O'Connor and Daniel Watts. I am also grateful to the anonymous reader.

Notes
[1] See for example *Phaedo* 74 (esp. 74d5–8), 78–9 (esp. 79a6–7), 100b1–e7; *Republic* 475e9 ff.; *Symposium* 210e6–211b5; *Timaeus* 27d6–28a4, 51d3–52a7 (I am assuming that the *Timaeus* is a late dialogue); *Philebus* 58e4–59a9, 61d10–e3.

[2] παντελῶς ὄντα (*Republic* 477a3 and *Sophist* 248e8–249a1; see below). Also εἰλικρινῶς ὄντα (e.g. *Republic* 477a7, 478d6), ἀληθινὴ οὐσία (e.g. *Sophist* 246b8), ὄντως ὄν / οὐσία (e.g. *Timaeus* 28a3–4, 52c5 and *Sophist* 248a11), and sometimes simply οὐσία (e.g. *Phaedo* 78d1 and *Sophist* 246c2). Plato's terminology is not fixed, indeed reconciling, or otherwise, his terms is an inquiry of long standing.

[3] i.e. the relation of one-way dependence which Plato sometimes refers to as 'participation' and 'communion' (μέθεξις, κοινωνία).

[4] The conclusion is stated at 249c10–d4. It is important to observe (as we shall see in

section 6) that this conclusion sums up not only the immediately preceding argument (248e7–249c9), i.e. the argument against the friends of the forms (which is our present concern), but also the earlier argument against the materialists (246e5–247c8, which is not our main concern at present).

⁵ Brown 1998, 204. Moravcsik (1962, 31 and 35–41) argues that Plato defends an 'all-inclusive' and 'tier-insensitive' answer to the question 'What exists?' So too Owen 1986b [originally 1966], 41–4 [336–40]. A tier-insensitive interpretation is also defended by Teloh 1981, 194–5 and Bordt 1991, 514, 520, 528.

⁶ See Ross 1951, 110–11; Cherniss 1965, 352; Frank 1986; Frede, 1996, 196; and Silverman 2002.

⁷ I believe this vital point has not been properly recognized by critics on either side of the two interpretations. Frank (1986, 14), for example, who defends a tiered interpretation, still construes the opening question without paying attention to the crucial qualification παντελῶς: 'I construe the passage: "Are we to be so easily convinced that change and life and mind and understanding are not part of reality (τῷ παντελῶς ὄντι ...)?"' Brown (1998, 201) translates 'what completely is' but immediately construes this to mean simply 'things that are', and in general pays no attention to the qualification παντελῶς. Moravcsik (1962, 39) also construes this passage to be saying simply that 'there is mind, life, soul, etc.' (likewise Silverman 2002, 154).

⁸ That this phrase, τὸ παντελῶς ὄν, is indeed ambiguous in this way is due to the ambiguity of the adjective τέλειον, which may mean either 'complete', in the sense of 'all-inclusive', or 'perfect'. παντελῶς is an intensification of the adverb, and so may mean either 'utterly completely' or 'utterly perfectly' (cf., e.g., πάσσοφος, 'utterly clever', *Tht.* 149d6, and παναληθής, 'absolutely true or real', *Rep.* 583b3). The ambiguity of τέλειον has of course been at the root of another famous controversy of interpretation, that is, that surrounding Aristotle's claim (in *Eth. Nic.* 1.7) that *eudaimonia* is the τελειότατον and τέλειον ἁπλῶς ἀγαθόν for humans. On the so-called inclusive reading, Aristotle's claim is that *eudaimonia* is constituted by *all* final goods whereas on the so-called dominant reading the claim is that it is constituted by *a single* final good, the perfect one.

⁹ 'τὸ μὲν παντελῶς ὂν παντελῶς γνωστόν, μὴ ὂν δὲ μηδαμῇ πάντῃ ἄγνωστον'. Translation by G.M.A. Grube, revised by C.D.C. Reeve, in Cooper 1997, 1103.

¹⁰ This claim is relatively unexciting in part because it is already familiar especially from the *Republic* (477a2 ff.), in part because the position of the friends of the forms, as it was characterized earlier in the dialogue (246b6–c4), is already committed to it. Nor is it plausible to suggest that they may not initially recognize this commitment, for their position is directly modelled on that described in the *Republic* passage (see below).

¹¹ One might, for example, argue that Plato invokes the distinction between two tiers of reality not to answer the question 'What is there?', but to answer the question 'What has an essence?', or to answer the question 'What is being?' (i.e. 'What is it for something to be?'). I would not, certainly, find such an argument plausible, because I think these three questions – 'What is there?', 'What is being?', and 'What has an essence?' – are inseparable from one another in Plato. But this is a large issue.

¹² I accept Badham's conjectured addition of πάντων to line 249b6, adopted by the new OCT.

¹³ See Owen 1986b [originally 1966], 43 [40], n. 15; Teloh 1981, 195; and Brown 1998, 202. Some critics (e.g. Frank 1986, 16–18 and Silverman 2002, 155), especially if (like Frank) they defend the tiered interpretation, argue that this conclusion is only

about *some* changing things. But clearly this is not a viable option. Other critics (esp. Cherniss 1965) who likewise defend the tiered interpretation simply ignore the problem that the conclusion is not committed to a tiered ontology.

[14] This is clear from the formulation of the conclusion at 249c11–d1: ἀνάγκη διὰ ταῦτα μήτε τῶν ἓν ἢ καὶ τὰ πολλὰ εἴδη λεγόντων τὸ πᾶν ἑστηκὸς ἀποδέχεσθαι… The former is apparently a reference to 244b6: παρὰ τῶν ἓν τὸ πᾶν λεγόντων… (Parmenides is mentioned by name at 244e2). Plato is assuming, as something familiar, that the Parmenidean One is changeless.

[15] For an excellent account of this battle, see Brown 1998. But I take issue with her tier-insensitive interpretation of the final argument against the friends of the forms (248e7–249d5).

[16] The claim is that the *dunamis* proposal provides a ὅρον for ὁρίζειν τὰ ὄντα (247e3–4). I read this to mean that the proposal provides, in the first instance, a mark for marking out or delimiting the things that are. It is addressed, therefore, primarily to the question, 'What is there?' It is a further question whether this mark is also supposed to amount to a definition proper of what it is for something, anything, to be a being, i.e. whether it is also addressed to the question, 'What is being?'.

[17] This last argument has been thoroughly examined by Keyt 1969, Vlastos 1973 and, more recently, Brown 1998.

[18] For this line of interpretation, see Frede 1996.

[19] See esp. Brown 1998, 199–200, who also refers to other critics in favour of this interpretation.

[20] Frank (1986, 11–12) argues that the friends of the forms reject the *dunamis* proposal because they reject the view that knowledge of the forms is like sense-perception of sense-perceptible things. While I am attracted by this idea, it is not required by our interpretation. Plato may accept that there is an analogy between sense-perception of sense-perceptible things and rational cognition of rationally knowable things while at the same time rejecting, because of his commitment to fundamentally tiered ontology, the view that these two kinds of knowledge, and their respective objects, strictly have something in common and that a single account applies to both.

[21] See nn. 7–8 above.

[22] See n. 9 above.

[23] See Brown, 1998, 201, quoted below.

[24] Brown (1998, 205), who defends this reading, calls it 'eirenic'.

[25] Leaving aside the difficult issue of how the soul that knows the immaterial forms is related to the bodily senses that know material things. This issue is hardly less difficult than that of how the immaterial forms are related to material things.

[26] Brown 1998, 201.

[27] Brown 1998, 199–200.

[28] *Tim.* 29d7 ff. This interpretation has even become enshrined in Liddell-Scott-Jones, which mentions *Sophist* 249a under the entry νοῦς in the sense of '*Mind* as the active principle of the Universe'.

[29] For a careful criticism of this interpretation, and of some of its defenders, see Vlastos 1973 and Brown 1998.

[30] The interpretation which says that it is the forms that have a changing, rational soul was originally defended by Plotinus, who says: εἶτα καὶ κίνησις ἦν ἐν τῇ δυάδι τῇ πρώτῃ καὶ στάσις, ἦν δὲ καὶ νοῦς, καὶ ζωὴν ἦν ἐν αὐτῇ· καὶ τέλεος νοῦς καὶ ζωὴ τελεία…

καὶ ζῷον παντελὲς ἦν (*Enneads* 6.7.8, lines 25–31). We may note that here Plotinus ingeniously relates *Sophist* 249a to *Timaeus* 31b1 (cf. τὸ παντελὲς ζῷον).

Bibliography

Bordt, M.
    1991   'Der Seinsbegriff in Platons "Sophistes"', *Theologie und Philosophie* 66, 493–529.

Brown, L.
    1998   'Innovation and continuity. The battle of gods and giants, *Sophist* 245–249', in J. Gentzler (ed.) *Method in Ancient Philosophy*, Oxford, 181–207.

Cherniss, H.
    1965   'The relation of the *Timaeus* to Plato's later dialogues', in R.E. Allen (ed.) *Studies in Plato's Metaphysics*, London, 339–78.

Cooper, J.M.
    1997   *Plato. Complete works*, Indianapolis.

Cornford, F.M.
    1935   *Plato's Theory of Knowledge*, London.

Frank, D.H.
    1986   'On what there is: Plato's later thoughts', *Elenchos* 6, 5–18.

Frede, M.
    1996   'Die Frage nach dem Seienden: *Sophistes*', in T. Kobusch und B. Mojsisch (eds.) *Platon. Seine Dialoge in der Sicht neuer Forschungen*, Darmstadt, 181–99.

Keyt, D.
    1969   'Plato's paradox that the immutable is unknowable', *Philosophical Quarterly* 19, 1–14.

Moravcsik, J.
    1962   'Being and meaning in the *Sophist*', *Acta Philosophica Fennica*, vol. 14, 23–78.

Owen, G.E.L.
    1986b   'Plato and Parmenides on the timeless present', in Owen, *Logic, Science and Dialectic*, London, 27–44.

Ross, D.
    1951   *Plato's Theory of Ideas*, Oxford.

Silverman, A.
    2002   *The Dialectic of Essence. A study of Plato's metaphysics*, Princeton.

Teloh, H.
    1981   *The Development of Plato's Metaphysics*, University Park, Pennsylvania.

Vlastos, G.
    1973   'An ambiguity in the *Sophist*. Appendix I: On the interpretation of *Sph.* 248d4–e4', in Vlastos, *Platonic Studies*, Princeton, 309–17.

8

WHY DOES PLATO BELIEVE IN A TIMELESS ETERNITY?

Andrew S. Mason

I

At *Timaeus* 37c ff., Plato introduces, for the first time in western thought, the idea of a timeless eternity.[1] He may not have been the first to conceive of timeless existence, for that idea is frequently ascribed to Parmenides.[2] But Parmenides, if he believed in a timeless existent, did not apply to it such terms as αἰώνιος (*aiōnios*), ἀΐδιος (*aïdios*) and ἀεὶ ὄν (*aei on*), whose primary application seems to be to what is everlasting in time. Plato, on the other hand, applies all these terms to the intelligible model of the world, while still affirming its timeless status. From him there descends a tradition, among both pagan and Christian thinkers, of applying the description 'eternal' to a timeless mode of existence, a tradition which culminates in Boethius' famous definition of eternity as '*interminabilis vitae tota simul et perfecta possessio*', 'the perfect possession of eternal life *all at once*'. Since Boethius it has been a frequent, though not universal, practice, among both philosophers and theologians, to reserve the name 'eternal' for what is timeless, using other terms for what is everlasting in time.

Plato contrasts eternity with time (χρόνος, *chronos*), and this in itself might be taken to show that, for him, eternity is a timeless mode of existence. In fact the matter is not so simple: for in the *Timaeus* Plato uses *chronos* in a restricted sense, meaning by it not any kind of succession or duration, but rather time as measured by the movements of the heavenly bodies – days, nights, months and years, together with the periods of the planets.[3] Hence, something might lack this measured kind of duration while not lacking all duration. However, in the course of contrasting eternity with time, Plato makes two points which seem to show that it is timeless in a deeper sense. First, 'was' and 'will be' are aspects of time, which we apply improperly to 'the eternal being' (*Tim.* 37e4–5). Second, what is eternal 'becomes neither older nor younger through time' (*Tim.* 38a3–4). The precise sense of the statement that it does not become younger is something of a mystery: but that it does not become older seems to mean that it is not subject to temporal passage; it is not constantly adding moments to its span of existence. (It does not mean that it does not decay: even the universe, which *is* a temporal being, is ageless in that sense.)[4] Hence, we should accept that Plato sees the eternal as timeless in some important sense, even though this may be hard to define.

There has been controversy over whether Plato really believes in a timeless eternity, and, if he does, over just what this might mean. However, my main concern is not with either of these questions; I assume that Plato's eternity is timeless, and set on one side the question what, exactly, this amounts to. My primary aim is to inquire what Plato's reasons were for believing in a timeless eternity.

II

In the passage cited above, Plato uses several terms that may be translated as 'eternal'. At 37d3, the model is *aiōnios* (αἰώνιος); and at 37d5 and 6, 38a7 and c2, the name *aiōn* (αἰών) is used for its condition, which is contrasted with time. At 38b8 and 39e2 the term *diaiōnios* (διαιώνιος) is used of the model. At 37d1 the model is *aïdios* (ἀίδιος); the same term is used at 37e5, the passage in which it is argued that 'was' and 'will be' cannot be applied to the eternal. *aïdios* is also used of the Forms at 29a3–5. At 38a3, in the passage which claims that the eternal does not grow older, the expression used is τὸ ἀεὶ κατὰ ταὐτὰ ἔχον ἀκινήτως (*to aei kata tauta echon akinētōs*), 'that which is always unchangeably in the same state'. The expressions *aei on* (ἀεὶ ὄν), 'always existing' and *aei kata tauta echon* (ἀεὶ κατὰ ταὐτὰ ἔχον), 'always being in the same state' are of course frequently applied to the Forms, in the *Timaeus* as in other dialogues[5] – e.g. 28a2 (ἀεὶ κατὰ ταὐτὰ ὄν, *aei kata tauta on*, 'always existing in the same state'), 37b3 (τὰ κατὰ ταὐτὰ ἔχοντα ἀεί, *ta kata tauta echonta aei*, 'the things which are always in the same state'). The expression *aei ōn* (ἀεὶ ὄν), 'always existing', is also applied to the creator at 34a8 and 37a1.

All these terms naturally refer to a temporal existence. *aiōn* (αἰών) normally means a period of time, or age: *aiōnios* (αἰώνιος), a word which seems to originate with Plato, would most naturally mean 'age-long' or life-long'. At its one previous occurrence, at *Rep.* 2.363d2, a reference to 'eternal drunkenness' in the afterlife, it clearly refers to a period of time, though perhaps an infinite one. In the very passage of the *Timaeus* which we are considering, it is used to describe time itself (αἰώνιον εἰκόνα, *aiōnion eikona*, 'an eternal image', 37d7). *aïdios* (ἀίδιος), formed from *aei* (ἀεί), is a standard term for 'everlasting', and within the *Timaeus* it is used not only of the Forms, but also of the heavenly gods, the stars, who are clearly temporal beings.[6] As for *aei*, its obvious reference is of course temporal: within the *Timaeus* it is often used in a temporal sense, e.g. at 52a6 it is used in relation to the motion of sensible things – πεφορημένον ἀεί (*pephorēmenon aei*, 'always in motion').

Plato's use of these terms poses a double problem. First, we may ask how these terms, whose obvious connotation is everlastingness in time, came to be applied to what is timeless. Secondly, there is a problem to which Richard Mohr has drawn attention.[7] We might suppose that Plato has introduced a new sense for these terms, distinct from that which they have when used of temporal things. But in fact he does not seem to recognize that his usage is equivocal. At 37d the creator, recognizing that the model is eternal (ἀίδιος, *aïdios*), strives to make the world as similar to it as possible. The following lines expand this point: the model is eternal (αἰώνιος, *aiōnios*), and no generated thing can achieve this *completely* (παντελῶς, *pantelōs*); for this reason time is made, as a 'moving likeness of eternity', intended to make the world as close as possible to its eternal model.[8] This point is emphasized again at 38b–c[9] and 39d–e.[10] Thus, it seems that the world is supposed to be eternal, *like* its model, though not perfectly so. But if 'eternal' is used in two quite different senses, this is not possible; one can only compare the degree to which two things are eternal if this really is a property which, at some level, they share. If, however, 'eternal' sometimes stands for timelessness, sometimes for everlastingness in time, it seems to stand for two properties which are not only distinct, but incompatible.

III

A solution to this second problem has been proposed by Mohr.[11] He argues that there must be some property possessed both by the eternal model and by time, though less perfectly so by time. Accepting that the 'eternity' of the model is timelessness, he claims that the complex of celestial motions which makes up time can itself be seen as, in a sense, timeless. He proposes that this timelessness is that appropriate to standards of measurement, of which, he argues, temporal judgements cannot intelligibly be made.

It is by reference to standards that we ascribe properties to things and make judgements of sameness and difference. It seems to follow that such judgements cannot be made of standards themselves, since this would imply comparison with a further standard. Moreover, it is by reference to standards that we make judgements of change and stability; for instance, when we say that a child has grown, or that an adult has not, we are comparing them with standards of length. It follows that we cannot say, of standards themselves, either that they have changed or that they have not; for this, once again, would imply reference to a further standard. Hence, Mohr argues, standards 'are not in the category of things which either change or abide'[12] and thus 'fall outside of the class of things which change or fail to change'.[13] It follows from this that we cannot say of a standard that it 'was' or 'will be' such and such, or that it has a quality for a greater or lesser length of time.

Mohr argues that, while Forms are standards in this sense, the celestial movements which make up time are also standards, in that they enable us to tell the time and to compare periods of time. If we accept them as standards, we cannot strictly make temporal judgements about them. For instance, we cannot say that the moon takes a month to circle the earth, for a month is defined by reference to the moon's period. Nor, while treating the moon's motion as a standard, can we say that its period was once different from what it now is, nor that it has stayed the same; for this implies comparing it with a further standard. In this sense, therefore, the heavenly motions are timeless, in that temporal judgements cannot intelligibly be made about them.

However, while the heavenly motions are under one aspect standards, they can also be seen as ordinary sensible processes, and in that respect they are subject to ordinary temporal judgements. Forms, on the other hand, cannot be seen under any aspect other than that of standards. It follows that there is no respect in which they are not timeless, whereas the celestial motions are timeless in one respect but not in others. It is for this reason, Mohr suggests, that time can be described as eternal, but not perfectly so.

IV

However, it is possible to object to this interpretation on two main grounds. First, it seems to rest on a philosophical assumption that is controversial, and which it is not obvious that Plato accepted: that if a judgement cannot be informative, it is unintelligible. From this the corollary is drawn that such judgements cannot be intelligibly made or denied, nor can the question be raised whether they are true.[14] In the present case, if the moon's motion is accepted as a standard of time, then a month *is*, by definition, the period of the moon's motion; hence we do not say anything informative about the moon when we say that it takes a month to rotate.[15] Therefore, it is argued, it *makes no sense* to say either that the moon's period changes, or that it does not change; the moon's motion 'falls outside of the class of things which either change or fail to change'.

However, it is possible to take another view of such judgements, on which they are not unintelligible, but only pointless; judgements such as 'the moon has always taken a month to circle the earth' are true, and their negations false, but they are normally uninformative, and indeed misleading, since if they are presented as informative they will lead people to suppose that things might have been otherwise. Such judgements are comparable to 'seven has always been a prime number', something we would not normally have cause to say, but which is still arguably true. We do not say it, because it is so obvious that its assertion would be deceptive; but we might have cause to say it, either in speaking to a child, to whom conceptual truths are not obvious, or in philosophical discussion, where we have reason to reflect on the status of conceptual truths. In such contexts, we are not using it to rule out a genuinely possible (or imaginable) alternative, but precisely to affirm that there *is* no alternative. Likewise we might have reason to say that the celestial motions do not change, not comparing them with another standard, but rather affirming that just *because* they are the standards they cannot possibly change. In that case, judgements that they have been and will be the same are perfectly intelligible.

It is hard to tell which of these views is Plato's, or indeed whether he had reflected on these matters in such a way as to discriminate between them; but it is at least unsafe to assume that he would have seen the heavenly movements as timeless by being standards.

The second possible objection to Mohr's view is that it answers only one of the two problems raised earlier about Plato's use of the concept of eternity. It explains how *aiōnios*, whose primary application is to the timeless, can also be applied without equivocation to time itself. But it does not explain how this and related terms came to be applied to the timeless in the first place. The most natural reading of *aiōnios* (αἰώνιος) would seem to be 'everlasting'; and this is certainly true of *aïdios* (ἀίδιος) and of *aei on* (ἀεὶ ὄν) or *aei kata tauta echon* (ἀεὶ κατὰ ταὐτὰ ἔχον). These terms are frequently applied to the Forms before 37c, and no one would suspect, in advance of this passage, that anything other than endless duration was being ascribed to them. Moreover, it is not only time itself which has a limited eternity; the world as a whole, in virtue of its possession of time, is made as like as possible to its eternal model.[16] At 38c1–3 the way time images the eternal seems to be linked to its infinite duration:

τὸ μὲν γὰρ δὴ παράδειγμα πάντα αἰῶνά ἐστιν ὄν, ὁ δ' αὖ διὰ τέλους τὸν ἅπαντα χρόνον γεγονώς τε καὶ ὢν καὶ ἐσόμενος.

for the pattern is, being, for all eternity, but it [time] for the whole of time has become and is and will be.

Here, there seems no reluctance to apply temporal judgements to time itself; it is its permanence which links it with the eternal.

In the light of this, it seems that the idea of the eternal should not be wholly divorced from that of the everlasting. We are not dealing here with an uninterpreted technical term of Plato's philosophy, which can be understood simply in the light of what he says in this passage. He does not use a single term, but a number of related terms, all of which have the natural connotation of 'everlasting'. He is writing about a property with which his readers are already familiar; here he elucidates more clearly what the perfect possession of that property involves. In the course of this our understanding of the property may change to some extent, but not in such a way that we lose all contact with its original use.

V

We need, then, some point of similarity between the timeless and the everlasting in time: some property which is possessed by both, though more completely by the timeless. I suggest that this property is that of being subject to neither generation nor destruction. The intelligible world is often contrasted with the sensible world, which is subject to generation and destruction; for instance at 28a,[17] or 51e–52a,[18] where the Forms are described as ἀγέννητον καὶ ἀνώλεθρον (*agennēton kai anōlethron*, 'ungenerated and indestructible'). In the present passage, at 37d4, we are told that the generated cannot attain to full eternity, though the world attains to it in a partial way, presumably by being exempted from destruction.

If this is right, Plato's conception of eternity will be a negative one; the Forms exist for ever in the sense that they have no beginning or end. In insisting on their eternity, Plato is not concerned that they should enjoy an infinite number of moments of existence, but rather that they should not perish.

If eternity is understood in this negative sense, it will indeed be a property shared by the timeless and the everlasting, though of course they possess it for different reasons; for temporal things it is a contingent matter that they do not come to be or perish, while timeless things, of their nature, cannot do so. Once again, in affirming that the timeless does not perish, we are not ruling out a genuinely possible alternative, but rather affirming that there is no alternative.

It is often recognized that in this passage Plato is ascribing some kind of permanence to the Forms, but it is sometimes thought that this shows some confusion on his part;[19] the language of stability should not be used in connection with timeless being, since stability is persistence through time. But if permanence is understood in this negative sense, there need be no confusion. Certainly the concept of permanence is linked with time, in that it is contrasted with becoming and perishing, which do happen in time; if we lived in a timeless world (and if thought were still possible in such a world) we would have no need of the concept of 'always'. But it does not follow that the things to which we ascribe permanence must *themselves* be capable of becoming and perishing; given that there are things which become and perish, we can define permanence by contrast with them; and in this case timeless things will be permanent precisely in that they are beyond any possibility of becoming and perishing.

VI

We now have an explanation of how one property, eternity, can be seen as belonging both to the timeless and the everlasting; but it remains to be seen why *only* the timeless can be eternal in the fullest sense. Could not something be wholly free from generation and destruction merely by persisting throughout time? The world, indeed, cannot be fully eternal, simply because it is generated. But this does not explain why the eternal cannot grow older, or why 'was' and 'will be' do not apply to it. The answer can be found at 38a2–3; 'was' and 'will be' are changes, while the eternal is described as 'what is always *unchangeably* in the same state'. This, as Owen among others has pointed out,[20] gives us one central premise of Plato's argument: what is wholly changeless must be timeless. But if we are to derive from this the conclusion that what is fully *eternal* must be timeless, we need a second, implicit premise; what is fully eternal must be changeless. On the present interpretation, this will mean that only what is changeless can be wholly free from becoming and perishing.

The first premise has frequently been discussed. As is often noticed, the passage echoes two passages in the *Parmenides*, in both of which it is argued that what is in time grows older and also, paradoxically, younger, and is subject to the descriptions 'was', 'is' and 'will be'. In the first passage, *Parm.* 141a5–d6, it is argued that, as the One does not have these properties, it cannot be in time: in the second, *Parm.* 152a3–b2, that, as it *is* in time, it must have these properties.

The discussion in the *Parmenides* is conducted against the background of the assumption that what is not in time cannot exist (*Parm.* 141d6–e10, 151e6–152a3). This is sometimes taken to show that Plato, when writing the *Parmenides*, had rejected the *Timaeus*' idea of timeless eternity. However, an alternative view is possible: that this idea of timeless eternity was introduced by Plato in response to the arguments considered in the *Parmenides*; given that these arguments seem to show that whatever is in time is in change, the changelessness of the Forms can only be guaranteed by ascribing to them a kind of timeless existence. If the *Timaeus* is later than the *Parmenides*, it may well be the case that the idea of timeless eternity, which is not found explicitly in earlier dialogues, was introduced after the *Parmenides*, as a result of Plato's considering the arguments presented there. Alternatively, it might be the case that Plato had already formed the idea of timeless eternity before writing the *Parmenides*, but is there making the assumption that there is no timeless existence for the sake of argument.

Richard Patterson[21] has plausibly argued that the centrality of changelessness explains why time, the pattern of celestial motions, brings the world closer to eternity. These motions give the world the greatest possible stability, first by being circular – the most uniform of motions, as Plato points out in several places[22] – and secondly by forming a pattern in which the world returns at last to its original position.[23] Hence, the world does indeed change, but according to an unchanging pattern, and so approaches as close as it can to the changelessness of its original.

We may still ask, however, why only what is changeless can be wholly eternal. Might not an object exist for ever, and so be free from generation and destruction, but be subject to qualitative change? In an Aristotelian system, this is certainly possible; for Aristotle makes a clear distinction between those changes in the world which constitute the generation and destruction of substances, and those which are mere alterations. Plato, however, does not seem to have such a clear distinction. Rather, there is evidence that for him material things are seen as constituted by changes or motions; body is referred to as *genesis* or process. The soul is also seen as a kind of motion, a motion which moves itself. On this view, we do not have an ontology of enduring things to which changes happen. Although there are, in some sense, persisting things in the world, these are constituted by a series of changes.

One passage which supports this view is *Laws* 896a1–897b8. There the Athenian defines soul as a motion which moves itself, and takes this to establish that it is the primary motion, prior to any motion produced in a thing from outside. However, the conclusion drawn is not simply that soul is prior to bodily movements, but that it is prior to bodies themselves.[24] The reason for this becomes clear at 897a: soul, with its motions, takes over the motions of bodies and 'leads everything to increase and decrease, separation and combination, and following on these heat and cold, weight and lightness, hard and soft, white and black, bitter and sweet'.[25] The qualities which constitute bodies are seen as motions or the effect of motions, and so as dependent on soul.

This view of the nature of bodies can also be supported by reference to the metaphysics of the receptacle in the *Timaeus*.[26] This is the only truly self-existent object outside the intelligible world; bodies are qualities manifested in it, not entities in their own right.

When the world is viewed in this way, change on the one hand, and generation and destruction on the other may be seen as two aspects of one phenomenon. From one point of view, all generation can be seen as change. Something persists through every change; there is no generation *ex nihilo* or destruction *in nihil*, and therefore every change in the world may be seen as an alteration in whatever persisting thing is involved (in the case of the most fundamental physical changes, in the receptacle). But from another point of view, all change is generation; any change may be seen as the coming into being of new motions and qualities, and the perishing of the old. Hence, while bodies and souls may indeed be seen as persisting, for so long as the motions and qualities which constitute them retain sufficient coherence, from another point of view they are constantly being destroyed and regenerated.

A view of this kind is famously stated, in respect of the human body and soul, at *Symposium* 207c–208b. There, Diotima argues that both the body and the soul are constantly changing in composition. Because of this, she claims, we cannot fully attain to immortality; we do not in fact wholly persist, even in this life, but rather leave a new self behind as the old one passes away. Yet this is not something *wholly* new, but is under some aspect identical with the old; *we* are made new, and in some sense *we* are preserved by this process.[27]

The lines which conclude this passage seem to imply that only what does not change at all can be, in the fullest sense, immortal (*Symp.* 208a7–b4):

τούτῳ γὰρ τῷ τρόπῳ πᾶν τὸ θνητὸν σῴζεται, οὐ τῷ παντάπασιν τὸ αὐτὸ ἀεὶ εἶναι ὥσπερ τὸ θεῖον, ἀλλὰ τῷ τὸ ἀπιὸν καὶ παλαιούμενον ἕτερον νέον ἐγκαταλείπειν οἷον αὐτὸ ἦν. ταύτῃ τῇ μηχανῇ, ὦ Σώκρατες, ἔφη, θνητὸν ἀθανασίας μετέχει, καὶ σῶμα καὶ τἆλλα πάντα· ἀθάνατον δὲ ἄλλῃ.

In this way, everything mortal is preserved, *not by being altogether the same for ever, like the divine*, but by leaving behind, in the place of what passes away and grows old, another new one like it. By this device, Socrates, the mortal shares in immortality, the body and everything else; *but the immortal does so in another way*.

Even in the *Symposium,* then, it seems that Plato adopts the view that only what suffers no change at all is, in the fullest sense, indestructible. Yet there the denial of immortality applies only to the human body, which is clearly changing in composition, and the human soul, whose content of thoughts, feelings, desires etc, is constantly shifting. Immortality in the fullest sense may still be allowed to the gods, whose thoughts are presumably unchanging (as they explicitly are at *Timaeus* 40a8–b1). What the *Timaeus* adds to this is the perception that whatever is in time is in change, since it is subject to growing older and to the changes expressed by 'was' and 'will be'. When this is combined with the doctrine of the *Symposium*, it seems that only a timeless existence can guarantee complete permanence; and in this case only the Forms, and perhaps the creator, are in the fullest sense indestructible or eternal.

However, some temporal things are nevertheless able to be everlasting in some respect, in that they are given enough stability and coherence to maintain their identity across time, even though they are in some sense perishing and being renewed. This is true of the world, the heavenly gods, and the rational human soul. These, therefore, are in a secondary degree eternal.

Andrew S. Mason

Acknowledgements
This paper was presented at the Celtic Conference in Classics at Glasgow, and also to audiences in Edinburgh. I am grateful to all who contributed to the discussion, and especially to David Robinson and Theodore Scaltsas.

Notes

[1] '"Was" and "will be" are generated forms of time, which indeed we ignorantly ascribe to the eternal nature, not rightly. For we say that it was, is and will be, though according to the correct account only 'is' belongs to it, but it is right to apply 'was' and 'will be' to generation which proceeds in time – for they are changes; but that which is always unchangeably in the same state (ἀεὶ κατὰ ταὐτὰ ἔχον ἀκινήτως) may never become older or younger with time; nor is it the case that it once became, nor that it now has become, nor that it will be in the future, nor in general can it have any of the attributes which generation has attached to perceptible things that move; but these are generated forms of time, which imitates eternity and rotates according to number' (*Tim.* 37e4–38a8).

[2] 'It neither was nor will be, since it is now, all together (ὁμοῦ πᾶν, *homou pan*), one, continuous' (Parmenides B8, Diels-Kranz, 5–6).

[3] 'As he ordered the heaven he made an image, moving by number, of eternity which abides in unity, that to which we have given the name of time. For days and nights and months and years did not exist before the universe was made, but he contrived their generation then, at the same time as he created it' (*Tim.* 37d5–e3). See also 38c3 ff., 39c5–d2.

[4] 'That it might be ageless and free from disease' (*Tim.* 33a2).

[5] See for instance *Phaedo* 78b ff, where Forms, which are constantly in the same state, are contrasted with sensible things, which are in constant change; e.g. at 78c6 ἅπερ ἀεὶ κατὰ ταὐτὰ καὶ ὡσαύτως ἔχει, 'those things which are always in the same state and unchanging'. Another passage which draws a similar contrast is *Symposium* 211b1–2, where the Form of Beauty is αὐτὸ καθ' αὑτὸ μεθ' αὑτοῦ μονοειδὲς ἀεὶ ὄν, 'itself, by itself, with itself, single in form, always being', by contrast with sensible beautiful things which are 'at one time beautiful, at another not'.

[6] 'From this cause arose those stars which do not wander, but are living creatures, divine and eternal, and always remain turning with the same motion in the same place' (*Tim.* 40b4–6).

[7] Mohr 1985, 70–1.

[8] 'When the father who generated it [the world] recognized that it was moving and alive, a generated image of the eternal gods, he was glad, and in his joy he planned to make it still more like its pattern. Therefore, since that is an eternal (ἀίδιον) living creature, he tried to make this universe like it, so far as was possible. The nature of the living creature was eternal (αἰώνιος), and it was not possible to bestow that quality completely on what was generated; but he decided to make a moving image of eternity, and as he ordered the heaven he made an image, moving by number, of eternity which abides in unity, that to which we have given the name of time' (*Tim.* 37c6–d7).

[9] 'Time, then, came into being with the universe, so that being generated together they should be destroyed together, if destruction of them should ever come to pass, and

according to the pattern of the eternal (διαιωνίας) nature, so that it should be as like it as possible. For the pattern is, being, through all eternity, but it [time] has come to be and is and will be throughout the whole of time' (*Tim.* 38b6–c3).

[10] 'In this way and for this reason were generated those of the stars which have turnings as they travel through the sky, so that this [the world] might be as like as possible to the perfect and intelligible living creature by its imitation of the eternal (διαιωνίας) nature' (*Tim.* 39d7–e2).

[11] Mohr 1985, 67–75.

[12] Mohr 1985, 69.

[13] Mohr 1985, 74.

[14] The assumption on which Mohr's argument rests has been criticised in many places, e.g. Searle 1966, and, in a context related to the present one, M. Kneale 1968–9.

[15] It is only while we are using the moon's motion as a standard of time that the claim that its period does not change is uninformative; it is, as Mohr notes, possible to treat the moon's motion as an ordinary sensible process, and compare it with other standards. If we do this – e.g. by comparing it with the sun, and calculating its period as a fraction of a year – it might well be a discovery both that the moon's motion has the specific period which it has, and that it is unchanging.

[16] *Tim.* 37c6–d2 (see n. 8 above).

[17] 'That which is grasped by intelligence with reason is always in the same state (ἀεὶ κατὰ ταὐτὰ ὄν), but that which is an object of belief by opinion with unreasoning perception comes to be and passes away, but never really is' (*Tim.* 28a1–4).

[18] 'Since this is so, we must agree that there is one thing, the Form which is always the same, ungenerated and indestructible...but that which shares its name is second, like it, perceptible, generated, always in movement, both coming to be in some place and perishing again from it' (*Tim.* 51e6–52a7).

[19] See, for instance, Owen 1966, 335; this argument is discussed by Mohr 1985, 72.

[20] Owen 1966, 334.

[21] Patterson 1985.

[22] 'A movement in the same place according to the same pattern, [suited] for one who always thinks the same thoughts about the same things' (*Tim.* 38a8–b1). See also *Laws* 898a–b.

[23] 'The perfect number of time completes the perfect year when the relative speeds of the eight revolutions have been completed together' (*Tim.* 39d4–5).

[24] *Laws* 896c1–2; cf. 892a2–b1.

[25] *Laws* 897a6–b1.

[26] *Tim.* 48e2–52d1; see especially 49d4–e7, according to which fire and the other primary bodies should be called not 'this' (τοῦτο, *touto*) but 'such' (τοιοῦτον, *toiouton*); while the interpretation of this passage is highly controversial, on a traditional reading this means that they are not things in their own right but rather qualities of the receptacle.

[27] 'A man is called the same though he never has the same things in him, but is always being made new, and in other respects perishing' (*Symp.* 207d6–8); see also 208a7–b4, quoted below.

Bibliography

Kneale, M.
    1968–9 'Eternity and sempiternity', *Proceedings of the Aristotelian Society*, n.s. 69, 223–38.

Kneale, W.
    1960–1 'Time and eternity in theology', *Proceedings of the Aristotelian Society*, n.s. 61, 87–98.

Mohr, R.D.
    1985 'Plato on time and eternity', in R.D. Mohr, *The Platonic Cosmology*, Leiden, 53–81.

Owen, G.E.L.
    1966 'Plato and Parmenides on the timeless present', *Monist* 50, 317–40.

Parmenides
    1951 Fragments, in H. Diels and W. Kranz (eds.) *Die Fragmente der Vorsokratiker*, vol. II, Berlin.

Patterson, R.
    1985 'On the eternality of Platonic Forms', *Archiv für Geschichte der Philosophie*, 67, 27–46.

Plato
    1901 *Parmenides*, in J. Burnet (ed.) *Platonis Opera*, vol. II, Oxford.
    1901 *Symposium*, in J. Burnet (ed.) *Platonis Opera*, vol. II, Oxford.
    1902 *Timaeus*, in J. Burnet (ed.) *Platonis Opera*, vol. IV, Oxford.
    1907 *Laws*, in J. Burnet (ed.) *Platonis Opera*, vol. V, Oxford.

Searle, J.
    1966 'Assertions and aberrations', in B. Williams and A. Montefiore (eds.) *British Analytical Philosophy*, London, 41–54.

Sorabji, R.
    1983 *Time, Creation and the Continuum*, London.

Whittaker, J.
    1968 'The "eternity" of the Platonic Forms', *Phronesis* 13, 131–44.

9

AN ARISTOTELIAN PERSPECTIVE ON PLATO'S DIALOGUES

Stephen Halliwell

What did Aristotle think of Plato's dialogues, and how did he suppose they should or could be read? According to one contemporary authority on both philosophers, we are in a position to formulate brisk, uncomplicated answers to these questions. Terence Irwin has claimed that Aristotle 'shows no hesitation in attributing the views of the Platonic Socrates to Plato', and on the basis of this claim Irwin enjoins us to 'follow Aristotle in believing that the arguments and conclusions of the Platonic Socrates (and other main speakers) generally [*sic*] represent the views of Plato'.[1] Now, if it could be demonstrated that Aristotle did indeed have an unambiguous conception of the relationship between the dialogues and their author's independently held views, I do not deny that this would deserve to carry substantial, though not necessarily decisive, weight with modern readers of Plato. However, part of the purpose of this essay is to challenge the unguarded confidence with which Irwin (enunciating a thesis that is widely shared) affirms the existence of such a conception on Aristotle's part. In the first and longer section of my argument I shall undertake a close interpretative scrutiny of a single sentence of Aristotle's, a sentence which though little studied happens to contain the richest comment on the nature of Plato's philosophical *writings* to be found anywhere in the Aristotelian corpus. The second part of my case will address certain features of the larger context of this sentence, a context which itself contains the most extended discussion left us by Aristotle of any portion of Plato's texts. My ambition is not to replace Irwin's unequivocal stance with an equally unyielding alternative, but rather to suggest that we would do well to tread warily and avoid reductive simplifications in making assertions about Aristotle's attitudes to the Platonic dialogues. I do not at all presume that Aristotle must have held a single, unwavering model of the dialogues. I hope instead to establish that in his most explicit pronouncement on the subject he sketches a perspective which is intrinsically complex. That perspective will not settle the question of how 'we' should read Plato, especially if, as I believe, there is no *one* way in which Plato ought to be read. But for both historical and philosophical reasons the Aristotelian perspective to be investigated here merits careful pondering by all serious interpreters of the dialogues.

So much has been asserted on so many occasions about Aristotle's reactions to the philosophy of Plato that it is surprising how little notice has been taken in print of the most revealing remark – indeed, the *only* general evaluative remark – made by Aristotle on the character of Plato's written works. The remark in question occurs in *Politics* Book 2, ch. 6, in the course of the well-known critique of the communist scenarios of both the *Republic* and the *Laws*. In fact, the precise juncture at which Aristotle makes the remark is the first thing of note about it. He introduces it when his focus has already shifted from the earlier to the later work (though with a comparative eye still on the *Republic*), and it actually seems to be prompted by a specific detail in the *Laws*, namely the size of the military class under the posited system of communism. Yet he frames his observation on Plato's writings as an aperçu about 'all the discourses of Socrates' (πάντες οἱ τοῦ Σωκράτους λόγοι). Opinions on the significance of this detail are divided: first, over whether it implies that Aristotle in some sense identifies or equates the Athenian of the *Laws* with 'Socrates' (i.e., with the Socrates figure of other Platonic dialogues); secondly, over whether, if he *does* make this identification, it constitutes carelessness, an unwarranted hypothesis, or a reasonable assumption on Aristotle's part.[2] These questions are not central to my own enquiry, so I will state baldly that I do take Aristotle here to be treating the *Laws* as an extension of, or continuous with, the class of Plato's 'Socratic dialogues'. That proposition entails at least (though perhaps no more than) that he thinks of the Athenian as possessing a broadly comparable ethos or as playing a broadly comparable role to that of the figure called Socrates in most of Plato's other dialogues, and, in consequence, that the dialogic nature of the *Laws* is not different in kind from those other works. But regardless of exactly what one makes of this aspect of the passage (and the late Trevor Saunders went so far as to suspect 'ironic jesting' behind the implication of the *Laws*' putatively 'Socratic' status),[3] the generalization which Aristotle goes on to make about Plato's Socratic dialogues provides a vital clue to his evaluation of the *oeuvre* as a whole.

Before we pursue the details of that evaluation, one further issue of preliminary interpretation needs briefly to be registered. Strictly speaking, Aristotle refers here to a whole class of Socratic dialogues or discourses; taken in isolation, the reference might be supposed to include more than the writings of Plato. Other texts, for sure, suggest that Aristotle had a conception of Socratic dialogues as a more-than-Platonic genre of philosophical writing. In his own dialogue *On Poets* Aristotle ascribed pre-Platonic Socratic dialogues to Alexamenus of Teos (though text and interpretation have been disputed);[4] in Book 3 of the *Rhetoric* (1417a20–3) there is a reference to 'Socratic (discourses)' which clearly has generic scope, since the label οἱ Σωκρατικοὶ λόγοι stands here in contrast to 'mathematical discourses', οἱ μαθηματικοὶ λόγοι; and the same is probably true, given the classificatory nature of the passage (and the link with the fragment of *On Poets*), of the listing of 'Socratic discourses' as one kind of prose mimesis in chapter 1 of the *Poetics* (1447b11). It would be perverse, however, to treat the phrase 'all the discourses of Socrates' in *Politics* 2.6 as having this purely generic sense. Plato's *Republic* has been the topic of analysis for almost the whole of Book 2 up to this juncture. Its contents have been consistently cited and paraphrased in terms of the positions adopted by the figure of Socrates (a point to which I shall return in the later part of my paper). The *Laws*, as already noted, has been brought into the discussion alongside the *Republic* immediately before the key sentence on which I wish to focus; but no other author of Socratic dialogues has been mentioned. So Aristotle's remark must be a remark about Plato's writings alone. Even so, its phrasing does show that Aristotle is consciously thinking of those writings as Plato's achievement *in* the genre of Socratic dialogues or discourses. If he conceives of Socratic dialogues as a (mimetic) genre, which we know that he does, and if he conceives of Plato's written work as a whole as belonging to that genre (which we have seen that he seems to), then his interpretation of that work presumably reflects those assumptions. Against that backcloth, then, let us turn to Aristotle's compressed yet striking summary of the character of Plato's writing, and in particular to the four qualities which it singles out as salient in that body of writing.

Aristotle's *obiter dictum* on Plato's dialogues reads as follows (*Pol.* 2.6. 1265a10–3; I deliberately withhold my own translation but provide Trevor Saunders' for basic orientation): τὸ μὲν οὖν περιττὸν ἔχουσι πάντες οἱ τοῦ Σωκράτους λόγοι καὶ τὸ κομψὸν καὶ τὸ καινοτόμον καὶ τὸ ζητητικόν, καλῶς δὲ πάντα ἴσως χαλεπόν.[5] Saunders (1995, 32) translates: 'Now all the Socratic dialogues display extravagance, brilliance, originality, and a spirit of inquiry; but it is perhaps hard to succeed in everything.'

We need to be alert from the outset to the delicately poised structure of Aristotle's remark (signalled by its μέν/δέ contrast), which encompasses admiration for Plato's writings in the same breath as hinting at reservations about them. This in itself should inhibit us from jumping to any easy conclusions about Aristotle's considered view of the dialogues. With this in mind, it will prove worthwhile to examine the full evidence of Aristotle's usage of the four adjectives which appear in nominalized form in the first part of the sentence just quoted; as we proceed, we shall find it illuminating to take into account the data of Platonic usage as well.[6] Throughout what follows, 'Socrates', together with 'Socratic', will denote the Socrates figure of the dialogues of Plato, unless otherwise indicated. This distinction mattered to Aristotle himself: I believe that 'Fitzgerald's canon', so called, justifiably takes it as Aristotle's standard practice – with a few, though no truly problematic, exceptions – to designate the Socrates of the dialogues as ὁ Σωκράτης, while keeping Σωκράτης without the definite article for the historical Socrates.[7] The relevance of this practice to my case will emerge in the later parts of the paper.

First, then, τὸ περιττόν. Uncertainty over the scope of this noun betrays itself in the range of translations offered by scholars. While Jowett plumps for the litotes 'never commonplace', Rackham has 'brilliance', Barker 'original[ity]' (likewise Aubonnet's Budé translation), and Lord, Simpson and Reeve '[the] extraordinary' (cf. Schütrumpf's 'außergewöhnliche Ideen'). But Sinclair renders it as 'exaggeration' and Saunders as 'extravagance', while differently again Gigon has 'Kühnheit' and Bertelli 'magnificenza'.[8]

Broadly speaking (and leaving aside the word-group's technical denotations in mathematics and biology), something or someone counts as περιττός for Aristotle when remarkable in the dual sense of being both exceptional (even to the point of uniqueness) and at least *prima facie* impressive or admirable. περιττός can thus be readily combined with θαυμαστός/θαυμάσιος ('amazing', 'wonderful', etc.), but unlike general usage, which includes both negative and positive ways of being 'out of the ordinary', Aristotle never attaches the term to the merely odd or aberrantly peculiar.[9] Typical is his application of the word to phenomena in the animal world: bees, for instance, are a remarkable species (περιττὸν γένος) in virtue of features which are not just unusual but zoologically marvellous (hence also the use of the adjective θεῖος, 'divine', of them), and the same holds for dolphins or the beaks of birds.[10] According to two passages of the *Rhetoric* things that are περιττός tend to be treated as objects of value or honour (τιμή), and they constitute one class of things which count as admirable (καλός) to a high degree.[11] In keeping with this last point, in the *Politics* Aristotle praises certain aspects of the Carthaginian constitution by the adverbs καλῶς καί...περιττῶς (2.8.1272b24–25), 'admirably and exceptionally'. Individuals can be περιττός in various respects. The epithet is appropriate to any action that is the cause of a good reputation (*Pol.* 5.8.1312a27). Aristotle himself is prepared to use it of intellectual and philosophical abilities of a rare kind: he speaks in the *Topics* (6.4.141b13) of the acute and exceptional acumen (ἀκριβοῦς καὶ περιττῆς διανοίας) needed to grasp certain mathematical properties, and in the *Metaphysics* he applies the term to the philosophically wise in general.[12] Pertinent to our understanding of his comment on Plato's dialogues, however, is the fact that in the *Nicomachean Ethics*, when contrasting *sophia* and *phronēsis*, Aristotle uses the adjective to describe the contents of the wisdom (sc. of things higher than human) attributed by some people to such philosophers as Anaxagoras and Thales, who are said, on this view, to know what is 'extraordinary, wonderful, difficult, divine... but of no practical use' (περιττὰ μὲν καὶ θαυμαστὰ καὶ χαλεπὰ καὶ δαιμόνια... ἄχρηστα δ' ...)[13]

Though this last passage in no way diminishes the importance of *sophia*, it does help to show that something or someone can in principle count as περιττός while still failing to meet every test of philosophical value. The figures in question are regarded, on the view Aristotle adduces there, as possessing a higher wisdom (*sophia*) but lacking truly human, practical wisdom (*phronēsis*): their knowledge is therefore 'beyond the ordinary' in a somewhat double-edged sense. As it happens, a passage which illustrates a comparable but harsher nuance combines the word with one of the other three terms in our sentence of the *Politics*, namely κομψός. At *De Caelo* 2.9.290b14, Aristotle states that the doctrine of the 'harmony of the spheres' is one that has been expressed κομψῶς...καὶ περιττῶς (let us say, 'cleverly and unusually') but is nonetheless false.[14] The suggestion here is of something whose distinctiveness is more superficial than substantial, though Aristotle's terminology shows that it is hard to separate 'style' and 'content' in such judgements. But a similar point at *Metaphysics* 10.1.1053b3, where those who proclaim the Protagorean tenet of 'man the measure of all things' are convicted of saying 'nothing' while appearing to say something 'exceptional' (οὐθὲν δὴ λέγοντες περιττὸν φαίνονταί τι λέγειν), confirms an important inference: Aristotle's use of περιττός, unlike (as we shall shortly see) that of κομψός, never carries pejorative force in itself but can sometimes be associated with criticism of intellectual ideas that are more meretricious than cogent.[15] Moreover, when Aristotle reiterates his verdict on 'the harmony of the spheres' later in that same chapter of the *De caelo* (290b30–1), he now describes the doctrine as one that has been formulated with a kind of musico-stylistic cultivation, ἐμμελῶς καὶ μουσικῶς, 'elegantly and charmingly'. Although Aristotle is analysing what he takes to be a pseudo-musical theory, those two adverbs, themselves musical metaphors (and both common in Plato), can hardly be ironic. They acknowledge a certain attractiveness of language and perhaps a poetic imaginativeness in the terms in which the doctrine is couched: both pick out ways of 'sounding good', but their positive force is offset by adjacent notes of doubt. The affinity between these adverbs and the earlier pair, κομψῶς...καὶ περιττῶς, gives us a clue to at least part of the range of qualities, and the potentially attendant risks, covered by our sentence in the *Politics*. It may not be going too far, given the implications of the *De caelo* contexts and the parallel conjunction of περιττός and κομψός in that work, to surmise that the *Politics* hints at what Aristotle thought of as a quasi-Pythagorean streak in Plato's uses of language and imagery. In the latter connection we should recall a final passage, from the *Poetics*, where epic mimesis is deemed to be exceptional (περιττή) in metrical and verbal terms (24.1459b36): here the adjective marks out a certain stylistic elevation, even in relation to that of the spoken verse of tragedy. There is enough reason here to suppose, at any rate, that Aristotle's use of τὸ περιττόν (plus τὸ κομψόν) at *Pol.* 1265a10–1 could cover stylistic-cum-'literary' as well as more narrowly intellectual properties.[16]

The provisional conclusions warranted by the first term in Aristotle's list of Platonic qualities already open up complex ramifications. On the one hand, the ascription of τὸ περιττόν to Plato's work clearly conveys a judgement that the dialogues sustain an extraordinary impressiveness of both ideas and writing (more specifically, as examples of the mimetic genre of Socratic dialogues). However, two possible overtones of reservation, whose strength will need to be tested by the other three items in Aristotle's list (as well as by the shape of his remark as a whole), may be detected: first (as suggested particularly by the *Nicomachean Ethics'* contrast between *sophia* and *phronēsis*) that the dialogues may in some degree, and precisely on account of their exceptional qualities, be removed from the realm of practical wisdom; secondly (if we press for a more 'suspicious' reading of περιττόν), that their *prima facie* impressiveness may not always fully pass the test of closer, more rigorous scrutiny. As a rider to these conclusions I note that the use of περιττός as a word of strong approval, so common in Aristotle, not least with reference to intellectual activity, is almost entirely absent from Plato's own vocabulary.[17] We shall see, however, that this is not true of the other three terms in Aristotle's sentence.

I move now to the second substantive in our sentence of the *Politics*, τὸ κομψόν. Here again the evidence of the translators points towards instability of interpretation: we find 'grace' in Jowett, 'cleverness' in Rackham, 'ingenuity' in Barker, 'brilliance' in Sinclair and Saunders, 'sophisticat[ion]' in Lord and Reeve, 'exquisite[ness]' in Simpson, 'Geist' in Gigon, 'geistreiche Erfindung' in Schütrumpf, 'finezza' in Bertelli, 'subtilité' in Aubonnet.[18] Unlike the situation documented earlier regarding τὸ περιττόν, all these renderings do share a positive force. But to that extent they arguably miss the mark, since in Aristotelian and much other Greek usage (including the traditions of literary/rhetorical criticism) κομψός is a far from straightforwardly laudatory term.[19] We have already seen that, as here, the term is juxtaposed with περιττός in another passage of Aristotle (*De Caelo* 290b14), a passage which contrasts this combination of qualities as *ostensible* merits in the framing of a philosophical thesis with the falsehood of the thesis. κομψός there implies something like 'fine-sounding (but not wholly cogent)', and in general it is a much more ambivalent adjective in Aristotle's lexicon than περιττός.

The force of the word comes through at its bluntest at *Meteorology* 1.13.349a30, where a particular theory (that all winds are really one wind) is called a κόμψευμα and said to be 'evidently false'. The unusual noun κόμψευμα (its only surviving classical occurrence) is formed from the verb κομψεύεσθαι, which always implies a deliberate striving after effect.[20] It reflects that end of the semantic spectrum of the word-group at which what may come into play is not just inventive ingenuity but the danger of (intellectual) posturing. Distinguishing between this pejorative zone of meaning and more favourable usage is not altogether easy, however. In *De Caelo* (2.13.295b16), Anaximander's view of why the earth supposedly does not move is said to be formulated in a way whose attractions are not matched by truth (τοῦτο δὲ λέγεται κομψῶς μέν, οὐκ ἀληθῶς δέ); but does that mean that the view is ingenious though wrong or merely specious? Aristotle seems to have some liking for employing κομψός terms in this contrastive type of judgement (as we earlier saw to be the case with περιττός too): he does the same thing elsewhere in the *Politics* (4.4.1291a11), in a passage with particular resonance for our present concerns, where the basic class-structure of a city is said to be a topic handled κομψῶς ('elaborately' or even 'ostentatiously'?) but 'not adequately' by Socrates in Plato's *Republic*;[21] and a variation of it occurs once more in *De Caelo* (3.5.304a13), where one possible ground for positing fire as the only element is said to involve more sophisticated reasoning than another (κομψοτέρως contrasted with ἁπλουστέρως), though in this last case the context allows the word a sense of complexity rather than speciousness. The doctors who are called κομψοί in the *Protrepticus* believe it is appropriate to their profession to possess a general understanding of nature; as the context indicates, they aspire in their own way to a kind of 'theoretical *phronēsis*' or philosophy.[22] To behave in that way does not seem to entail a pretentious pose of any kind, but it does betoken the possession of conspicuous aspirations.

We can see, then, that κομψός, extended from its reference to purely physical good looks,[23] always implies in Aristotle's hands that an idea, theory, or piece of reasoning is *prima facie* eye-catching and lays claim to high intellectual-cum-stylistic ambitions. The underlying basis of those ambitions always requires closer inspection, however, and in cases where it is found wanting, the material in question may be thought all the worse for its superficial appeal. With all this in mind, we may legitimately suppose that when Aristotle attributes τὸ κομψόν to Plato's dialogues he is paying them a genuine compliment, but is also holding in reserve, as it were, a conceivable hint of ambivalence. The dialogues have an immediately alluring flair and finesse, he is suggesting – but (if one chooses to discern the sometimes suspicious connotations of the term), to be κομψός is not and cannot be everything in philosophy. The combination of τὸ κομψόν with τὸ περιττόν does not make the interpretation of Aristotle's tone any easier. περιττός in itself, as I have shown, is more directly commendatory in Aristotelian usage than κομψός, but in the one other passage where the two terms are coupled – the *De caelo*'s comment on the 'harmony of the spheres', cited above – the pair of predicates is nonetheless sharply set against the supreme philosophical value of truth. As I earlier argued, considerations of imaginative and metaphorical elegance seem to be active in Aristotle's mind in that passage, and this could be a factor in his description of Plato's writing in the *Politics* too.[24] One particular if speculative possibility in this regard is that τὸ κομψόν embraces Plato's penchant for philosophical myths.[25]

But there is a further, far from negligible factor to add into the scales at this point. Is it coincidental that Plato himself displays some fondness for the vocabulary of κομψός and its cognates? These terms occur in fact considerably more frequently in his work than in Aristotle's (more than forty times as against no more than ten). It would perhaps be rash to think that Aristotle had Platonic usage consciously in mind when framing his remark on the dialogues, but we need to allow for the chances of at least subliminal influence. Now, contrary to what is sometimes maintained, it is certainly possible to find a few passages of Plato where κομψός is used as an unambiguous term of commendation: even if we put on one side, as arguably tinged with irony, the passage of the *Republic* where Socrates calls the contrasting reactions of dogs to acquaintances and strangers κομψόν (impressively clever) and 'truly philosophical' (2.376a11), no such doubts attach to the same adjective when applied to the kind of physical training he envisages for the young Auxiliaries (3.404a9) or to arithmetic as a subject for philosophical study (7.525d1).[26] But the dominant semantics of Platonic usage centre on the notion of a subtlety which at best is of merely technical intricacy, at worst a symptom of sophistic and rhetorical speciousness, and which includes the propagation of (artfully) paradoxical propositions.[27] In Plato as in Aristotle, that which is κομψός may be explicitly contrasted with the truth, as most emphatically at *Republic* 6.489b8 (in allusion to a *bon mot* of Simonides'). Socrates sometimes refers with various shades of irony to the ideas or theories of others (occasionally to his own pronouncements) as κομψός.[28] The word-group can also be applied to social pretensions.[29] All in all, Platonic usage tends to remind us of, so to speak, the 'sophistic' in sophistication; in doing so, it builds on the κομψ- root's existing connotations of artifice or showiness (not least in manner of speech).[30] If Aristotle had ever consciously framed the issue in his mind, we are entitled to believe that he would not have expected Plato himself to find the attribution of τὸ κομψόν to his writings as the most welcome or unequivocal of compliments. This underlines the difficulty of being sure about the tone of the term in the setting of the *Politics*' remark, though it would nevertheless be crude to suspect any obvious irony in Aristotle's choice of it.

The third term in Aristotle's characterization of Plato's writings is τὸ καινοτόμον, a substantive which is very rare in all periods of ancient Greek. The only other certain occurrences of this word-group in the Aristotelian corpus are all, as it happens, in the *Politics* itself.[31] There are three of them, each involving the verb καινοτομεῖν. One picks up the sentence in 2.6 to the extent that it refers to the unprecedented status of some of the communistic ideas expounded in Plato's texts; the other two both refer to radical, even revolutionary, political change. At 2.7.1266a35, Aristotle states that no other political thinker than Plato 'has introduced the ground-breaking principles' (κεκαινοτόμηκεν) of holding children and women in common or arranging communal dining for women; later on, at 2.9.1274b9, he categorizes these same ideas as a peculiar or unique feature (ἴδιον) of Plato's work (see below). This use of the verb καινοτομεῖν, whose literal sense refers to the opening of a new vein in mining or quarrying, probably carries overtones of decisive political innovation, as though Plato the writer were playing the part of a radical reformer or even a revolutionary in airing such proposals: at both *Politics* 5.6.1305b41 and 5.12.1316b19, Aristotle attaches the verb to the activities of impoverished oligarchs who resort to political agitation (even to the point of fostering tyranny) in order to promote their own interests. Given that the generalization about the dialogues in 2.6 occurs within the critique of unprecedentedly radical ideas in the *Republic* and *Laws*, Aristotle must at some level be thinking of the quality of τὸ καινοτόμον as embodied in politically bold gestures. But at the same time he must mean the concept to have broader scope: he could hardly imply that all or even most of Plato's dialogues ('all the Socratic discourses') have politically drastic import in this primary sense. Most fundamentally, however, and over and above the specific implications for the communism of the *Republic* and *Laws*, τὸ καινοτόμον implies a deliberate pursuit of ground-breaking thinking, perhaps with a marked colouring of utopianism. To that extent it forms a pair with the final item in the list, τὸ ζητητικόν, just as the first two items in the list form a pair. While most translators just opt for 'originality', 'novelty' or something similar, Schütrumpf is therefore justified in going for the stronger rendering 'Kühnheit der Neuerungen', which helps to convey the sense of a thrusting commitment to exploration.

Plato's own usage of the καινοτομ- word-group is confined to two works, but there is an intriguing observation to make on its relationship to Aristotle's sentence. In *Euthyphro* the verb occurs in three places (3b6, 5a5, 16a2), once in Euthyphro's mouth and twice (both times with an ironic slant) in Socrates', always with reference to the charge against Socrates of being an

Stephen Halliwell

innovator in religious matters. In the *Laws* we find the verb applied four times, and the noun (καινοτομία) once, to the idea of change or innovation in artistic practices (2.656e2, part of a famous passage on the supposed prohibition on such innovations in Egypt), in politics (4.709a6), in children's play and upbringing (7.797b4, c1), and in the social fabric more generally (12.950a1):[32] all these occurrences are stamped with an attitude of disapproval or deprecation on the part of the Athenian speaker. Remarkably, therefore, nowhere in Plato does καινοτομ- terminology appear in a positive light: its only Platonic associations are with, firstly, the (false) religious charge against Socrates, and, secondly, the dangerous, destabilizing nature of political, social, and cultural change in general. I do not wish (or need) to press a confident claim about the likelihood of Aristotle's conscious recollection of Platonic usage. But, as with κομψός, subconscious influence is harder to rule out. When we add the details just documented to the dual facts that καινοτόμος makes a unique appearance in Aristotle's own lexicon, while his employment of the cognate verb elsewhere in the *Politics* is limited to radical politics of a rather turbulent kind, it is difficult to avoid the inference that by identifying τὸ καινοτόμον as a prominent feature of Plato's writing he is expressing himself in a calculatedly thought-provoking, even piquant, manner.[33] Read Plato, the subtext seems to run, and expect to face some radical challenges to your settled ways of thinking.

After Aristotle's somewhat unusual choice of the metaphorical τὸ καινοτόμον, the final term in his list, τὸ ζητητικόν, is the easiest of the four to deal with. It is not, however, without interesting nuances of its own.[34] Apart from Jowett's weak rendering of it simply as 'thought', retained even in the revised Oxford translation edited by Jonathan Barnes, translators rightly converge on the idea of keenness of enquiry and investigation, giving some weight to the *-ikos* suffix.[35] Aristotle's expression is nonetheless striking. As with the preceding item in the list, the precise choice of word represents a rarity in Aristotelian vocabulary; in fact, he uses this adjectival form nowhere else, though it does appear at *Problemata* 14.15.910a30 (in a context which links it to *sophos*), to denote the quality of being mentally or intellectually industrious. Of course other members of the word-group – most notably the simplex verb, but also the compound verb ἐπιζητεῖν ('to enquire') and the noun ζήτησις ('enquiry') – occur ubiquitously in the corpus to designate the quintessential activity of philosophical questioning.[36] But the suffix *-ikos*, a productive contributor to lexical growth in classical Attic, intensifies the bare sense of enquiry by implying a practised disposition or strong bent for hard philosophical exploration.[37] That is how Plato himself uses the term in three passages which describe those who are indefatigably committed to searching for truth: *Meno* 81e1 (where ζητεῖν, 'enquiry', as well as μανθάνειν, 'learning' or 'understanding', is reinterpreted as a matter of 'recollection'), *Rep.* 7.528c1 (where the adjective denotes the type of people who pursue the difficult study of solid geometry), and *Rep.* 7.535d (characterizing the diligent attributes needed by the philosopher-to-be). It is conceivable Aristotle is here consciously paying Plato the compliment of adapting a term which appears with some epistemological weight in those very Platonic contexts. Whether or not that is so, I suggest that his use of ζητητικός is meant to stress the process more than (or as much as) the results of philosophical exploration, seeking rather than finding.[38] An immediate reason for discerning this nuance is the coupling with τὸ καινοτόμον, whose focus on exploration or 'breaking new ground' has already been discussed. A further, more far-reaching reason, and one which brings me to the stage at which to start drawing together the threads of my analysis of the four terms in Aristotle's sentence, is this: taken both individually and as a group, these terms imply very little at the level of philosophical *doctrine*, and much more at that of philosophical ethos, mentality and, in the broadest sense, style. I will return to this point shortly, and relate it to a larger feature of Aristotle's treatment of the *Republic* and *Laws* in this part of the *Politics*, after first reviewing what I believe I have shown about his synoptic statement of the character of Plato's dialogues.

Aristotle's remark has a clearly admiring slant to it; only a deeply cynical reader, with an over-eager eye for irony, could dispute this. The admiration is particularly apparent in its first and last elements, since substantial Aristotelian usage demonstrates that for him περιττός is intrinsically laudatory, and the same must be true of ζητητικός. However, the sentence does exhibit touches of ambivalence.[39] Its phrasing can be read as comprising two pairs of qualities (the first pair stressing exceptional flair and subtlety, the second originality and questing commitment), though there is some overlap and interplay between the two pairs, especially as περιττός is itself associated with originality. Comparing Aristotle's four terms with Plato's own vocabulary, we have found that in the latter: (a) περιττός is simply never used in the same positive way, (b) κομψός and cognates are very common but have a markedly ambivalent and sometimes pointedly ironic force, (c) καινοτόμος and cognates are always associated with negative judgements on change and instability, and (d) ζητητικός is a rare but unequivocally favourable term. In so far as Aristotle might be taken to have a subliminal sense of the Platonic connotations of the vocabulary in question, these findings augment our reasons for detecting a complex tone in his evaluation of his teacher's writings. At the very least, Aristotle is employing a critical diction that only partially reflects the 'Socratic' values of Plato's dialogues: in particular, the Platonic Socrates appears περιττός only in the eyes of his enemies, and he is not a figure who wishes to be thought of (unironically) as κομψός. Yet it is precisely as a comment on Plato's writings *qua* Socratic dialogues that Aristotle frames his sentence. By doing so he abstains from giving a complete characterization of Plato's philosophical mind or thought. His viewpoint seems of a different kind from the one he takes up, most obviously, in his much-cited remarks on Plato in the first book of the *Metaphysics*, where, without adducing any texts, he sketches a set of Platonic philosophical allegiances that were forged under the combined influences of Heracliteans, Socrates, and Pythagoreans.[40] The sentence of the *Politics* constructs for Plato an authorial 'profile' which is both emphatic but also delicately nuanced. It accentuates extraordinary flair, sophisticated stylishness, ground-breaking radicalism, and indefatigability in tracking philosophical problems. But, as already mentioned, it says nothing about specific ideas, positions, or doctrines.

That last point now calls for some expansion. If my interpretation is correct, how are we to relate Aristotle's comment on the dialogues in general to the extended discussion of the *Republic* and *Laws* which surrounds it? What I want to suggest is that in addition to the particular resonance of each of its four terms, Aristotle's *obiter dictum* about Plato's writings has a bearing on the spirit in which he reads the texts of the *Republic* and *Laws*. Why else make the remark at all in this context, midway through the critique of the communistic programmes of those two dialogues? We can go further, though, than this basic appeal to context. To see how, we need to turn our attention to an important but neglected feature of this larger section of *Politics* Book 2, namely the fact that Aristotle treats the ideas and arguments cited from the *Republic* and *Laws* for the most part independently of any putative authorial endorsement.

Once the *Republic* has been authorially identified at its first mention (*Pol.* 2.1.1261a6), Aristotle refers to its communist proposals in terms of what Socrates 'says' (φησί/λέγει: 1261a7–13, 1264a29, 1262b10, etc.), subsequently as what Socrates 'thinks' (οἴεται, 1261b19, 1262b6, 1264b38), what Socrates 'wants to construct' (βούλεται ποιεῖν, 1261b22), what Socrates commends (ἐπαινεῖ, 1262b9), how Socrates 'establishes the rulers' (τοὺς ἄρχοντας... καθίστησιν, 1264b7), what Socrates 'stipulates' (διορίζειν, 1264b29, cf. 1264b37), and, finally, Socrates' principles or premises (ὑπόθεσις, 1261a16, 1263b30–1). As his analysis proceeds, Aristotle specifies or alludes to the *Republic*'s arguments in several other ways: at 1261b32–3 he speaks simply of τὸ λεγόμενον ('what is said' in the text in question), at 1262a26 of 'those who are devising this communism' (τοῖς ταύτην κατασκευάζουσι τὴν κοινωνίαν),[41] at 1262a33 of 'one who makes/posits' (ποιεῖν) children held in common (for this use of the verb cf., e.g., 1264b1, 7), at 1262b4 of 'such a law' (νόμος; cf. e.g. 1261a11, 1263b15). But at no point does Aristotle attribute any element of the *Republic*'s communist scheme directly to Plato himself.[42] When he switches to the *Laws* in 2.6, he again identifies the work authorially at the start (1264b27), just as with the *Republic*, and after resuming some further points about the latter, still in terms of what 'Socrates' maintains, he makes his controversial statement that most of the *Laws* consists precisely of laws (1265a1–2).[43] He then starts to characterize the contents of the *Laws* with a series of verbal forms that have no explicit subject – 'he has said little about the constitution, but while wishing to give it more in common with existing cities...he brings it back round...' (1265a2 ff.) – before going on, immediately after this, to introduce his general pronouncement on 'all the discourses of Socrates'. In linguistic terms it is easiest to treat those subjectless verbs as continuing the manner in which Aristotle has so far analysed the communistic ideas of the *Republic*: indeed, most of the verbal forms occurring here have close parallels in the preceding pages.[44] So it is actually an option to treat Aristotle as implying 'Socrates' in each case. But in keeping with what I earlier said about the ostensible classification of the *Laws* itself as a 'Socratic' dialogue, it is preferable to modify that approach by assuming that Aristotle is carrying over his manner of citation from the *Republic* but tacitly acknowledging (by the subjectless verbs) that Socrates is no longer *strictly* the speaker in the *Laws*. The result, on this view, is a slight haziness of reference, though one which intelligibly mirrors the anonymity of the Athenian protagonist in the *Laws*. The alternative of supposing that Aristotle slips here into locutions which refer to the author himself involves a more abrupt switch from 'Socrates' to Plato, from one mode of paraphrase to another, and is harder to reconcile with the fact that no position advanced in Plato's text has been previously read as authorially underwritten.[45]

Now it is true that this picture is complicated by the fact that Aristotle does subsequently appear to make several claims about Plato's authorial position in relation to the arguments of the *Laws* (and, to a lesser extent, of the *Republic*). There are four such passages: (a) at 1266b5 he says, 'Plato when writing the *Laws* thought that one should allow [variations of property] up to a certain point...'; (b) at 1271b1 he apparently ascribes criticism of Sparta in the *Laws* directly to the author (see below); (c) at 1274b9 he observes that several communistic ideas (some found in both dialogues, some only in the *Laws*) are peculiar (ἴδιον) to Plato; (d) at 1293b1 he refers to Plato as an example of a thinker who enumerates only four kinds of constitution. What weight should we attach to these passages as evidence for Aristotle's conception of authorial intentions or commitments in the dialogues?[46] Two of them, (c) and (d), need tell us nothing on that score; they purport to be no more than factual statements about the contents of the dialogues. The other two, (a) and (b), do both apparently identify Plato with the thrust of arguments found in his writings. However, (b) is weaker in its entailment than (a), since its formulation, 'as Plato has criticized in the *Laws*' (ὅπερ καὶ Πλάτων ἐν τοῖς Νόμοις ἐπιτετίμηκεν), could readily be understood as conveying no more than 'as with the criticism made in Plato's *Laws*' – an interpretation, moreover, which is easily paralleled in some of Aristotle's citations of poetic texts, where there can be no question of a 'biographical' extrapolation to the author's personal views.[47] In (a), however, there is a strong *prima facie* case for taking Aristotle to be drawing an inference from text to author, since the participial phrase τοὺς Νόμους γράφων at 1266b5 is unlikely to be a merely temporal marker. It is not impossible that in stating 'when he wrote the *Laws* Plato thought...' Aristotle means simply that 'this is the position Plato set out in his *Laws*', but as he sometimes uses similar locutions elsewhere when making broader statements about Plato's philosophical convictions (independently of passages in the dialogues) it is reasonable to take him to be making a steady inference of this sort here.[48] But do we have good warrant to suppose that since Aristotle speaks of Plato's own beliefs in connection with just one (relatively technical) point in the *Laws*, and does so in a somewhat awkward parenthesis within the discussion of Phaleas of Chalcedon, his references to Socrates' statements and beliefs in the *Republic* are all code for 'Plato's statements' etc.? I think not. If Aristotle had wanted to count all the ideas and arguments cited from the *Republic* as unconditionally those of Plato himself, why would he have repeatedly and scrupulously cited them with formulations that ascribe them to the Socrates-figure in the dialogue?[49] Such an interpretative leap is both intrinsically implausible and unsupported by the rest of the corpus, in which, it must be stressed, Aristotle nowhere combines such Socrates-based paraphrase with direct criticism of Plato.

What we are left with, then, is an extended treatment of the communist scenarios of the *Republic* and, to a lesser extent, the *Laws* in which Aristotle makes more than twenty citations of the contents of these dialogues in formulations that assign ideas and arguments to the speaker Socrates, but only two citations (neither of them referring to the *Republic*) which arguably draw inferences to authorial beliefs.[50] These data complement my earlier scrutiny of Aristotle's general comment on Plato's Socratic discourses, a comment in which none of the four qualities predicated of the dialogues carries any implications of 'doctrinal' status, while all of them foreground features of a more questing, open-ended philosophical style and mentality and two of them explicitly highlight a commitment to innovation and exploration. So I conclude from both 1265a10–3 and the wider evidence of *Politics* Book 2 that at this (early?) stage of his career Aristotle had a strong sense of, and some considerable respect for, the dialogic finesse and dramatic form of Plato's writings – so much so that he went out of his way to discuss the *Republic* in a fashion which avoids equation of its ideas with the author's personal beliefs, while following a similar though slightly less sustained hermeneutic method in the case of the *Laws* as well. All this is in keeping with the conception of Socratic dialogues attested at *Poetics* 1.1447b11 and in *On Poets* fr. 15 (Gigon) as a mimetic genre of writing and therefore, by Aristotelian criteria, a medium for something other than first-person authorial statement.[51] *Politics* 2, in other words, manifests a marked inclination to argue dialectically with Plato's texts, treating their contents as material for serious philosophical debate but not primarily or predominantly as the expression of authorial tenets.[52] These circumstances are all the more revealing for occurring in what, as I noted at the outset, is the most extensive citation of the dialogues anywhere in Aristotle. Surely one moral of this tale is that absolute assertions about Aristotle's construal of the Platonic Socrates as a 'mouthpiece' or 'spokesman' for Plato himself are badly in need of revision. The question of Aristotle's practice in this area is not open-and-shut.

I have tried to show that *Politics* 1265a10–3, if carefully pondered, provides a valuable clue to at any rate one Aristotelian perspective on Plato's dialogues. This is a perspective that gives salience to essentially non-doctrinal qualities, and it is borne out by the manner in which Aristotle declines to assume authorial endorsement of everything said by Socrates in the *Republic* (or, a shade less unequivocally, by the 'Socratic' Athenian in the *Laws*). I would like to suggest, in conclusion, that we might detect a double layer of motivation behind Aristotle's decision to make his general remark about the dialogues in this context. Both layers might be called 'apologetic', but in different senses of the word. In the first place, Aristotle is partly concerned to justify himself for his robust disagreements with some of the ideas developed in the *Republic* and *Laws*. His sentence intimates that although Plato is an extraordinarily subtle and inventive philosophical writer, that cannot exempt the arguments found in his works from rigorous scrutiny. At the same time, however, and just as importantly, Aristotle's remark tells any shrewd, attentive hearer that precisely because Plato's dialogues are so extraordinary, the kind of selective scrutiny of them he is undertaking cannot and does not purport to do full justice to their many-sided virtuosity.[53] Aristotle indicates simultaneously that even the products of genius are open to questioning (since that is the essence of philosophy), *and* that what makes such products great may sometimes be occluded by the down-to-earth tenor of such questioning. The counterpoint between the first two clauses of his sentence thus shapes a poised gesture which balances emphatic (but not entirely unambiguous) praise against an expression of reserve that is typically Aristotelian in its tentativeness. What's more, that tentativeness ('but it is perhaps hard to do everything excellently') may itself communicate an additional hint to those inward with Plato's writings, since it evokes the expression 'excellent things are demanding' (χαλεπὰ τὰ καλά) for which Plato himself had some fondness.[54] Aristotle offers his critique of Plato's texts as an incisively dialectical but even so a partial, incomplete engagement with their rich resources of thought and language. His pregnant aperçu signals his awareness that those texts permit and invite readings that might take a different form from the approach he himself adopts on this occasion. If the whole complex story of Aristotle's response to Plato is ever to be attempted, these considerations deserve to occupy a more prominent place in it than they have so far received.[55]

Acknowledgements
I am grateful to my fellow Plato panellists at the Celtic Conference in Classics, September 2002, for their helpful discussion of this paper.

Notes
[1] Irwin 1992, 77, with 88–9 (n. 83) for the further claim that the critique of *Republic* and *Laws* in *Politics* 2 'provides a striking example' of how Aristotle equated the arguments of the dialogues with their author's views; cf. Irwin 1995, 6. But Irwin, here and elsewhere (incl. Irwin 1988, 199), fails to engage with the detailed implications of *Politics* 1265a10–3 discussed in my text and does not adequately report the complexities of Aristotle's citations of the dialogues in *Politics* 2; cf. nn. 42, 46 below.

[2] Aristotle is convicted of error by, e.g., Susemihl in Susemihl and Hicks 1894, 249, but defended by Hicks in Susemihl and Hicks 1894, ibid., and Morrow 1960a, 146 (cf. n. 53 below); Schütrumpf 1991, 221–2 denies that Aristotle strictly identifies the Athenian with 'Socrates'. Cf. n. 45 below.

[3] Saunders 1995, 128 bases this view on the supposed disparity between the 'staidness' of the *Laws* and the qualities picked out by Aristotle's generalization about the dialogues.

[4] Fr. 15 Gigon (fr. 72 Rose), *apud* Athen. 505b–c (retaining πρώτους in Athenaeus' text); cf. *P. Oxy.* XLV 3219, fr. 1. Haslam 1972, 17–24, and Laurenti 1987, I 250–3, 289–91, discuss what Aristotle may have believed about Alexamenus' dialogues. Deman 1942, 25–33 documents various views on Aristotle's references to Socratic *logoi*.

[5] Schütrumpf 1991, 222 mistakenly prints ὀρθῶς for καλῶς in the second clause.

[6] The existing commentaries do not document either the Aristotelian or Platonic material thoroughly: Schütrumpf, for example, in his substantial notes, does not cite any Aristotelian usage of περιττός or its cognates. The significance of the sentence is often ignored in discussions of this part of the *Politics*, most recently by Calabi 2000 and Vegetti 2000.

[7] For the best defence of 'Fitzgerald's canon' (citing Fitzgerald 1850, 163) see Ross 1924, i.xxxix–xli, arguing cogently against Taylor 1911, 41–51, and dealing with exceptions; for (qualified) acceptance cf. Irwin 1996, 338 n. 6 (with Irwin 1995, 355 n. 12), Kahn 1996, 87, Newman 1887–1902, ii.219, Schütrumpf 1991, 156, Vlastos 1991, 97 n. 67. Cf. n. 50 below.

⁸ Jowett 1905, 68 (reprinted unaltered in Barnes 1984, ii.2007); Rackham 1932, 101;Barker 1946, 57; Aubonnet 1960, 65; Lord 1984, 64; Simpson 1997, 46; Reeve 1998, 37; Schütrumpf 1991, 22; Sinclair 1981, 122; Saunders 1995, 32; Gigon 1973, 79; Bertelli 1977, 44.

⁹ The association with 'the wonderful' can be seen at *EN* 6.7.1141b6 (knowledge: see n. 13 below), *Pol.* 8.6.1341a11 (musical skill). Examples of περιττός with an uncomplimentary sense can be found in Plato, n. 17 below; for others see LSJ s.v. περισσός, II. In Aristotle, *Pol.* 2.8.1267b24 is the only case where the word has an ambiguous force (Newman 1887–1902, ii.267 therefore exaggerates the implications of this passage for Aristotelian usage as a whole); the word apparently covers unusual attributes either good or bad at pseudo-Ar. *Probl.* 30.1.954b24, though the context (cf. n. 12 below) is concerned with exceptional talents. I note that Aeschines 1.119, 2.114 uses περιττός of Demosthenes with an ironic inflection, i.e. ostensibly admitting his exceptional abilities yet simultaneously throwing them under suspicion.

¹⁰ *Gen. Anim.* 3.10.760a4, with 761a4 (bees), *Hist. Anim.* 7.2.589a31 (dolphins), *Part. Anim.* 4.12.692b16 (birds' beaks).

¹¹ *Rhet.* 1.6.1363a27 (with Cope 1877, i.116), 1.9.1367a26; cf. pseudo-Ar. *Virt.* 1250b29.

¹² *Met.* 1.2.983a2. Cf. the application of περιττός at pseudo-Ar. *Probl.* 30.1.953a10, 954b28, 955a39 to those with exceptional talents (as well as a tendency to melancholy) in philosophy, politics, poetry and other arts; *Rhet.* 2.15.1390b27 also has wide reference; at *Pol.* 8.2.1337a42 τὰ περιττά apparently denotes the more abstract realms of philosophy (cf. n. 37 below). Compare the parallel form περιώσιος in Empedocles' description of Pythagoras as περιώσια εἰδώς, 'knowing extraordinary things', Emped. fr. 129.1 DK.

¹³ *EN* 6.7.1141b6: although characterizing a viewpoint of others, Aristotle's unusual phrasing (with four positive adjectives in the μέν-clause, and a negative judgement in the δέ-clause) interestingly resembles the sentence-structure at *Pol.* 1265a10–3.

¹⁴ Could Plato *Crat.* 405d, alluding to the harmony of the spheres as a doctrine of those κομψοί in music and astronomy, have been at the back of Aristotle's mind here?

¹⁵ Compare, in a very different setting, the place of τὸ περιττόν in the critical scheme of Longinus *De Subl.*: intrinsically a feature of sublime greatness (esp. 35.3), it can nonetheless produce faults in those who strive for it without sufficient substance of thought (3.4).

¹⁶ *Contra* Hicks in Susemihl and Hicks 1894, 249, one need not focus on 'thought' to the exclusion of 'style' with either of the first two terms in Aristotle's list; Cope 1877, i.116, by contrast, takes Aristotle's whole remark to concern Plato's 'style'. Bertelli 1977, 44 reads greater emphasis on the 'form' than 'content' of Socratic argument in Aristotle's sentence; but this judgement too needs refining in the light of my further arguments.

¹⁷ περιττός has the sense 'superior' only at *Laws* 5.734d7. It is at best neutral, but by insinuation negative, in the mouth of the imaginary interlocutor at *Apol.* 20c6; it implies something irregular or untoward at *Symp.* 219c7, and something excessive at *Rep.* 3.407b5, *Laws* 1.645c5. Cf. n. 37 below for a spurious Platonic instance.

¹⁸ See n. 8 above for all page references to translations.

¹⁹ The semantic range of κομψ- terms is illustrated by LSJ s.v. 976–7, though some of their suggested translations are now dated; cf. nn. 28, 30 below. For later instances applied to various kinds of literary affectation and lightweight 'prettiness', see, e.g.,

Demetrius *De Eloc.* 36, Dion. Hal. *Isoc.* 12, Marcus Aur. *Med.* 3.5, Longinus *De Subl.* 41.1. Lucian *Pisc.* 22, with or without satirical overtones, makes Chrysippus speak to Plato admiringly of τὰ κομψὰ ἐκεῖνα, 'those gorgeous works of yours'.

[20] Cf. the reference in the same context of *Meteorology* to those who want to speak with an air of cleverness (349a20, τῶν σοφῶς βουλομένων λέγειν). The easy association of κομψός with striving to create a certain sort of impression is nicely reflected in comedy at Aristophanes *Wasps* 1317.

[21] Cf. also *Probl.* 17.2.916a35: κομψῶς (but 'provided one doesn't analyse it too precisely...') used of Alcmaeon's idea that people die because they cannot connect the beginning to the end.

[22] *Protrep.* B46 Düring. For κομψοί doctors cf. pseudo-Ar. *De Respir.* 27.480b27, Plato *Rep.* 3.405d4, 408b6 (with n. 28 below).

[23] In the corpus this basic sense appears only at pseudo-Ar. *Physiog.* 5.809b9: females of all species have πόδας κομψοτέρους, 'prettier feet', than males. A comparable extension from physical beauty to *prima facie* attractiveness of ideas can be seen with εὐπρόσωπος, facially 'good-looking', which Aristotle applies to the communism of the *Republic* at *Pol.* 2.2.1263b15.

[24] Note, in a different but perhaps related vein, Aristotle's dismissive comment on (Platonizing) use of 'poetic metaphor' at *Met.* 1.9.991a22 (cf. 992a28–9), 13.5. 1079b26.

[25] Cf. the κομψὸς ἀνήρ, author of an eschatological myth, at Plato *Gorg.* 493a5, a passage with Pythagorean colouring; see Dodds 1959, 296–8.

[26] Other positive uses: *Phdr.* 230c3 (natural beauty), *Crat.* 400b3 (the verb κομψεύεσθαι applied to phonological refinement); cf. pseudo-Plato *Epist.* 13.361a4 (sculptural beauty).

[27] Associations with technical difficulty: e.g. *Laws* 3.689c9; cf. the pretensions of certain craftsmen at *Rep.* 6.495d4, the ingenuity of a technical device at *Phlb.* 56c2. Links with rhetoric and/or sophistry: e.g. *Gorg.* 521e1, *Rep.* 6.499a6, *Soph.* 236d2 (the sophist as manipulator of appearances), *Laches* 197d7 (in the mouth of Laches); at *Gorg.* 486c6 Socrates equates κομψά (quoting Eurip. fr. 188 Kannicht) with 'nonsense', ληρήματα/ φλυαρίας. Paradoxes: *Tht.* 171a6, *Phdr.* 227c7, *Rep.* 4.436d5; cf. *Lysis* 216a1.

[28] Various notes of irony are discernible at e.g. *Euthph.* 11d7, *Crat.* 399a4, 402d3, 429d7, *Phaedo* 101c8, *Rep.* 3.405d4 (cf. 408b6), the latter referring to doctors (cf. n. 22 above). Even so, it is an exaggeration to say, with De Vries 1967, 37, following Norden 1909, i.69 n. 1, that Plato 'never' uses κομψός without irony, as my references in the text and the preceding notes demonstrate. LSJ 977, s.v. κομψός 2, go to the opposite extreme of claiming that in Plato (and Aristotle) the word has 'at most a slight irony'.

[29] See *Hp. Maj.* 288d4, *Rep.* 9.572c6.

[30] Examples of non-philosophical usage which highlight artifice or pretension include Soph. *Ant.* 324, Eurip. *Cycl.* 315, *Suppl.* 426, *Tro.* 651, fr. 16 (quoted by Aristotle himself at *Pol.* 3.4.1277a19: cf. Newman 1887–1902, iii.161), fr. 188 Kannicht (with Plato *Gorg.* 486c: n. 27 above), Aristoph. *Kn.* 18, *Wasps* 1317 (n. 20 above), *Frogs* 967, Men. *Peric.* 299. On the semantics of κομψός cf. Chantraine 1945.

[31] The use of the verb in fr. 598.1 Gigon (fr. 580A Rose), *apud* Pollux *Onom.* 9.77, is not Aristotle's own.

[32] καινοτομία also occurs at 4.715d1, apologetically, with reference to novel nomenclature.

[33] The use of the verb καινοτομεῖν by Aristophanes' Praxagora, in the build-up to the announcement of her communistic scheme, at *Eccl.* 584 (noted by Schütrumpf 1991, 222), should be treated as no more than coincidence, regardless of the vexed issue of the play's chronological relationship to *Republic* Book 5.

[34] If one wanted to look for possible traces of ambivalence even here, it would have to be along the lines of 'striving [for effect]', *vel sim.* (cf. *Pol.* 2.1.1260b33–4, where Aristotle deprecates an equation of ζητεῖν with σοφίζεσθαι); but that would be gratuitous.

[35] 'Keenness of inquiry' (Rackham); 'spirit of enquiry' (Barker); 'urge to investigate' (Sinclair); 'searching' (Lord); 'spirit of inquiry' (Saunders); 'probing' (Simpson, Reeve); 'Energie des Forschens' (Gigon); 'eindringendes Forschen' (Schütrumpf); 'impegno di ricerca' (Bertelli); and, somewhat differently, 'sagacité' (Aubonnet): see n. 8 above for all page references to these translations.

[36] Bonitz 1955, 309 documents a selection of evidence. 'Enquiry', ζήτησις, distinguishes philosophers from non-philosophers: *Meteor.* 1.13.349a27.

[37] It is used by Socrates of himself in pseudo-Plato *Axiochus* 366b6; interestingly, the noun τὰ περιττά occurs in the same context with reference to special objects of knowledge (366b8): cf. n. 12 above.

[38] Aristotle's familiarity with Plato's own dialectical habits may have been at the back of his mind: *EN* 1.4.1095a32 couples ἀπορεῖν (to be puzzled) and ζητεῖν (to enquire) in speaking of Plato's practice in terms (both verbs in the imperfect) which seem to record personal recollection rather than reference to the dialogues; see Burnet 1900, 17, with, e.g., Ar. *Met.* 1.9.992a20–2, 13.8.1083a32 for parallel cases. The term ζητητικός was later taken over for a class of Platonic dialogues by Thrasyllus, *apud* Diog. Laert. 3.49; see Tarrant 1993, 46–57. Compare the application of the term to the Sceptics, Diog. Laert. 9.69–70. Of course, a process of philosophical 'seeking' can move towards a stable conclusion: note the two uses (significantly, of Socrates) at *EN* 6.13.1144b18, 7.5.1147b14.

[39] Bertelli 1977, 44 briefly detects ambivalence in Aristotle's sentence, but his comments fail to do justice to the differences, as well as partial affinities, between περιττός and κομψός.

[40] *Met.* 1.6–7.987a29–988a17: in outlining Platonic concepts of non-sensible forms etc., Aristotle twice speaks of what Plato 'held' or 'accepted', ὑπολαμβάνειν (987b1, 5); he also uses 'say' (φάναι, λέγειν: 987b15, 24), 'think' (οἴεσθαι), and 'posit' (ποιεῖν: 987b26, 30); and he sums up by saying 'these are the distinctions which Plato stipulated about the subject of enquiry' (Πλάτων...περὶ τῶν ζητουμένων οὕτω διώρισεν, 988a7–8). A scrupulous interpretation of the passage would attempt to relate all this phraseology to the absence of any reference to the dialogues. Cf. nn. 48, 55 below.

[41] The verb κατασκευάζειν could be used of practical implementation of a plan or proposal, as 1264a6 shows; but at 1262a26 it must have a looser sense.

[42] Clay 1988, 270 n. 11, and Vlastos 1991, 97 n. 67, briefly note the consistency with which in *Pol.* 2 Aristotle separates 'Socrates' from the author of the *Republic*; cf. Simpson 1998, 93 n. 37. Stalley 1991, 183–4 n. 5 resists the implication that Aristotle uses this method of citation to acknowledge 'distancing' between author and speaker, but his counter-argument is weak: see n. 46 below. Irwin 1995, 6, maintaining that Aristotle reads Plato's dialogues doctrinally, finds in *Pol.* 2 an 'identification of Plato with the Platonic Socrates': to do so he ignores the total evidence of Aristotle's practice of citation and assumes that 1274b9–10 must imply authorial commitment (cf. nn. 46–7 below).

Hicks, in Susemihl and Hicks 1894, 214, speaks of Aristotle's 'cautious manner of referring controversially to contemporary thought', and question-beggingly claims that 'Plato lurks under Socrates', shortcircuiting the whole question of how Aristotle read the Platonic dialogues. Mayhew 1997, 6–7 sidesteps the issue of what Aristotle's references to 'Socrates' may mean for his reading of the *Republic*. The view of Henry Jackson, cited by Susemihl and Hicks 1894, 247, that Aristotle had a 'characteristic dislike of Plato's indirect method of approaching the doctrines which he wishes to enforce', is multiply tendentious. It is odd of Blondell 2002, a hermeneutically sophisticated work, to refer without explanation (94 n. 201) to 'Aristotle's notorious failure to distinguish between Plato and his Sokrates'.

[43] On this vexed issue, see Morrow 1960a.

[44] εἴρηκεν, 1265a2 (cf. 1264a12, 1264b24); φησί, 1265a8 (cf. 1261a7–13, 1262b10, 1264a29, 1264b13–16); βουλόμενος, 1265a3 (cf. 1261b22): the clause 'wishing to make...' refers to the words of the Athenian in such passages as *Laws* 5.739a–e and need not invoke authorial intention; so Aristotle does not here depart from his preceding protocols of citation.

[45] Some translators retain the non-specific phrasing at *Pol.* 1265a2 ff., but Rackham 1932, 99 makes 'the author' subject at 1265a2 (cf. his earlier intrusions of Plato's name, not in the Greek, at 1262b21, 1264a7: Rackham 1932, 83, 93); Schütrumpf 1991, 20 adds '(Platons Irrtum)' at 1264a5. In a later passage, at 1265b19, Jowett 1905, 70 (oddly allowed to stand by Barnes 1984, ii.2008) actually makes 'Socrates' the subject of a statement about the *Laws*. Cf. n. 2 above.

[46] Irwin 1992, 89 (n. 83), and likewise Irwin 1995, 6, adduces the first three of these passages to show that Aristotle treats the *Republic* and *Laws* 'as evidence of Plato's views': but he does not discuss the exact interpretation of each of them, nor does he confront the fact that in the *Politics*' entire treatment of the *Republic* Aristotle never once ascribes an argument to Plato himself. Stalley 1991, 184 n. 5 is wrong to think 1274b9–11 sufficient to establish that Aristotle sees direct authorial endorsement of the communism of the *Republic*. Cf. n. 42 above.

[47] See *Hom. Probl.* fr. 379 Gigon (fr. 155 Rose), where the narrative voice at Hom. *Il.* 6.234 is read in terms of the poet's own criticism (with the same verb ἐπιτιμᾶν). Aristotle, like other Greeks, readily uses expressions such as 'Euripides says...' to mean that something is said in Euripides: see, e.g., *Pol.* 3.4.1277a19; *EN* 5.11.1136a11–12. Cf. n. 51 below.

[48] The verb οἴεσθαι, 'think' (whose strength need not be unqualifiedly 'doctrinal'), occurs in ascriptions of philosophical convictions to Plato at *Metaph.* 1.6, 987b19, 7.2.1028b18–20, 12.6.1072a1 (none of which involves a straightforward citation of a dialogue); the same verb is used of the historical Socrates at, e.g., *EN* 3.8.1116b4, 6.13.1144b19, 29, 7.2.1145b23. In describing the ideas of Plato and other thinkers, Aristotle employs a wide range of locutions: these call for a systematic investigation that they have never received. Cf. n. 40 above.

[49] Morrow 1960b, 74–5 revealingly struggles to combine his unargued assertion that Aristotle 'evidently' interprets the Athenian in *Laws* as 'spokesman' for Plato with a sense that 'dramatic form is always something of a mask' and that 'the real Plato, more than most authors, remains inscrutable'.

[50] There are five later passages in the *Politics* (4.3.1291a11–12, 5.10.1316a1–3, 1316b26–7, 8.7.1342a32–4, 1342b23–5) where arguments from the *Republic* are again

ascribed to Socrates rather than directly to Plato: the last of these, ostensibly problematic on the terms of Fitzgerald's canon (n. 7 above), may involve interpolation; cf. Ross 1924, i.xl–xli.

[51] Aristotle's view of the relationship between mimesis and authorial statement is most forcefully declared at *Poetics* 24.1460a5–8: on this and related passages see Halliwell 2002, 164–71. When, however, Brumbaugh 1993, 242 n. 4, apparently with *Pol.* 1265a10–3 in mind, attributes to Aristotle the notion 'that Plato's Socrates, in the *Republic*, is always literature but perhaps one cannot have such literacy [*sic*] and serious truth at the same time', his paraphrase is bizarrely loose and tendentious.

[52] See Bertelli 1977 for more detail on the dialectical methods of *Politics* 2.

[53] The selectiveness of Aristotle's critique has sometimes troubled modern scholars; but Aristotle does not claim comprehensiveness for his treatment. Cf. Morrow 1960a (positing use of an early, incomplete draft of *Laws*), Bertelli 1977, 42–52, Stalley 1991.

[54] Susemihl and Hicks 1894, 249 plausibly detect an allusion to the saying χαλεπὰ τὰ καλά in the second clause; Plato's own liking for it is apparent from *Hp. Maj.* 304e8; *Crat.* 384b1; *Rep.* 4.435c8, 6.497d10.

[55] The whole story would encompass responses to the person, oral teaching, the surviving dialogues, (perhaps) other writings of Plato's, the 'unwritten doctrines', and the views/writings of other 'Platonists'. No single item in this list should be allowed to predetermine our understanding of the others – nor of the whole. Where Aristotle's criticisms of Platonist metaphysics are concerned, see esp. Fine 1993, who argues (28–9, 34–6) that Aristotle criticizes a 'reconstructed version' of Platonic arguments and assumptions. For a recent overview of Aristotle's intellectual relationship to Plato, see Graham 2004.

Bibliography

Aubonnet, J.
    1960   *Aristote, Politique livres I et II*, Paris.
Barker, E.
    1946   *The Politics of Aristotle*, Oxford.
Barnes, J. (ed.)
    1984   *The Complete Works of Aristotle: the Revised Oxford Translation*, 2 vols., Princeton.
Bertelli, L.
    1977   *Historia e methodos: analisi critica e topica politica nel secondo libro della 'Politica' di Aristotele*, Turin.
Blondell, R.
    2002   *The Play of Character in Plato's Dialogues*, Cambridge.
Bonitz, H.
    1955   *Index Aristotelicus*, 2nd edn, Graz.
Brumbaugh, R.S.
    1993   'Four types of Plato interpretation', in G.A. Press (ed.) *Plato's Dialogues: New studies and interpretations*, Lanham, 239–48.
Burnet, J.
    1900   *The Ethics of Aristotle*, London.

Calabi, F.
  2000   'Aristotele discute la *Repubblica*', in M. Vegetti (ed.) *Platone: la Repubblica*, vol. IV, Naples, 421–38.
Chantraine, P.
  1945   'Grec ΚΟΜΨΟΣ', *Revue des études grecques* 58, 90–6.
Clay, D.
  1988   'Reading the *Republic*', in C. Griswold (ed.) *Platonic Writings, Platonic Readings*, New York, 19–33 (notes, 269–72).
Cope, E.M.
  1877   *The* Rhetoric *of Aristotle*, 3 vols., Cambridge.
De Vries, G.J.
  1969   *A Commentary on the* Phaedrus *of Plato*, Amsterdam.
Deman, T.
  1942   *Le témoignage d'Aristote sur Socrate*, Paris.
Dodds, E.R.
  1959   *Plato,* Gorgias, Oxford.
Düring, I.
  1961   *Aristotle's* Protrepticus, Göteborg.
Fine, G.
  1993   *On Ideas: Aristotle's criticism of Plato's theory of forms*, Oxford.
Fitzgerald, W.
  1850   *A Selection from the* Nicomachean Ethics *of Aristotle*, Dublin.
Gigon, O.
  1973   *Aristoteles Politik*, Munich.
  1987   *Aristotelis Opera III, Librorum Deperditorum Fragmenta*, Berlin.
Graham, D.
  2004   'Aristotle's reading of Plato', in J.J.E. Gracia and J. Yu (eds.) *Uses and Abuses of the Classics*, Aldershot, 61–74.
Halliwell, S.
  2002   *The Aesthetics of Mimesis: Ancient texts and modern problems*, Princeton.
Haslam, M.
  1972   'Plato, Sophron, and the dramatic dialogue', *Bulletin of the Institute of Classical Studies* 19, 17–38.
Irwin, T.
  1988   'Reply to David L. Roochnik', in C. Griswold (ed.) *Platonic Writings, Platonic Readings*, New York, 194–9.
  1992   'The intellectual background', in R. Kraut (ed.) *The Cambridge Companion to Plato*, Cambridge, 51–89.
  1995   *Plato's Ethics*, New York.
  1996   'Art and philosophy in Plato's dialogues', *Phronesis* 41, 335–50.
Jowett, B.
  1905   *Aristotle* Politics, Oxford. Original edn 1885.
Kahn, C.H.
  1996   *Plato and the Socratic Dialogue*, Cambridge.
Kannicht, R.
  2004   *Tragicorum Graecorum Fragmenta Vol. 5: Euripides*, Göttingen.

Laurenti, R.
   1987   *Aristotele: I frammenti dei dialoghi*, 2 vols., Naples.

Lord, C.
   1984   *Aristotle. The* Politics, Chicago.

Mayhew, R.
   1997   *Aristotle's Criticism of Plato's* Republic, Lanham.

Morrow, G.R.
   1960a   'Aristotle's comments on Plato's *Laws*', in I. Düring and G. Owen (eds.) *Aristotle and Plato in the Mid-Fourth Century*, Göteborg, 145–62.
   1960b   *Plato's Cretan City*, Princeton.

Newman, W.L.
   1887–1902   *The* Politics *of Aristotle*, 4 vols., Oxford.

Norden, E.
   1909   *Die antike Kunstprosa*, 2nd edn, 2 vols., Leipzig.

Rackham, H.
   1932   *Aristotle,* Politics, Cambridge, Mass.

Reeve, C.
   1998   *Aristotle,* Politics, Indianapolis.

Rose, V.
   1886   *Aristotelis qui ferebantur librorum fragmenta*, 3rd edn, Leipzig.

Ross, W.D.
   1924   *Aristotle's* Metaphysics, 2 vols., Oxford.

Saunders, T.
   1995   *Aristotle* Politics *Books I and II*, Oxford.

Schütrumpf, E.
   1991   *Aristoteles Politik II/III*, Darmstadt.

Simpson, P.L.P.
   1997   *The* Politics *of Aristotle*, Chapel Hill.
   1998   *A Philosophical Commentary on the* Politics *of Aristotle*, Chapel Hill.

Sinclair, T.
   1981   *Aristotle. The* Politics, rev. T. Saunders, Harmondsworth.

Stalley, R.F.
   1991   'Aristotle's criticism of Plato's *Republic*', in D. Keyt and F.D. Miller (eds.) *A Companion to Aristotle's* Politics, Cambridge, Mass., 182–99.

Susemihl, F. and Hicks, R.D.
   1894   *The* Politics *of Aristotle*, London.

Tarrant, H.
   1993   *Thrasyllan Platonism*, Ithaca.

Taylor, A.E.
   1911   'On the alleged distinction in Aristotle between Σωκράτης and ὁ Σωκράτης', in A.E. Taylor, *Varia Socratica*, Oxford, 40–90.

Vegetti, M.
   2000   'La critica aristotelica sulla *Repubblica*', in M. Vegetti (ed.) *Platone: la Repubblica*, vol. IV, Naples, 439–52.

Vlastos, G.
   1991   *Socrates: Ironist and moral philosopher*, Cambridge.

INDEX RERUM

ability   9, 87 f., 90, 106–8
action   22, 61, 78, 81–3, 85 f., 88, 90 n. 6, 91 n. 19, 96 f., 102–4, 109, 112–14, 116, 119 f. n. 4, 120 n. 13, 121 n. 20, n. 21, 122 n. 30, 123, 192
affect   83
affectation   205 n. 19
affection   64 n. 8, 139 n. 1
Anaxagoras, Anaxagorean, Anaxagoreans   60, 69 n. 57, 73, 193
Anaximander   19 n. 35, 195
anger   75, 83, 86, 89
aporia   155
appear   22, 125–48 *passim*, 193
appearance   v, 14, 80, 125–48 *passim*, 206 n. 26
appetite, appetitive   17, 82, 84, 93, 96
Aristotle   vii f., 1–3, 18 n. 17, 19 n. 33, 20, 65 n. 8, 69 n. 47, 81, 129, 130, 142 n. 13, n. 14, 143 n. 14, n. 19, 146 f., 173 n. 8, 184, 189–211 *passim*
art   2, 14, 96, 116
assimilation, assimilate   17, 96 f., 102, 107, 119 n. 3
authorial   200–3, 207 n. 42, 208 n. 44, n. 46, 209 n. 51

bad   3, 9, 15, 18 n. 12, 80 f., 85, 89, 106, 205 n. 9; see also evil
beautiful: the beautiful, the Beautiful   43, 47–9, 51, 53 f., 65 n. 15, 67 n. 31, 68 n. 35
belief   v, 96, 125–48 *passim*, 187 n. 17
benefit   6, 9 f., 95–124 *passim*
bodily   10, 14, 57, 78, 85, 91 n. 22, 96, 108, 174 n. 25, 184
body   14 f., 46, 49, 56, 65 n. 12, 78 f., 81 f., 84, 89, 90 n. 10, 92 n. 23, 107, 109, 158, 167 f., 171, 184 f.

capacity   23, 55, 78, 95 f., 109, 151, 165 f.; see also faculty, power
change   v, vii, 48 f., 58, 85, 131, 149–75 *passim*, 177–88 *passim*, 197–9
character   82, 84, 95, 97, 106, 116, 119 n. 3, 209
chronology   4, 18 n. 18, 20, 73
cognition   23, 30 f., 39 n. 5, 61, 76, 78–83, 86, 88 f., 90 n. 9, 174 n. 20
cognitive   30, 40 n. 17, 70, 82 f., 88, 90, 96, 107, 109, 119 n. 3, 166, 168
communion   43, 158 f., 172 n. 3
community   3 f., 15, 83, 103, 122 n. 26; see also society
complete   102 f., 106, 149–74 *passim*, 179, 182, 185, 186 n. 8, 187 n. 23; see also perfect
composition   185
  dramatic composition   55, 64 n. 6
conative   96, 107, 109
consciousness   79 f., 88 f., 91 n. 12
constituent   62, 97 f., 110–12, 117 f.
constitution   116, 192, 201
content   31 f., 35 f., 79 f., 90 n. 9, 91 n. 14, 144 n. 23, 144 f. n. 28, 185, 193, 201–3, 205 n. 16
convention, conventional   1 f., 11, 14–16, 88
craft   14 f., 55, 98, 111
craftsman   7, 15, 102, 111, 206 n. 27

decide, decision (epist.)   80, 88,
definition   vii, 2, 5 f., 14, 18 n. 13, 32, 41 n. 22, 44–6, 48 f., 55, 57, 62 f., 64 n. 3, 66 n. 20, 67 n. 31, 79, 85, 91 n. 19, 123, 133, 144 n. 23, 174 n. 16, 177, 180, 182, 184
desire   15–17, 75–8, 80, 82–5, 87–9, 91 n. 22, 92, 95–124 *passim*, 185
destruction   51, 182–4, 186 n. 9; see also generation
dialectic, dialectical   66, 110, 137, 161, 165, 170, 175, 203 f., 207 n. 38, 209 n. 52
Diogenes of Apollonia   60, 69 n. 57
disobedience: see obedience
distinguish   22 f., 26, 31, 38, 39 n. 7, 76 f., 79, 81, 140 n. 4, 144 n. 23, 166, 170, 208 n. 42
divine   3, 5–10, 16 f., 59, 61, 97, 101, 111, 128 n. 28, 185, 186 n. 6, 192 f.
dramatic date   4
dramatic form   202, 208 n. 49, 210
dunamis   158–60, 167, 174 n. 16, n. 20

education (and 'upbringing')   12, 32, 80, 85, 88 f., 91 n. 22, 95, 98, 104, 106–11, 116 f., 119, 121 n. 20; see also upbringing
emotion   75 f., 79, 82–4, 87, 89, 96, 107
envy   83, 86 f., 89, 123

213

Index rerum

epistemology, epistemological   vii, 21–3, 31, 38, 41 n. 20, 46, 61, 146 f., 199
equity   2
essence   5, 55, 61, 66 n. 20, 67 n. 29, 157, 173 n. 11, 175
eternity   v, vii, 61, 177–88 *passim*
eudaimonia   173 n. 8
evil   1, 9, 14; see also bad
existence   24, 28, 33, 38, 39 n. 7, 47, 61, 65 n. 14, 66 n. 20, 177, 182–5

faculty   55 f., 75, 79 f., 82 f., 86–9, 106; see also capacity, power
feeling   75, 78, 80, 140 n. 3, 144 n. 32, 185
form   15, 23–5, 28, 33 f., 36–8, 39 n. 7, 40 n. 16, 41 n. 22, 42 f., 54, 58, 60, 66 n. 20, 67 n. 28, 68 n. 35, 96–105, 108, 110, 112 f., 115, 117, 119, 120 n. 11, n. 14, 121 n. 17, n. 18, 122 n. 23, 149–75 *passim*, 178, 180–3, 186 n. 5, 187 n. 18, 188, 207 n. 40, 210

generation   51, 168, 182–4, 186 n. 1, n. 3, see also destruction
genre   190 f., 194, 203
god   3–6, 8, 11, 15, 18 n. 14, n. 16, 40 n. 15, 45, 64 f. n. 8, 67 f. n. 31, 68 n. 39, 134, 154 f., 175, 178, 185, 186 n. 8
good: the good, the Good   14–16, 47, 49, 58, 65 n. 15, 84 f., 96, 100 f., 110, 120 n. 14, 121 n. 17
goodness   15–17, 56, 119
goods   1, 17, 85, 88, 98 f., 104, 122 n. 27, 173 n. 8

happiness, happy   v, vii, 83, 95–124 *passim*
harmony   59 f., 85, 91, 95–124 *passim*, 126, 165, 193, 196, 205 n. 14
Heraclitus, Heraclitean, Heracliteans   19 n. 35, 137, 200
honour   6 f., 10, 12, 84, 87 f., 155, 192

illusion   21, 38 n. 1
image   v, 21–42 *passim*, 44, 144 n. 23, 178, 181, 186 n. 8
imagery   194
imagination   81–3, 89, 91 n. 17, n. 18
imitation, imitate   5, 21, 100–3, 107 f., 120 n. 14, 186 n. 1, 187 n. 10
inclination   86, 107, 133, 140 f. n. 4, 203
individuality   75, 89 f.
injustice, unjust   1–20 *passim*, 80 f., 83, 86 f., 98 f., 120 n. 6, 121 n. 21, 137 f., 157, see also intention, intentional   28, 119, 120 n. 13, 122 n. 30, 201, 208 n. 44
irony   196 f., 199, 206 n. 28

judge, judgement (leg.)   3, 9, 14, 16, 87

judgement, judge (epist.)   27 f., 31–3, 81, 91 n. 16, 91 n. 19, 125–48 *passim*, 179–81
justice, just   vii, 1–20 *passim*, 49, 56 f., 81, 83, 85–7., 89 f., 91 n. 19, 96–104, 106, 111 f., 118, 191 n. 4, 120 n. 5, 121 n. 21, 122 n. 29, 123 f., 132–4, 137 f., 145 n. 32, 157, see also injustice, unjust, law
justness   103, see also justice

knowledge   21–42 *passim*, 55, 59, 67 n. 25, 76, 78, 80, 82 f., 85–9, 95 f., 101, 104, 107–11, 115, 117, 119, 121 n. 17, n. 18, 125–48 *passim*, 151, 153, 163, 165, 168 f., 174 n. 20, 175, 193, 205 n. 9, 207 n. 37

language   32, 42, 59, 63, 63 n. 2, 70 f., 91 n. 22, 132, 140 n. 4, 182, 193 f., 204
law   v, vii, 1–20 *passim*, 88, 114, 117, 121 n. 21, 200
  (language of)   69 n. 50
lawgiver   114, 116
learning   21, 23, 42, 49, 80, 107–9, 199
legal   1–5, 9, 13, 17, 19 n. 34, 58
legislation   2, 4, 6, 14, 16 f.
likeness   vii, 21–42 *passim*, 179
literary   194, 205 n. 19

materialist   63 n. 1, 149–75 *passim*
measure   107, 177, 179
measure doctrine   125–48 *passim*, 193
memory   82 f., 91 n. 17, 106 f.
mentality   122 n. 26, 199, 202
metaphor   58, 62 f., 63 n. 2, 68 n. 38, 69 n. 50, 91 n. 16, 132, 137, 145 n. 32, 154, 193, 196, 198, 206 n. 24
metaphysics   70, 147, 149, 152, 172, 175, 184, 209 n. 55; see also ontology
mimesis, mimetic   101 f., 106–8, 119 n. 3, 120 n. 7, 123, 191, 194, 203, 209 n. 51, 210
mind   65 n. 12, 80 f., 108, 128, 139 n. 1, 173 n. 7, 174 n. 28,
moral   2, 7, 11, 15, 17, 18 n. 13, 20, 41 n. 20, 108, 199, 121 n. 17, 124, 211
motivation   17, 83, 85, 89, 92, 100, 104, 110–14, 118 f., 120 n. 13, 121 n. 17
myth   57, 154, 196, 206 n. 25

nature   v, vii, 3–5, 14 f., 18, 43, 55–9, 61, 66, 91, 95–124 *passim*, 186 n. 1, n. 8, 187 n. 9, n. 10, 195
normative   1, 96 f.

obedience, disobedience   2, 4 f., 7, 9 f., 12–17, 19 n. 26, 19 n. 28, 19 n. 32, 20, 96, 112
obligation   11–13, 18 n. 13, 19 n. 29, 98
ontology, ontological   vii, 22 f., 43, 60–2, 63 n. 1, 64 n. 8, 71, 149–52, 156–61, 163–70,

214

Index rerum

172, 174 n. 13, n. 20, 184; see also metaphysics
opinion   7, 10 f., 31, 48, 80–3, 85–7, 89, 128, 131, 142 n. 13, 143 n. 16, 187 n. 17
oratory, orator   2, 4, 14, 44; see also rhetoric
order   3 f., 9 f., 14–18, 60 f., 82, 86, 97, 100–2, 106, 112, 121 f. n. 22, 186 n. 3, 186 n. 8

Parmenides   28 f., 40 n. 16, 49, 59, 65 n. 19, 67 n. 28, 70 n. 57, 73, 154, 160 f., 169 f., 174 n. 14, 175, 177, 183, 186 n. 2, 188
participation   50 f., 71, 172 n. 3
perception, perceptible   24 f., 27 f., 32–7, 39 n. 7, 41 n. 24, n. 29, 46, 78–86, 89, 90 n. 9, n. 10, 91 n. 17, 107, 125, 132–8, 139 n. 1, 140 f. n. 4, 141 f. n. 6, 143 n. 18, 144 n. 22, n. 23, 144 f. n. 28, 145 n. 34, 147 f., 149 f., 159 f., 162, 165, 168, 174 n. 20, 185, 186 n. 1, 187 n. 17, n. 18
perfect   81, 85, 95 f., 98–101, 104 f., 107–18, 120 n. 9, 121 n. 18, n. 20, n. 21, 122 n. 22, 149–75 *passim*, 177, 179–82, 187 n. 10, n. 23; see also complete
persuasion   12, 91 n. 22
philosopher   viii, 22 f., 32, 38, 39 n. 3, n. 7, 72, 84, 91 n. 82, 92 n. 23, 97, 99, 101 f., 104, 108–10, 113, 116–18, 121 n. 18, 123 n. 32, 142 n. 11, 153, 168 f., 193, 199, 207 n. 36, 211
philosopher-king   v, vii, 95–124 *passim*
philosopher-ruler   123; see also philosopher-king
philosophy   7, 17, 80, 85, 89, 95, 113–15, 195, 203, 205 n. 12, 210
play   198, see also upbringing
pleasure   14, 16, 23, 80, 82–4, 86, 88 f., 91 n. 22, 107, 120 n. 11, 123
poet   7, 91 n. 22, 107, 193 f., 202 f., 205 n. 12, 206 n. 24, 208 n. 47
poetic   193, 202, 206 n. 24
politician, political, politics   7, 9, 12, 15 f., 85, 95, 100, 102–4, 106, 113–16, 121 n. 21, 122 n. 26, 197 f., 205 n. 12, 209
power   56–8, 68 n. 39, 79, 81, 89, 138, 158, 167 f., see also capacity, faculty
property   7, 44, 46, 54–6, 58 f., 62, 65 n. 8, 85, 90 n. 9, 102, 104 f., 122 n. 23, 145 n. 28, 179, 181–3, 201
Pythagoras, Pythagorean, Pythagoreans   60 f., 63, 63 n. 3, 69 n. 57, 70–2, 194, 200, 205 n. 12, 206 n. 25

reality   v, vii, 50, 59, 66 n. 20, 115, 130, 149–75 *passim*
reason   14, 43, 50–4, 75, 77 f., 80, 83, 85, 88, 92, 93, 96 f., 123, 131 f., 143 n. 16, 152 f.,

158 f., 163, 165, 168 f., 187 n. 17
recognition   v, vii, 21–42 *passim*, 78–81
remind   7, 24–8, 33–7, 40 n. 12, n. 14, 41 n. 23, n. 28
rhetoric, rhetorical   8, 194, 196, 206 n. 27; see also oratory
rule   14 f., 96–8, 100 f., 108, 111, 113 f.

senses   31 f., 41 n. 20, 56 f., 128, 131 f., 136 f., 141 n. 4, 145 n. 28, n. 30, 158, 174 n. 25
shame   75, 86 f., 89
society   3, 88, 101 f., 109, 117, 122 n. 26, 146; see also community
sophist, sophistic, sophistry   1, 14, 115, 196, 206 n. 27
soul   v, vii, 10, 14–6, 24, 28, 32, 38, 47, 49, 60, 65 n. 12, 75–93 *passim*, 95–7, 101–4, 107, 109, 112 f., 119 n. 3, 119 f. n. 4, 121 n. 21, 131 f., 135, 143 n. 16, 151 f., 158, 160, 164–9, 173 n. 7, 174 n. 25, n. 30, 184 f.
spirit   96, 107, 109
stable, stability   58, 95, 100, 106, 113, 179, 182 f., 185
standard   3, 5–7, 102 f., 121 n. 21, 179–81, 187 n. 15
Stoics   91 n. 12
style   193, 199, 201, 205 n. 16

technical   43 f., 54 f., 57, 63, 63 n. 2, 64 n. 6, 70, 181, 192, 196, 202, 206 n. 27
temperance   15, 17, 102
tendency   95, 100, 104, 107, 129, 205 n. 12
Thales   193
thinking, thought   26, 30 f., 34–6, 41 n. 24, 44, 78–82, 86 f., 89–90, 91 n. 12, 125, 133 f., 185, 187 n. 22, 198
tripartition   v, vii, 7–93 *passim*
truth   10, 58 f., 61, 63, 65 n. 16, 65 n. 19, 69 n. 48, 90 n. 10, 96, 106–8, 117, 128, 169, 181, 195 f., 198, 209 n. 51

understanding   9, 14, 33, 46, 48, 96–8, 101, 110, 112 f., 117, 119, 119 n. 3, 121 n. 18, 142 n. 14, 195, 199
unjust   see injustice
unwritten   3 f., 6, 10, 16, 18 n. 14, n. 17, 209 n. 55
upbringing   12, 112, 198, see also education

virtue, virtuous   1, 57, 65, 83, 86, 96–8, 102, 107, 109, 119 n. 3, 122 n. 28

wisdom   7, 10, 57, 109, 138 f., 193 f.
world   3, 31 f., 39, 60–3, 91 n. 12, 119, 121 n. 22, 123, 130, 177, 179, 181–5, 186 n. 8, 187 n. 10

INDEX LOCORUM

Aeschines 1.119, 2.114   205 n. 9
Aeschylus
  Agamemnon 647, 929   61
  Seven against Thebes 187   61
  Suppliants
    384, 388–90, 395–6, 405–6   18 n. 11
    426   206 n. 30
    437, 673   18 n. 11
Alcidamas, *Messeniacus*   18 n. 16
Anaximander DK 12B1   19 n. 35
Andocides, *De Mysteriis* 20.6, 59.2,
  138.4   65 n. 16
Antiphon the Sophist, DK 87B22   61
Aristophanes
  Ecclesiazousae   207 n. 33
  Frogs 967   206 n. 30
  Knights 18   206 n. 30
  Wasps 1317   206 n. 20, n. 30
Aristotle
  De anima
    3.3   142 f., n. 14
    422b8–10   130 f.
    428a16, 20–2   143 n. 19
    428b2 ff.   130
    428b4   143 n. 14
  De caelo
    290b14   193 f.
    290b30 f.   193
    295b16, 304a13   195
  De generatione animalium
    760a4, 761a4   205 n. 10
  De insomniis
    I 458b28 f., II 460b18–20   143 n. 14
  De partibus animalium
    692b16   205 n. 10
  De poetis
    fr. 15 (Gigon)   190 f., 203 n. 4
  Historia animalium
    589a31   205 n. 10
  Metaphysics
    983b2   205a12
    987a29–988a17   207 n. 40
    987b1, 5, 15   207 n. 40
    987b19   208 n. 48
    987b24, 26, 30, 988a7–8   207 n. 40
    991a22   206 n. 24
    992a20–2   207 n. 38
    992a28 f.   206 n. 24
    1028b18–20   208 n. 48
    1053b3   193
    1072a1   208 n. 48
    1079b26   206 n. 24
    1083a32   207 n. 38
  Meteorologica I
    345b1–3   143 n. 14
    349a20   206 n. 20
    349a30   195
    349a27   207 n. 36
  Nicomachean Ethics
    1.7   173 n. 8
    1095a32   207 n. 38
    1116b4   208 n. 48
    1129a26–1130a14   1
    1129b11–14   2
    1134b18–35, 18–37   3
    1136a11 f.   208 n. 47
    1137b11–13   2
    1141b6   205 n. 9, n. 13
    1144b18   207 n. 38
    1144b19, 29, 1145b23   208 n. 48
    1147b14   207 n. 38
  Poetics
    1447b11   191, 203
    1459b36   194
    1460a5–8   209 n. 51
  Politics
    2.6   189–211 *passim*
    1256a10–13   205 n. 13
    1260b33 f.   207 n. 34
    1261a7–13   200, 208 n. 44
    1261a11, 6, b19   200
    1261b22   200, 208 n. 44
    1261b32 f.   200
    1262a26   200, 207 n. 41
    1262a33, b4, 6, 9   200
    1262b10   200, 208 n. 44
    1262b21   208 n. 45
    1263a30 f.   200
    1263b15   200, 206 n. 23
    1264a5   208 n. 45
    1264a6   207 n. 41
    1264a7   208 n. 45
    1264a12   208 n. 44
    1264a29   200, 208 n. 44

Index locorum

1264b1, 7   200
1264b27   201
1264b13–16, 24   208 n. 44
1264b29, 30 f., 37, 38   200
1265a1 f.   201
1265a2 ff.   201, 208 n. 45
1265a2, 3, 8   208 n. 44
1265a10–13   vii, 189–211 *passim*
1265b19   208 n. 45
1266a35   197
1266b5   201 f.
1267b24   205 n. 9
1271b1   201
1272b24 f.   192
1274b9   197
1274b9 f.   201, 207 n. 42
1274b9–11   208 n. 46
1277a19   206 n. 30, 208 n. 47
1291a11   195
1291a11 f.   208 n. 50
1293b1   201
1305b41   197
1312a27   192
1316a1–3   208 n. 50
1316b19   197
1316b26 f.   208 n. 50
1337a42   205 n. 12
1341a11   205 n. 9
1342a32–4, b23–5   208 n. 50
Protrepticus
   B46 (Düring)   206 n. 22
Rhetoric
   1363a27   205 n. 11
   1367a26   205 n. 11
   1368b7–10   4
   1373b1–17   3, 18 n. 17
   1373b18   18 n. 16, 19 n. 33
   1375a26–b18   4
   1390b27   205 n. 2
   1417a20–3   191
Topics
   102a, b   65 n. 8
   141b13   192
[Aristotle]
De respiratione
   480b27   206 n. 22
De virtute
   1250b29   250 n. 11
Homerica Problemata
   379 (Gigon)   208 n. 47
Physiognomica
   809b9   206 n. 23
Problemata
   910a30   198
   916a35   206 n. 21
   953a10   205 n. 11
   954b24   205 n. 9
   954b28, 955a39   205 n. 11

fr. 598 (Gigon)   206 n. 31
Athenaeus 505b–c   204 n. 4

Demetrius *De elocutione* 36   206 n. 19
Democritus DK 68B2c   61
Demosthenes
   18.2   18 n. 6
   18.275   4
   19.179   18 n. 6
   20.118   18 n. 10
   25.17   18 n. 6
   39.40   18 n. 10
Diogenes Laertius 9.45 f.   61
Dionysius of Halicarnassus, *Isoc.* 12   206 n. 19

Empedocles
   31B135   18 n. 15
Euripides
   Andromache 1068   65 n. 16
   Cyclops 315   206 n. 30
   Hippolytus 1070 f.   142 n. 11
   Troades 651   206 n. 30
   fr. 16 (Kannicht)   206 n. 30
   fr. 188 (Kannicht)   206 n. 27, 30

Heraclitus
   22B30, B114   19 n. 35
Herodotus
   1.196   1
   9.85   61
   7.28   68 n. 40
Hesiod
   Works and Days
      276 ff.   18 n. 3
      213–83   18 n. 9
Homer
   Iliad
      6.234   208 n. 47
      18.493–508   2
   Odyssey
      14.106   128

Isaeus 5.9.2, 5.11.12   65 n. 12
Isocrates
   3.7   18 n. 6
   15.179   18 n. 6

Longinus, *De sublimitate*
   3.4, 35.3   205 n. 15
   41.1   206 n. 19
Lucian, *Piscator* 22   206 n. 19

Marcus Aurelius, *Meditations* 3.5   206 n. 19
Menander, *Perikeiromene* 299   206 n. 30

POxy XLV 3219   204 n. 4
Parmenides
   DK 28B4.8   65 n. 19

DK 28B8.5–6   186 n. 2
DK 28B8.32–8   67 n. 28
DK 28B32   65 n. 19
Philolaus
  DK 44B5   60
  DK 44B6   59–62, 69 n. 54
Plato
  Apology
    20c6   205 n. 17
    21a4–7   7
    21a6–7   8
    21e5   8
    22a4   8
    22e1   8
    23a5–b4   7
    23b4–7   8
    24d2–25a11   9
    25a12–c4   9
    28b5–9   9
    28d6–10   8
    28d10–29a1   8
    29d3–6   8
    29d7–30b4   9
    30c8–d1   9
    30d5–31b5   8
    31c4–32a3   9
    31e2–4   9
    32b5–c3   9
    36c5–9   8
    37e5–38a1   8
    39a8–b8   9
    41c8–d2   9
  Charmides
    156b   56
    168b–169a, 168b3, 168c, 168c4–168d7   55
    168d   56 f.
  Cratylus
    384b1   209 n. 54
    385e4–386a4   141 n. 5
    386a1–3   126, 140 n. 4
    389a6–b4   91 n. 14
    399a4   206 n. 28
    400b3   206 n. 26
    401c2–4   61
    401c   62, 63 n. 3
    402d3   206 n. 28
    405d   205 n. 14
    429c7–d6   144 n. 23
    429d7   206 n. 28
    432, 432c7–d3   26
  Crito
    44b5–46a8   10
    44e5   64 n. 5
    47e6–7, 48b3–9, 49b7–e2   10
    49e5–50a2, 49e6   11
    50a–b   13
    50a2   11
    50a9–b5, 50b1–52c4   12
    50d, 51a   13
    51a2–c3, 51c8–52a3, 52a8–53a7   12
    52d8–e5   11
    53b2   64 n. 5
    54c1–8   12
  Euthydemus
    283e7 ff., 286b8 ff., c2   144 n. 23
  Euthyphro
    2b1–2   4
    3b6   197
    3e6–4e3, 4e4–5c3   5
    5a5   197
    6e10–7a1   5
    7b2–8a8   6
    7e5–8b6   5
    7e6–8   6
    9c1–11b5   5
    11a   65 n. 6
    11a6–b1   5
    11a6–b5   45
    11d7   206 n. 28
    11e4–15a7, 12e5–8, 14e9–15a4, 15b7–c2   6
    16a2   197
  Gorgias
    447a3   69 n. 49
    448c   58
    462b8–466a8   14
    467e7   58
    472   59
    472b   55
    472b3–c2, 472b6   58
    474c4–479c6, 477c6–479c6, 482c4–484c3   14
    486c   206 n. 30
    486c6   206 n. 27
    486c1   64 n. 5
    491d   15
    491d4–500a6   15
    493a5   206 n. 25
    497e–498e   58
    503d5–504d3   15
    503e2   91 n. 14
    503e4   58
    504d1–3   15
    504d5   91 n. 14
    504d5–e4, 507e6–508a4   15
    510a6–e2, 510e3–511a3, 512d8–513c2   17
    515c4–517a6, 521d6–8   16
    521e1   206 n. 27
    521e3–522a6, 522c7–e3, 522e3–6   16
  Hippias Major
    288d4   206 n. 29
    304e8   209 n. 54
  Laches 197d7   206 n. 27

Index locorum

Laws
  636d7–e3 91 n. 13
  644c9 f. 91 n. 18
  645c5 205 n. 17
  646e10–647a2 92 n. 25
  656e2 198
  662b2–4 91 n. 13
  689c9 206 n. 27
  709a6 198
  715d1 206 n. 32
  717d5–6 91 n. 19
  734d7 250 n. 17
  739a–e 208 n. 44
  797b4, e1 198
  892a2–b1 187 n. 24
  896a1–897b8 184
  896c1–2 187b24
  897a 184
  897a6–b1 187 n. 25
Lysis 216a1 206 n. 27
Meno
  71b3–4 45
  72a6–b9 44 f.
  72b22 63 n. 3
  72e f. 65 n. 11
  80d1 67 n. 25
  91b2–93a4 19 n. 27
Parmenides
  132d5–7 29
  132d1–4 40 n. 16
  141a5–d6, d6–e10, 151e6–152a3, 152a3–b2 183
Phaedo
  61d, e 60
  65d 64 n. 6, 65 n. 11
  65b9–11 90 n. 10
  65d9–35 46
  66a3 65 n. 16
  66a8 65 n. 19
  68e3 85
  72–77 24, 32–38
  73c6–8 34
  73e9 40 n. 9
  74 172 n. 1
  74a2–3 41 n. 28
  74a5–8 40 n. 14
  74a6, 6–7, 8 25
  74b 49
  74b2 48
  74c11–d2, c13–d1 41 n. 28
  74d4–e4 26
  74d5–8 172 n. 1
  74d6 48
  74d6 f., d9–e2 25
  74e2–5 27
  75b1–2, 5–6 48
  75c10–d4 48 f.
  75d 66 n. 20
  75d2–3 66 n. 20
  76b 65 n. 20
  76d–77a 47, 65 n. 18
  76d7–77a5 46 f.
  76d8–9 67 n. 21
  78 f. 172 n. 1
  78b ff., c6 186 n. 5
  78c6–d9 47–9
  78d 49
  78d1 48
  78d1–5 65 f., n. 20
  78d3–5 49
  78d4 65 n. 19
  79a6 65 n. 15
  79a6 f. 172 n. 1
  80b 67 n. 28
  84c3, 91–4 142 n. 7
  92c8, d8–e2 49
  92d9 65 n. 18
  95a–107b 43, 60
  95b5 f. 68 n. 32
  95e 60
  95e10, 96e 51
  96c6–97b7 51 f.
  96e8–97a1 52 f.
  97a3, 4, 4–5, a5–b7 52
  97a7, b2–3 53
  100b1–e7 172 n. 1
  100b10 ff., c–d, c4–5 51
  100c9–101c9 53
  100d6–e6, e ff. 51
  100e2 f. 67 n. 31
  100e8, e8–101c9 51
  101b, c 60
  101b10 f. 51
  101b9–c9 53 f.
  101b10–102a2 50
  101c2 ff. 43
  101c3 54
  101c3 f. 51
  101c5–7 68 n. 32
  101c8 206 n. 28
  101d1 ff. 60
  102a10–d4 90 n. 8
  102d 60
  102b1 43
  104b 60
  104b9 43
Phaedrus
  227c7 206 n. 27
  230c3 206 n. 26
Philebus
  31 ff., 31d4–32d8 82
  32b9–c1 91 n. 18
  33d2–34a6 79
  34a10 f. 82
  34b10 f. 91 n. 17
  37 144 n. 23

38c12–d1   80
39a1–7, b3 ff.   81
46c7   140 n. 3
47d5–48a4   83
48a8–50b6   87
56c2   206 n. 27
58e4–59a9, 61d10–e3   172 n. 1
Politicus
295a–b   2
Protagoras
309a1   128
320d5, e2, 321c1   57
326e8   69 n. 44
327c5   128
327c7   69 n. 44
329c3–d1   56
330a4   57, 69 n. 43
330a6–7, 330b1   69 n. 43
330c1, 4, d4 f., 331a8, 332a5, 337d4
   69 n. 44
330d   57
330c1, 4, d4 f., 331a8   69 n. 44
331d6   69 n. 43
332a5   69 n. 44
333a5   69 n. 43
337d4   69 n. 44
349   57
349a8–c5   56 f.
349b   55
349b3 f.   69 n. 44
349c1   57, 69 n. 44
349c5   57
352d3   69 n. 44
356c4–357a5   143 n. 17
359a7   57
Republic
Book 1   122 n. 29
Book 2   97
Book 3   107
Book 4   75–93 *passim*, 104, 107
Book 5   22, 27, 40 n. 17, 84, 207 n. 33
Book 7   22, 78
Book 8   76
Book 9   76, 82, 89, 91 n. 13, 120 n. 5
342e6–11   111
345d5–e4   116
346e3–7, 350a6–9c1–5   111
352d8–353e6   91 n. 14
363d2   178
369a8–b1   121 n. 22
370a7–b2   106
375a5–b10, c1–e5   107
376a11   196
388a2   107
395a4   95
395b3–5   106
395b4   121 n. 22
395b8–d1   107

395b8–d3   96
395d1–3   108
396a4, 398b–400e, 401b1–4, d6–8   107
401b1–402a4   96
401d5–402a4, 402b9–d5   119 n. 3
404a9   196
405d4   206 n. 22, n. 28
407b5   205 n. 17
408b6   206 n. 22, n. 28
410d6–10, e1–3   107
412d9–e8, 413e6–414a2   108
419a1–3 , 419a4–420a1   104
420b3–421c6   122 n. 22
420b4–8   104, 116
420d5–e1   104, 109
421a2–8   103
421a8–b1, b6–c2   109
421c4–6   104, 122 n. 22
421c5–6   110
429c5–d1, 430b2–5   86
433a5–6   106, 122 n. 22
433c7 f.   86
435a1–c2   96
435c8   209 n. 54
435c9–d8, 436b8–c1   76
436d4–437a3   77
436d5   206 n. 27
438c1–4   90 n. 7
439a1–8, b3 ff.   75
440c1–d3   83
440c2   140 n. 3
441b1–5   96
441b3–c2   88
441e4   96
441e4 f.   86
441e5–6, 442a2–b3   96
442a4–b4   84
442b11–c3, c5–8   86
442d1   85
443c9–444a2   96 f., 102 f., 107
443c9–444e3 119 n. 4
443e6   102, 119 n. 4
444a1   119 n. 4, 121 n. 21
444c10   119 n. 4
444c10–d1   96, 107
444d8–e3   96
444e7–445b7   97
465b5–d1   98, 122 n. 27
475a5–b10   84
475b8–10   82
475c6–8, e2   23
475e9 ff.   172 n. 1
476a4–7, c2–4, 5–7   22
476c5–d3, d1–3   23
476e6   39 n. 7
477a2 ff.   173 n. 10
477a3–4   150, 163
477a6   150, 162

Index locorum

477c1–d6   91 n. 14
478b5–c2   144 n. 23
479e1–5   81
485b10–487a8   107
485d3–8   82
486a8, b1–5   107
486b3   115
486b6–13, c1–d3, d7–12, c3–d5, d10–e5   107
487a2–5   96
487a2–8   106
487a7–8   107
489a5–6   115
489b8   196
490b2   82
490d6   115
491d1–492a5   106
492a1–5   111
495b8–496a10   115
495d4   206 n. 27
496a11–497a5   117
496c5–e2   108
496c7–d5   118
496d3   117
496d4–5   108
497a4   117
497d5   118
497d6   117
497d10   209 n. 54
497a3–5   109
499a6   206 n. 27
500b7–d3   102
500b8–d3   101
500b8–d9   103
500c9–d3   101
500d4   102, 113
500d4–9   101
500d5, 6, 8   102
504e7–505b3   86
505d11–506a3, 506a9–b1   101
511e1   143 n. 19
515a5–c3   39 n. 2
515b4–5   39 n. 2
516e1–517e2   98
517b–c, b7–8   133
518b7–c3, c4–d8, c5, d9–e2, 518e2–519a1   109
519c4–6   101
519c8   114
519c8–d2   101
519c9   113
519c10   101
519d7   121 n. 18
519d8–9   114, 122 n. 23
519e1–3   116
519e1–520a4, 519e1–521b11   114
519e3–520a4   98
519e4, 520a8, d2   113

520a5–c1   98
520a6–d5   112
520a6–e3   113, 121 n. 21
520a7 f.   98
520a9–c1   112
520d6–e1   100
520d7–e1   112 f., 121 n. 16
520d8–9   98
520e4–521a1, 520e4–521a2   115
520e4–521b11   115 f.
521, b1, b1–2, b2, 9–10   115
523   32
523a10–b4   79
523d3–5   90 n. 9
524e4   79
525   54
525d1   196
527d7–e1   121 n. 18
528c1   199
534a1   143 n. 19
534b3   66 n. 20
535d   199
538d6–e3   66 f., n. 20
539e2–540c2   110
539e3   113
540b3   98
540b4   101
540b4–5   113
540d1–541b5   117
554c11–e2, 555b9 f.   85
561e6–d7, 562b3, 9–10   85
572c6   206 n. 29
575e2   39 n. 6
580d3–9   84
580d8   86
580d10–581a1   84
581b5 f., 582c8   88
583b3   173 n. 8
585   54
586d4–e3   86
589a7–b1   89
592a5–9   113
596b7   91 n. 14
602c7–603a8   131 f., 143 n. 16
602c8, d7, 8   131
602e4   143 n. 16
602e4–6   132, 143 n. 16
602e5   131
603a1   132
603a4, b10   143 n. 14
603c11–d2   131
611e1–612a3   82
Sophist
217a   69 n. 44
219   54
235e5–236a3   131
236–264   155
236d2   206 n. 27

222

240b   39 n. 6
244b6, e2   174 n. 14
245e6–248e6   154–160 *passim*
245e6–249d5, 246a4, a8–b3   154
246a8–c4, b1, b6–c2   171
246b1   158
246b6–c4   154, 171, 173 n. 10
246b7   154
246b8   154, 172 n. 2
246c, c1 f.   154
246c2   154, 172 n. 2
246e5–247c8   150, 153, 157, 169, 173 n. 4
247a8   154
247c9–248e6, 247d3   158
247e3–4   174 n. 16
248a4–5, 7   154
248a7–8   154, 158
248a10   154
248a10 f.   158
248a11   154, 172 n. 2
248a12   154
248a12 f.   158
248b2–6   159
248b7, d, e2   154
248c1 f.   159
248c7–9, d10–e5   158
248e7–249a1   160
248e7–249a2   150
248e7–249b7   152 f., 163
248e7–249c9   173 n. 4
248e7–249d5   149–175 *passim*
248e8–249a1   150, 172 n. 2
248e8–249a10   162
249a   173 n. 28
249a10   161, 166–168
249b2–3   161 f.
249b6   173 n. 12
249b8–c9   152 f., 163
249c3–4   151
249c10–d4   150 f., 153, 161, 169–171, 172 n. 4
249c10–d5   153, 155
249c11–d1   154, 174 n. 11
249d3 f.   161
249d4   151, 161
263e–264b   140 n. 4
264   136
264a–b   135 f., 141 n. 4
264a10   91 n. 15
266bc   40 n. 15
Symposium
199c, d   68 n. 39
202e   68 n. 39
207c–208b   185
207d6–8   187 n. 26
208a7–b4   185, 187 n. 26
210e6–211b5   172 n. 1
211b   67 n. 28

211b1–2   186 n. 5
219c7   205 n. 17
Theaetetus
144e3   143 n. 14
148b6–8, d4–e6   133
149a1–151d3   144 n. 23
149d6   173 n. 8
150a8 ff., a8–b4, b9–c3, e6–7, 151c2–d3   144 n. 23
151d–187a   125–148 *passim*
151–160   144 n. 22
151d ff., d–e 139 n. 1
151d–160c, 151e   133
151e1–3   125, 132
151e4–c.184a9   145 n. 33
151e5 f.   144 n. 23
151e8–152a1   139 n. 2
151e8–152b9   140 n. 3
152   135
152a1–2   139 n. 2
152a6–7   126
152a6–8   125–7, 132, 136 f., 139, 140 n. 4
152a7   145 n. 32
152b2–9   125, 133
152b10 f.   140 n. 3
152b10–c1   133
152b12   136
152b12–184   140 n. 4
152c5, 7   133
154a3–5, a3–9   127
154b1–6, 156d–e   145 n. 28
156e   134
157c7–d3   144 n. 23
157e1 ff.   134
158a   127, 140 n. 4
158b2   144 n. 22
158d2–4   135
158d4   136
158e   134
158e3   136
158e5–6   134
159 ff.   135
159b–e   142 n. 13
159c11 f., d   127
159c–e   145 n. 28
160c7–d4   134
160e2–3   144 n. 23
160e7 ff.   134
160e7–161a4, 161e4 ff.   144 n. 23
161d2–3, 161d2–162a3   135
161d3   139, 144 n. 26
161d5–7   135
161d6–7   144 n. 23
161e8   136
162d1   134
162e   139
163b8–c5   80
165e8–168c5   134

Index locorum

166c7–9   139
166e–167a   135
166e3–4   135, 142 n. 13
167a6–b4   144 n. 28
167a7–8   144 n. 23
167c4–6   144 n. 25
167c6   144 n. 26
169e8–170a5 ff.   145 n. 31
170c2–4 ff.   145 n. 31
170d4–e3   81
171a6   206 n. 27
171a6–9   144 n. 23
172a1–4   144 n. 25
172a3, b1–2   144 n. 26
172d–177b/c   138, 145 n. 33
173b–c   145 n. 33
174c6, d1   142 n. 11
177d4, 178b–c   144 n. 26
178b3–7   144 n. 23
179c1–2   145 n. 31
179c3–4   145 n. 28
182a–b   133, 145 n. 28
182d1–7   145 n. 28
184–7   125, 127, 139 n. 1
184a9–b1   144 n. 23
184b8–d5, 184b8–185a3   79
185 ff.   139 n. 1
185e5–7   79
187c7–200d4   145 n. 33
188b3–5   39 n. 4
188d3–189b6   144 n. 23
189e4–190a5   81
191d6   91 n. 17
201b   39 n. 6
201b5–c7   91 n. 16
201d4–206c2   145 n. 33
210b4 ff.   144 n. 23

Timaeus
27d6–28a4   172 n. 1
28a   182
28a1–4   187 n. 17
28a2, 29a3–5   178
29d7   174 n. 28
31a4, b1   163
31b1   162, 175 n. 30
34a8, 37a1   178
37c   181
37c ff.   177
37c6–d2   187 n. 16
37c6–d7   186 n. 8
37d   179
37d1, 3   178
37d4   182
37d5–6   178
37d5–e3   186 n. 3
37d7   178
37e4–5   177
37e4–38a8   186 n. 1
37e5, 38a3   178
38a3–4   177
38a7   178
38a8–b1   187 n. 22
38b–c   179
38b6–c3   187 n. 9
38b8   178
38c1–3   181
38c2   178
38c3 ff., 39c5–d2   186 n. 3
39d–e   179
39d4–7   187 n. 23
39d7–e2   187 n. 10
39e1   162
39e2   178
40a8–b1   185
40b4–6   186 n. 6
48e2–52d1, 49d4–e7   187 n. 26
51d3   172 n. 1
51e–52a   182
51e6–52a7   187 n. 18
52a6   179
52a7   172 n. 1
65d3 f.   129
70d7–8   84
87c1–88c6   92 n. 23

[Plato]
  Axiochus 366b6, 8   207 n. 37
  Epinomis 983a   143 n. 14
  Epistles 13, 361a4   206 n. 26
Plotinus, *Enneads* 6.7.8, ll. 25–31   175 n. 30
Plutarch, *Moralia* II.158c   128
Pollux, *Onomasticon* 9.77   206 n. 31

Sophocles, *Antigone*
  324   206 n. 30
  447 ff.   3
  456–7   18 n. 14
Stobaeus, *Eclogae* 1.21.7a1–8.3   59

Thucydides
  3.22.8   65 n. 19
  4.108.5, 6.60.2, 7.8.2   65 n. 16
Xenophon
  Cyropaedia
    5.4.7, 6.3.7   65 n. 19
  Memorabilia
    4.4.12–13   2
    4.4.19–21   3
    4.4.19–25   3

INDEX VERBORUM

ἀγαθός, -όν   43, 46, 49, 58, 68 n. 31, 85, 173 n. 8
ἀγέννητον   182
ἄγραφος   4
ἀδικεῖν   83
ἄδικος   1, 9 f., 128
ἀεί   vii, 47, 134 f., 177–88 *passim*
ἀίδιος   vii, 177–88 *passim*
αἴσθησις   46, 65 n. 12, 79, 82, 89, 134 f., 139, 145 n. 28
αἰτία   43, 50–3, 60
αἰών, αἰώνιος   vii, 177–88 *passim*
ἀκίνητος, -ον   149, 151, 161, 169, 178, 186 n. 1
ἀληθής   58, 69 n. 50, 128, 130, 133–5, 144 n. 23, 173 n. 8, 195
ἀληθινός   115, 154, 162, 166, 168, 171, 172 n. 2
ἅμα   77 f., 130, 143 n. 16
ἀναγκάζω   58, 113
ἀναγκαῖος   46, 114
ἀνάγκη   46, 48, 59, 102, 113 f., 174 n. 14
ἀνεμιαῖον   144 n. 23
ἄνθρωπος   89, 95, 102, 106, 121 n. 22, 128, 140, 140 n. 3, 141 n. 5
ἀνώλεθρον   182
ἀρετή   44, 56, 67 n. 25, 91 n. 14, 102
ἄρχειν   115, 131, 200
ἀρχή   59 f., 84, 86
αὐτὸ καθ' αὑτό   43, 48
ἀφομοιοῦν   97, 107

γένεσις   67 n. 29, 154, 164–6, 168, 171
γένος   69 n. 44, 152, 155, 192
γίγνεσθαι   46, 50, 52 f., 67 n. 31, 70, 158, 181
γραφή   4

διανοεῖσθαι   46, 65 n. 12, 134
διάνοια   81, 91 n. 15, 192
δίκαιος   1, 9–11, 49, 83, 98, 112

δικαιοσύνη   vii, 1, 14 f., 56 f.
δικαιότης   15
δίκη   4, 18 n. 3
δόγμα   135 f.
δοκεῖν   134, 141 n. 5, 142 n. 11, 143 n. 19
δόξα   80 f., 84, 86, 89, 91 n. 15, nn. 18–19, 92 n. 25, 135 f., 138 f., 142 n. 11, 143 n. 19, 145 n. 28, n. 30
δοξάζειν   91 n. 19, 92 n. 25, 134 f., 143 n. 19, 144 n. 22
δόξασμα   136
δύναμις   55–57, 68 n. 39, 91 n. 14, 109, 158
ἐθέλειν   112 f., 121 n. 18
εἶδος   43, 54, 58, 60, 63 n. 2, 63 f. n. 3, 70 n. 61, 70–3, 84, 91 n. 14, 154, 174 n. 14
εἴδωλον   144 n. 23
εἰκών   26, 44, 81, 178
εἰλικρινῶς   162, 172 n. 2
εἶναι   43 f., 46 f., 49, 59, 63 f. n. 3, 64 n. 7, n. 14, 65 f. n. 20, 67 f. n. 31, 126–30, 132, 134 f., 137, 140 n. 3, 150, 162, 185; see also ὄν
   ὃ ἔστιν   47–9, 53, 67 n. 25
ἕκαστος, -ον   46–50, 53, 56, 64 n. 6, 66 n. 20, 106, 121 n. 22, 141 n. 5
ἑκών   101
ἐμπειρία   14
ἔμψυχον   153, 166–8
ἐπανόρθωμα   2
ἐπιείκεια   2
ἐπιθυμητικόν   78, 80, 82, 84 f., 87, 89–90, 91 n. 22
ἐπιθυμία   82, 84, 87
ἐπίσκεψις   79
ἐπιστήμη   48, 55, 80, 98 f., 140 n. 3, 153
ἐπωνυμία   43, 49
ἔργον   80 f., 86–9, 91 n. 14
ἔρως   82
ἐστώ   60–2, 69 n. 55

Index verborum

ζητεῖν 198, 207 n. 34
ζήτησις 198, 207 n. 36
ζητητικόν 189–211 *passim*
ζῷον 162 f., 175 n. 30

ἡγεῖσθαι 91 n. 19, 136
ἦθος 4, 102, 119 n. 3

θαυμαστός 192 f.
θεῖος 59, 61, 101, 185, 192
θεός 5, 18, 68 n. 31
θυμοειδές 75 f., 80, 83, 86–90
θυμός 83

ἰδέα 43, 54, 60, 63 n. 2, 63f n. 3, 67 n. 29, 71, 73
ἴδιος 43, 50 f., 53 f., 56 f., 65 n. 8, 67 n. 29, 102, 141, 197, 201

καινοτόμος 189–211 *passim*
καλός 10, 43, 46–9, 51, 53, 67 n. 31, 102, 114, 192, 204 n. 5, 209 n. 54
κατά τι 77 f., 90 n. 6
κινεῖσθαι 149, 151, 153, 161, 169
κίνησις 151, 153, 163, 174 n. 30
κοινωνία 15, 43, 172 n. 3, 200
κομψεῖος 50, 54
κομψός 189–211 *passim*
κόσμιος 15, 97, 101
κοσμιότης 15
κόσμος 15, 59–61
κρίνειν vii, 78–81, 83, 88, 91 n. 16
κριτής 134

λογιστικόν 78, 84, 86, 88 f., 91 n. 22
λόγος 65 n. 11, 65f n. 20, 68 n. 32, 86 f., 119 n. 3, 190 f.

μανθάνειν 199
μέγεθος 43
μέθεξις 172 n. 3
μέν 39 n. 6, 190, 205 n. 13
μεταλαμβάνειν 43, 58, 71
μετέχειν 43, 50 f., 53 f., 58, 60, 63 n. 2, 68 n. 32, 71, 185
μιμεῖσθαι 97
μίμησις 106, 108
μονοειδές 48, 67 n. 28, 186 n. 5
μορφή 43, 60

νόησις 79
νοητόν 80, 91 n. 14
νομίζειν 39 n. 2, 136, 142 n. 9, 144 n. 26
νόμιμον 2, 15, 18 n. 15
νόμος vii, 1, 3, 14, 17 nn. 2–4, 106, 200
νοῦς, νόος 65 n. 13, 73, 153, 165, 174 n. 28, n. 30

οἴεσθαι 51, 91, 134, 136, 144, 200, 207 n. 40, 208 n. 48
ὅμοιος 23, 40 n. 16, 56, 59, 65 n. 12, 67 n. 28, 106 f., 121 n. 22
ὄν-
 τὸ ὄν 47, 49, 59, 65 n. 19, 67 n. 27, 151, 153, 155, 161, 169
 τὰ ὄντα 47, 59, 65 nn. 15–16, 69 n. 50, 141, 174 n. 16
ὄνομα 57
ὄντως 154, 162, 166, 168, 171, 172 n. 2
ὄρεξις 82
ὁρμή 82
ὅσιον 5, 45, 64 n. 7
οὐσία vii, 5, 43–73 *passim*, 141, 154, 158, 162, 166, 168, 171 f.

πάθος 5, 45, 64 f. n. 8, 65 n. 10
πᾶν, τό 151, 153, 161, 169, 174 n. 14
παντελ- 162
 παντελές 162 f., 175 n. 30
 παντελῶς 153, 161, 172 n. 2, 173 nn. 7–8, 179
 τὸ παντελῶς ὄν vii, 149–75 *passim*
παράδειγμα 163, 181
παρουσία 43, 58, 61
περιττός 189–211 *passim*
πιστεύειν 130, 143
πίστις 143 n. 19
πλεονεξία 99, 111 f., 118
πρᾶγμα 56 f., 59–62, 69 n. 44
πρός τι 77 f., 90 n. 8

Σωκράτης 44–6, 48, 128, 185, 190–2, 211
Σωκρατικός 191
σῶμα 46, 49, 84, 90, 167, 171, 185
σωφροσύνη 15, 55 f.
σώφρων 85

τάξις 15
ταὐτόν, ταὐτά 47 f., 73, 76–8, 143 n. 16,

226

Index verborum

155, 171, 178, 181, 186 n. 5, 187 n. 17
τέλειος, τέλεος   173 n. 8, 174 n. 30
τελειόω   106
τέλος   181
τέχνη   14

ὑπόθεσις   43, 60, 200

φαίνεσθαι, φαίνεται   vii, 125–48 *passim*
φαντασία   81, 91, 133, 135 f., 138, 140, 142 n. 14, 143 n. 19, 144 n. 28
φάντασμα   144 n. 28
φιλία   15

φιλοσοφία   82, 85, 115
φρονεῖν   109
φρόνησις   153, 169
φύσις   vii, 1, 4, 14, 18, 59, 61, 95, 105 f., 121 f. n. 22

χαλεπόν   191, 193, 204, 209 n. 54
χρόνος   177, 181

ψευδής   130, 133 f., 144 n. 22
ψυχή   10, 46, 49, 65 n. 12, 90 nn. 8–9, 135, 153, 165 f.